Spuds, Rabbits and Flour Bags

An Australian farming family
share their stories of yesteryear

Joy E Rainey

Printed in Australia

First Printing: March 2021
2nd Edition

Shawline Publishing Group Pty Ltd
www.shawlinepublishing.com.au

Paperback ISBN- 9781922444530

Ebook ISBN- 9781922444554

CONTENTS

To Rosa, kind, ever generous,
and to all who have their feet on the earth
and their eyes on the flower.

INTRODUCTION

Lost to this generation is much of the wisdom of its elders. The stories of people who have lived in earlier times, what they've learned. Our communities are rich with stories. Sadly, most will never be told.

A reminder of the enduring nature of the old came with the death in 1941 of the bush poet Banjo Paterson, who wrote the 'Man from Snowy River.' This poem epitomised the rugged individualism of early Australia. It is interesting to note that until 1921 there were more people who lived in the Victorian bush than in Melbourne.

Stubborn strength and authenticity remain characteristics of the bush to this day. The Brutons represent many Australian rural families who coped stoically, dogged as their draught horses, during the devastating depression. This decade of sunken-eyed hunger was well before the birth of the welfare state, and many died, especially in the cities. Then there were more calls on the rural resilience. Following hot on the heels of the depression was the 1939–1945 war. Many farmers' sons, formidably fit, did not return.

These rigours were survived by the Brutons on the smell of an oily rag. Their staple, a good degree of home-grown ingenuity, vegetables, and 'poor man's mutton.' Rabbits, also referred to as 'underground mutton' were already a major Australian commodity. Earlier, in 1906, Australia was to earn more by shipping away rabbit meat and skins than from frozen beef. It was not until the 1950s that the introduced virus, myxomatosis, began to decimate this pervasive pestilence.

No 'throw away' society in those days! Everything was skilfully recycled. Necessity was indeed the mother of invention. All before the gods of consumerism and chemicals wreaked toxic havoc with western minds and environment.

Times past, painted with a different palette, were still vividly remembered by the older Brutons. Memories crying to be archived. The relatively modern invention, a tape recorder, was enlisted. This valuable tool worked hard in the late nineties, as I questioned and gradually captured their stories. Courage has been the Bruton hallmark. Still is, and this is strongly evidenced by a preparedness to share their lives openly, without artifice.

The six Bruton children, those still living of the twelve, speak for themselves. Their words, their stories. Many of these reminiscences, told and heard for the first time, were now able to be laid to rest. Discussions are not rigidly constructed, nor is the oral rephrased. I have endeavoured to indicate contexts, rhythms and other communication pointers like body language. Sometimes the speakers may not be able, occasionally unwilling, to express otherwise. The inclusion of these aspects is in my opinion essential. Otherwise, the accounts are incomplete, and risk being flattened into dry equanimity and so-called objectivity.

There is both good and bad news in the Australian past, as there is with every family. These stories tell us something about the struggles of all families, about the ways in which we all resemble each other. Our understanding of the past shapes our sense of identity and provides an accumulation of experience to guide us through the present and into the future. Families are like holograms, simple and complex. The observer can be drawn into a vivid, unexpected universe.

This is a different sort of writing for me. It is not analytical, which is my practice as a clinical psychologist. The collection of material from my aunts and uncles and my mother, Rosa, has been challenging. As the observer and participant of this, my family of origin, I am inevitably biased to some degree. Roots still grow from my toes, from the world I experienced as a child. I try to share some of this, providing mortar between the bricks of the narrations.

Harry and Olive were the last generation to grow up experiencing clean water, soil and air. Country living too, the social mores, were less complicated. Ready assistance and support were given to neighbours, thoughtfully anticipated, not requested. These were times when socks were darned, not discarded. When a person's word was binding, and financial transactions took place with a handshake. When doors were left unlocked.

Those times have gone, and I feel a yearning for some of the old values, and for unspoilt land and ocean. Since no era is perfect, there are aspects, the passing of which I celebrate. I'm not sorry that the authoritarian parenting model and rigid gender boundaries have gone. Nor am I sorry the ecologically devastating rabbit plagues have been, in the main, stamped out. Unrestricted hospital visits are a welcome relief, especially for small children. I'm glad that pain is more easily controlled.

May you, the reader, enjoy and ponder these verbal sketches, through whatever lenses you bring from your own experiences.

Outcomes of suffering poverty can be meanness of spirit, a grasping for what one has lacked. Or a giving generously, knowing poverty's sting. Olive and Harry shared the little they had, and most of their children were of the same ilk.

Bob

War

On this day, winter 1998, we talked about Bob's war-time experiences in New Guinea.

'The date I was discharged was 22nd of January 1946.'

Bob surprised himself at his ability to recall details, considering initial concerns of not being able to remember very much. This date, burned on his memory, was the culmination of three years active war service. Later, other dates emerged. Important markers of experiences. Mementos not to be forgotten. Not to be blurred or overshadowed by subsequent events of his life spanning nearly sixty years.

It was earlier in July Bob and I began discussions concerning his childhood, spent initially on the Bruton market garden at Cheltenham. Then, from age ten to twelve, the farm at Taradale, followed by the family's mixed farm at Little Hampton. Our focus had gradually crept closer to the war years. That long shadow that had been cast over the Bruton family.

When Bob was conscripted in 1942, there was already his older brother Tom and a younger brother Stan at war. Bob was the fourth child, and second boy of Harry and Olive Bruton's dozen. Eventually, at twenty-seven, he was to spend three years of almost continuous service in the inhospitable and dangerous jungles of New Guinea.

He may have been there even longer if he'd joined up at the beginning, as was his original intention.

'When war broke out, Ted Shelden and I were digging spuds at Ginger Rothe's. We heard news they were looking for people. Thought we'd go down and join up. I told Nell. She said, 'Think it would be better if you leave it because we have to get married!' By the time I was conscripted I had one child Dorothy, and the next child Barry was born just before I went to New Guinea.'

When I visited Bob, he and Nell had been living for some years at Kyneton, a good half hour drive from the old Bruton farm at Little Hampton and several kilometres from their previous home at Fernhill. The present simple brick home contrasted sharply with their earlier house, which had been decorative with the trappings and meticulous detail of Victorian architecture. Kookaburras embellished the iron lace at the corners and the decorative brickwork was richly toned in two contrasting sunburnt shades. Here they had reared their family, grown hay, milked cows, then later grown potatoes.

Various vignettes of past sojourns in this house and on the farm came to mind. Many an enjoyable summer holiday was spent exploring with my cousins. I particularly appreciated these times with Dorothy, the same age as myself. I slept in a temporary bed in her bedroom. At one stage when I was thirteen, while my family were moving from our house at Avonsleigh in the Dandenong Ranges to another one at Emerald, I spent two or three months with them. I attended the local Kyneton High School with the Bruton kids.

My uncle's opulent stands of gladioli and dahlias there, at Fernhill, are special memories, emblematic of his gardening prowess. These were as dramatic as his large patches of peas and any other vegetable which took his fancy.

Although winter in the garden at Kyneton too, sported cottage flowers and the smaller back garden brimmed resplendently with vegetables. Bob's skills as a grower bore testimony to his market gardening heritage. He had descended from two green-fingered families, the Brutons and the Bluhms, pioneer gardeners in the sand belt southeast of Melbourne.

We sat at the grey Laminex kitchen table. Nell, replete with crutches, having been in the Bendigo Hospital after fracturing her leg, was sitting in the adjoining lounge room watching television. I wondered what sort of experience it was for Bob, leaving his young family to go to war.

Bob was pensive as he searched his archives. He looked down and fiddled with a teaspoon. 'I enjoyed married life a lot. I didn't want to leave the family. I don't remember a lot. But I do remember our unit marching through Melbourne before we got straight on the train to go to New Guinea. I remember clearly! We were nearing the Princes Bridge to march under it and along the parkland near the river.'

His face lit up. His tone incredulous. 'I spotted Nell and the two kids on the bridge! I happened to spot her!'

It seemed as though he was talking about yesterday. His voice had slowed, 'It was a terrible feeling, but it was something that had to be done. You had to live through it. There was a bugler down below where we were. Ever since whenever a bugler plays, Nell shoots through. She can't stand it!'

My memory was active. Bob was playing with a teaspoon, then, too. A cameo which has remained with me since childhood. The scene—the ample and homely kitchen at Fernhill. Bob and Nell had their four children by this time, after the war. The two younger boys, Graham and Peter, were born after his return from New Guinea. There was that certain closeness Bob and Nell had, which as a child I observed and felt, without, I suppose, recognising it intellectually.

A typical scene flashed across my mind. Morning tea-time! Bob would sit at the end of their big dark wooden extension table with the rounded substantial legs. Nell sat next to him on his right at the side. The kettle would be singing on the straw-coloured Rayburn wood stove. A cheerful reminder that another cuppa could be ready at a moment's notice. It was a happy sound. Softly singing kettle with a trickle of steam drifting from the spout. The hot spout which was carefully turned away from the front of the stove.

The kettle sang of happy times. A comfortable sound. It seemed to express my happiness and that of the family. Apart from cups of tea, the oven was also kept busy with Nell's industry. Various cakes were produced. I especially recall large wedges of rich fruitcake. Nothing spared!

But it was the tinkling teaspoon which triggered my memory. The picture was etched with clarity. The image of Bob absentmindedly, slowly stirring his cup of black tea. It rang of music. The teaspoon seemed to caress his cup. The caress of his eyes was on Nell. The breathless, lingering glances seemed to last an eternity. She, dark haired, smooth bloomed, bosomy under her bibbed floral apron. Large brown eyes, soft as a cow's, were locked with his blue. They talked, but the spell would continue. Sometimes the spoon and the cup seemed to have a dance all of their own. This was something my parents never did. Something indefinable was happening, and it left a rosy glow.

'I joined the 58th, my number was VX147040,' Bob was saying. 'We later amalgamated with the 59th just before we went to New Guinea. I was in the infantry, a mortar man. After about twelve months, I was promoted to N.C.O. First, we went to Albury, where we joined the battalion and did training, then up at Casino, New South Wales, we did exercises. We camped there, then we went to the Atherton Tablelands out of Cairns where we camped again. The area is now covered with a lake.

I went up in '42 after Pearl Harbour. That was the start of it. When we first went over, it was on the Taroona. They put me up on the crow's nest, up top to spot submarines. I said, 'I'd better come down, I'm going to be sick!' The officer said, 'No you're not.' I was up there two or three hours until I sprayed an officer. Then they let me down.'

'Did Nell see the boat off?'

Bob responded kindly to my naivety. 'Oh no. It was very hush hush. Couldn't even tell her I was heading off. Every letter was censored and some of the officers who censored were no good at all! Nell could not make sense of some of them. When I was over there, I got to the stage where I was going crook at an officer and getting into trouble. A Catholic padre, Father English said, 'Sounds as though you're in trouble.' I said, 'It's just this censor business! They are chopping everything out of it. Things nothing to do with the army.' He told me not to say anything to anyone. 'Drop your letter into me.' He'd say, 'You haven't put anything in you shouldn't, have you?' I'd say, 'No.' He'd just seal and sign it.'

There was something very nice, very straight about Bob. I imagined the padre had seen this. And he had a certain charming quality which I had admired as a child and still did. An attractive man. His slow drawl was deceptive. His eyes held a lazy alertness. Kindly eyes. Laughing eyes. His infectious smile would spread slowly from lips to lids. Easily. Lighting up those eyes. Like soft butter on toast.

He never seemed in a hurry to speak. He took things in, assessed, weighed. He seemed to sift through deeply within himself, feeling his way. But expressing those feelings was probably something else. In a sense, he held his cards close to his chest. Yes. I remembered him well in his youth and my childhood. Suntanned, rolled up sleeves, a ripple of muscle. Often, he had a cigarette in his mouth, savouring the aroma as he squinted through the smoke. One sensed Bob's strength was not only to do with his physical. There was a firm inner core.

In later years Bob shared he had been smoking since his early teens. His father Harry was an avid anti-smoker and a staunch churchman.

Little Hampton. Father. Farming.

'Dad and I were digging spuds in the top paddock. Dad said, 'If you're going to get into the smoking you can pack your swag and go!' Bob looked slightly bemused when he recalled his reply. 'If you can throw me over the fence!' I thought, I'm not going to be pushed around! Dad had a small smile on his face and said no more. He'd said the same to Tom. I think Tom was swearing at the horses. He went. He went when he was about fifteen.'

It was in February 1926 that Tom turned fifteen, and Bob notched up to eleven one month later. The family had not long moved from the rental property at Taradale, to the forty acres of Little Hampton red soil. Harry took out a mortgage from his brother-in-law Moss Daff to buy the place. The house was an old weatherboard, with a corrugated iron roof, and a brooding front verandah. Too small to accommodate the family comfortably. Harry's finances were limited, and he must have felt desperate.

The late twenties were soon to be overtaken by that long difficult decade of economic and social hardship, the depression.

In the absence of Tom, Bob was now the eldest boy. He became skilled at many important activities. He'd help Rosa, his eldest sister, punch up the bread, sometimes offer to fill in for her when she needed some time off. At thirteen, he was the one designated to slaughter any beast for the table. 'I was taught by the man next door,' Bob had told me in his usual amiable manner. 'I was never an expert. The family weren't able to pay someone. Bartholson, in Connie Suitor's place, told us how to kill a pig. To stun him first. George and I must have opened the coop and out he went. We had to chase him to catch him. I used to be the butcher then. I'd kill some of the calves too if we run out of feed. We'd have veal now and again.'

'And your father, would he do it?'

'No! He'd be missing.'

'I had to be independent. Tom wasn't there much earlier, either. He was at the Sanatorium two years. That's why we had to move from Cheltenham to Taradale. Tom had T.B. and the doctor said it would be better for him to live in an inland climate.'

Bob was farmer, horseman and a support to his mother. It was he who rode his horse into the black night, looking for his distracted mother after an angry outburst from his unpredictable, short-tempered father.

'Oh. No! Oh. Well, well yes. She was pretty upset. Just got to breaking point. But she used to get over it. The old man—he'd do his block. I know he done it twice. He'd up a chair and bash it on the table and break all the crockery. And I think that might have been the time. He'd be very sorry afterwards, I think. Mum didn't agree with everything but was very loving.'

'Quite frightening too.'

'Gee whiz, I used to have nightmares about it.'

'How old were you?'

'Six or seven, I suppose. Oh no, ten, I suppose. The last time was at Little Hampton.'

Bob was pensive, his right hand active, agitated even, as he tapped the table repeatedly with the teaspoon. 'I used to think I could straighten up the old man a bit. He was a blustering sort of a coot. He never talked much. Not sure if I'd try to get him talking or put him right on some things. He was a bit bigoted.'

There was a great similarity between Bob's appearance and demeanour and that of his mother. I never observed any resemblance between Bob and his father's dark looks or behaviour.

15

Bob's voice was blunt. 'Oh. I suppose I just didn't like being told what to do.'

Again, Bob was quiet, and so was his hand. 'I think his bark was worse than his bite.'

On reflection, Bob and his father did have something strong in common. Bob had a special place in his heart for horses, too. Inherited by both, probably, from Bob's grandfather, William Bruton. William, who owned a market garden at Cheltenham, was renowned as a horse doctor and grower of fine asparagus. A charismatic character, he was reputed to have saved many a horse's life.

'The others had a bike. I preferred a horse. I bought a pony. Dot. Used to ride her, also used her in harrows and the gig. She was a very good strong little pony,' he added with the softness of affection in his voice. 'I ended up with two or three different ponies over the years. I rode all over the place.

Mick the draught horse. I remember. Very lively. And when the white one Con backed down the steps at the mineral springs....' Bob was laughing, 'I wasn't there. I think I might have went to give help to get him out again.

Dad didn't believe in horses having bits in their mouths. When we were scuffling spuds, I'd go okay with an old horse. The horse would know what to do. But, generally, I don't think you can control a horse well without a bit. Don't know how Dad paid for all the carts and jinkers hat were wrecked going through the bush to Drummond. We'd crash into a few trees. Going around a tree, he wasn't able to control the horse with no bit. I never heard Dad yell at a horse in my life! He'd break a wheel or a shaft. He'd cut a sapling and make a shaft. If Dad had a jibbing horse, he'd put a sugar bag over his head, and get him walking two or three steps and slowly lower the bag, and the horse would just get going. I remember if a horse had a cut, we'd put boracic acid powder on it and a bandage.

He was good with animals. Always be chaff for the horses. Twelve ton in the barn. He always fed the animals before he fed himself.

When we moved up to Little Hampton, Dad brought his plough, a mouldboard. It had wooden handles and beams and a cast-iron shear. It was a good little plough, but it was no good up there with two horses in it. It was a little one they used down at the market gardens in the sand with one horse, but at Little Hampton, the soil being heavier, we'd have two horses in it and hit stones and bust it.

Dad would go down the bush and get a new beam, some wattle that was just bent the right way, and bore holes in it. He'd just go and do it, no growling. Eventually he got Scala's, the blacksmiths in Trentham, to make a steel one, because the other was breaking all the time.

Dad made stone drains to drain the bottom paddock. Lot of hard work digging all the drains. A local farmer would not have done it. He grew things down there, but it wasn't a place for a market garden. Farmers plough when the ground is damp, not soft. This was hard clay soil. Dad would not overwork his horses and plough when the soil was dry or damp. He'd plough when wet. Easier then. If the ground is soft and slightly moist, you'd have to scrape off the shear more often too. The earth would build up on the plough and make the horses work harder. But ploughing when wet, the ground would slide off the shear. He'd plough and till the grass, kill it, so he could grow veggies on it.'

The question of how Bob had learned land and farm management interested me.

'I remember walking between the handles of the plough with the old man behind me. But I learned mainly from the Rothes. Tom was never interested in farming; he was more a technical man.'

Comments made by Bob on another occasion came to mind. When I asked Bob if he regretted leaving school early, he'd answered, 'No! School was something I didn't like. I wasn't a scholar. I was going to be a carpenter.'

There had been a silence as Bob stared down at the brightly flowered tablecloth. 'There was this local who said he would take me on as an apprentice. Dad took me over to see him, and as we were getting there—he was a terrible man to swear—he let go an earful. Dad didn't even stop! He just turned the jinker around! I remember he said, 'You're not going to work with that man!' '

Perhaps in later years, Harry may have learned Bob chose to swear himself, to use what expletive fitted. This was no compromise of Bob's good plain decency, integrity, fairness and compassion. Perhaps the swearing, unacceptable to Harry, attested to Bob's inner rebellion against his father's rigidity. 'The future of a boy, barely in his teens, decided in a couple of seconds!' I voiced my indignation.

'Oh. Was something that happened,' said Bob as he dismissed the subject, his expression remote, momentarily closed off like a curtain.

'Transport in the thirties?'

'Jinker mostly we used in those days. And we didn't get the cab till we went to Little Hampton.'

He noted my puzzled look. 'Had a cab, and a buggy and a jinker. The cab was covered in, a step at the back and seats each side, along sideways. The buggy is like a gig, only it's got four wheels, one main seat and just a little one. The jinker has only two wheels. But sometimes a jinker is called a gig!' he said, chuckling.

'Dad used to head off and walk to Drummond Church through the bush on Saturday afternoons and stay the night sometimes at Drummond with friends, and we'd come in the gig on Sunday. People used to walk in the bush a bit. The distance to the church would have been about twelve or fourteen miles, I suppose. I was walking to Jeffrey's one day a few miles on the other side, and I saw the biggest kangaroo I'd ever seen! He just stood in the track in front of me, and I stood too, and after a while he went on his way.'

Siblings

The war threw a milieu of men together. Sleeping, training, military action! Teamwork and mateship were crucial. Co-habiting in a community was not foreign to Bob having been brought up in the large Bruton brood. As with all families, there was a wide mix of personalities.

Bob and Tom! Interestingly, Tom too eventually became a man of the land, owning and working his own properties. Tom had citrus orchards, later he moved north to Queensland and grew sugar cane. Usually, he invented something or other for his farm. Bob took a different road, that of mixed farming, spuds, dairy, sheep and beef. It seemed from the beginning they both lived in different worlds.

'Tom was always tinkering. He built the first valve radio at Little Hampton. I'd sit up and listen, and so did he. Was in Tom's room because Dad didn't believe in it. Prior to this, he made crystal sets. He really had a great talent for that. It's a great pity he didn't go on further with his education. We used to get short wave from overseas. Long wave and short wave.'

On this particular day, all the while Bob talked, he fiddled with a pencil. Up and down, up and down, went the pencil. Sometimes slow, sometimes fast. The motion seemed like a barometer. A measure of the intensity of his feelings. It was fast when he had mentioned 'education.'

'Your father didn't like having a radio?'

'No oh no! He wouldn't allow it in the house. No. No that was a sinful thing that! Well, I think I might have been the only one who used to go and listen to the wireless. I don't remember Minnie. It's a wonder Minnie wasn't there. I suppose she was, but I don't remember her. Sometimes I'd be there pretty late, really. Tom was pretty clever with his wireless's he built himself. When Bess and Fred got married, I remember, he made them a wireless for their wedding present.'

I was silently recalling that Tom was torn away from home for a lengthy period on the brink of adolescence, due to his T.B. The young patients were allowed to roam the bush and explore. Perhaps this was a prelude to Tom's acceptance of further absences. Privations to be endured for the prize of freedom already tasted, away from his fanatical father.

'Tom worked up in the Mallee after he suddenly went away. There was a rat plague, and he slept in an old tin shed. He told me he had a fear of going to sleep, frightened of them gnawing his feet.' remembered Bob.

'Tom and his father?'

'A clash of personality, perhaps. His son may have been a lot like him.

Tom also built his room. Was at the western end of the verandah near the laurel tree. When Tom was away, I'd dive in there. I usually slept in the other end in the bigger boys' room.

The boys' room had been a shed. They used to put bags in it. I remember either Dad or s'pose Tom, jacking it around or pulling this room around on logs. Jacked it up, put it on the eastern end of the verandah there. It was the boys' room then. This was Stanley, George, me and then when Uncle Will and anyone come up, the girls would have to come out and we'd have to double up. Quite a few of us would sleep there. Was no lining in it. We used to have trouble with the condensation from the pretty flat tin roof. And a frosty morning it would drip, drip, drip! We put a chain on the roof to stop it, but it wasn't effective.'

'It would have been pretty cold out there, I reckon,' I said, shivering at the thought of the freezing Little Hampton winters.

Bob's voice had that usual optimistic tone. 'It wasn't the best. It was one way of getting out of bed.'

I remembered that small room added by Tom. Apparently, this was soon after the family moved from Taradale to these less commodious conditions. He would have been about fourteen when he built it.

Bob was recalling more about this room too. 'He made it from waste timber. The mill edgings. They'd throw them into a pit and burn them. A lot of sap wood. If you wanted it, you'd take your lorry down the bush to the mill and grab it. Maybe it was Thrum's. Ord's mill had finished and gone then. The room Tom built was only about seven-foot-long and about five foot wide. I think Tom or someone got this second-grade timber for the washhouse too. It's still standing.'

Occasionally, I too, had slept in Tom's old room. The basic iron bed, with the stretched hessian bag base and flock mattress. I'd doze to the rustle of the wind in the large, shiny, deepest green leaves of the laurel. Its arms would sway as it played scrappy music against the wall, irregularly punctuated by the sharp clickety creaks of the windmill. This duet would inspire my candle to glimmer and shimmer against the dark. Another dimension. The dervishes danced, gambolled, frolicked, improvised. Pauses, then renewed motion. Playful whirling to the wind. And all this entertainment only limited by my imagination. But when these dancers turned into ghosts, that's when I would draw the curtain. The finale! With moistened fingers, I'd extinguish the candle. Then take flight, burrowing into my feather pillow, blankets pulled high.

Even as a child, I was struck by the simplicity of this room. The bed pushed against the outside wall, which followed the verandah's front. Walking space, just large enough, sandwiched between bed and rudimentary shelves, made from two or three fruit cases placed atop each other. This chest of sorts backed on to the original house weatherboards. Across the front of this storage hung a cotton curtain gathered on a string. A flower pattern, not too bright—against background black.

On the top of it, providing a fine white smoothness, draped a large cotton cloth. In my eyes, this cloth, bordered by an inch or so of hand crocheted lace, somehow resurrected this structure from the mundane.

Sitting on this white was usually a slightly chipped enamel candle holder, also white. Replete with a box of 'Bryant and May' matches and a big stub of white candle, two or three spent matches, a few globs of candle grease, it waited for instant use.

There was, I know, another curtain diagonally across the corner at the foot end of the bed. A space for hanging clothes on the wooden rod inside. The latch on the door was simple and home fashioned. A piece of string or a bootlace threaded its way through the round hole. Pull the string and up went the bar over the latch! Bootlace one side, and from the inside, use your finger! All bent to make it fit.

Bob elaborated 'The hinges on the door may have been bought, but not necessarily. Every time Tom made a chook house, he'd cut the leather off an old boot and use it for hinges.'

I guess what took my eye, though, was the mat. Placed next to the bed, it was a welcome respite from the cold of bare floorboards. What amazed me was my grandmother Olive had somehow found time among her many chores and childbearing, to create such an attractive artefact. It was cleverly fashioned from colourful pieces of material and old stockings, which were inserted into that versatile helper. The venerable hessian bag. Bright, compact, and refreshingly warm. I discovered in later years it was called a 'rag' mat.

The free pattern stands out in my memory. Swirling soft turquoise, a touch of pink here and there and along the border. The cool colours of the sea juxtaposed against the richness of warm earthy browns. The delicate greys, soft browns, biscuit tones of the stockings, provided a background for this flowing artistry. In the centre two flowers were edged with black. One a rich blue, the other, the warmth of pink. Then, what I considered a master touch! A dot. Just one! Of a different hue, vibrant, the size of a thumbnail, lower in the corner. Larkspur blue.

'George?' I was asking.

'George was a good singer. Mrs Dunell said he should be trained. He stayed in tune. Stan and Bess were off key with singing. George sort of took over the family during the war.'

'He seemed to be very conscientious.'

'I suppose he would be. We all were, weren't we?'

My memories of George were of a dark eyed, good looking, fairly serious man. 'Did he used to have some fun?'

'Oh yes. He was quiet. At home, in the kitchen, we had a table, and between it and the wall was what we called a wooden form, like a long bench seat. And us kids had to sit on the form at mealtime. Of course, the one at the end would get in, and then the others would have to get in underneath. And George was there, and Minnie was annoying him. Anyhow,' Bob gave a loud laugh, 'and suddenly there was a hell of a yell, and Minnie's yelling 'George's bit me ear!' He'd have been three or four, I suppose. Oh no, he'd have been older than that.

Oh, George was just there. He was a fussy little fellow, didn't like his vegetables.'

'How old was George when he left school, and what might he have chosen as an occupation if he'd had the choice?'

'George was about fourteen. I'm only guessing. Farming probably. We used to get upset when Dad sat under a tree or lay down in the paddock sometimes. George and I made up rhymes. 'Are you sitting idle, still there's work to do,' and so on. Actually looking back, Dad might have been sick then. Could have had the diabetes. He was always thirsty. He'd come in and have coffee essence with sugar, had an enlarged heart.'

'Who would you have talked to most in the family?' I asked.

Bob's answer was quick. He did not need to reflect. 'Min!'

I brought up another important subject again. 'How did it affect you, Tom's being away so much, and his not being particularly interested in farming? You being the next eldest boy?'

Bob tackled this in his inimical style. 'Tom had a lot of brains and no sense! He was a bit of a loner. S'pose I had to be independent.'

'Who do you think had it the hardest?'

'Daise, always thought she was the worst done by.'

'Why, do you think?'

'But that's her nature. The way she was. Just her. I suppose... Don't think anyone had it harder than anyone else.'

Bob was quietly reflective, 'I have a memory of us kids picking peas or supposed to be.

Rosa and Dad were picking, Min and I would be there eating them. Rosa would say, 'Come on. Well, I'm going to tell Dad if you don't hurry up! Get going!' Rosa took her duties more seriously. She'd have her light moments too. Had a lot of responsibility. Harold was good for a tease, easy to bait. Percy kept away from controversy. Nothing seemed to worry him much.'

Recreation

Those gold diggers' holes in the bush. Probably an irresistible attraction for young boys. When Bob was a lad, they were not yet a century old. As I thought of them, a shiver crept down my back. 'Did you ever go down the diggers' shafts?'

'Yep!'

'Use a rope to get down?'

'No! The ladders made of saplings from the bush were still there, that the diggers used. They'd dig down, then tunnel off.

You'd find bottles down the mine shafts and get marbles out of them. She'd be dangerous now. They had tunnels branching off. There was one up the back of Percy's,

Meuser's hill. Used to be a pub halfway down there during the gold rushes. The miners who were mostly Chinese had vegetable gardens. When the gold ran out, they ran out. The vegetable gardens were up near Percy's. Leylands—farmers at Percy's up the back, burnt out. Percy is on the original Leyland's property. Then Alexander's got it. Still a few belladonna lilies at the house site, they're pretty tough. Was up that way that two or three of us would get around and go down the mines. We'd get down the hole into a tunnel.

But I didn't like going into the tunnels, I felt a bit nervous. It was completely dark. Whereas when you are down the mine, the main shaft, you could look up and see a patch of sky at the top. We'd go down about forty feet. I suppose many of the mines would have been eighty, ninety, a hundred feet! George and me. Tom would be up directing, as he usually did. Bet Minnie'd be in it. I don't remember Rosa being there. Oh, we used to get around alright. We'd walk. Wonder we didn't get lost!

'Rabbiting?'

'We had some ferrets. What happened to most ferrets is they'd stay down the burrows. They were pretty hard on the chook house, because they were pretty good on chooks! Every time I'd go ferreting, the ferret would stop in the burrow. I suppose you couldn't blame it, could you!' added Bob, chuckling.

'I'd have to dig him out. We used to light a fire in the burrow. If you could get a bit of a breeze like today, and if you can get on the burrow, the side the wind is coming from, it would help blow the smoke through, and the ferret would come out a hole higher up. But that was pretty desperate.

We were doing that down back of Rainey's one day, us kids. And Maxwell, who used to own it, came down. Didn't go crook at us, it was summertime. He explained how we could start a fire. He was quite good.'

'It's not the fashion, ferreting now, is it?'

'Apart from that, you've got to go to the house and find the owner and the owner's absent. To get on the land, I mean. And they won't let you in, they'll. ooh!'

Bob's eyes were spitting fire. 'They're mongrels these property owners now! No. And they don't trust people at all. They're real city slickers. They're not country people! Go in there mushrooming and I get abused.'

Bob was tapping the table erratically with the side of the pencil.

'I had a pet wombat at one time, and I'd still like to know what happened to it. It was only a little one, and we were trying to work out how to feed it, and we thought someone might of taken it quietly down the bush. I don't know. I got up next morning, and it was gone. We were trying to feed it on roots. Mum said, 'That's no good, you'll have to give it milk for a while.' Bob gave a deep sigh.

'What do you think happened?'

'Well, I sort of think my father might of had something to do with taking it. But I just don't know. Have no idea. But it disappeared. I suppose it just wandered off.'

'The ordinary milk may have given it the trots, anyway.'

'Trotted off.' quipped Bob.

There were other pets too, in the Bruton household. A dog, Min's cats, calves sometimes, a lamb given by a passing drover.

'There were no sheep around here then. I think sometimes during a drought they'd drove through and that's how we got the lamb. Used to come from up north and drove around our roads. That lamb grew into quite a big sheep. It put its flamin' foot into the dough rising in front of the fireplace. Didn't matter who said no. It still came in.

Had some silkworms. Fed them on mulberry leaves. Think we put the cocoons into hot water, used to tease the silk out somehow. Don't remember.

Oh, we had family concerts sometimes in the main room near the fire. Dad used to do something too. I remember him reciting 'Patrick Magintie, an Irish man of note, came into a fortune and bought himself a goat!' I can see him there saying that, standing in front of the clock, by the fire. Then he'd want to know, 'Why can a mosquito bark?' It was climbing up the gum tree and bark or some such thing. I know I'd do something in the concert. Can't think of what it was.

Used to play footy for Lyonville. Freddy Bremner and I both played.'

Depression

A sinister, dark shadow, the looming gloom of the thirties, was waiting around the corner to pounce. Relocation of the large family from Taradale to Little Hampton, different soil and climate, a new community, was another unwelcome challenge. Obviously desperate to make ends meet after the move, Harry had taken on that distasteful job.

'Dad did the toilets after we moved to Little Hampton for a year or two. McArthur, we bought the place from used to do the job and Dad took it over. He used to empty the last load on the paddock. The rest he'd tip down the old mines at Trentham. He reckoned the worst ones were from the nunnery, always in a mess. Tom helped him. He eventually jibbed on Dad. Tom reckoned Dad made him do the dirty work.'

Then the depression struck, gradually tightening its grim grip.

'Mum got the job collecting the mail. I was working at home then because when it was snowing and raining, I'd go in her place. Fifteen, I s'pose. Whenever that was. That was nearly seventy years ago. We used to bring the paper out and get paid for that. How much, I don't know. The Argus, The Sun or The Age. She'd leave the papers and mail at the Little Hampton Post Office with Sadie Price, and people would collect them. Oh, there were quite a few when you think about it around the district. Suiters, Belyeas, Brutons, and the Barrows, Rothes, Rawlings, McGraths, Justices, Moloneys. Yere. I know we had quite a bundle of papers!'

Money was hard to come by! Olive's income, though a mere miniscule, was an important contribution to the family economy. The older children dug deep into their pockets and supplemented this out of meagre earnings. It wasn't always easy to find the mortgage payments.

'Mum would take the interest, to pay the Daffs in cash. Phyllis Daff still remembers her going down there on the train and hanging on to her bag. Eventually, when George had a really good year with potatoes, he said 'I'll give you the money to pay off the mortgage, but the house has to be in Mum's name too.' Mum was always afraid Dad would sell the place; he was a bit unpredictable.'

Fortunately, the Bruton family was basically self-sufficient. Many weary work-seeking men from the cities roamed the country, despairing for their starving families.

'Swagmen? Nice old fellows. Mum and Dad would always give them something. Often Dad would invite them in for a meal and a sit by the fire. They'd come to our place pretty well every year. I think the swagmen used to have a sort of code. Perhaps they put a stone on the gatepost or something like that, to indicate to the other swagmen that there could be food got there. I grew up in the Depression, I didn't know anything else.

The susso workers worked hard. They used to be paid 'sustenance' wages by the Government to cart timber for producing charcoal for the powering of cars.'

'What's about the best thing to have in a depression?' I asked.

'A feed! The only difference in a depression, I suppose, is the difficulty to make a living. All I know is that it was hard times money wise. Things were cheaper, but you didn't have the money to buy anything. It doesn't matter how cheap something is, if you don't have the money.'

The family grew potatoes, peas and various vegetables like swedes, to hopefully sell at the Kyneton market, or put on the train at Trentham for selling at Castlemaine or Melbourne. They had a domestic vegetable garden to the west of the house near the windmill and the deep, never-dry well. Also, a handful of fruit trees.

'Surprising the food you can grow in a little spot.' said Bob.

'Was a good thing that Harry had been a market gardener.'

'Yes. It helped. We'd buy flour in large bags, about 186 pound or so, from Jim McKenzie's or Co-op in Trentham. Dad preferred to grow vegetables like peas, turnips, swedes, but he had to diversify at Little Hampton and grow wheat and other things. No irrigation. He always grew enough oat chaff for the horses. The cow? She'd have chaff, not necessarily oats. Only gave her what the horses didn't want. The cows came second in those days.

We sent spuds and peas to Melbourne. When we lived at Taradale, I'd take the spuds to Castlemaine Market. They've just now done up the market where I would take them. I remember taking them in the spring cart. May have had some caulis too. Put the spuds into hessian bags for market. They were sixty-five pound, fifteen to the ton.'

'What's a spring cart?'

'A dray with springs on it. A dray is used for heavy loads.' answered Bob patiently.

'We had a pit to store potatoes, made it near the fence, so no one would walk on it. Lined with straw, straw put over the top, then six inches of soil over it. The pit would be, oh, about six-foot-wide, about a foot deep, then up to a peak about four feet high. We'd have rails to build it up a bit. I remember Bill Moloney had pits there in McGrath's. Oh, they were a hundred yards long. I was there picking spuds out of the pit for weeks. He'd keep them in the pit from April, May into September, through the winter. Then sell it off during the spring. You couldn't leave them too long; they'd get too many shoots and get soft.

We were never allowed to use good spuds for the kitchen or animals. Used ones too small. Gave them to the pigs. Boiled them in a four-gallon kerosene tin. Better boiled, didn't stick in their throats. And for the chooks, some people used to add bran and pollard. Generally, we didn't put much bran or pollard with them. Too expensive. Got scraps from the kitchen too. Some people would fill their copper with spuds to cook for their pigs.

We didn't have a binder for cutting the hay. Belyea did across the road and he used to go round contracting. They don't do it these days. There are no binders at all, stopped in the 1950s and 60s. Work horses like good oaten chaff, cut with the binder, left to cure, and then cut into chaff with a chaff cutter. There are still a few little hand chaff cutters around.

If you gave the horses too many oats, they'd get boils under the collar, get frisky, inclined to get foundered. I can get itchy after oats!

The tractor revolutionised farming. I think a lot of horses were shot for pet food.'

Pre-War Employment

As Bob grew up, he did farm work, both at home, and on land he'd rented for potato growing. He also worked for his orchardist uncle, Will Bluhm, and another orchardist, Handyside, at East Burwood near Melbourne. More often it was labouring for various locals, like Ginger, Dave or Fred Rothe.

'John Rothe, that is Ginger, was the ploughman. He'd walk behind the four horses and three furrow plough. I'd come along behind with a kero bucket of spuds and throw them in the furrows. Fill up from a bag of spuds each end of the paddock, perhaps two bags in the middle. Sow about four acres a day.

Hard work was a challenge. Digging spuds. See if I could get an extra bag or throw a sheaf higher! We'd load two ton of spuds on to the lorry with two horses, unload them on to the railway platform at Trentham. Be hundreds of tons stacked up there. The merchant would offer you a price. McBeth we used to sell to in Melbourne. They'd pay the farmer eighteen shillings to five pound a ton. That was a terrific price! About twenty-four shillings was usual through the late 1930s.'

There was something else Bob undertook during latter years of the Depression to earn those precious pennies. Just before those desperate times of a different nature. That cataclysmic conflict which would cut cruelly into the fabric of his life.

'For a year or so, I did wood cutting, charcoal for cars. We cut the wood out of the bush. Don't remember the pay, one pound a week or a day. Was good money compared with what you used to get. Susso.

In my twenties, I did the wood cutting in between some farm work. The wood was felled so we would have to cut it. Would take off the bark. Have to be same lengths, about six feet and thick as your head. If it was too green to burn, then we'd lay it there for a few months or so.'

It was interesting to hear about the charcoal burning.

'Be quite a few charcoal burners down the bush. They would stack up the wood, put a hole in the centre with some bark to light it, the fire in the centre. Air holes on the side. As soon as it got burning properly, they closed up the air holes. Just smoulder. If it burnt too long, it was useless. It would be a long burn for roughly four or five days. They'd then tear it to pieces and spread it out, but they had to be quick. They'd sell the charcoal in bags.

There were a lot of Italians doing this work. They would make kilns with dirt. Later on, big, covered steel drums were used, steel burners. They'd turn off the flow to stop the fire. They'd use crosscut saws and wedges, put the wood on to sledges pulled by the horses. Lovely wood for burning. It was messmate, I think. That's why they didn't like planting trees. Spent their lives getting rid of them.

When war broke out, the Italians were placed in internment camps and Australians did the work. Fellows doing the charcoal would be pretty black when they were going home. Sally's brother Ned Plant, we used to call him 'Ned Kelly', worked there. He'd say, 'I have to have a bath! A bath every night makes you weak!'

It was a beautiful forest, according to some of the elderly people. When we first went up to Little Hampton, we rode through the forest there; it was fairly open to Glenlyon. Now there's a lot of wattle. Be 200 years to get back to what it was. The tree fellers must have come in. They done a good job, just took the good ones out. Thrashers from Glenlyon used to come up along the old wagon tracks. Boys found a piss pot from somewhere and stuck it up high in one of the trees. Got this piss pot from somewhere. Just boys.

Those big dead trees that used to stand in the paddocks at Little Hampton. That's where most of them went. Into charcoal burning. They'd been ringbarked a hundred years before that. A hundred feet to the first branch! They were cut into six-foot lengths, stacked up like tepees. She'd be a pretty big job. Covered with dirt in the paddock. Had a way with bark. Let the air in a bit so it would burn. When everything was bright, they'd put a shovel of dirt here and there, where the air was coming in. Watch them day and night. Domenic Debenardi was one fellow who did it.

Yes. Those great big old trees. I used to help clean up those. We'd make jacks and tree pullers. Put cable around as high as we could, get a jack hooked on and gradually tighten it. These trees give you an idea what the country used to be like. Must have been bush. The first name of Little Hampton was Forrest, Nell's Auntie Janie Jackson used to tell us. She remembered they'd dig these big holes and put the big logs in them to burn. She lived next door to us when we lived in Hunt's old place. We used to have a look every night to see how she was. Babe found her dead. Seventy-eight when she died.'

It was after 1946, though, that Bob and his family lived at Hunt's. Much was to occur in Bob's life before this.

War. Padre

Now today, as we talked about the war, Bob returned to the subject of correspondence. There was a tightness, a sadness in his voice. 'When up in the islands, it would be nearly a month before Nell would get a letter. The boys would say, 'How's Mum and the kids?' The boys were terrific! One day I flopped on the bed to read my letter. She'd put in two blank pages by mistake. I said, 'She's not talking to me today!' he added, laughing.

Bob's voice was rarely loud. He spoke in a particularly softly now as he continued the thread of how the padre had been that major assistance to him during his letter writing crisis. One imagined the frustration on both sides. Trying to maintain closeness through the written word would have been difficult. No warm touch, look or kiss. No companionable talk.

Letters written under difficult circumstances, awaited at home after weeks of hope and disappointment. Weeks of watching and waiting. And wondering. The gnawing of worry. Today might be the special day when life would feel lighter. Then, written evidence would testify to a dear one's survival. At least until the date scribbled inside the letter by hot steamy hands. The run of ink. Letters torn open with hungry fingers. A curse at having to rely on such a thread, easily impaired by a censor's brutal razor. Father English's assistance in preserving that precious lifeline was indeed a critical contribution.

'He was a lovely man, Father English. A real Irish twang, he had. There was also a protestant padre Father Pedric. He got wounded in the behind! He dived into a hole when the bombs were coming. He dived in and he was on top of the others, and his behind was sticking out.' Bob was chuckling. 'Father English was trying to tell some fellows that Father Pedric had been wounded in the buttocks, but they could not understand his lingo. Then he finally exploded. 'He was shot in the blooming arse, you stupid!'

Father English had a church later on at Mordialloc. I think he was there when he came out of the army until he died. He wasn't much older than me. He had to do our burials, and I was escorting him a bit if he had to go over the ridge. When someone died, he'd do the protestant service if the person was protestant. He was a marvellous bloke.'

I was amazed at Bob's ability to recall details, considering his earlier claim of a poor memory. I now ventured to ask something more about paperwork. The nitty gritty of the pay packet! His comment was detailed. 'As a private, six bob a day. Three and six was taken out of it for the family. Nell would get extra as well from the army.'

Further discussions with Bob elicited that he had authority to take that extra, which was over and above Nell's allowance, for his own use. 'That was my privilege! I could've kept six shilling if I'd wanted.'

War. Training. Arrival in New Guinea

'I quite enjoyed the training. The long route marches. When we had to sit in a tent and do nothing for two weeks, that made me mad. Sometimes they'd take us out in trucks and drop us somewhere, and we'd be told to find our way back. Some poor blighters didn't know how to get back.'

Bob was no stranger to camping and finding his way around the bush. The Bruton family had lived close to the state forest on the western side of their property. On both west and south it was many miles through the bush to Lyonville and Daylesford. The Bruton children roamed all over this big forest.

'We used to go for long walks. Yes, as kids we used to camp down the bush too. Took a box of matches and tommyhawk. We'd get some bark from the logs which had been felled and we'd make a hut out of that. We used to have our little fire and cook some spuds.'

'And finding your way in the bush?'

'No trouble with that! Just naturally we headed for home. It was easy.'

'Would you have preferred a different unit than the mortars?' I asked. Bob had a father who was very much a pacifist; perhaps he would have preferred a less active role.

'No, I think the unit was very good,' said Bob.

Bob had later joined the A.I.F. which was fairly common. The major reason for this was apparently so he could be transferred overseas if necessary.

'The A.I.F. could go anywhere. The Militia, made up of 'nashos', had to stay in Australian territory. This included at that time Papua New Guinea. The battalion would be sent somewhere else and the 'nashos' would have to be left behind.'

'And they'd want to be with their mates. So, is this the main reason you switched?'

'Yes. The main reason yes.'

'You didn't want to desert your mates, part of the group, and you wanted to see the group through, type of thing.'

'Well, you've got the right idea, yes.'

'If a fellow hadn't joined the A.I.F. and the other boys knew it, would they feel as if the side was being let down, would you think?'

'No! No. There was none of that. They were just mates.'

'Sounds as though most of the conscripts joined the A.I.F.'

'Yes. In our mob most of them did, yes. I mean, it didn't really make a lot of difference to us. Well it could've.

No I think it was very, very good. The mortars were six in a detachment. I was the mortar commander, and we'd be in headquarter company. This company consisted of odd bits and pieces. The signals communication telephone blokes they were in headquarter, machine gunners and tank attack. We'd be allotted to a particular company perhaps for the day, perhaps six days to support their action. We sort of got around the other battalions.'

His tone was enthusiastic. 'It was nice to get to know a terrific lot of fellows. All champions.' He paused. 'Or mostly.

We disembarked at Port Moresby, shrapnel valley, near the airfield where the zeros used to come over. There the Aussies had anti-aircraft guns and would shoot at the Japs' zero bombers. There was fallout of shrapnel here and there. It would put holes in our tents, but no one was hurt.'

My unspoken thought was that Bob's introduction to New Guinea was indeed a baptism of fire. But the rest of his story paled these episodes into insignificance.

'From Moresby we went by plane to Wau. At Wau there was a landing strip. One end of it was in Bolola Valley. The planes got down and got up again. At least some did. Some didn't. Some crashed. Too short a runway. Was a fairly big plane carrying about twenty of us. We had to charge straight into the jungle because they reckoned the nips were there, ready to knock us off. We had to cross Double Mountain to get behind the Jap position at Salamaua. We were there for four or five months. This was our first action and there was a lot of it.'

War. Tropical Tangles

Now I felt I was entering a man's world very much. The world of a soldier. I pressed on with questions. I felt I needed to know and understand some of the perhaps unspeakable. The impossible to fully describe. Conditions these men had to face.

'See any Japanese?' An underestimation, I knew. The appropriate questions were difficult. I was pleased Bob was prepared to share with me.

Midst a slow considered drawl, glances and pauses, Bob searched the recesses of his memory. Sometimes his face lit up with a ready grin. Sometimes fast, sometimes there was a slow spread to the rest of his face. This was punctuated by the third finger of his right hand producing a staccato tap tap on the table. But later, during the last hour, he had taken hold of an orange fly swat. As we talked, he tapped a regular beat. A restless quality. The tick tock of time.

When I looked into his eyes, soft and weary, I saw a man tired in spirit. Physically he was less agile and his frame now thinner. I invited him to visit us at Bairnsdale four hours' drive away. Verbally he was affirming, 'Yes,' he'd like to. His eyes did not convince. I wondered what those eyes were really saying. Was it that Bob had given up hope of going anywhere? A heavy feeling. My memory drifted back again to that strong, muscular and handsome man. The same drawl and sense of humour. But laughing eyes with a devilish glint sometimes. These eyes did not have that life. The tap-tapping continued with a relentless beat until Nell swept into the kitchen and suddenly grabbed the fly swat from his hand.

'I captured a Jap one time!'

I lifted an eyebrow.

Bob was looking past me. 'We had a little patrol. I could see this Jap. Regular, he'd go down this little track, come back real early in the morning. Was a little fellow. Was word from headquarters they wanted a prisoner. I had the job of jumping on him. I jumped down as he came past, from behind a tree.' He paused, his voice almost inaudible. 'They got quite a lot of info from him.' He responded to my worried look. 'Torture? They wouldn't, I don't think. He didn't fight. Just as well.

Another fellow we caught in about 1943. He talked better English than we did. This bloke was quite sure he was only a hundred miles from Brisbane. He thought he was in North Queensland. They were told they were in Queensland. They printed money especially for the invasion. At that stage they all had a pocket full of this money. They were quite sure they were in Australia! There was another one we captured; I think we ambushed him. We had a patrol there, went past. One of the blokes jumped out with an Owen gun. I think the rest of his patrol were knocked off, and he was at the tail end.'

'What an extreme test for one's nerves,' I commented. 'How did the men cope with the continuing stress?'

'Everyone seemed different. Some would sit down and howl like a baby for days on end. Others would go stupid, be talking all the time, gibberish. Then you'd get another one who'd want to clean up the Japs on his own. Bit of a problem when you're unable to send them back because of being in the jungle. Some of them would be hospitalised.'

I wondered how Bob had coped. His voice sounded tight, 'Having loved ones at home helped. I had that to look forward to, something to battle for. I did not notice the married blokes go off as quickly as the single blokes did.'

Tropical tangles, brooding, dense. I felt a shudder within me. A perfect setting for hiding and attack. The continuous strain on one's nerves. Not knowing when the unpredictable would strike. Ambushes were another subject.

'I remembered one time our whole mortar crew, five or six of us, went to another company through the jungle. When we arrived, the captain asked me if I'd take over the forward position because all of their blokes, their nerves had gone. Some of the best. They were sitting in their holes howling. The Japs attacked us too, we stopped them, and they didn't come back. Anyways those fellows were crack patrollers. They all cracked up because they'd been ambushed eight times. They were fired on but never saw a Jap. For some reason the Japs would fire high and they'd miss. They weren't used to being in the jungle, and they only managed to kill one of our blokes.'

How hard it must have been to keep one's feet moving! One step and then another. Each step an act of defiance against one's survival instincts. Each step closer to perhaps somewhere one did not want to go. Closer to someone one did not want to encounter.

My memories were stirred of the lush jungles I had seen in Sumatra and Malaysia. The deep brooding myrtle forests of southern Tasmania. Impenetrable. Small slithers of filtered light playing upon opulent green tapestries. The hidden habitations of watching eyes. I usually felt a certain sense of companionship when I walked in the Australian bush. A friendly relatedness to those concealed animal observers.

But what if those eyes belonged to one who stalked me, wanting my life? A homo sapien with fire and sword who would show no mercy. Perhaps I would be killed outright or left to die in agony. Vulnerable. Pitiful. Bleeding.

Every shadow, every bush, would shimmer with threat. A sudden innocent flap of wings was now a rustle of hand upon sword. The warm darkness, shadows in day or night, were now sinister and malevolent. That which I cannot see becomes ominous. My sweat is cold. Fear, my constant companion, becomes frozen numbness. Get the job done. Keep going. Don't think.

I pulled myself back to Bob. This was my fantasy. I wondered how he would express the reality of the nightmare. What feelings did he recall of living constantly on the edge, when the stench of death was real? The images of blood crimson through a bandage, filling a boot, a stain of dark slashed across a shirt. Waxen faces. Empty eyes. The staring of the dead.

My voice was apologetic when I returned to this question, 'How did you cope?'

'Don't know. I think I just took it in my stride, more or less. I don't know. Just did what we could and kept going. Could not think too much. Yes, the smell of death was real. The Japs smelt a lot worse.'

I ventured a little further. Tentatively, very tentatively. 'Have you some pictures that come back and haunt you?' I knew I was treading on delicate ground. His answer was affirmative.

'What do you do with them?' I asked.

'I've consciously worked at blocking them out.'

Bob shifted in his chair, uncomfortable. 'I just forget them. Make myself. There was always some who were gamer than others, and some who would avoid the risks, not many. Some would be so frightened they would tremble, couldn't speak, but still they did what they needed to do. They were the real good ones, they lived with it.'

To press further, I felt would have been a gross intrusion. The door to those memories was shut tight. Memories which had been placed in cold storage. Forever.

He went on, 'I don't know if I realised it at the time consciously, but after the first campaign I had a bit of shrapnel in my shin bone and it turned into an ulcer, and I was put in hospital. I never realised then I was a lot worse than I thought. They kept me there for three weeks, then convalescent camp for three weeks. My nerves were a lot worse than I thought.'

'And how did your nerves affect you?' I asked.

'I had nightmares then. Still have nightmares that a Jap is sneaking up on me. Once every three or four years now.'

War. Sickness

'While I was in hospital, I got malaria and they could not diagnose the type, and they thought I had dengue fever. But I got dengue fever up in the Ramu Valley. I was plain euchred, high temperature. Dengue knocked me out, I think I was unconscious for three days. I was put into the tent hospital; I remember we went out on a working bee the morning I went to the doctor. The doctor said, 'Oh gee, can't put everyone in hospital, take a couple of aspirins.' I sat under a tree. It was Thursday, and that was the last I remembered. I saw a church parade, I said 'Why are you having a church parade on Thursday?' Someone said, 'You're dinkum! You're talking sense at last!' I apparently had been raving. The convalescent camp was on a deserted rubber plantation. I remember the cuts around the trees and the little cups collecting the sap.

A few days later, I said I was alright. The doctor said, 'If I asked you to walk up the top of the peak there, you'd not make it.' Thought I was better than I was.

I got dengue two or three times. I think dengue was bad if not worse than malaria. Knocked me around more. It was caused by mosquitoes. About half the people who got it didn't get over it. It was sort of a rash to start with, like flea bites.'

Bob was now pondering something else. 'I'm thinking of this fellow. Only him and I left in our company. No one else. All had gone sick or something or out. I found him that day out on the track, out to it. Got him to the hospital quickly. He was lucky. Knocks you properly. We didn't have half our strength because of sickness.'

'What were your symptoms of dengue fever?' I asked.

'Blowed if I know. A fever.'

I wondered how a soldier managed if he caught dengue fever away from camp.

'If you caught it on patrol, you didn't cope very well. Well, I don't know, you just had to keep going! A lot were carried back to a temporary tent hospital by the boongs.' I found later that this was an affectionate nickname for the natives.

'At the tent hospital there would be an army doctor, sometimes orderlies, they were good. Apart from nurses in Moresby, it was all men.'

My mind flashed back, and I shared this with Bob. 'I remember you having malaria. You were lying on your bed in a terrible sweat. You were tossing backwards and forwards. Someone said you were delirious.'

Bob looked surprised at my disclosure. 'Yes, for a couple of years I had relapses. Old Lincoln, the doctor, got on to it in the end. 'I think this will cure it,' he said. I never went back to him again. It really done it.

Yes, we had tablets to keep the malaria down in the islands. We were told one tablet per day. The name? 'Abrin, adobren'. Can't properly remember. Oh! It sent you quite yellow, nearly as yellow as the Japs, but it used to do the job, mostly. When we were in camp, they'd line us up, make sure we swallowed them. Some of them didn't.'

'Any side-effects you knew of? Why did some not want to take it?'

'Only the yellow skin. Always a crank somewhere!'

By now the jungle felt even more deadly. My mind went from ticks, mosquitoes, to crocodiles—these cunning animals being on the top of my fear list.

'I saw one croc about five-foot-long. We were going to wash in his pool. We left him to it.' added Bob with a wry grin.

'Leeches?'

It seemed that leeches were the lesser of Bob's concerns. 'There were leeches, but I don't remember them worrying me.'

I imagined the presence of leeches may certainly not have worried him, he being already familiar with their habits from his childhood. He had told me, with his characteristic humorous twist, 'Mr Parker at Little Hampton was one of my teachers when I was about ten. He taught us lots of love songs because he was getting married and he was in a bad way. During school time we'd be sent down to the creek to collect leeches for the hospitals. Tommy got a prize for getting the most. We'd collect them from the edge of the water. Lift up sticks and stones. We'd put them in a jar. Some kids would put their feet in the water and pick off the leeches. I wasn't the brave type. But we'd get a leech on us now and then.'

'Worms?'

'Yes, yes.'

'Give you worm tablets, or what?'

'Bloody oath. Yes! I had to go to the hospital and get starved for a night. I was in there just after the war finished and we'd just come back from Moresby, I think. Not sure. Anyhow, one of our fellows got into the Military Police Force. Apparently, he had to wait to get home after the war, so he decided to join the police. He had a jeep to drive. It was six or eight months, might have been twelve months before they got home, and they had to do something. He reckoned it would be good, and it was!

But anyway, they had me in hospital and starved me this night. And then he come in, in the jeep and he said, 'We're going to open some bottles tonight, better come with us.' So I sneaked out the tent.' Bob was chuckling now.

'The next morning the Matron did her round. I thought, 'Now I'm in for it!' So she just looked at me, and she said, 'You might as well have some breakfast this morning. You won't be going up today.' I thought I got out of that pretty good. But he drove his jeep right down the centre of the tent when he brought me back. I remember some of them saying, but I don't remember anything. He plonked me on me bed.'

There must have been more to this worm story, hopefully a successful conclusion.

'Well, I had it the next night. I had me breakfast, and then I had to starve to the next morning. And they give us this bomb or so. By crikey, you'd have to be sitting down before you took it! My word!'

'Tape worms up there?'

'I think so, yes. Oh gee, I can't think of the name of this worm! But it was very bad you know. We were pretty near useless, but after we got rid of that, it made a heck of a difference.'

'Snakes?'

'I don't remember any snakes. I remember a cassowary. Lovely bird. I was observing up on the hill with glasses and he was on the creek bed. Also saw other birds, lots of different colours. I saw a lot of fungus. Showed up white and blue in the dark, even when it was really dark. You wouldn't notice them in the daylight, think that was up in the ranges back of Salamaua. They were about the size and shape of Iceland poppies, but I don't remember all of the colours. They were bright. Some of them may have been bright green. They were large, could be big as a small cup, small as a two bob. Different sizes and types. One doctor said the phosphorous on the fungi was penicillin, which was the new wonder drug in the tropics. You'd get ulcers from shrapnel wounds, mainly rest was the cure then, penicillin was just coming in at that time.'

Bob recalled when these fungi became important signposts. 'One of the times I remember these flowers, we were going to shift. We were carting stores and leaving. Intelligence platoon, a map reader, came down to guide us because we were going to be in the dark. We had been on the track before and followed this intelligence guy. At one stage there were five different ways we could go. I knew he went the wrong way! I yelled out, 'You're going the wrong track!' He replied, 'I'm from the Intelligence, I don't do those things!' There was this phosphorescent flower. Gee, it was pretty. Later we saw the same bush again. We realised we were going round in a circle. Two of the blokes and I sat down and had a snooze, then after a while we heard them go past, heading the wrong way again. I think I talked him into it, going the right way. I think he had the only torch, but a torch only buggers things up worse.

We got there eventually. It was this phosphorous looking flower which was the marker. I still remember it. At the army reunion a couple of years ago, I asked Fonz Ryan if he remembered it. He was a schoolteacher, used to teach at Harcourt North. He remembered it too. Fonz used to barrack for Castlemaine footy and I used to barrack for Kyneton. Fonz and I and another bloke used to barrack for different teams, and we'd meet up there in Bendigo at the matches.'

Bob was in full swing, his memory acute. 'There were lots of blowflies when I was in hospital. They brought a native policeman in. I don't know how many bullet holes he had in him. They'd gone right through. He'd laid out there for three days when they found him and brought him in. I used to help the nurse to clean him up. There were maggots coming out of him. They reckoned it was the maggots that saved him. All those bullets missed his heart, lungs, and vital organs. One in a million I s'pose. He just lay there moaning. I was in the next bed to him. They gave him a blood transfusion when they brought him in. Used my blood. It was straight from one to the other. On our meat tag, they also had our blood group as well as our name.'

'Meat tag?'

'Identification. We wore these metal tags with our names and numbers around our necks on a string, or bootlace. When an Aussie died, we'd take the meat tag, but it had to be handed to an official as soon as possible, as you could be knocked off the next day. We also gave a description of the place where he was buried or not buried, to the padres attached to the brigade or battalion.'

Yes. The possibility of death was ever present. I recalled how Bob's parents, and brothers and sisters back home, had coped with this constant, ominous threat to their loved ones in service. Every night there were prayers for Tom who had been taken prisoner in Greece, for Stan who was overseas at the same time in Palestine, and Bob who was in New Guinea. There would be prayers of a morning and prayers at night. The boys were surrounded very much by the care of their family. Mercifully, they all came home.

War. Equipment

Our discussions returned to the Ramu Valley, where Bob had been flown in. 'Big wide valley.' he said. 'Kurnai grass high. As high or higher than us. And sharp! After the wet, the whole valley would be covered with it. Bit like Australian sword grass, but not as severe.

One of our main jobs was cutting it down to make an airstrip in the location of the Bolola Valley. I remember one zero strafed us once, otherwise it was okay. We were issued with machetes. It was green, then went hay colours later on, like oats. I don't think anyone liked it. It was long, full length over six foot high. When we were cutting it, there were a lot of rats living in it, you'd step on them. Don't remember ever seeing a snake up there. I heard a few yarns about them.

After two weeks there I got dengue. I was pretty tired then. After I'd come good, the battalion had gone up into the Ranges. I had to make my way up there, could have been two or three of us. Then they sent me and my crew with the mortar to Bogadjim to patrol. We were there in C Company for three weeks.'

His final comment, 'It really wasn't very nice,' seemed to be the underestimation of the year.

How the soldiers coped in the high country, and how much gear they carried seemed important. Bob said he wore a belt and braces over his shoulders. Attached to the belt was a haversack. 'On one side there would be pouches on the strap for ammo.'

On his back he, as the mortar commander, carried wire, compass, watch, a distance finder but no binoculars. Bob explained that only the commandos were issued with these. Additionally, he would carry three ten-pound bombs. The mortar gun came apart into three pieces, the base plate, the barrel, and the tripod, and the men would carry these heavy pieces between them. The fine wire was for his bush telephone.

'I'd take it with me when I was finished if I could. More often I'd have to break the wire and leave it there. I would run the wire out. I could talk to the boys on the wire.

Our rations would fit in our pouches nicely when we went out on patrol. We'd have just enough food for a few days. We were issued with salt tablets too. If we were out more than three days, they would send out food with another patrol. Our field rations were in tins. Ours weren't very good. Bully beef and a packet of dry biscuits. But not dry for long!' he quipped. 'Then they were trying us on the American rations, but they got too sweet. We'd swap with the natives, some chocolate for a pumpkin or a marrow. Our vegetables were dehydrated carrots and stuff. At one stage the nips got on to the dropping ground, frightened the natives away who picked our provisions up, and all we had for the two weeks was dehydrated carrot. We were glad when we got a few biscuits.'

'Would you say you were generally well nourished?'

'Not really. We had the dehydrated carrots for a week, was all we had. Even when things were going well, we didn't eat well. Had to get supplies too, they had to be dropped. The planes were lucky to get out. A lot crashed. Called them 'biscuit bombers.' Other than that, it was good with food. Most times you had bully and biscuits and things. Other times you had very little.' He added on a characteristically optimistic note. 'It's all good when you're hungry.

We carried rifles, these and ammo in the pouches were heavy in themselves. As mortar commander I had a pistol, not a rifle. I seldom had a map; they were few and far between. You wouldn't want to get cleaned up with one on you either. Sometimes we'd have a range finder.' He tried to explain the range finder to me. 'It's really two photos, you look in with mirrors. They were very good, but not much good in the jungle. I often wished I had some binoculars.'

'Did you have a first aid kit?'

'I could wonder the same thing,' said Bob, as he searched his memory. 'What comes to mind is a bandage, Vaseline sort of stuff, a safety pin I remember was stuck on this bandage. It was pretty basic, just a little bundle.'

'Were you taught first aid?'

'No. Only through practical experience. Everyone had the same basic kit of bandage and pin which we used to wrap around a wound. I remember helping a fellow out. He got a bullet through his knee. We had two or three bandages around it, and I got him halfway back to headquarters and he was in agony. The pain was catching up with him. Percy Finn C Company. In the end we carried him. He died the other day.'

Bob's memory appeared vivid. It was hard to believe that sixty years separated these events.

Carrying the mortar and bombs was heavy going. 'The mortar bombs used to be done up in three ten-pound bombs. Often we'd have a pack in each hand. As a rule, everyone had three bombs, but they could have one pack extra. We were always carrying mortars.'

'Who would carry the mortar pieces?'

'Well, there were supposed to be five or six in the mortar crew, and we'd take a piece each. A mortar commander, usually a corporal or a sergeant, well, he wouldn't have to carry a piece because he'd be up with the company commander. He wasn't supposed to carry anything.'

'And that included you, didn't it?'

'Yes. That was me, yes.'

'I bet you did though!'

'Yes, oh yes, we did. We weren't supposed to.'

'You weren't supposed to because you were keeping an eye on things going ahead, doing reconnaissance too?'

'Yes. And then they used to have the three bombs in a cardboard parcel with a sort of handle on for carrying it. Each one would carry one of these parcels. We were very unpopular with the company, the rifle boys, because they'd have to carry some for us too. They'd take a very dim view of that.' Bob laughed, 'Can't blame them either!'

'Carry thirty pounds of bombs as well as a mortar piece?'

'As a rule, no. The mortar pieces were about sixty pounds. Each mortar piece.'

The weight these soldiers had to carry continued to stun me. 'Would have been much easier to carry the bombs.'

'Oh yes!'

I imagined the strength these men had to maintain, carrying much more than a bushwalker, with the added stress of constant vigilance, often illness. Just how far did they usually have to walk?

'Easily two to three kilometres, sometimes longer. We were sometimes carrying the mortar all day, other times just an hour or so. We always measured distances in hours, 'that hill' was two-and-a-half hours away.'

'And what about a typical day?'

'We'd be up before dawn; we'd all be waiting for them. The Japs used to attack at dawn and in the dark. If it was okay, we'd go patrolling then around the area to check out if there were any Japs. Depending what the call was from the company commander, we'd often have to go somewhere else and drop bombs.' Bob suddenly remembered that they also carried mosquito repellent, salt tablets, and tablets for malaria.

On the beat in the jungle. Funk holes came to mind. What were these and how were they constructed? Perhaps this would further stimulate Bob's memory and lead to another interesting tangent. In this case it led to yet another piece of equipment which they had to carry.

'We always carried a shovel. We'd dig little holes, a funk hole for yourself but not trenches as such. I would have great fights with the second in command of the mortar. When we'd get somewhere, officially the first job you do, would be to dig a hole and put your mortar up. He used to put up his two-man tent first. I just could not stop him. He dropped into my hole one day when bombs hit. I said, 'Now you know what I mean.' But he still continued with the same behaviour. Then the officer would come along and see a tent up but no funk hole, and I'd be in trouble, not him!' Bob added in his kindly fashion, 'He didn't like that rain. It was always damp in the jungle. 'Dry,' meant just if it did not rain for two or three days. You could go for a week without dry clothing it was that warm. If it was here in Victoria, you would get pneumonia.'

For a moment I pictured Little Hampton. Frankly, I thought, given the inclement conditions there, and the very basic nature of the Bruton boys' sleeping quarters, it was surprising even with the driest of dry clothing the boys did not get pneumonia.

Now Bob continued matter-of-factly in his understated style, 'I usually used my boots and socks for a pillow.'

'Bare feet?'

'Mozzies would get them a bit. Saved me some foot diseases, though. They used to issue us with a mosquito lotion in a screw top bottle. That was the best tinea cure there was. We'd put it between our toes. Then if we wanted a light, we'd tear a bit off our pants, make a wick and light it. I'm not sure it was so good for the mozzies. Good for everything else.'

Another item the men carried was a ground sheet. Bob recounted they slept on this, but if it was raining, they'd put it over themselves. 'We seldom carried a blanket, usually a ground sheet. If we had it. This was a waterproof rubbery thing. It was used as a cape to keep the rain off. Very handy when we went over Double Mountain. I had a spare pair of boots. I pitched them away, couldn't carry them.'

'You often didn't have a ground sheet?'

'That's right.'

'So you'd just be on the ground, would you?'

'That's right, yep.'

Bob saw my stunned expression. 'We slept like a log!'

I was unconvinced. 'You'd be a bit damp though.'

'Oh yes.'

'You'd sleep in those funk holes?'

'Often slept in them.'

'But you didn't always have a funk hole?'

'No. Oh no. Very often not. Only made a funk hole if we were staying a few days. Was the first thing we'd do. Or, even just for the night sometimes. You know depends on circumstances.'

'Tents?'

'Yes. Sometimes we had a two-man tent, and we'd have canvas with holes, and cut saplings and made bunks out of it. We'd have a tent over these two bunks.'

'You'd have to carry that, wouldn't you?'

'Yes. The canvas. The tent was much lighter stuff. I mean, that was when we were going to stop out for a few days.'

'What weight would you normally have to carry?'

'I think fifty-six pounds was the limit. I'm not sure. It was usually more over the limit than under it.'

War. Bathing

'We shared two-man tents. Slim said to me, 'Louie stinks! He won't have a bath. He just goes down to the creek and comes back.' I walked behind him, got him in the river, made sure he took off his clothes and washed them. It was quite a struggle. He was just being a spoilt little boy. We'd wash our clothes, hang them on a bush, then get back into the same clothes again.'

I imagined bath times to be occasions of great vulnerability. Naked men being fired on by the Japs. No clothes. No protection. Bob was more concerned about implications of not washing than possible attack by the Japs.

'Your skin could go rotten if you didn't wash, and clothes would get that stiff you would not be able to put them on. Even when things were crook, we'd come to a river, have a good wash. Half would go on guard and half would go in. I think that saved us too.

One fellow, he was a corporal. When we left there, he would not take his boots and socks off or have a bath in a creek. Didn't want to be caught without them. Well, he ended up a cripple with scale which took the skin off up the legs, even dug into the bone. Was a lot of it there, we'd have to battle it all the time. This fellow didn't wash for weeks. I was in his crew and we were sent out to this place, and he had us dig his funk hole and he never shifted out. The company commander would ring up and I'd answer the phone and go up, and I'd have a talk to my sergeant. I thought the sergeant would straighten him up, but he stayed there in the funk hole.'

Probably the reason was obvious, but I asked my stock question 'Why?'

Bob's blue eyes were direct and confrontative. 'Because he was frightened! He ended up in the hospital. I never saw him again. But someone told me he gradually got better. He never took his boots and clothes off, started stinking so much that they ended up chucking him in the lake. But it was too late, his legs were gone.

That scale! We had tinea too, but it was worse than tinea. Used to go right up your legs, crutch. Very itchy red rash. Anyone who neglected personal hygiene! But others got it too. They used to put mosquito oil on the rash, was the best cure for it. The fellow who didn't wash his feet looked horrible, like chops. Pure flesh. It hurt him to have his boots taken off.'

I was reminded again that Bob was brought up in the damp. But it was a cold damp and windy. The chill winds swept across the Bruton farm at Little Hampton near Trentham, northwest of Melbourne. They would knife you in half. Double you up. The big open fire in the front room of the small house was a saving grace. Many a cold body backed on to this fire, craving its warmth. The glow illumined the crammed floor to ceiling bookshelves, made from fruit cases, at the side of the enormous fireplace.

In the winter the men sometimes worked in driving sleet, even snow. They dug spuds and picked them up, the frost crusty on the ground. All day the frost stayed in the shadows. No gloves then! For most of the year the big work horses pulling ploughs and lorries snorted hot steam, shiny coats licked dry by the piercing wind's insistence. The damp of sweat. Hot sweat on a cold day.

Yes! Bob was indeed no stranger to damp or sweat for that matter! Damp everywhere, even the toilet seat, a cold walk past the well. And the squares of newspaper on the nail, cold on one's nether regions. All added up to damp, damp, damp!

Brilliant green lichen. This verdant velvet, delicate thin, embellished the lower boards of the weatherboard house. It covered the jinker shed, tall chaff shed, and the stables. It crept up on the southern edges of the slender gum trunks behind the pig stye.

The bottom paddock was always damp. A case for gumboots to clamber down, gather fresh minty watercress growing in the permanent spring, a soft trickle from the side of the hill. In later years, one of Bob's brothers, Percy, put a large dam in the boggy area at the bottom.

I remember more evidence of this invasive chill. The wash house out the back, opposite the well, was not impervious to the deathly wraith-like windy fingers. They reached through the chinks between the grey rough-hewn weathered timbers. An inhospitable place. Built by teenage Tommy under his practical mother's watchful eye. Braved by the Bruton offspring every week when they lit the copper for their baths. Oldest first, with less water. Another bucket or so of hot water for each new occupant. The youngest, Harold, the last, could stay in for a longer soak. Large and high, the white enamel bath somehow shielded one's bare shoulders from gasping goosepimply draughts. If one crouched low enough! And kept vulnerable skin from cold enamel. Puffs of breath and warm steam were a welcome contrast.

The New Guinea damp was not of this variety, that is, apart from the surprising chill high on misty mountain ridges. Better the New Guinea warmth? Or better not. This tropical heat fostered an insidious, more vicious variety of deadly diseases. And, in wartime, that was the least of it!

War. Action. Fuzzy Wuzzy Angels

'We had to attack this place sometime. Was this major. And the only time we had a tank with us. It was my job to guard him. The major walked behind the tank calling, 'Corporal, are you there?' I would be in the bush; I could guard him better there than beside him. I said to him, 'Why are you yelling out? Don't you attract the crabs?' 'What do you think I yell for?' he said.'

Bob answered my puzzled look. 'Drawing the crabs, that is the Japs, was what he was doing.

At one time the tank was firing on a position a bit further, and he said to me, 'Get over the other side of that tree will you!' The bark flew off the tree! A jolly woodpecker had fired! I just happened to be on the right side of the tree. Our tank stopped him.

But this time a couple of jeeps were following us with lots of cases of ammo. The major was sitting on the boxes of ammo, telling me what he wanted. We heard a shell coming, and we tipped over backwards because we thought it was going to hit! As we were picking ourselves up, we heard 'The major and Bruto are gone!' We stuck our heads up 'Like hell we are!''

A subsequent discussion indicated that 'woodpecker' meant a machine gun.

Bob said earlier that the plentiful water probably saved them from fungal diseases. They had bathed regularly. My bushwalking experience indicated caution concerning the drinking of it.

'We had tablets to put in the water,' said Bob. 'We had the salt tablets too to take every day. We'd get very tired otherwise. We'd be euchred! It was okay to drink water if it was near a spring. Been a blue there one time, and we were on a little creek. Fairly flat country. About 200 yards along the creek were machine gunners. They were supposed to patrol upstream, us downstream. They were doing their patrolling, and we were drinking the water out of the creek. After they left there we went up, and there were two Jap bodies in the water. Put us off! Our blokes who had been patrolling should have told us! They weren't doing their job. They had just been through and we were behind them.

There were quite a few Japs we'd bury. We did not take identification, nowhere to put the tags as we were pretty loaded up. We started collecting them at one stage.

We were told don't worry about that, just get rid of them. No system for the collection of Jap identification. We handed some in and they probably chucked them away. Just buried them in their holes. One glance. We cleaned up a lot of them. Buried a lot.

One night one of the blokes looked out his tent and said, 'There's some wacker out there digging up the Japs!' Fellows going through their pockets to see what they could find. I ordered them out of it, and they went. I don't even know where they came from, but they were real scroungers.'

We moved from death to angels. A mutual relief.

'Fuzzy wuzzy angels was true,' said Bob. 'The natives did a lot more than they were given credit for. Boongs was an endearing name really. Never heard anyone speak a word against them! They were mainly stretcher carriers; they'd carry the wounded. We carried all our own gear. Sometimes the natives would carry a bit more, like supplies. The natives would bring supplies—our ammunition and food, from the dropping ground to us. The only way was for a gang of natives to pick up the air drops. The Japs got on to them one day and they scattered them. That was when we had no food for a few days. We had to clean the Japs out before we could get more tucker. It was pretty hard to get the natives back. Then they would disappear into the bush. Could be right beside you and you would not know they were there.

I've seen them carry a bloke out and he stopped moving and he died on them, and the natives sat down and howled. They didn't know him from a bar of soap. They just sat down and howled and howled. Would be mainly six to carry them out.'

'Would they be paid to assist?' I wondered.

Bob sounded unsure, 'Yes, well, might have got their rations. I don't know, very little anyway. The native police boys were terrific. I saw one mid track, rifle poised, standing motionless all night. The natives were very loyal to the Aussies.'

'Why?' I sounded blunt.

'The Japs give them hell! Would rape their women.' He saw my shock. 'Oh no! They were horrible!

The natives would build me an opip up the tallest tree. They'd tie steps with vines. Kunda vines. Could be a hundred yards long or more. Could be as thick as your arm down to a thumb size. They'd tie steps with vines especially for us, right up high. We could see from the top sometimes little wisps of smoke or missing trees where the Japs might be hiding, sometimes we'd pick out their fox holes. The natives. Oh yes. They were good. They'd take a vine from one side of a river to the other, to save us from being swept away. They were marvellous.' he exclaimed vigorously.

'An opip?'

'An observation post. Talking about opips. One time, oh they were mad. An American corporal wanted to use my opip. He got up the top and started shouting out he could see the nips! We had to scatter; the nips started firing on us. As I was getting down the tree, the Japs guns started blazing. Hit the tree further down, he'd given away our position!'

Bob scratched his head, then ran his fingers through straight brown hair. 'We were on patrol one-time round Bogadjim and the Finisterre Ranges. Was Ernie Doherty, Whitey, Ocka Powtie, Bob Gillespie, someone from Shepparton. Names hard to come by these days. Normie Hore, another fellow. We were supposed to harass the Japs. They were withdrawing along the coast.

Were such a terrific crew. We all got home. Just together for that patrol and for three or four weeks. We'd get back to the platoon and be given a new lot of fellows. The officer-in-charge said he'd like to recommend me for a decoration. 'Not on your account, for your blokes.' But our next in charge blew it. I think it was crook, and the boys did such a good job. Usually, patrols would be only half a day. Well, three days I remember being out. Oh well, this Bogadjim patrol, that was three weeks. That wasn't right though, I reckon that lieutenant should have been bagged for that. But he wasn't, anyway.'

'That would have been pretty gruelling—a big strain for the men on duty.'

'Oh terrible. Yes. Yes. They just about cracked up.'

'The lieutenant go out with you too?'

'No! Oh no. That was his job from headquarters, just to send us out. But this bloke, he used to get under our skin. He'd be there annoying us all the time until there was something coming up and he'd have to go off to a gas or a water school. Or a machine gun school or something. He missed nearly all the action. But he was uncanny, the way he could do that!

Old Lululiei. Gee, he was an ugly old coot! The ugliest bloke I've ever seen. He was the leader of the village. He had the sort of face you'd never trust. He'd trade pumpkins and bananas and taro for salt tablets and chocolates. He'd come every morning. I think the Japs had cleaned his village up and burned it down. The natives had moved what was left up into the hills a bit, he'd never tell us where he was.

But anyway, he'd say, I forget how they used to count. He'd say, 'Two hundred Japs coming from that way!' And sure as eggs, they'd attack us. He'd point, 'From there.' In the end, one day he came and said, 'Japan man come from that way.' He pointed west, then he pointed east, and then he pointed south, 'that way and that way and that way!' We all got out. We got up the track, we were walking along the ridge in the rain. We could hear the Japs come to where we'd been, could hear the bombs and the mortar guns. Old Lululiei alerted the company several times. This last time, that was it. That was when the Japs were pulling out and going to Wewak and trying to consolidate there.'

Bob went on to recount another memory of this particular camp, and another, perhaps even closer shave. A memory which may have been hard to share. A memory close to his heart.

'Us mortar group were there in the C Company for three weeks instead of the usual one week. We did a lot of good, but the boys were just about rebelling on me, because they wanted to re-join our battalion 58 and 59, because this was out of the firing line. We had averaged three hours sleep a night. The nips were at us nearly all the time. The boys wanted some peace, could not stand much more of it. I went to the boss who said, 'I don't know what we're going to do without you fellows.' I remember I went and lay down on a hammock, then I seemed to nod off.'

Suddenly Bob's gaze and words faltered, his eyes filled with tears. 'Nell came along and said, 'You stop there! The boss said you could go. Stay where you are.' Bob was fighting now for his composure. 'I must have gone to sleep and dreamt it. But it seemed she was there. We stayed. The next day, we could see along the track where the Japs had been lying in wait to ambush us.

Saved my life,' he said in a tight voice. 'We used to use this track every day to go up the hill for provisions. But for safety's sake, we'd never go through first thing in the morning. We'd get off the track through the jungle, about ten feet away from it. The track was mostly up and exposed. We took turns doing it.'

'Taking one's life in one's hands,' I said.

'All dangerous jobs,' was Bob's resigned remark. 'We did not often walk on the tracks, we got off them. If you went on the tracks, you'd be ambushed very quickly.'

I was aware of standing back, but now I was very much in the present. For a moment I recalled a dream of my own. A dream about Bob a few days earlier. I dreamed he was worried about his health, that he was unwell. But I drew a blank with Bob concerning my worried question.

'I'm alright,' Bob had said.

Perhaps dreams are in the family, I mused, considering my mother also had a tendency to dream that different sort of dream.

'It was the day after my dream that old Lululiei warned us about the Japs coming from three directions. After this we had two or three days on Bogadjim beach, a lovely beach. At the end of this beach was a Jap hospital. They'd left the hospital with everything still there. We didn't touch anything either.' Bob seemed to be making some sort of inference.

'Why not?' I asked.

'Because it would have been booby-trapped. They were buggers for that! This was about the time when the Japs were pulling out from Bogadjim and going towards Wewak to consolidate further up the coast.

I remember seeing a woman, she came along with a load of wood. She had a dog sitting on the load, its feet on her head, a pig on one tit and a baby on the other. There were two kids walking along in front and she'd give them a kick along. I said to the boys with us, 'Gee. she's too old to be having kids.' Turned out she was eighteen! They say the women never lived to be more than thirty. The awful life they had!

Another day we were having a rest, and a mob of six young blokes and one girl came along. The girl had a big bundle of wood on her head. The boys never walked with her and never carried one stick. I had trouble controlling our boys then!'

War. Japanese Swords. Booby Traps

Bob was stirring his spoon round and round in his black tea. He spoke amid the tinkling, which was light compared with the next subject. 'We were on patrol one time. A fellow pulled us up. There was a Jap sword buried to the handle in the ground. This forward scout had the sense to leave it alone. We stood guard over it when we went past, and I reported it. A company commander sent down a person to dismantle it. He didn't get there. Another patrol went there the next day, and a fellow grabbed it. Killed him, and one each side.'

This having to be alert all the time must have been exhausting. The tension. The strain. Now Bob was alluding to the importance of good observation. 'Bit like when we used to go trapping rabbits. If we saw fresh dirt on the track, we'd know it was being used. This was the same. If we saw fresh earth on the track, we'd go well around it, be a booby trap.

Those Jap swords! Everyone wanted one. But there was no way of getting them home. They were difficult to carry. We were loaded up anyway, and we couldn't send them home. Hard enough to carry it out. No way of posting home. They'd just cover the bomb itself with dirt and had wire from the sword to the bomb. I remember I jumped into a foxhole, were two Japs in it, but they had no use for their swords. We put our packs in a heap with the swords. We were going to go back and get them! One of the fellows went back later, and this pile had been blown to bits. We didn't get our shaving gear or shave for weeks.

Those swords seem to be unlucky. Those who got them the next day they seemed to be knocked. Was uncanny. After that I give it away, I didn't want one. At this same place the boys set up the mortar. I was telling them what to do. I jumped into my hole and a mortar shell from the Japs came and landed on its side next to me. And this little Freddie Conway. He was always scared. He saw it and threw it out! Bang it went. We used to think that these shells that did not land the right way were duds, after that we weren't so sure.'

I returned to the safer ground of rabbits. Bob's down-to-earth observations from his rabbiting days. I wondered if the country boys coped better in the jungle.

'Probably yes, but a lot of the city boys, they adapted very quickly. One guy would stand as forward scout, he'd see a fly on a bush right away. He grew up in Brisbane.

He'd have only been about twenty. We'd take it in turns to be forward scout, had to lead ten yards in the front.'

'Lonely?' I queried.

'Sometimes safer, because sometimes the Japs would leave the forward scout and concentrate on all of the rest of the bunch, therefore we had a wide gap between all of the fellows. Talking about getting ambushed. We'd booby trap tracks as well.'

I wondered about other hapless creatures which might activate these booby traps. 'Bet some jungle animals were caught in the traps as well,' I muttered.

My comment was carefully considered. 'Yes, possums and wild pigs would set off booby traps. Made a mess. We wouldn't know if the noise was caused by the Japs or not. Black pigs were in the bush. When the Japs cleaned up the villages, their pigs went off into the bush. There was a saying 'Never abuse a native's pig or their garden in that order.' We'd make booby traps out of a lot of things if we didn't have grenades. I run out of grenades and there was a construction group coming up behind us. We used wire for some booby traps. Actually we used a lot of sig wire for booby traps.'

'Sig wire?'

'Signals, telephone wire. When using it for communication, it was supposed to be my little phone, so I'd look after it at night too. I lay on the wire. No good getting up all night looking at it. I'd go to sleep laying on it. That's right, yere. The slightest little vibration and I'd wake up.

I think the major was in charge. Anyway, we knocked the Japs off a little hill that was in the way, and we were only out for the day. Ended up being three days. And after we'd pulled out from there, we were dragging our sig wire with us. But then, we couldn't get through. The Japs had found it and cut it. And I wanted to drop it there and then. But the major said, 'Keep running it out, we might join it up one day, one time.' We didn't know. We hoped we didn't because that's how they used to trap us. They'd cut it and then they'd sit and wait for us to come along and find where the break was.'

'So, that would be rather nerve wracking then.'

'Yes. It wasn't the best. It wasn't the best at all.'

'Did you ever follow up your telephone wire to find you were being ambushed?'

Bob's voice was tense. 'Yes, oh yes! Oh yes, we've done that. But I mean, we've been very careful. Saw what was going on. I know one mob, or one patrol that got into trouble that way.'

'About how long would the wire be?'

'Oh, several miles. Oh yes. Fine wire, very fine. Shellacked covering, like a paint. But it was out of a roll, copper, about the size of a billy. Well, you'd get about two or three miles out of it.'

'And the Japs. Did they have telephone wires? Did you cut theirs too?'

'Yeh. Yes. Yes. I remember one time. Not us. Another unit. They done that. Oh, they got the Japs too. The Japs had much the same wires.'

46

'All a battle of wits. Not only fire power and manpower. A battle of every part of everything.' I said, feeling a vast abyss between Bob's experience and my understanding.

We sat quietly for a moment; Bob's expression reflective. 'Funny after the war, even with the motor cars. It was psychological I know. Fellow over here, used to do the Fergie tractors up. He said, 'Come and look.' Was a Jap car! I opened the door. I swore I could smell Japs in it. The car was made in Australia! Yes, you could smell the little stinkers, could smell where they'd been.'

'I suppose when you could smell them, you'd be on alert?' I said.

'Oh yes! We were on alert anyway. Sometimes in the jungle we would come across only ferns or bamboo. The Japs used to get the young bamboo shoots. You could tell if we ever came to a heap of bamboo, we'd have a look and see if the young shoots had been cut off recently. If they had, we'd know there were Japs around.'

Bob's eyes had that faraway look again, 'We were on this ridge, and Paddy Barnes, he was a machine gunner. I think he was a sergeant. He came to me and said, 'I'll show you where our booby traps are down the ridge, because I'm leaving to go to an officer training school.' Well, Paddy tripped over his own booby trap! He should have laid down immediately! He should have been flat, but he hid behind a little bush. I dived over the ridge, and he got it in the face. I saw him recently. He had a lot of scarring.'

War. Mateship

It was amazing to me that any of these men were able to survive both the rigours of war and jungle. The Japs, the mosquitos, the ticks. The continuing dampness of the climate. Sickness. Sometimes lack of food. Dealing with explosives. The stress of it all. The extreme stress. I imagined life long-links would be forged between men and discussed this with Bob the following day.

'Friends for life. Been through a lot together. Bloke down in Melbourne just died. Percy Finn was in the rifle company. He got that bullet through the leg, and I carried him for quite a while. He was helpless. He never forgot that. He was a stranger to me before this. Stiffy Anstis. He was a great swimmer. Got drowned in the Murray a few years ago. His girls still keep in touch with us. Whitey, Roy White, he was a mortar man with me too. Lives up in the Mallee, Sea Lake way, near Manangatang. We've always kept in contact. Loves talking, gets a bit fantastic. Been a good mate. Ordinary decency. We were on the Bogadjim patrol together. We're both country boys, made a difference.'

'Difference?' I underlined.

'Yes. We sort of spoke the same language. Finding ways in the bush like me. Whereas the others had no idea. We could talk about things that the townies would not talk about and vice versa. We were all good mates, but there was something about the country fellows.

Shorty at Mildura. He was special. Shorty Davis was in the canteen when we were in camp. He'd look after me. He was a little short fellow, and when out in the bush, I'd look after him. I remember we were going over Double Mountain to get at the back of the nips. We had orders not to stop more than two minutes. Hard to get the group up there, we'd be sweating, and it was bitterly cold. We were well back west of Salamaua, crossed the Bolola Valley over to the back of Salamaua. The highest point of it was 9500 feet. There were millions of years of vegetation lying there to climb over. Going up some of those steep pinches on the mountain, Shorty's legs would not reach from one foothold in the vines to the other. 'Come on you little bastard!' I'd say, 'I can't!' I'd put the rifle down and lift him over. Shorty was carrying a dixie and it would click with each step. When it stopped, I knew he'd stopped. Even the big blokes would have to find footholds.'

It was on another day when talking with Bob that I returned to the subject of dixies. What were they?

'A dixie was our tin for food. Was aluminium, had a folding handle. You'd eat out of it, put it on a fire. We had one each plus an aluminium mug. 'It would go clink, clink on the back of Shorty's pack.'

Bob was thinking more about Shorty. 'He was always pretty resourceful in more ways than one. At Mildura he'd go round the empty pokies and pick up the stuff people left. Died seven or eight years ago.'

Bob had that faraway look again. 'They put a bridge over this river. There were boards on it. Shorty was followed by Stiffy Anstis. A board was missing. Shorty missed the board and fell down the gap! Stiffy grabbed him by the braces and hoisted him up. Been a hell of a lot of rain and the river was raging. Fall would have been death.'

It was a week or two later I discovered from Bob that this hazardous crossing was tackled during the night. 'The boards were just tied on with vines on to thicker vines, made by the boongs, some blokes with short legs could find it hard.'

I was wondering if Bob's training from carrying his brother Allan, a polio victim, when Bob was of school age may have assisted his ability to carry a man. Or perhaps throwing around all those heavy bags of spuds had been another type of training for the job.

'Sooner have a bag of spuds any day.'

'Why?'

'Wouldn't have the responsibility then. A man is much the same as weight goes.'

Allan. Mentone

'Yes. I used to stay at Grandma and Grandpa Bruton's at Mentone and take Allan to the Children's Hospital. I don't know if it was four days a week, was several days, for him to have a massage. Uncle Joe built a box cart out of broom sticks and bolts and plough wheels. I remember taking Allan to Mentone from Little Hampton. We'd go on the steam train to Melbourne, then it was electric from the city. At Mentone, I'd cut through Booker's paddock.

When we went to the Children's Hospital, I'd wheel Allan from Mentone, leave the box cart at the Cheltenham Railway Station. Never thought of it being pinched those days. The cart made a big noise on the gravel. No springs. Allan never complained. But it was easier than carrying him on my back. In Melbourne we got the tram to Grattan Street, carried him two blocks after we got off. Well-wishers one day gave him a big apple. Allan hated people giving. Sometimes it would be a threepence, sixpence, or a shilling.

Got on the wrong train one day, ended up at Tunstall, now called Nunawading. I got out and wanted to go to the other side to get back. Showed the conductor my ticket, but he wouldn't let me! I bawled. A nice old bloke came along and wanted to know what was wrong. He went and saw the stationmaster and we got over to the other side.

I remember going with Min in the train to Melbourne. She was a great help. Don't remember her being at Mentone when I was taking Allan in. They reckon it was Min and I who got his arm moving. Laying there in the 'Thomas splint.' Laying there. The splint stretched out his arms. Was terrible! Mum took them off eventually. No one could stand it any longer. I remember Mum, she'd been told to keep his arms tied into it, and to feed him. Min and I used to whip out his right arm and try and get him to feed himself. Could be what saved it. We'd get into trouble. Strap it up quickly when Mum was coming. We were trying to help him. Then years later, the treatment was changed for polio patients. A woman introduced this treatment, to use the limbs, exercise them, which was very successful. By this time Allan had had numerous operations, including one to stiffen his leg, so the treatment may not have worked. Don't remember him crying, seldom he'd go crook.'

'Did you have a special way of being able to carry him—piggyback or what?'

'Piggyback. Yere. I used to pitch him. Sort of put my arms under his legs and shoulders and sort of pitch him over me shoulder and then grab him round that way. Yere, oh yes, I used to piggyback him.'

'And did Allan have any strength to hold on?'

'Oh, very little. Oh yere. Oh well, one hand. He'd put the good arm around and catch hold of his bad arm you know, around under me neck. But that used to get a bit choky sometimes. No. I had no trouble carrying him. I just developed this idea of pitching him up!'

'You were pretty fit.'

'I must have been, yes.'

'You were only about what, thirteen, fourteen?'

'I was twelve.'

'I must have left the Little Hampton School at thirteen. One of the reasons to help Allan. Got leave to be away. Four months at Mentone, but I was that far behind when I got back. Grandma and Auntie Elsie were always asking when I was coming down. My word. Auntie Elsie did a lot of work massaging Allan's legs, either staying at our place or Mentone.'

'How did Allan get around at home?'

'Taradale he was in hospital. At Little Hampton he'd sit on the sledge sometimes. Boards across, chain attached to the horse. We had the box cart to take him to school. You'd get into it like putting a horse into a dray or buggy. The sledge, the horse would pull it. We'd take him for a ride. We had to use the sledge a lot for carting spuds in the paddock. Us kids could load the spuds then. Drive along beside a bag of spuds and tip it over on to it. Also could roll stones on it, and cart them off.'

'These days they don't use sledges much.'

'No! They've got good tyres, wheels these days.'

'And when Allan went to school, did the kids pull the box cart?'

'We used the box cart, would put a rope on the front and oh, it was muddy sometimes. And George would pull him and I'd push. But if it was too muddy, we'd just carry him. Well, I remembered I carried him.'

'Red mud. I remember it very well.'

'Lovely friendly mud. It would stick.'

'Was the teacher helpful with Allan?'

'Yes. Yes. I never noticed. Don't remember anybody against. I think he just fitted in and they done what they could.'

'Did Tom help too?'

'No. Tom didn't help. No. No. Wasn't Tom's thing. No, I don't remember Tom doing anything like that. Was more into the wireless, all he could think of. He'd have been fifteen, sixteen. He'd have been into his wireless by then.

When I stayed at Mentone for the stretch of three or four months, they gave me the job of the sled. Don't remember the horse's proper name. They used to call the horse in the sled 'Lizard.' Well. They always called everybody by a nickname.

They had a shed Uncle Albert built, and the women used to do most of the packing of the asparagus. They used to tie the asparagus bundles with flax. And I remember Auntie Eva being there one stage. Whether she was just in there with a cup of tea or working, I don't know. She ended up getting and died with creeping paralysis.

The blokes used to wash all their veggies. They'd bunch them out in the paddock ready and bring 'em in. Then wash them and stack them on the lorry to go to market.

There was a well with a windlass on it, up near the shed. Was a row of fig trees, was at the top end of that. That's where we used to do the washing.

Grandma and Auntie Elsie used a wood stove. They used to burn tea-tree wood in it. Where they got it from, I don't know. The cooking? I just enjoyed it full stop.'

'The tea-tree would spit, I imagine.'

'It did too. The clock from Auntie Elsie that I gave Paul my grandson, I remember on a mantel piece. But I don't remember if it was in the kitchen, over the stove, or the front room.

Grandma used to have a cow. I think everyone had a cow. She was a lovely little jersey. Grandma would tether it out on the side of the road on the grass. Part of our job used to be to go and bring the cow home or shift it.'

Bob's eyes lit up; he spoke enthusiastically. 'By gee. She was a lovely little cow too. Grandma used to carry her bucket and her stool and sit down and milk her. She didn't have a cow shed or stall. The cow would just stand while she milked it.

When I stayed at Grandma's with Allan, Uncle Ted used to put his pony in the gig on a Sunday afternoon, and we used to go to Uncle Reuben's. They'd be out in the stables, the barn there, sitting on a bag of chaff or something, and Reub would pull this thing out of his pocket and he'd play old tunes. Like a mouth organ, the jew's harp. Ted used to get on with Uncle Reub.

A nice fella. Good sense of humour. A lovely man to know. Nellie, his wife was nice. She was different. I remember the rhubarb. He had a few lands of rhubarb, a few lands of cabbages, carrots, a lot of lettuces. He used to walk along with a bucket of water and a tin, must have been seedlings he was watering. He'd have two horses in the plough at once, compared with Ted and Joe had one horse. He used to plough a bit deeper at Heatherton, he said. Perhaps because of the sand. I used to know Snowy, one of Reub's kids. He used to come to Grandma's for dinner. There was Clarry, he limped.

Uncle Reub came up to Little Hampton several times. I remember in later years after we married, we went down to Jack Talbot's mushrooming. Kero tin full of mushrooms and Uncle Reub was there at our house, Rainey's, on the hill, when we got home. And we had mushroom till we looked like it!

When I was older, I went on my own on the market garden picnics down at Cheltenham. Used to go with the Porters and Alf Fankhauser to the fruit growers' picnic too. I met a girl Mavis on one of the picnics. Liked going to meet the girls.'

Certainly, Bob was no stranger to the Melbourne vegetable growing sand belt. His grandparent's market garden was thoroughly familiar to him as a young child, long before he began staying there at age twelve. The areas Cheltenham to Mentone had been the haunts of the Bruton children when they lived on their parent's market garden in earlier years, at Chesterville Road, Cheltenham.

Cheltenham

'Can't remember anything about school there. Well, I can remember a little bit. Being in trouble because I was left-handed. The other schools didn't worry about it. Can remember coming home from school with a mob of kids and the cab went past us. Someone had climbed up on the step at the back and some of the older ones sung out,

'Whip behind!' and the cabbie swung his whip around. Copped whoever had climbed up on the step.' Bob laughed.

'Black cab with a step at the back, pulled by a horse. We had one at Little Hampton too, to fit us all in, used to go to Drummond. Ours had two or three steps at the back. The cabs used to have a partition up and the driver couldn't see through there to the back. Were just the same as taxis.

The cabs used to go from the station to the asylum. They'd come up Chesterville Road and up Bernard Street, and across that way. It was an asylum then, now it's Kingston Centre for elderly people.

There was an old man, Jack Green, who used to come to Mum. He might have come from the old peoples' home, the asylum, I don't know. He'd usually be drunk, and he'd ask Mum for something to eat, which she'd give him. In the end Dad threatened him. Dad didn't have a gun, but he said, 'Jack Green, if you come inside the gate again. I'll shoot you!' Jack went away saying 'What a shame. What a shame.' Bob was chuckling and hiccupping with mirth.

'What sort of good times did you have with your father in those days?'

'Oh yeah. When we were having those singsongs, he was happy enough. I can remember being in the jinker, sitting in the front, coming home from Grandma Bruton's. And we were just coming down Latrobe Street, got down to Point Nepean Road, and there was this line of cars, and we had to sit there for quite a while. And then when a gap came, he'd say, 'Get up Doll.' And Doll said, 'No. I'm not going.' And she wouldn't go. And in the end, she decided, but by that time the cars were all in the front again. I don't know how long that went on, but Dad was very patient, didn't raise his voice.

On a Sunday we'd be at Grandma's for tea. All looked forward to it after church. Must have been a Sunday. All these cars would go from Melbourne down to the beach, to Mentone and Mordialloc mainly. And they'd be coming back just before dark.

Dad used to take us all on the lorry sometimes for a drive, us and Auntie Eadie Porter's kids. I remember that. And he used to get mussels and periwinkles down at Mentone too. He used to swim out a long way to some rocks with a bag. Must have been a good swimmer.'

'Your father, did he talk about his earlier life, before marriage?'

'He talked quite a lot about his trip up to Queensland. Think he must of gone up there after his first wife died. The sugar cane, and bananas, putting bananas on that flying fox. He talked a bit about his mother. We didn't hear much about his father.'

Given that Bob's grandfather, William, apparently used to frequent the local pub, and that his son Harry became an avowed teetotaller, I wondered out loud about their eldest child Harry's relationship with him.

'No. Think it was alright. When I was there with Allan, Grandpa would cross that ditch, a plank across the drain next to the road. He'd get to the plank, and because he was almost blind, he'd get down on his hands and knees. But generally someone would come back with him from the pub to help him across the road.'

Bob remembered another difficulty with this deep drain.

'Dad had a problem with Little Doll, getting the pony over the drain. She used to jib! She'd go, eventually. The old man. Gee, he was patient with horses. The drain had water in it, run along Point Nepean road, come down Latrobe Street. Dad would talk to her softly; he'd just sit there and wait. We had her until we moved to Little Hampton. Died there of old age.'

'Fun times with your mother?'

Bob had been quiet, I recall, as he searched his memory. 'I can remember coming home from school and we'd have been learning a song. And I can see Rosa and Minnie sitting one each side of her. Some sewing, I don't know what. I sung this song for her, which we'd been learning. Drink to me only with thine eyes, and I sung that. And she said, 'That's not what I used to sing to that tune,' and she sung me a song, 'Down in a green and shady bed a modest violet grew.' '

Bob's tone of voice became especially soft. 'She sang that for us. I have an awful job of remembering anything, but I can still remember that song.

I liked Uncle Moss and Auntie Rose Daff. When I suppose Stan was born or when Daisy was born, George and I were sent to the Daffs for a couple of weeks. They called us the twins. We were just little, George and me. We went to school from there. George Daff was named after George. I remember Rosa used to take Daise everywhere.

We used to play with our cousins, the Clayton kids too. Pearson and Mavis. We'd just walk across the paddocks to their place.'

Another picture surfaced. Bob was chuckling again, 'Min was up a tree after a bird's nest. The magpie attacked me and Min. Min was calling out 'Rosa! Rosa!' Rosa chased the bird away. This was often a catch cry. 'Get Rosa!' '

Another memory Bob launched into with obvious enjoyment. 'I don't remember ever going with Dad to the Victoria Market. But I used to enjoy Dad coming home from market. I remember going to meet him coming home towards dinner time. He'd leave about two in the morning and come back about lunch time. Went about three times a week. We used to get a few bananas, p'raps that's why we went to meet him! But I can just remember those bananas. He had a canopy that went over the seat, think it was a bag, could have been canvas. Whether the frame was made of steel or wood, I don't know. Cosy. He'd be sound asleep! The horse knew how to get home.

We'd know which way he was coming. To me it seemed a long way but was probably a few hundred yards. There was one road, wasn't Chesterville Road, it had boards for the wheels to run on, like tram tracks. And the horse would walk in between them.

No. I don't remember much about Dad's market garden at Cheltenham. I was quite young when we were at Chesterville Road. The men in the paddocks would be weeding the carrots, parsnips and beetroots. They used to have a bit of a bag tied round their knees and they'd crawl along. To save their pants. I suppose their knees would get wet and cold too. They'd just tie it around with string, as far as I remember.'

Those versatile bags. Like kerosene tins, they fulfilled many functions. Bob mentioned another one. 'We used to turn the bottom of a corn sack bag, pull one corner into another corner, and hang it over our head too, for a shelter.

When we left Cheltenham and moved to Taradale, I was eight. I do remember moving. We had to get going early. I was the driver of the spring cart, went down trailing the cow. Min sneaked her cats on in a box. The lorry went too, our two horses. And the pony and gig. Uncle Ted came too, to help. I think he came back on the steam train.'

Taradale

'School at Taradale. I remember Miss Morgan. I used to like her correcting my schoolwork because I enjoyed looking at her tits when she bent over! The only other teacher I particularly liked was Parker at Little Hampton.'

Bob had spoken of Parker before. He stood out in Bob's memory as the lovesick teacher of romantic songs who sent the class on leech collecting errands for the hospital.

'At Taradale we generally went to school with bare feet. Even frosty mornings. Better than the flamin' boots. George and I got new boots. Went to school and halfway to school we parked them. Forgot them coming home! We didn't like these new boots at all. Think we had boots at Little Hampton. We'd have got the boots broke in then.

I seemed to have more friends at Taradale than Little Hampton. Used to be an old hut at our place. Used to play mothers and fathers in there with the Pickins. George Pickin, Mary, Min's age, and Anne, Rosa's age. We'd use pine needles under the trees too sometimes, to make walls.

We used to play on the railway bridge, the viaduct bridge. Tommy took a cotton reel and an umbrella. When we were at the middle of the bridge, he reckoned he wanted to do an experiment. He said, 'You know, you can jump off this with an umbrella!' Stanley was considered first, then he looked at me. 'You're the smallest, you can do it!' Was I worried. Rosa told Tom, 'No! He's not going to!' Was I glad. We all jibbed.

Tom led us astray a bit. He was just a boy. Another time we had a big fire. We were sitting around it and the rocks were exploding with the heat. That gave us a shock.

We were only at Taradale a couple of seasons. Dad grew vegetables, potatoes; we had two or three cows, some fruit trees. Dad used to have some weird ideas too. I remember he was doing some hoeing on a paddock across the creek. Thought what he was hoeing was cabbages. Clinton, I think was his name, said it was not cabbages but tobacco. Dad dropped the hoe and came home. He was employed to do it and jacked up. Against his principles.'

Harry, I imagined, would have had to adapt to different farming methods. Just some of the adjustments all members of the family were forced to confront due to this move for the sake of Tom's health.

'Were you aware of a major adjustment personally?' I'd asked Bob.

'No. I've got no idea of that at all.'

'Of your parents?'

'No. You didn't notice. We were kids.'

We returned to a more enjoyable topic.

'We used to play in the water race. We'd hop into it, and float along. It went partly underground. We'd float down in the dark. Wouldn't see light at the opening, or at the other end till you got along a bit. There was lovely wildflowers on the edge. We used to dog paddle. We wouldn't let George do it, thought he wasn't good enough at swimming.'

'Didn't Grandma Bluhm come up to stay? What was she like?'

'Oh. Oh, she seemed a weak little old lady to me. I remember she died at our place. I still remember the snoring noise. Oh. When she died, she was there for several days before they could move her. No. it was a terrible smell. Mum didn't know where to put us all to get away from it.'

Bob remembered having been asked in the late 1980s, to write a few lines concerning the Brutons for a small historical publication of the area. I asked him for a copy.

BRUTON

The Brutons arrived in Taradale about 1922, with a large family. They lived on top of the hill, on the Melbourne side of Taradale, where he grew vegetables and took them to Castlemaine in the spring cart to market.

The older kids did quite a bit of panning for gold in the back creek, at one stage they had a junket bottle full of gold. To this day nobody can remember where that junket bottle went.

The Brutons moved from Cheltenham to Taradale because certain members of the family were ill, and the doctors suggested that a move to the country would be the best thing.

Mr Bruton was a very religious man, so much so that he was the local preacher at the Church of Christ. When the local pub burnt down, he was heard to say, 'The Lord is on our side.'

Then we eventually moved to Little Hampton. Mr Bruton would drive from Cheltenham to Taradale in a lorry drawn by two horses with a spring cart attached to carry garden tools. The trip took two days, stopping at Woodend overnight.

ROBERT BRUTON

Having returned from his foraging, copy in hand, Bob sat down. He was stirring his black tea briskly. That tinkle again.

The old house at Taradale. Last time I'd seen it, it looked weather beaten and woebegone. 'Perce was saying he thought the house had collapsed,' I said.

'Oh, it's gone! We looked for it and couldn't see it. Think they've cleared it away. It was full of hay for a long time.'

Bob had something to show me in the garage. We walked through the billiard room, brushing against several large pots of maidenhair fern. Some were tiny leaved, like cobwebs. Results of Bob's forays into damp bush gullies.

Bob switched on the light, illuminating various decorative objects he'd created. 'You choose one if you like it,' he said.

As I left, I clutched the pretty shell decorated vase. Bob had spoken one day of different types of shells, nicknamed poms, by soldiers. The next day, we returned to the war.

War. Action

'Salamaua was probably the worst experience we had. My group suffered casualties. We lost a couple of blokes, quite a few of them were wounded. A couple of them got scrub typhus. We thought we'd lose them both, but one turned up here after the war. We got nearly to Salamaua, and we were told to come back. Could've taken it. What they were doing was to get the Japs that were coming from Lae, they were coming around to deal with us. But there were plenty of them left at Lae. When we attacked the Jap positions at Salamaua, we had heavy casualties. The heads would say withdraw, go back to a certain place, then start again. We were trying to knock off the Japs before they got back to Lae.'

'How would the generals know when and where to deploy their troops?' I pondered aloud.

'There were lots of ways the intelligence worked,' said Bob. 'They got info from the natives too. There were a couple of companies of commandos. They were good. They were mad, but they were good. They were in the front line. They'd hit the Jap patrols. Quite a few of them went a bit troppo. Their job had its advantages. They would not have to counterattack, they'd clean them up and move on. They had a roaming job and were seldom in a place for more than a day. One day the Japs were coming into our range. Commando boss said, 'We want you! Bring a pack of grenades.' The nips were in the village, had knocked off the natives. I had to take the first hut, throw them in and shoot back. They'd do that. Clean it up and shoot through. When we got back, I was told I could go. I was off and on with them for two or three weeks after that.'

I had to remind myself again that Bob was talking about events which had occurred sixty years previously. His memory was immediate. It seemed that these experiences were etched within him forever.

'The Aussie commandos blew up a mining town. Was a scorched earth policy. They even blew up a swimming pool with a hot spring. Gee. I was crooked on that. There had been several mining towns. Wau at one end of the Bolola Valley was known as one of them. The track was of many steps carved by the natives into the earth up the sides of the Bolola Valley. To get out of the valley took us all day. We walked up through grass then the jungle. We went up and up to get out. We had been flown in to sneak in behind the Japs at Salamaua.'

Bob's expression had been intense for some time as he talked about these difficult and dangerous campaigns. Quiet words and steady gaze. His soft tone and economy of words only hinted at hardships experienced. I felt sure our discussion had stimulated other memories, too painful to be shared. Memories written in blood.

Now Bob's expression changed. Replaced momentarily with lightness like sunshine. 'I'd have loved to see the country in peace time. Beautiful country.'

I ushered him back to the thread. 'It was after Salamaua that we saw the deserted Jap hospital. We spent three or four days at a beach while waiting further orders. We went by boat to Milne Bay for a short time. I remember it. They had a bake house tent. It was the first time we had fresh bread for four or five months. We'd been having biscuits or nothing, or biscuits and bully beef. Sometimes American rations. Sweet, but good. At Milne Bay we got bread and fresh meat stew, but we were up all night with diarrhoea! Just couldn't take it. After this we were sent back to Moresby.'

'Were there any other differences between the Americans and Aussies, besides a penchant for sweeter rations?'

'They had hammocks. We weren't game enough to use them because the hammocks were up high. We liked to sleep below ground level. They didn't seem to worry about smoking either. You could not walk into our camp without being stopped by a guard, a picket. But you could walk straight into an American tent.

It was towards the coast, near Bogadjim. We patrolled down there and just walked straight into their camp. Oh Yes. Yes. They made us welcome. It seemed funny for us just to walk in and not be challenged or anything. Don't know how they got away with it. Must have been just the big numbers that done it. That day when the Yank officer in the artillery asked if he could use my opip. He was drawing their fire! Jumping up and down. Made a big noise when he saw Salamaua. They were mad that way, would get excited. They'd do things in big numbers, not do-little patrols.'

A saving grace for Bob, I discovered, was his ability to have short naps. 'I was quite good at snoozing. I could go to sleep anywhere. Could be up half the night picketing. Could be up for two days. Little stinkers used to attack us at night sometimes. Funny! Our artillery units could be going all night and our own guns would not wake us up. But if the Japs opened up, we'd hear it to billyo, and we'd be in our trenches as quick as lightning. Spent a lot of time thinking about that one!

We went back to other ranges in '44. The Finisterre Ranges between Ramu Valley and the coast. We had to chase the Japs out. Mostly there'd been an Aussie unit there before us, and we took over from them. We knew the Japs were starting to pull out and going to Wewak to consolidate further up the coast. We were there two or three months flushing out Japs, then went to Bogadjim and Madang.

When we went to Madang, I think it was where we camped in a coconut grove, in a beautiful lagoon. There were coloured fish. We weren't allowed to swim in there. I don't know why. I hated leaving it. It was in a creek near there where we saw the croc.

I remember the rivers up there were pretty wide in places. Big rivers you could walk across. Sometimes the water would come down from a volcano, could be very warm. In the wet weather the rivers were twice as wide, up to our hips or so. Hold our rifles up high. The boongs would pull a vine from one side and take it over to save us from being swept away. I remember the Mogiai River at Bougainville, that was a particularly big river.

I remember at one stage towards the end of the war; we got some TNT dynamite. We'd run out of grenades fishing. Was silly. We cut it into three and we'd light them and chuck them in the river. The fish were stunned unless they were right near it. I remember struggling back with a big bag, and then we got only two little feeds out of it. Took it to the cookhouse, and we had to give them a few, then the fishermen in the fish shop who cleaned them. He and his mates had to have a feed, and so on and so forth. But this was the last time we ever did this. We saw some black heads of natives watching us at the time. The natives realised what we were doing. We never thought we were taking their food. When we saw them watching, we realised what was going on; we stopped doing it straight away.

Another time we were patrolling around, don't know where, but somewhere in the jungle. Half the patrol had to go home 'cause they were crook or broke a leg. I ended up in charge. I was only a corporal. Started with a major in charge. Very difficult terrain. There were Australian, New Zealand and New Guinea Administrators with us called ANGOW. We didn't find any Japs. Found some very interesting natives. Very nice too. We'd never seen anything like it. Their ways of life. A lot of them hadn't seen a white man before. I was supposed to write up a report, but you know what I was like at writing reports. The natives were very shy. Saw two albino natives. Don't know how they survived. We knew we were being looked at from the jungle. They gradually came out. I remember us eating quite a few coconuts.'

Leave. War Finish

'Before we came home on leave, we were doing a lot of guard duty and ceremonial things. I liked it. Something to do. They were giving us something to do to keep our spirits up. At the end of '44 for about two weeks I was on leave in Australia for the first and only time. We had to go back to the Atherton Tablelands in Queensland for a couple of months. We were taken to Bougainville from Queensland and were there until the end of the war. Things were easing up a bit. We hoped to get away to the

Salamaua campaign. Ended up going to Madang and the Ramu Valley, and it was getting lively there too.'

I wondered how it had felt leaving the war zone, then having to return to it.

'Hard, but we had to do it. Had to get rid of them. A few blokes had had enough. Didn't want to go back. When I returned from leave, it was on the troopship Waroona. I enjoyed that. I must have been one of the last ones to go on board, so I had to sleep on deck in a hammock. It was better than being in the hold with the blokes chucking on you. I think we also went on the Waroona on the trip home after the war, but I wasn't with our mob. It depended on points acquired. I had a hundred points because I was married with two kids, so I was given a higher preference. Still took six months.'

It was on another day, about a week later, that I again saw Bob. He was waiting with his usual good-humoured patience to continue. I wondered how he had heard about the finish of the war. 'I don't remember. I think just our company commander told us that we had instructions not to shoot a Jap, because we could be up for murder.'

My tone was incredulous, 'But what if the Jap soldiers hadn't heard about the cessation of the war and they shot you?'

Bob spoke with feeling. There was a rough edge to his voice. 'I nearly got court martialled over that! I took the boys out. With us was an officer, a young new recruit who had just got his pips. Wanted to make a name for himself. We were supposed to obey him. None of us wanted to go very far. He wanted to go up the hill. He told the boys to get going. Normally they did what you said. Those fellows were not going to move. They sat down. I tried to get them to come along. 'It's stupid,' they said 'We'll be in trouble either way. If we shoot a Jap, we'll be in trouble, and if we don't follow instructions we'll be in trouble.'

I was the go between; I talked them in to getting up. I suggested to the forward scout that every time he came to a tree, to go around the left of the tree, so we'd swing around from the hill. We finished up at the Salvo's coffee stall. We had no intention of going up into the hills. We kept doing the same thing. He could not do anything about it. He had the authority. He reported it to the commander. Anyway, when we got to the coffee stall, the officer met someone there. While he was talking, the boys shot through back to the battalion.

I had disobeyed the officer, and that was pretty serious. Our company commander got us out of it.' Bob shook his head. His tone was explosive. He spat out, 'He was wanting us to go into the war zone. Ridiculous circumstances. You get used to those things in the army. Doing those silly things. But that was the worst. There were Japs around still. Paper was dropped telling them. Whether they got the pamphlets, who knows. Had to patrol to see if the Japs were sneaking up on us, but venturing further, that was looking for trouble. The officer was a new chum. We were supposed to tell the Japs the war was over. How to tell them. I don't know! We weren't told that. Think we'd shoot first, ask questions later.'

'The news the war was over must have had a tremendous impact, it must have been hard to believe.' I said.

'It was a big relief when we started thinking of getting home. Then we discovered it could take six months. With most, it took longer. I was on the water at Christmas. I'd hoped to make it home but didn't. Some men didn't get home for twelve months. So many men to move.'

Something lighter drew my attention. The coffee stall. A long shot from today's cappuccinos and a cosy, aroma filled coffee shop.

'No matter where you were going, there'd often be these small stalls run by mainly two Aussie Salvos. Be under fire sometimes. They were really wonderful blokes. Coffee for nothing. They'd put it in a little can.'

'Do you remember the day you came home?'

Bob's glance was steady, 'Don't remember. We stayed in New Guinea for quite a while after the war. The war was finished in August. I didn't get home till after Christmas. The boat would have docked at Sydney and all our gear was in Melbourne. All we had was a shirt, shorts, boots and socks and we were freezing. We weren't too happy.'

Now I detected a slight change in his tone. Sardonic. 'So they opened their hearts and gave us all an overcoat. But about the day I came home I don't remember.'

I was listening to the silence as Bob, lost in thought, was apparently searching his memory.

Suddenly Nell's voice was heard. Like gunfire. Loud. 'You got full!'

Bob's response was fast. 'I got home under my own steam, didn't I!'

Mementos

'Any mementos you bring home?'

'Darl, do you know where there are any doilies I made in hospital? People would be interested.'

'Fiddle!' said Nell.

Bob continued on track. 'Your brooch I sent home. Forgotten where it was. Made out of Perspex.'

Bob and Nell both disappeared, Nell hobbling painfully with a stick. It was just two weeks since she had been in the Bendigo Hospital. I remembered her earlier comment about being in a bad mood. 'I'm frustrated, I want to be able to walk,' she said. Bob had been aghast when I'd mentioned the availability of community home assistance. 'I'm the chief cook and bottle washer! Don't need any help,' he'd replied indignantly.

Now Nell returned with the brooch. A simple heart hanging from a bar, both in a soft bluey coloured Perspex. Across the bar was the somewhat formal statement, 'Wife.'

'A mate made it from the windscreen of a plane,' Bob explained.

Bob was now carrying two small tins which he carefully placed on the table. One tin as long as your finger. The other considerably smaller and square. The larger had a sunflower gold lid embellished with a scroll, colour of tangerine. 'Log cabin' it stated boldly. Below, delicately written, shiny, 'Flaked gold leaf tobacco.' The other tin sported a white dog listening intently to an old, fluted loudspeaker, aptly labelled 'His Master's Voice gramophone needles, loud tone,' with a caution, 'Use once only.'

Bob sat still for a moment, pensive. He was thinking about his lost doily. 'It was fancy work, a type of crochet, made from unravelled parachute silk. There was a girl on the staff at the hospital that showed us.'

He was now opening the larger tin. Here was some paper money carefully preserved. The smaller tin held aluminium coins with holes through the centre. I weighed a few in my hand, their lightness unexpected. 'This money was Jap money printed ready for the invasion. The Jap didn't need it anymore,' was his answer to my question of how he came by the items.

I was looking at the tobacco tin 'How did you get your smokes in New Guinea?'

'Often the Red Cross. They'd turn up with a tin of tobacco, Havelock H and Log Cabin.'

'How many years since you opened these boxes?'

'Twenty or thirty years or something.'

While I was looking at these mementos, Bob disappeared. He reappeared with some papers. Here was his discharge certificate. He didn't mind my copying the details. 'VX147040. Corporal Robert David Bruton 58/59 Australian Infantry Battalion 23rd April 1942—22nd September 1943, Australian Imperial Force from 23rd September 1943—22nd January 1946. 1371 days which include Active Service. In Australia from 472. Outside Australia 899 days. Discharged from Royal Park 22nd January 1946. 5 feet 9 inches. Hazel eyes.'

War had cast a long shadow over many lives. Three years spent as a soldier. A life irrevocably changed by events outside Bob's control.

'Did the war change you?' I asked back from my reverie.

'I don't know.'

'Did you feel you would survive?'

Bob shook his head, 'No, I had a strong feeling sometimes the other way. But we did.'

There was a long pause. It seemed miraculous to me that Bob had survived all the physical and emotional rigours of the New Guinea war experience. Suddenly he added, 'I was home on leave and Mum said, 'And don't you be like Tommy and be captured!' I said, 'Oh no Mum! They don't take prisoners up there!' It was a terrible thing to say, I could've cut my tongue out.'

'Beats me,' I said, 'how so many came home. If the Japs didn't get you, it seemed the mosquitos would.'

For a moment Bob's eyes were following the magpies outside. There were three hopping around in the garden. 'There used to be about ten, twelve months ago. But the crows came, and the magpies must have told each other, because they all disappeared, and now there are only three.'

I thanked Bob for sharing his kaleidoscope of memories with me, which I appreciated must have been very difficult on occasions. Bob ran his hands through his hair, a familiar gesture. 'Wish I'd written it down, spoken about it before. If people knew what happens, they might be put off war.'

Post War. Fernhill

Now to the plough. The earth. Sowing and growing. The style of farming had not changed in this relatively short time, during the eternity of Bob's war ordeal. His three-year absence must have been forever for Bob's family. Dorothy was nearly six, and Barry three, when their father returned.

'I knew Babe. She knew me before I left. But Barry was a bit of a problem. I suppose I was too. Anyway. He made it in the end. Barry didn't think I had any right to be with his mother.

When I came back, it was four years before I was granted a soldier settlement property. We rented Rainey's at Little Hampton. Four rooms. The kitchen and wash house were at the back.'

This small, Edwardian miner's cottage, with the simple front verandah, still stands proudly on the hill. As a very small child I recalled staying there, presumably while Bob was at war. My cousin Judith, a toddler, was there too, and of course Dorothy, whom Nell and Bob call 'Babe' to this day. A highlight for me was sitting on the back of Cherry, their placid jersey cow.

'Yes Cherry,' said Bob softly, as he remembered with a smile.

We explored his return to the land after the war, before he was able to call a block his own. 'Planted spuds first year I was home and we had peas. Made a few bob because it was too late to plant spuds. I was working around, mostly with Fred Rothe. I got a paddock off the Moloney girls, planting spuds there. They got a third and I two-thirds, I think. Then we moved to Hunt's and rented sixty acres there for three years. Lived in the old Hunt's home opposite the Little Hampton School. Had spuds and oats. Always had two or three acres of peas.'

The silence was punctuated by Bob's drumming fingers of his left hand. It reminded me that he and his mother were both left hand dominant. I was quietly recalling Percy's recent remark 'Bob was a champion pea picker.' Bob seemed to tune in to my train of thought.

'Must have been in March we were picking peas, because I had Graham down there and Nell was in hospital having Peter. Because Graham would fill himself up with peas, then he'd fill his nappy up with peas.'

'How did you come by land through the soldier settlement scheme?' I wondered. 'Did you have any choices?'

'Yes and no. They'd advertise blocks, and you'd have to apply, you'd have a look and apply for what you wanted.'

'And did it work out well for you?' My hope for an affirmative answer was granted.

'Oh yes, I got what I wanted! Was the second or third I applied for, was two blocks on that property, I had one. Some people applied for fifty properties, quite a lot of competition. I was very lucky to get one. Depends on your previous experience with farming, war record and a few different things. Then the next few years we were paying off the loan, of course.

I remember the steam train. A spark from it set fire to some of our paddocks. That was just after we got down there, about 1950. Oh, with the help of neighbours, the Drews, we soon put it out.'

'It was an overgrown farm,' I said, recalling the piercingly prickly scotch thistles.

'Must have not had the men during the war to keep it trim,' said Bob. 'It took some years and hard work to make it viable. The house had not been lived in for about ten years and the scotch thistles were very tall. I can still see Mum standing there at the front of the house. She was tall, and the thistles were nearly as high as her. I left the thistles to seed and sprayed for five years. Pretty toxic, it's banned now.'

'Did you use horses after your return from the war?' I asked.

'The old fellow still had horses at the farm. I bought a Ferguson tractor, cost 600 pounds, grey. At that stage you took a risk. There were no planting machines then, but you could use it for planting spuds. We had a mechanical planter the horses pulled, but a few years after that we had two of these planters put together and we could use them behind the Fergie. Had it for a few years before we could adapt for spud planting. But used it for scuffling, hilling spuds up. This was usually done with one horse and you'd be walking behind the horse with the scuffler or moulder.' Bob pointed 'I've got my single furrow plough and a scuffler out there. We'll have a look at it before you go.'

'It sounds as though you were a bit more adventurous than some people were!'

'Yes, I was young. I had the first tractor in the district and then Percy got a David Brown, which did the same job as the Fergie. Then everyone had them. Eventually had to sell your horses, most of them were took down the bush and shot, and a lot of them were sold for pet food. Some horses, thoroughbred, you didn't want them to be sent to the knackers. Quite a few kept their old horses, put them out to grass. That's what we did.

No. I didn't play footy or tennis. Why? I didn't have the time. We'd go and watch the footy sometimes. Followed Kyneton. Sometimes went to Echuca or Bendigo. Nell played the organ at the Tylden Presbyterian Church. Later years we'd go to the trots, Melbourne, Kilmore, and Maryborough. Just wanted to see the horses. We liked our horses!'

After eradicating the stubborn spiky scotch thistles, Bob made a beautiful flower garden which graced their elegant Victorian house. Nell was never short of a vegetable for the table either.

The saga of the thistle comes to mind. A stick had to be enlisted to push away the brutal, blood-hungry leaves, as we tackled the hard job to sever one or two stalks. But once secured, us gaggle of girls, the three of us, Dorothy, Judith and I, had an important use for them.

Clandestinely creeping into the bedroom of some unsuspecting body, we'd work our magic. Or malevolence. The leafy barbs would be hidden under the bottom bed sheet. They were placed carefully to coincide with someone's bottom as he or she sat and bent to remove shoes—or further down in the bed, to produce a sudden adrenaline rush as feet fell victim.

Now I look back and realise these playful ten-year-old pranks, the cruel planting of painful prickles, must have been an acid test for the unfortunate recipient's patience. Not so Nell and Bob. One particular occasion stands out in my mind. We had confided our plan to Nell. Poor unsuspecting Bob. He was, we said, the target, or so we inferred.

Nell and Bob usually retired early. Our bedroom adjoined theirs. Us girls all in our summer nighties listened breathlessly, ears to the wall near the marble fireplace, for signs that Bob was entering prickle territory. Nell kindly kept the secret. Or, thinking back, did she? Perhaps Bob's yell was orchestrated. But the next yell, Nell's, certainly was not! We three shrieked with laughter in the big double bed we shared. We rolled, fell about holding our sides, scarcely gaining a breath between bursts.

Suddenly, a thistle, airborne through the open window, fell upon us. The light was bright on Nell's face. Her arm, silhouetted against cotton night gown, held another repeat reprisal. She waved and waggled the thistle, a grin not far away. 'You girls, I'll get you!' There was much, though fairly short-lived, yelling and screaming that night. We retired to bed, having had as usual, a satiety of fun.

Those holidays at Bob's and Nell's. Halcyon days blessed by the sun, our youthful vigour and enthusiasm. Days of abandonment. Running, shrieking, climbing, collecting, exploring. Our energy was fuelled by Nell's flavoursome and plentiful food. No matter if we committed the folly of overindulgence! This was always forgiven. Those excesses of extra bread and jam bathed liberally in running sweet cream straight from the dairy. Food was meant to fill.

We roamed the world. Our territory stretched as far as our bicycle could take us, as high as the highest tree or the biggest leapfrog we could jump. We all got on well, save for Barry's infernal teasing. But that did not deter us.

I do not recall it raining. That is, on our summer holidays. But memories of the cold biting winter wind and rain and freezing frosts are seared uncomfortably on my memory. This was when I, aged twelve, stayed at the farm and attended school for a while.

'What type of farming did you enjoy the most?' I now asked Bob.

'I like the spud farming and mixed farming, sheep, beef. I never enjoyed the time we had dairy cows. Too much of a tie, I think. Morning and night. If I was digging spuds or ploughing, I would have to break off to do the cows. Spuds were always a challenge. Always a challenge to get a few more bags each day. Yes. I employed spud cutters and diggers, and casual workers at harvest time. Used to have the same blokes from Tylden and some blow-ins.'

'Remember I earned some pocket money picking up spuds at your place in my early teens?'

'I thought you'd kill yourself. Pig-headed Bruton!'

Perhaps Bob was right. But I wish he'd told me back then. Never one to give up, I drove myself. Fell into bed at night completely exhausted. In the main I was alone in the paddock, that is apart for some fellow or other digging and leaving me to it. In earlier years I'd picked up spuds for Percy, who had dumped my bags up and down to settle the potatoes. I missed this camaraderie too. I did the dumping of those heavy bags, almost as tall as myself. Don't know how. Yes, it was madness!

'There was a spring down the paddock, I put a dam on it. Got a water diviner to go all over the place and put down a bore. Struck water in one of the paddocks. Had a well too, back of the big shed. Put in a high tank and windmill, was good quality.'

Bob of course grew hay for his animals. 'I used to grow oats, was wheat too. Was twelve sheaves in a stook like a tepee. Fred Dobinson from Tylden had a thrasher and a chaff cutter, and he'd go all over the district. Jack Thrum had a thrasher too. The crop would either be thrashed or cut into chaff. The oats were cut into chaff. Needed the chaff for the horses. More waste if you give the whole stalks to the animals. The stalks would be all over the place. When it's chopped up, you get the heads and straw together, it's better. We always had chopped chaff for the cows too.'

The crop was frequently harvested on a warm summer's day during our school holidays. Hay making, a special time on the farm, was a special time for us kids too.

While Bob and the men were busy with the binding and stooking of sheaves, we too were busy. In our way. There would be Dorothy, Barry, the Drew boys and myself. We'd play in the stooks wriggling in to make a small hole. The golden dry fresh-smelling sheaves would form what looked like endless cubbies. Well, that was our activity at the beginning of the day. It wasn't our main interest. We were waiting for the big drama when only a small strip of crop remained. The big boisterous fun run. A race between us and the rabbits.

We ran like the rabbits too, but rarely caught one. When we did, we'd let it go. Or if it was a young one, take it home and feed it.

The red rash around our ankles caused by the short stubble, and slivers of chaff in our socks, was a small price to pay for the fun we had. Though I remember Bob sitting with John, one of the Drew boys, trying to pull a small seed of oats from his ear. They sat for quite a while on the couch in front of the fire, the small protruding hair attached to it illumined by the warm blaze. The local doctor eventually was successful in removing it.

Bob himself, I learned, had suffered with a foreign body in his ear when he was a boy. He said his mother poured castor oil into it and a well-oiled dead fly had floated out.

At one stage, us kids would dig out poor hapless rabbits from the security of their burrows. We would poke a long stick in first, checking if fur had attached to its end. Bob's spades were then vigorously employed. Another chase would ensue. Nell patiently allowed my pet rabbits, fed in a big box with wire over the top, to reside in her commodious pantry. This had been one of two bedrooms for servants of the house in its heyday. The rabbits were eventually let go. At least I believe so.

We never, ever thought of snakes. Not even on that day when Dorothy and I caught a number of mice amongst the stacked hay in the big shed. This was in the big truck-turning yard at the back of the house. Our hands would dart after these bright-eyed be whiskered beauties. We were quite successful in capturing a number which we placed in a big empty drum. At the end of the day, we would let them go, and they'd rush back into their hay homes.

It was over lunch, and halfway through the generous mound of mashed potatoes, fluffy with milk and butter which I had left until last, that I felt the tiny claws on the nape of my neck. A shriek from me, and the confused little rodent tried to hide itself in the security of my hair. 'I'll have no mouse in my kitchen!' yelled Nell. Mouse and myself were quickly banished outside until I had found the culprit.

Never a dull moment. The clang of the elegant wire gate which lead into the house garden and kitchen door usually announced a visitor. Often men, they'd come and go. The spud carting contractor, the man to fix the windmill, a friendly visitor, a neighbour. Fred Rothe sometimes dropped in. 'How are you, Doffo?' he'd ask cheerily. Dorothy, his only granddaughter, was the apple of his eye. The kettle sang, always ready for a cup of tea. Dot and I did our bit. We hung out loads of washing, we peeled countless potatoes, podded many peas, helped milk the cows.

On one memorable occasion, we swept the dirt under the end of the seemingly endless hall carpet runner. A short-cut to something more interesting. Nell's roar indicated our discovery, and we had to make good—immediately. All the while the wireless played. The hit tunes were more jolly than classical, and I began to like them. There was Buddy Holly. 'I love, oh I love you, Peggy Sue.'

Amongst this childish fun, Bob came and went. The days were punctuated by a regular routine of tea breaks and mealtimes, and cow milking. During these times Bob and Nell clearly enjoyed each other's company. They talked about farm matters. What farmer was planting what, who was shearing. The condition of the land and animals. Always that loving eye contact, each flowing with the other. Bob's clothes would sometimes be grimy with red earth. His hat was a cotton beret, khaki. Pulled back from his forehead, it almost covered his straight brown hair. His body, muscular, was fit beneath thick shirts.

Heady holiday happiness, however, became substantially dampened with the passing of summer. School was never a favourite activity and eventually my sojourn at the Kyneton High School was upon me and so was winter. Surprisingly, apart from the embarrassment of an unreciprocated love letter written by me to a boy in our class— his name Neville Newnham, I still recall—school itself passed relatively easily. Probably due to the forbearance of Dorothy who, having had a cousin forced upon her, kindly made the better of it. The usual school day began with leaving home at 7.15am. Getting up at the crack of dawn was not my cup of tea. I reluctantly copied Dorothy's forthright jump out of bed on those cold, dark mornings. We rode along Chanter's Lane, which leads to the main bitumen road and the school bus stop. Our bikes would crunch over frozen mirror-like puddles on the gravel lane. Our breaths were white steam, our knuckles bloodless as they clutched cold handlebars.

My education gained considerable momentum. But not at the Kyneton High School. Rather, it was the rigours of farm life. Copulating cats and cows. Slipping on slimy, sodden cow dung. A lick on the lip from Snowy the steer. Being brushed off against a fence, suddenly and rudely, by a pretty and petulant Shetland pony. All was new to me. These surprises were my cousins' amusement. Their eyes, particularly Barry's, would dance. 'City slicker!' they'd call me sometimes, but not maliciously. And they weren't far wrong.

Something else comes to mind. Toughening? Sobering perhaps. Nell did not listen to my utterances that day I felt sick. Pulling the blankets off me, she ordered me to get ready for school. My only experience of an admonition from Bob came that morning. As I sat with eyes down turned, tears mingling with milky porridge, I heard his voice. It sounded fierce. 'Stop blubbering! You're going to school!'

We had half an hour to ride to the bus stop. Then we'd open the big farm gate of old Scotty and Mum Scott's who lived adjacent and deposit our bikes in their shearing shed. I remember Mrs. Scott. We went in there, into their white well-kept weatherboard house one day. A kindly aproned lady, she owned many fine bone china cups and saucers. I was quite impressed. But this was not the particular association with the Scotts which stands out in my memory.

It was one day when we alighted from the bus to go home. The farmers, felt hatted with short sleeves and overalls, were doing something with young lambs close to the fence. Piercing cries filled the air. A hasty sideways look saw a lamb atop a bench on its back, a knife like implement in the hand of the farmer, a tin of black tar.

Those cries, desperate with terror and pain, have plagued me from time to time. A reluctant reminder these days is when driving past the Scott's enroute to Percy's. It is as though the wind itself shrills the story as it blows through that weathered hand-hewn fence.

Another experience evocative of this, was hearing anguished cries, almost identical to these lambs, during my ill-fated nursing days. Cries not engendered by cutting off a tail, but by circumcision. I could see this procedure occurring at regular intervals through the plate glass which separated the surgery and the baby nursery, in the hospital where I worked. Every time the scenario was the same. The sudden sharp cry of pain, baby's legs kicking hard, defenceless. The baby would wail a sharp continuous crescendo. Then, as the painful protracted process became gaspingly overwhelming, the pitiful and powerless pleas would become exhausted whimpers.

As I recall, my born and bred country cousins, and Gloria and Elaine Cox, the kids from a neighbouring farm, did not make anything of the lamb tail incident.

There is another recollection of lighter note. This happened on an evening after school, too. We picked up our bikes from the Scott's and were riding along Chanter's Lane quite enjoying the clear day. But this ride turned out to be a little different. For me, anyway! I looked up from slow peddling and observed a pair of eyes upon me. A big staring face watching me in silence. The biggest Hereford bull I'd seen in my life. Dorothy, her equable self, wheeled my bike, while I, shamefully, walked along inside the opposite fence, away from my imagined charging bull. Occasionally still, I am reminded jokingly about this! I have no idea if Bob ever heard of it.

Perhaps I should have asked him if he had! Perhaps I could have also shared the lamb experience with him too! I have no firm idea how he may have responded.

A question about animals, I did ask. Something I recalled during our conversation. 'You had a white duck which slept with the dog in the dog kennel! I remember it when I was a kid staying at your place.'

'Yes! And the cat too.'

'Wasn't that lovely?'

'It was so! Oh, they were good mates those three.'

Earlier, during this last afternoon, amid the usual steaming cups of tea, there were other questions. Important. 'Looking back on your childhood, what would you say were perhaps your happiest times?'

Bob's voice had a lilting, optimistic quality. He hardly drew breath. 'I think they were all happy times, more or less! Few that weren't. A good childhood, really. A lot of people would say, 'Gee it must have been hard.' But it was a pretty good childhood!'

'And what about one of the saddest times?' Bob looked past me to scenes seemingly projected on the wall. 'I think seeing Mum when Bernie died. She was very upset. That's the most upset I've seen her. That was one of the hardest times,' he added in a gentle voice.

As Bob stared at the wall, he was seeing something else. 'Oh. Grandma Bluhm dying! The death rattles. This memory's plagued me all my life.'

'When you look back on your life, what have you enjoyed the most?'

Bob did not hesitate. Not one second. 'Having a wife and kids!'

'And what advice would you give future generations?'

Bob was not a man to moralise. Again, his answer came fast, firm with conviction. 'Find out for yourselves!'

This time when I left, Bob did not get up to let me out. He pointed to the large bag of garlic he had placed on the billiard table in the sunroom for us. My wave saw a man sitting at the table, bowed head resting on his hand. Preoccupied with his world. No ceremonial leave-taking. His expansive smile, good natured and optimistic, was missing. Perhaps knew his lack of energy was due to lung cancer.

This last glance is etched on my memory. Tanned arms emerging from the rolled-up sleeves of a heavy duty check blue shirt despite the cold day. Thinning brown hair, hardly grey, combed straight back from his forehead. Straight as a die. His plain brown pants, loose and large due to his weight loss, held up with the unexpected decoration of reddish-coloured braces.

Minnie

Queensland. Cheltenham

It was the feather that caught my eye. Standing upright, it gently waved to and fro, flowing with Min's brisk high heeled click. Minnie's face, round, dimple cheeked, was animated. Her greyish green eyes twinkled a welcome. This cameo was completed with ear length straight brown hair enhanced by a simple, smart, head hugging navy hat and the flattering flourish of the feather.

Min spied me as soon as I jumped off the red rattler at Flinders Street Railway Station. My mother had arranged for Min to meet me. We were going shopping for my first bought coat. A big expedition this, for a twelve-year-old, and paid for by my spud picking earnings at Percy's.

Trim, in her navy suit, Min's small matching leather handbag was clutched in her left hand as she propelled herself toward me. The feather, adding to her five-foot two stature, stood out like an exclamation mark. A jaunty quality. Like a cat with its tail straight up, it seemed to be a symbol of an optimistic, happy woman. The feather shimmered and shook gently, as it coped with the vagaries of wind and movement. Just like Min, whose philosophy was to maintain a harmony, and to remain anchored. Well, it seemed to me anyway, that her pattern was to keep any contentious thoughts to herself. Not a bad idea to be careful with one's speech. Though a passionate utterance from Min's good-natured lips might have been a breath of fresh air all the same.

Min, third eldest of twelve, had married nicely. Fred was of the land too, an orchardist, and his forbears were market gardeners, as had been the Brutons. He was the second youngest of eight, born to George and Elsie Mock. When Min met me at the station in the fifties, she and Fred already had three young girls and their youngest, a son, George. Their eldest, Judith, was a year younger than myself, but more sophisticated. Many an enjoyable school holiday was spent by me, and sometimes another cousin, Dorothy Bruton, at the Mock's orchard in East Burwood. Today, ever kindly, Min with her unerring good taste, quietly steered this gauche adolescent into the beginnings of a more sophisticated self-image. A bottle green woollen coat. Lapels just big enough for a small diamante bird or animal brooch, bought from the cheap jewellery section of Coles.

So much for my reminiscences. One snapshot of many memories. The smiling person facing me now, in 1996, was completely grey, and her hair had been waved. The dimple was still the same. Along with her twinkling eyes it lent a slightly mischievous note to her face betraying a sense of fun.

'Do you remember that feather?' I asked.

Min's memory was quick, although she had stated earlier it was poor. 'Remember we all went to the Zoo? A monkey grabbed it! It was a sad end to the beautiful feather.'

The strong afternoon light with the hint of pink hibiscus, illumined Min's soft-hued olive cheek. The Queensland sun seemed to suit her. She and Fred had spent over forty summers now in the pretty hilly inland country near Nambour, eighty miles north of Brisbane.

Expatriates of Victoria, they sold their orchard in Mahoney's Road, East Burwood in 1960, and courageously embarked on a new venture, sugar cane farming at Yandina. Now, in their twilight eighties, they had given up their home with the large fertile garden, lovingly worked by both of them. Their decision to move to a retirement village was difficult for Min. A saving grace for her was the small greenhouse allocated to their unit.

Here, the balm of a Queensland winter's day was comfortable compared with cold Victoria. It was no hardship to accompany Rosa on any trips to the Mock's. Not deterred by their smaller habitat, they were always warmly hospitable.

Rosa was suffering with a heavy cold. Min had persuaded her to rest. But not before they had toured the garden. My glance through the window saw two sisters walking together, engrossed, basking in the sunshine of each other's company. They had always enjoyed being together, each had been the other's favourite sibling and still was. Only fifteen months apart, they were different, both in looks and nature. But no sibling rivalry here! Simply companionable closeness. A look around the garden ended predictably in Min's greenhouse. After examining each pot, including Min's beautiful 'Dancing Lady Orchid,' they both sat and talked amid the colourful array of Min's proud and varied collection.

Min and I sat in the small lounge room, her treasures in the glass cabinet opposite. It was never easy to persuade Rosa to have a rest, but Min had managed it. The small dark polished mahogany table near the window was adorned with large orange centred daffodils. Some were still to emerge from their softly green sheathed buds. A happy portend of the visit. Sun-shiny saffron. They had been grown by Rosa in her garden in the Victorian Dandenong Ranges. This golden gift, carefully picked as buds and nursed enroute, had survived beautifully.

Cheltenham seemed a long way back. Much had happened in Min's life since those early days in the sand belt down south. Perhaps, I thought, we should start at the beginning.

'My earliest memories? Riding my horse. Broomstick! Around the house at Point Nepean Road. Of course, there were mainly horses then. That was about 1916. And I remember watching Dad washing carrots to take to market.' Min looked worried. She passed her hand over her eyes as though to see better, to remember. 'I left Cheltenham soon after turning ten, so I am afraid my memories are vague. I don't remember very well.

I remember walking along to the Cheltenham School with Tom and Rosa. I loved school, but I hated my boots! It was common to wear boots. I think I was a bit of a tomboy. I didn't want to wear them. Sometimes I would take off my boots and socks and hide them in bushes beside the path and collect them on our way home. Sometimes I would forget them, and I would get into trouble. Especially so one time, when the school photographer was coming! I'd taken my boots off and put them under the hedge near Grandma's. We had gone there for lunch, and I had forgotten to pick them up. I am still unsure if I was punished by being put in the front row of the photo, or if it was because I was the smallest in grades three and four!

I seem to remember mostly the play times at Cheltenham School. We made such lovely houses! Just walls of piled up needles from under the many pine trees around the school. Also, I loved the religious instruction given by Mr Mudge. He would set us a verse or a chapter to learn, and when we knew it off by heart, we were given a small bar of chocolate. It was beautiful chocolate!' Min was beaming. 'I learned the names of the books of the New Testament. One chocolate. Then the Old Testament I got about two-thirds through. No chocolate. I still get stumped after Psalms, Proverbs, Ecclesiastes, Song of Solomon—then I stumble. I also got a chocolate for repeating the Ten Commandments.

Tom, Rosa and I sometimes went to Grandma Bruton's market garden in Latrobe Street for lunch. To do this, we walked along the path beside the railway line, and then through a narrow walkway made in the fence, and into the edge of their asparagus farm. We followed a boxthorn hedge, then up to the house. Sometimes when crossing a paddock, a cow would be peacefully grazing not far from where we crossed. So just to convince ourselves it was not a wild bull, we would sing to ourselves, 'God will take care of you, be not dismayed,' as we hurried across! I think it was Tuck's paddock. Other times we had a penny to buy a piece of rainbow cake. Rosa usually looked after the money for us. There was a cake shop in Chesterville Road near the railway line. Sometimes we would pay two pennies for a pie. That would be three pennies we were given to buy our dinner with.'

'And what else did you do at playtime?' I wondered.

'I don't really remember playing with anyone except my brothers and sisters. I was friends with neighbours over the road who really were not very nice. We went over to buy milk as they had cows. I am still unsure if a bull did chase us once, and we spilt the milk getting under the fence, or if it is a dream that has stuck in my memory. I think lots of prickly pears grew in the paddock and we were shown how to safely eat them. I do remember playing on the roadside under the pine trees and being attacked by a nesting magpie. I also remember waiting in the drive for Dad to come home from the Victoria Market. I climbed up and stood on the very stout gate post. Then I jumped off, and my dress went over the post, and I was left hanging yelling for help! I think my big sister brought Mum out to help me down. I think it was always a special event Dad coming home from market. We used to look forward to seeing what he had brought home.

We always looked forward to going over to Grandma Bruton's too—she always made us so welcome to visit. Rosa and I loved to go there for dinner from school. She was lovely. I cannot recall a negative or cross word from Grandma. I don't remember Grandpa Bruton so well, as he had died earlier. He always seemed to me to have been old. He had a beard, and was to my mind, always sitting beside the kitchen stove to keep warm, drumming his fingers on the table. He used to make up rhymes about us, some of them funny. Like 'Rosie rode the roan cow around the rascals' hall,' is about the only one I can remember now. Also we always knew when he had been on a visit to the Royal Oak Hotel, as he would sit in his deck chair on the verandah and play his fiddle. The more he had imbibed, the faster he would play! Grandpa's violin expressed his mood so well. He would play quite jolly music. I cannot recall any particular tune that he played.

I don't remember Grandma actually packing asparagus, but Auntie Elsie and Auntie Eva I do remember at the bench. Grandma had enough to do supplying meals, and so on. The shed was long and narrow, a door at each end. There was a high bench running along one wall, stools to sit on to pack, and all these little box-like frames for each packer. The asparagus was laid on this heavy wooden block-type box and the ends were cut off to be level. Strings of flax were put in first to tie the bunch and then brought together and tied. The flax was grown on the property and had been cut and torn into strings.'

It was clear Min's entrancement was with her grandmother Elizabeth, rather than the vicissitudes of the market garden. She reverted with enthusiasm to her favourite subject. My eyes followed her gaze as it alighted on a small golden teapot in the glass cabinet. 'Grandma always used a little brown teapot. I think enamel with flowers on it. It seemed very small, but she would give cups of tea all round, with Auntie Eva and Elsie and Uncle Ted and Joe. Later on Auntie Elsie did the tea. The pot was always on the table at mealtimes. The men were hard working cutting asparagus, carting seaweed and spreading it over the land.

Grandma would always milk her cow at a certain time in the afternoon. There was a boxthorn hedge reaching from the shed to the paddock. I well remember running quietly down the other side of the hedge to try and make sense of what she was saying to herself. I never could. Perhaps just as well. Years later when I took Judith, she was about six months old, to visit by train to Richmond, and thence to Cheltenham, and a walk from there with the pusher, Grandma said 'You can have anything you like from that cupboard in the sitting room.' I chose an amber coloured glass jam dish which I had for years till it got broken. It was on a silver stand and very pretty. I remember the stove in the kitchen. It had an oven in the middle and a firebox under the oven, with another fire just under the top, like most stove tops. Only the top fire was used most times. For special cooking, the lower one would be used. I think it might have been called a Colonial Oven.

It was the next day when we continued. Rosa's cold had worsened, and with Min's encouragement and ministrations, including aspirin, she was glad to have a rest.

The conclusion of Min's first decade of childhood was indelibly inscribed on her memory, and she mentioned it once again. 'I was ten when we moved. The family moved inland on medical advice. Tom had developed T.B. They were told he should not be near the sea.'

This move, from their beloved Cheltenham and extended family, signified a dramatic change in family fortunes.

Taradale

'I was ten when we moved to Taradale. We were teased at Taradale School. I think it was because at one stage we had nits in our hair! So did other kids, but we had not been born and bred in Taradale. We were new and not welcome.

I remember Grandma Bluhm came to visit. I don't remember very much about her before this time. While she was at our place, she got pneumonia and died. Mum was heartbroken. I cried, I think because Mum cried. As far as Grandpa Bluhm is concerned I don't remember him, except I seem to see him at a trough near the well at Chesterville Road, Cheltenham, washing vegetables ready for market.

Bess was born during our two years at Taradale. She was born at home, and Dad told Rosa we were all to go down by the plum tree and play for a while. I remember visiting Mum at Doctor Scantlebury's in Cheltenham when Daisy was born. Rosa and I were so pleased to have a sister! We thought she was beautiful, and the doctor had such a lovely house and bedroom! And we were all pleased too to have another girl in the family when Bess was born. Even the boys! Later, I think Daisy resented the attention diverted to Bess. Rosa and I would want to go off, and Daisy wouldn't want to play with her little sister. She was always saying, 'Wait for me.''

Min spoke as though from far away. 'When we moved from Chesterville Road to Taradale, our lives changed. Then we milked cows morning and night, before and after school. We used to run home from school too for lunch because we weren't happy there. Mum would probably have a big scone loaf in the oven, or just out. Or if Dad was cook for the day, he would have a rice pudding in the oven or vegies and an egg.

We used to play among the mullock heaps left from the gold mining days. We also played in the creek and used to go for walks.'

Little Hampton. School

'When we moved to Little Hampton, the school was a one teacher school. Sometimes we'd run home for lunch. But not because we were unhappy. I was in grade seven and we eventually had Harold Parker as our teacher. He was fond of poetry and so was I. He was very patient and made us all interested and eager to learn the words and author's name. Especially the Australian poets. Mr Parker got married during the two years I was there. I thought he was very kind, but Daisy hated him. She said she didn't get on with him, said he wrapped her around the knuckles. He was, to my mind anyway, the perfect teacher.'

Min's voice quivered slightly. 'One episode I have carried with me all these years! I remember it clearly. Mr Parker had been to his home for the weekend. When he returned, he placed two bags of almonds in the shell, just inside the gate leading to his home next door. The contents were easily accessible to anyone able to reach across the fence. So guess who had a lovely feed. When Mr Parker found I was one of the culprits he gave me such a lecture but no punishment.' Minnie's voice had become even quieter than usual. She was looking down at her hands, embarrassed. 'I'll never forget the look he gave me. A pocket full! 'If I tell your father what you've done—he would die of shame!' I almost died of shame! I promised never to steal again. And I never did because he was so kind.

I had a special girlfriend at the Little Hampton School, Connie Suiter. I played with her and my siblings. Connie and I have been friends all these years, and she came to my eightieth birthday party. We shared most adventures, although she was interested in different things to me. She was a good dressmaker and later took a course and made use of her ability. I was more for poetry and cooking.

Most times we walked the mile or so to school. Sometimes we had a ride in the jinker with Mum when she went for the mail. The boys used to pull Allan in a cart.

Shoes? We wore shoes for school and Sunday school, then mostly no shoes. Especially summer. I don't remember getting new shoes, generally they were passed down. Sometimes we'd wear sandshoes in the summer, lace up canvassy things. We'd get white clay from the side of the creek to put on those. It was down behind the school. We'd also whiten the fireplace with this pipe clay.

Actually I liked all of school and I don't remember any teacher that I did not like. But I did find the mental arithmetic very hard. The teacher always called the numbers too fast for me to add up. I left school the day I turned fourteen. That was in October. Because I had failed in only one subject, mental arithmetic, I was allowed to return for two weeks in March and resit that subject. Thank God I did pass and received my Certificate of Merit. I left school because I was very anxious to contribute to the household budget.'

Food and Fun

'We always had porridge of some sort for breakfast. Rolled oats, digestive meal, sometimes boiled wheat. That was nice with honey. Then other meals we'd have lots of lovely thick beef stew with carrots and onions, lots of vegies, any vegetable that grew in the garden, or mince patties. These were cheaper than sausages. We ate plenty of potatoes, eggs and milk. Mum mainly cooked but sometimes Dad or Rosa did, after she left school in later years. Sometimes we took a cut lunch to school. Cut your own, and sometimes we'd run home. I do remember when Mum was in hospital with 'Percy baby' Auntie Elsie came up to help and then the sandwiches were dripping and pepper. Not bad, but the boys didn't like them. I did.

Us kids took turns to wash up after tea. We also took turns in peeling potatoes and so on. We'd have to make our own bed and keep the room tidy, sometimes milk the cow or go to the neighbour for milk. Feed the pig. I don't remember doing anything much as a small child. We'd wash up and sit around the front room fire, either knitting or reading or doing fancy work. Mum would be darning socks or sewing on buttons. There was always a family prayer before Dad went to bed. The boys, when they were old enough to work on the farm, might be too tired, so go to bed early, about nine. Dad would get tired, sometimes go to bed earlier. No machine sewing after tea. During the evening Dad would have one child on his knee. Mum, if not sewing, would be nursing the baby.

There wasn't much time for amusement except Saturday and Sunday afternoons, when the main thing was to go for a walk in the bush towards the mill or the mineral springs, or just walk through the bush. As the younger members grew up, they played tennis on Saturdays. They would press their grey, or white pants if they had any, themselves in the morning. I would only be visiting home then because I was away working. When we were younger, I remember, we used to amuse ourselves by making a swing in a tree, or climbing a large elm tree, or swimming in the dam, and riding bareback on 'Little Doll.' As we got older, me anyway, we took pride in cooking nice cakes and exchanging visits with neighbours. Sometimes we took part in church functions.

Rosa and I used to learn to act in plays, sing and recite. I used to love school sports. I could run. It was fun winning a championship or runner-up. Used to love flag relay races and Siamese races. Jumping was for boys, but I always wished I could join in! I even dreamed about winning the long jump. Just flying over the ground. So easy. I played marbles, cricket, anything that was going.

And talking about food for sweets. Mum would make what she called pancakes. Later we'd call them popovers, with golden syrup or honey. Dad loved to make a rice pudding. Just rice and milk, baked all morning in the wood stove oven. Used to have eggs on toast too, sometimes for breakfast. Dad did the dinner when Mum was on the mail run, or else Rosa did after she left school at thirteen and a half.

Sunday was always special! As an early teenager I remember going to Drummond to church, driving through the bush in the jinker, visiting member's homes for dinner, then going to Sunday school in the afternoon. Or else we'd go to the Methodist at Little Hampton. And I really did love the sing songs around the piano at the Price's at Little Hampton. I also loved to go to the dances. The school was the venue. But we were not allowed. The few times I did go, I had to sneak out! So when I was working and living at Trentham, the Community Singing was very enjoyable. It was held in the Mechanic Institute Hall each Friday or Thursday night, I'm not sure. Occasionally we drove from home to Trentham to go to the pictures. The first picture I ever saw was with Tommy 'Uncle Tom's Cabin'. I cried lots, but it was a wonderful experience.'

Excited, now I burst out. 'The pictures. You took me to see my first picture!
. Dorothy, Judith and I, to the State Theatre, Melbourne. We saw 'The Greatest Show on Earth.' Remember?'

Min smiled. 'Yes. That theatre was beautiful, wasn't it?'

We reminisced about the soaring ceiling—deepest heavenly blue, with the tiny twinkles of stars. And the breathless excitement of seeing an orchestra pit for the first time, the musicians seeming to magically rise up through the floor.

'Cornel Wilde and Charlton Heston were in it! Dorothy and Judith preferred Charlton, me Cornel. I now think their choice was better.'

Min returned to Sunday activities. 'I do especially remember the Sunday afternoon walks. We had a group who used to go with us. Sometimes Connie and the Higgins girls, Nellie and Mary. Ted Shelden, Rosa and George and so on, going to Ord's Mill. Especially to the mineral springs. Sometimes we'd have a competition about who could drink the most mineral water and walk across the creek via a plank stretched over. Then we'd walk up steep Mount Babington.

I was talking to Ted Shelden about these memories one day. He also remembers going to Price's for sing songs. George was quite a good singer, and he was singing pop songs on the way home. Ted remembered Rosa was going crook at them singing pop songs on a Sunday!

In grape harvest time, Ted was telling me he and George went to Nyah West. They each had a motorbike. George's was a Velocette, Ted's a Raleigh. They set off. George's bike broke down near Malmsbury. They left it there and double dinked on Ted's to get to Nyah in time to pick the grapes. It was quite a good paying job. At Easter on the Saturday morning, they left for home early, got five or six miles down the road and had a puncture. So they sat beside the road and fixed it. They carried no food as they expected to be home, and all they had left was some sugar. So they used water from a spring nearby in a paddock and put sugar in it. That carried them till they got home. Ted remembered too, that he and George used to go to the footy. Ted usually played but George went along to barrack. Sometimes he played.

Ted also reminded me of the Bible Study run by Mrs Dunell. I remember Mrs Hunt starting the Sunday school at Little Hampton. Later Mrs Dunell trained the kids for anniversary concerts. That was great fun. Everyone was expected to take part. George was good. Ted sang lovely. So did Stan.'

Employment. Outdoors

It was in 1927, during those last few years leading up to the devastating depression, that Min began employment outside the home.

'I was only fourteen when I went to North Drummond to work as a companion help for Blackwell's. I really enjoyed those months. I was working as a house help and company for their fourteen-year-old daughter, Dorothy. It was well out of town. I didn't really have to spend a lot of time inside. I was off with their two sons, going around the rabbit traps. That was more in my line. And many hours were spent doing this helping skin rabbits and stretching the skins.

Also, I was lucky enough to ride the horse to the post office to get the mail. I had one fall, but no bad hurts. There was a piano there too, but I did not learn to play, although I did love to sing. Probably out of tune, but joyful! What happened when I fell? I leaned over to close the gate between the Blackwell's property and the little post office at North Drummond. I don't know what frightened her. She bolted. Took off while I was getting the gate shut. I had one foot in, and one foot out. I was dragged. I could see those hoofs going past my head. It was a nice grassy paddock. I don't think I had anything wrong.'

It seemed that the outdoors was a special enjoyment for Min. There are vivid recollections from my own childhood of school summer holidays, and Min's happy involvement in family camping. She and Fred would take their four children in the pale green '35 Ford with the spare wheel on the back, pitch a tent, and spend many wonderful, sun-soaked days at Rosebud or Phillip Island beaches. I always felt greatly fortunate when I was invited to be part of it. It was the camping at Phillip Island I loved the most.

Our tent nestled behind the high dunes, a short climb to the excitement of sand and sea. Us happy tired kids were hushed to sleep by the muffled music of the ocean. The sighing song, the rhythmic symphony. Timeless motion. It rose to swelling crescendos and then a silence, almost inaudible. Velvet. Orphean.

Before our bedtime the flutters of hundreds of mutton birds, black against the evening sky, could be heard. Their screeches, like stringed instruments, provided an improvisation upon the ocean's ever flowing melody. Amid the cacophony of welcome, these amazing birds located their chicks in the near dark, disgorging fish into hungry beaks. As a child, and to this day, I marvel at the miraculous ability of those parent birds to locate their very own chicks, among a metropolis of many fluffy young. So many carefully concealed burrows amid the tangle of grassy tussocks.

On one occasion Judith and I slept in the Ford. It was exciting to snuggle down in our shared bed with an occasional peek through the window. As night fell, the lantern and Tilley lamp would be lit in the main tent. We could see Min and Fred's silhouettes as they companionably moved about in the soft glow behind the canvas. Exciting for a twelve-year-old. Especially as on this occasion one of the few tents in the area comprised some young men. We had giggle mania in those days. Even laughed at them cleaning their teeth as we spied through Uncle's binoculars.

Now we flicked back to the film of Min's life.

She was saying. 'I remember when I was fifteen, I worked for the people who owned the Lyonville Store. It was a grocery and petrol station. I walked home once a week through the bush. I was in the home with Mrs Millar and did housework. They were very nice people. I was the one who wasn't so nice. I had under my mattress 'Poppy's Paper'. A love story magazine! Whenever I could spare a minute, I would read it. The first time I did the washing there was quite a lot of starching to be done. I boiled the kettle to make the starch, and it went lumpy. I should have mixed the starch with cold water first. I put the lumps down the plughole. Mrs Millar said, 'Did you have trouble with the starch Minnie?' I asked, 'How did you know?' The pipe from the trough went into the drain outside and the lumps of starch were floating down the open drain. Mum didn't often use starch. I'd never watched Mum do the starching. Silver Star was the brand we used to get.

I used to work at Auntie Minnie Bluhm's at East Burwood too for quite some time, and then Rosa came later on. Another employer I had was Mrs Peter Drummond. That was when I was about eighteen. Her sister Miss Hollis lived next door to her. Mr Drummond would kindly drive me home in his horse and jig on my days off. He was the accountant at Trewella's Foundry in Trentham.

Another person I worked for was Mrs Weaver's at Boort. Housework. I didn't do any cooking. Three kids and a little one, twelve months old. Mrs Weaver did the cooking, and I did the cleaning. Three kids school age came home for lunch. She'd put a whole cauliflower in a big boiler, like you'd cook a pudding. Then put creamy cheese sauce all over it and the kids would tuck in. Lino floor. I'd take out the mats each day and sweep the floor. Usually cleaned things with hot soapy water. Ammonia was used sometimes.

I wasn't there for very long. I went down to Melbourne for Fred's sister, Elsie's wedding. Eckie we used to call her. I was a bridesmaid and Fred groomsman. He still had T.B. Had to go back to the Sanatorium at Mont Park for a little while. He was sort of on leave. I never went back to Boort. I'd given notice.

Before, when I was nearly twenty-one, Rosa had written to me from Boort and asked if I would be willing to share her job at Facey's. We worked very hard there. They had confectionary, bread, and a restaurant which held eighty people. We worked in the shop and in the house. Yes, Mrs Facey was very good to us. She showed us, I remember, how to cook beetroot with spices. On my twenty-first birthday on 18th October, she packed us a picnic basket with buns to take and have at the lake. Rosa and Audrey Burtt. We'd got to know the Burtt family at the church. Audrey was fourteen then, in 1934. Mrs Facey lent us a billy. I remember Rosa boiling it on the edge of the lake.

It was Audrey's birthday the next day after mine. I saw a bottle of Black Tulip perfume in a little gift shop in Main Street, Boort. I decided to buy it when I could afford it, knowing I could soon. So I went to get it and it was gone! Audrey had bought it. For me! A glass sweet set on pedestals, Rosa gave me. Still have them. They're lovely. Had them on the table thousands of times. The kids used to bring friends for Sunday dinner, and I'd always have those bowls. Fred sent two little crystal vases. Dot bought them for him. I have a photo of Audrey and I sitting on a tree. Several. Taken by Rosa.'

I was curious what gift Min had given Rosa for her twenty-first. Then I felt sorry, in a way, that I'd asked the question. Min's embarrassment was obvious. She sounded mortified. 'I didn't give her anything. Oh. I think I've been quite a selfish person in my life! All I could think of was Fred, I was so worried.

Eventually I was so devastated when Fred went into the Sanatorium, Rosa came to my rescue and worked in my place. At that stage I was at Facey's by myself. Think I then worked at Matheson's business and the post office on Burwood Road.

I went home for a few months and then worked at Sallmanns in Toorak in Melbourne. Four years from age twenty-one till twenty-five. I was at their daughter's for a little while, then Morris, but most of it was with the old people. I remember one day at the Salman's, Mr Robert Menzies, who eventually became Prime Minister, came to dinner. He came out to the kitchen and was talking to Rosa and me. He was a very nice man, not condescending or anything. At that time Rosa and I were together, probably one handing over to the other. We did the cooking. We would put the food into dishes on the dinner wagon. Mrs Sallmann would dish it out and Mr Sallmann carved the meat.'

Mother. Siblings.

'So your happiest childhood memories?' I asked.

'Swimming in the creek at Taradale. Going for long bush walks with Tom and the boys at Taradale. At Cheltenham it was just lovely to be taken on the lorry to the beach. Or even walk from Grandma's at Mentone to the beach.'

Now a more sombre subject. 'And who do you think had the least fun of all in the family?'

'I think my Mum had least fun of all. I don't remember Dad ever having fun. He did enjoy either driving or walking through the bush to Drummond and the 'getaway feeling.' But Mum couldn't share with him because of small children at home. Mum had her fun later, even though it was hard on her, getting out of the house to drive the pony and jinker on the mail run between Little Hampton and Trentham. I think that mail helped us to cope in the Depression. It didn't pay very well, but it helped pay the mortgage and feed us. The last two children were born while Mum was on this job. In some ways we were lucky to grow some vegies and fruit. Lots of potatoes, eggs, chooks, rabbits. The rabbits were trapped along the fence line. Uncle Will visited occasionally, bringing cases of apples and so on, and returning home with bags of potatoes, chaff for his horses. Mum's job as mail contractor helped her to get out of the house and meet people.'

'Memories of George?'

Min was smiling. 'What comes to mind was during the first year we were living at Little Hampton. George would have been about nine, me, twelve. We had a very hot summer. The house was very hot, and I found the coolest place was to lie flat out under the kitchen table. Auntie Elsie was keeping house while Mum was at Mrs Rodda's having Percy. Rosa would remember, I hope.

Anyway, George was feeling the heat too, but there was only room for one person under the table and I was there first. I don't remember what I did to keep him out, but I do remember George latching on to my earlobe with his teeth! He still didn't get the spot under the table, and I don't remember how he was punished.

George was still at home after I was married, and we travelled up for his wedding. I think maybe I was pregnant with Betty, so was too stressed to remember much about it.

When George's youngest boy was born, Ken, he was very unwell. He was having treatment at the Children's Hospital, and Freda and their next boy, Max, stayed with us at East Burwood. On the Sunday night George came to church with me. He was not a bit impressed with the service. I think he called it 'a lot of bunkum!' I was quite hurt but could not convert him to the Church of Christ. I think it was a baptismal service.'

'And which sibling might have had the hardest time, do you think?'

'I would have to say Daisy. Or Allan. Poor little Daisy. So envious of her elders and so anxious to be with them, but unable to relate to the younger ones. Most of us could always find some things interesting to do, or make, or chase.

When Harold was born, I was working at Drummond. He was a lovely, fun loving, mischievous beaut boy. No! I don't think he was favoured as the youngest. Perce and Harold were together a fair bit. Harold's hair was wavy; I remember putting Percy's straight hair in rollers to sit nicely. He was quite small.'

'And who do you admire the most of your siblings?' Min was quick to answer, her voice definite.

'Why it goes without even a question. My oldest sister Rosa, who was always there when needed! She always, in my mind anyway, just knew what should be done and did it to the very best of her ability. I did what I wanted to do most times. I think I also admired my older brother Tom, also younger one Bob. I think I talked most to my oldest sister, but I also had some very heart to heart talks with Tom. And Bob and I clicked. We enjoyed each other's company. Each of my older siblings were very different. But each of them was wonderful, to me, anyway.'

'And was Tom a rebel, do you think?'

'Rather than call Tom a rebel, I would say he was a free thinker. He was leaning towards communism I think, a red-hot commo! I am afraid I was not really interested in politics, therefore we did not talk about it in our young days. Tom was the sort of person who, when he was young, would talk with his sisters rather than his brothers in order to sort out the complexities of life. Sex, and so on. Later I think most talk was about farm and family matters.'

'Tom and your father?' I wondered about Tom's relationship with his upright father and imagined, particularly as the eldest, that this could have been a difficult area for Tom.

'I don't think that anybody could truly know Tom's feelings for Dad. Except to say, Tom was not interested in church, and therefore did not agree to anything to do with it. I think when Tom left home the second time it was not as sudden as it seemed. He had contemplated the trip and talked to his siblings about it. It was a combination of not being paid for work done at home. An impossibility. And being lonely for company of persons thinking as he did. He loved his mother dearly and would not think of doing anything he thought would hurt her, but could do nothing to earn money locally, to help feed and clothe our large family.

In later life, when he was farming in Queensland not far from us, he was often very sick, but was very determined to have something worthwhile to leave his family when he died, as he knew he would, before his old age.

In fact, you did ask me about my saddest memory the other day. My saddest memory is the weeks before Tom died, knowing that he did not have very long to live. And yet he was quite casual as he waved goodbye on his way to hospital on a stretcher. He was pronounced dead on arrival.'

On that dismal note, the balm of tea was especially welcome. So too, the savouring of more than one liberal slice of Min's special boiled fruit cake.

Father

Now, we returned to the more distant past. In previous conversations, Min had spoken very positively about her father. 'Yes. I have some lovely memories of my dad. When I was very young at Cheltenham. I can remember sitting on his knee as he told us stories about his year in Queensland before he married Mum, in the cane fields, riding on the train and so on. Also, he had a lovely quiet singing voice as he sang to us as young children on his knee. Always hymns. Never jolly songs. Yet he could also recite good poems or jolly ones. That was before the family grew too large for him to feed them properly or to control. The older boys all stood up to him and then ran away when he could not catch them. No. Dad did not share with me anyway, any of the things he did as a young man at home with his parents.

I just remembered another nice thing about Dad. I think I must have been anaemic for many years. When my turn came at night to wash the tea dishes, sometimes I was very, very tired. Dad would come and tell me to go to bed or sit by the fire, and he did the dishes for me. I was truly very grateful and loved him for it.'

Min's face shone with these recollections. It was rare to hear anything of a depreciative nature from either Min or Rosa concerning their father.

'And were there hard times with your father when you grew up a bit?'

Min seemed reluctant to be drawn on this subject. Her voice was hesitant. 'Dad got into tempers sometimes. No...... was I frightened?

'I don't think so.'

'Looking back, if it were possible, would you have changed anything concerning your childhood?' I asked. Perhaps this might lead to further discussion concerning her father.

'Nothing! Looking back, I had a wonderful carefree, happy childhood! I would not change a thing! But young adulthood. Yes. I should have insisted on going and learning to be a nurse. Instead of working for strangers. I could have helped the family more. However, I still enjoy my cooking, but I hate cleaning!'

Min quietly pondered my next question. 'What advice would you give the younger generation?'

'The same golden rule that we were taught. 'Do unto others as you would have them do to you.''

Fred

Min's voice was agonised. 'I couldn't stand going back to Boort. I could not visit Fred. That's why I went to Matheson's. I could have stayed with the Mocks as a maid, but I didn't want to. I was so worried about Fred.'

'Did you confide your pain to anyone?' I asked.

'No-one else knew how I felt. I kept it all inside. People said how come you were going together for eight years. How could you bear it! We were told not to get married until he was quite clear of T.B. A lady from Boort, a nurse, warned me not to marry until Fred was completely clear, and it would probably be eight years. But I was quite willing to wait that long!' Min's tone was soft and remote. 'We wrote to each other. I didn't seem to be able to think of anything else but Fred's illness. Everything else went by the board. I nearly had a nervous breakdown. It was July when he went in. He was twenty, I was nearly twenty-one. He went into the Cresswell Sanatorium the day Dorothy Bluhm was born. Was there nearly a year.

He wasn't allowed to work for another year after the Sanatorium. Then he worked at the garage at East Burwood. I stayed with Uncle Will and Auntie Min Bluhm at this time and worked at the East Burwood store.

Fred used to borrow the motorbike and sidecar from the garage, and he took me out in it. We married when I was working at the store. The proprietor, Mrs Mathieson, carried Semco fancy-work goods. To help keep the business going, she ran competitions. I won one. It was by embroidering and crocheting around the edge of two pillow shams. I won two beautiful blue vases. Still got them. I used to sit at night at my Auntie Min's too, do fancywork around the fire in the front room, or the stove in the kitchen. There'd be a hanging kerosene light.'

It seems that the young Min learnt quite a bit about keeping a well organised household. In later years, in her own home on their orchard at East Burwood, items would be carefully ironed and nicely stacked. Tasty meals were prepared on time, all with a minimum of fuss and quiet humour. Min and Rosa both owned a Fowler's Bottling Outfit and exchanged preserves. I used to look forward to Min's cherries and peaches. In exchange, Rosa gave bottles of our home-grown plums, also blackberries, which we helped gather from the profusion which grew around fences at Avonsleigh, in the Dandenong Ranges.

At twenty-six, in 1940, Min married Fred. An optimistic conclusion to those eight long stressful years of watching and waiting; hoping against hope that Fred would survive a usually fatal disease. Fred's father, George Mock, grew a wide range of produce including apples, pears and cherries. During the war they also grew flowers. Fred's grandfather, also George, was the only child of Thomas. It was in 1855 that Grandfather George, six or seven years old, arrived on the 'Birmingham' with his parents, from Devonshire, England. Thomas bought a market garden in the Melbourne sand belt, in the Black Rock area, and Fred's father was born there.

Interestingly, the Mock property was not far from where Min's forebears had also gardened! Fred's father was only twelve years old when his father died. An older brother, Walter, took over the reins, so to speak. He transported their market garden produce by horse and cart to the Queen Victoria Market. One of Walter's sons became an orchardist in Mahoney's Road, East Burwood, as did Fred's father. Others set up orchards further south-east of Melbourne at Red Hill.

Fred had explained. 'My grandmother acquired some land in Mahoney's Road, East Burwood. She gave Walter, George and Tom a block each. They all planted orchards. Later, in 1914, Pop bought another block on the Melbourne side of the road. They were mostly ten-acre blocks, for ten pound an acre. That was when I was born.'

Given the lack of opportunity of social activity for Min and Rosa as domestics, I was curious as to how Min had met Fred.

'He used to take his horse, the draft horse, old Brownie, down to the Mock house paddock to graze in Mahoney's Road. Over the road from the Bluhm's. I'd more or less talk to him over the fence.'

'And what happened to old Brownie in the end, on the advent of the tractor?' It was a momentary diversion.

'Think he went to the bone mills when he was old. Kept for a while after the tractor, then he went off to the bone mills.'

We returned to the happier topic. 'Fred used to go to the Methodist Church up on Burwood Road. I used to go to tea meetings with Fred. His young peoples' group always had a picnic up in the Dandenongs for Cup Day, and he asked me to go to this picnic with him. And I did.'

War

Ominous black clouds of war erupted as Min and Fred married in 1940. Like everyone, Min suffered disruptive, sometimes painful fallout. During those five long years of war, Min became a mother, giving birth to the first three of their four children. 'We had to take a dozen flannelette nappies into the hospital. We made them ourselves. Bought it by the yard. It was white and cost about one and sixpence a yard. A nappy was about one-yard square, or not perhaps as big as that, about 28 inches. We had to mark the nappies with our names—a black marking pen. Later, we made nappies from old sheets. I remember boiling nappies in a kero tin on the stove when Judith was six weeks old.

That was at Fred's Auntie Eck's. We didn't have a home of our own until towards the end of the war. We ended up living with Fred's parents on the orchard, that was in March 1941. The house was divided down the middle. Fred's brother Bert and his wife Grace had half, and Mum and Dad and us the other. We had one bedroom and a cot in the corner. It was pretty full. Fred took a few boards out of the wall and replaced them with flywire so we could close the door and get more air.

We moved into our own house for my birthday. It was in October 1945 when Betty was a few months old. Earlier, Fred's mother had had a stroke, and we helped to care for her. She was bedridden and then in a wheelchair. Grace and I took it week about. The first job I had to do was to give Mum an enema. This was the beginning of many shocks. I used to wash and dress and get her up and Fred helped too. His sister Dot from Mitcham helped also. Eventually Fred's mother had a nurse with her. Must have died in May. Betty was born in July and Mum died a month before Betty was born. When Judith was eighteen months old Fred got the measles.'

The young couple's lack of housing had obviously placed heavy strains on Min. The relief of finally finding a hearth of their own was enormous. She repeated, 'But we didn't have a home until 1945. Before our marriage Fred had that job in the garage in Timboon and we boarded in the boss's home. He and his wife welcomed us, and made the room a double room, so we could marry. Shortly after that the boss enlisted and was accepted, and went off to fight the Japs, leaving his wife the boss. Then the garage burnt down. Then we lived at Eckie's dairy farm for a while, and Fred helped. That was for a few months. Fred was needed at home on the orchard.

Fred built the house we eventually lived in, on the family property. We were not allowed to build until the third child was on the way. You had to get permission from the government because building materials had to go to the army. Also you couldn't use over 800 pounds, so it did restrict the type of home and the decisions you made. We ended up with a fibro cement house, tiled roof.

Fred asked me, 'What would you rather, a hot water service, or a toilet inside?' We could not have either in the beginning, but Fred had taken the precaution of having a spot to put the hot water service above the ceiling later. This was the very best birthday present! I had a holiday at Little Hampton. When we came home in October '45 Fred had finished the house enough to use it.' Min remembered her excitement. 'I tried the cold-water tap. I tried the other one! Hot water came out of it! We still had an outside toilet. We eventually had a spare room across the path on the corner of the lawn between the children's sandpit and the garage. It had a frame around it with passionfruit.'

This house I remember well. The front lawn, squarish, faced Mahoney's Road. A gravel road in the fifties. There were orchards on each side. Everywhere. Apple trees were predominant as I recall, but the row of cherry trees which stretched to the road along the drive is especially vivid. This, because I had gorged myself on them. All of us kids were allowed to eat as much of whatever fruit we fancied. Hopefully good sense would prevail or, as in my case, we would learn from experience the negative effects of gluttony.

My delight in this glossy, sweet tasting rubescent succulence began as a very small child. The Mock children's sandpit in the back garden provided us with endless entertainment, and sported in the centre, a big low branched cherry tree.

Judith ended up being the fortunate tenant of the new spare room not far from the sand pit. That must have been in our early teens. More confident than myself, more boy-wise, and more modern, she arrayed her windowsill with various small bottles of nail polish. Much time was spent by us painting and repainting. Nail polish was something my mother did not encourage. She could either not afford it or did not approve. Lipstick was certainly in the latter category.

That gravel road which passed the front of the house stands out in my memory. Stretching from the major bitumen Burwood Road and the Tally-Ho Boys' Home opposite, there was, at its beginning, a flower farm which in the spring glowed with thousands of daffodils. Then the orchards. There was Hughie Mullens, Albert Stock further up, then a fair bit further, the Mocks on both sides of the road. Over the hill past Uncle Will Bluhm's, the road ended, being cut across by bush. This arboreous area, typical higgledy-piggledy bush, was abundant with a wide variety of vegetation. It was enjoyable to amble along and pick a bouquet of wildflowers. Even a greenhood orchid or two, under the scraggly canopy of eucalypts—probably yellow box and stringybark.

That loose gravel! Capricious. Especially for the unpractised. That was where I came to grief on Judith's push bike! Judith owned a bike before I did, and she would kindly steady it for me as I balanced precariously. I had not completed my apprenticeship when the bike, seeming with a will of its own, gained frightening wind-whistling momentum. It propelled me, careering out of control down the hill past Ron and Dib Bluhm's. Instead of continuing straight, the pesky headstrong bike veered sideways. Colliding with a wattle in the bush at the bottom of the hill may have been kinder than that yellow pea-flowered, cruelly spiked gorse hedge!

Fred's cheery face appeared around the door. 'Cup of tea?'

'I'll take one into Rosa,' said Min. Rosa's voice could be heard. 'I'll take my vitamins too. They've helped my cold. They might help your memory Min.'

Fred was passing the door 'Vitamins? Oh, we eat pretty well, a salad every day.'

I stared through the gold and white of daffodils and net curtains, to the lilly pilly at the window. This tree, dramatic, like so many Australian natives, stood dark-pencilled in the dancing light. Clusters of small round pretty pink fruits festooned its strong branches. The brilliance of rainbow parrots babbling and feeding, blurring against the blue sky and blush of coral, was breath-taking.

'Oh,' said Min, on hands and knees as she rummaged through the bottom shelf of her jam cupboard. 'Here's some jelly I made from the lilly pilly.'

Then I remembered some entirely unfamiliar dark grape-like fruits I'd been given that morning by the local fruiterer to try. They were still in the paper bag. The name eluded me.

Min was quick 'Jabotacabo. They grow like grapes along the stems.'

Another small pot of jelly emerged miraculously, of a slightly different shade. Rosa's ears had pricked up, and she joined us. We dipped with teaspoons into these two perfectly set specimens. The rich pink jelly was a reminder of plum. The slightly tart edge to both was refreshing. Too difficult to choose a favourite. 'Gourmet!' I said.

War. Flowers. Orchard

'Wasn't there an Apple and Pear Board in the war?' Min asked Fred.

'Oh yes. The Fruit Marketing Board came in 1941. They fixed a price for all the different types of fruit. The price varied from one shilling, to three shillings and sixpence per case. In the late thirties, apples were bringing one and sixpence to five shillings for a forty-pound case! Compared with during the war, some apples and pears were estimated in quantity on the tree, and we were paid one shilling per bushel case for them to fall on the ground! We weren't allowed to sell or even give them away. We did, of course. That was for the stuff they wouldn't take. The others they paid about two shillings and sixpence. The cases were a bushel. A bushel is a measurement, not a weight.'

'We could not send it to England where it was needed. So there was a glut. It was terrible seeing the waste!' added Min.

Fred noted my bewilderment. 'A lot of our fruit prior to the war had been exported to England via the Suez Canal, but after the war broke out, there was a big limit on exports, because of lack of shipping and fuel. They couldn't afford space on the boats to send the fruit over, and the Suez Canal was closed. Apples weren't as difficult to handle as pears. Pears ripen quickly. We used to cart apples off to the packing sheds. The packing area was part of the big cool store in Burwood road, next to the East Burwood Post Office. Bert had a truck by then, a Chev, one ton, then a Dodge. He worked for the Board taking a load of fruit from the cool store most days to the Queen Victoria Market. He'd go about 5am, be back about 7 or 8am. The truck would be fully loaded, about a hundred-bushel cases on it. Was three of us in our orchard. Bert, Dad and I. We kept it going. In early '45 they discontinued the Board.

During the war we had to sell to the Board. We couldn't sell our own fruit at the market. Our sweet pea flowers were so much in demand that they paid better than apples. Also during the Depression, we used to grow sweet peas, and we lived better on flowers than fruit!

Mostly sweet peas were grown on stakes between the fruit trees. In all, we had a couple to three acres of them. We had numerous colours. The most popular being a pale violet called Valletta. We had been growing them before the war too, about the years 1933 to 1939.'

'That very nice mauve one people especially liked, and the darker ones, the men liked. The mauve one was popular with the florists for wreaths,' added Min.

'We also had stocks then. Sweet peas contained thirty stems. One penny per bunch. Stocks would be about one dozen stems depending on the size of the flowers, and the same price. We ended up discontinuing the stocks because they weren't as popular. My sister Dot before she married, she would pick flowers five days a week. And even after she was married, she would come down from Mitcham to pick flowers until 1940.

Originally, we had an old horse-drawn buggy, and Bert would take as many as twenty pineapple cases of flowers, at least three times a week, to the Blackburn Railway Station. The pineapple cases were larger. A bushel and a half. This required five dozen bunches. It cost five shillings for a box of sweet peas. The boxes were second hand from fruiterers. Originally, they used to store fruit in kero cases in the cool store. But the pineapple cases were square. They used to stack beautifully in the cool store. They had a cleat across the end. That was a good handle. The kero cases got their name because they had been used to carry two four-gallon cans of kerosene.'

Min smiled gently. 'Fred brought a bunch to me when I was working at Sallmanns before the war. I put it in my room sort of off the back verandah. Mrs Sallmann had two daughters, one a dressmaker and one a florist. The upshot of it was, she asked the Mocks to send a box of sweet peas once a week.'

'Even more often.' added Fred. 'We continued growing the sweet peas after 1940. Until the apples started to get better a year or two later. The price would vary. But we usually got threepence a bunch. Of course, the florist's price was set. They'd send a cheque each month. Bert would deliver them to the railway station in the truck. If we had any extra flowers, he'd take them direct to the Vic Market when he took in the fruit, at the end of the week. We'd also use other transport like the bus. We'd pay the bus and train for delivery. Might have been a shilling, I don't remember. Our market for the sweet peas was mainly florist shops, around Melbourne. The florists would collect what they ordered from the station. The stocks were too much work during the war years.'

Min was listening attentively. 'Clarry Bird. He started the bus from East Burwood to Tunstall Station. He would take a pineapple case full as a favour if we were stuck.'

'Yes. I used to enjoy picking the sweet peas. The salamander colour, the pink, was a particularly strong scented one. It was an easier and more pleasant job than picking apples, also a quicker return. Wonderful country to grow flowers. They were staked at about one foot high on tea-tree stakes taken from the creek, in a tea-tree row. Grew to about seven feet high. We had to reach up to pick them.'

Sweet peas are one of my favourites. I tried once to plant these colourful festive flowers with the heady scent. Shamefully, they shrivelled up soon after sprouting. It seemed miraculous when Fred recounted, they had grown these gems without irrigation.

'Dry farming. We used to plant them about Feb, then get the rains. Carry us through. But it was May before we picked any.'

Fred seemed to enjoy talking and Min happy to listen.

'In the old days the bakers and the grocers had horses, and Pop used to get a wagon load of manure from their pits. Later we got poultry manure. We'd put quite a generous furrow and plant the seeds on it, about six inches above the manure. We'd leave about six feet between the rows—give them room to breathe.

The tea-tree stakes came from down at the Dandenong Creek. Two or three people had blocks down to the creek edge. We'd find it and approach the owners. The tea-tree grew quickly. We'd go up Burwood Road towards Ferntree Gully. We'd get it mostly between Burwood and Highbury Road, only a mile. They'd be seven, eight, nine feet high and each stalk would be separate. Chop the feathery top off.'

Now my mind's eye had returned to view those other sweetly scented beauties, the stocks. What tips I wondered could Fred provide about the growing of them from seed, considering another of my recent dismal failures. I was astounded at the reply from an obvious expert.

'Some are the male, the double flowered bushes, and some female. The females have single daisy type flowers. So—we'd get a single, pull out the other singles near it, and put doubles around it. Say about four doubles. The more pollen on the female, the more likely it is to throw female plants. If the female doesn't get pollinated, that's lack of fertilised seed.'

So now I knew why my seed, bunches of little dark seeds I'd carefully harvested from crackly dry seed pods, had not grown.

Fred was saying, 'We got the colours controlled too. Used to have pink, dark and so on. Used to keep the same colours together. Two or three doubles around the one single, all same colours.'

'Your soil must have been pretty adaptable,' I said, thinking of the variety of produce grown by the Mocks.

Fred was enthusiastic. 'We had the best land apples could wish for! Six inches grey topsoil, one-foot yellow subsoil, about three feet of red clay. And the apples did really enjoy it. We had pear trees thirty feet high by the same across.

When my grandmother bought the blocks, one had umpteen different apples on it, and pears. We systematically changed over to the marketable types. There were cherry trees at the old house, seventy years old, 115 feet. There were forty or fifty sorts of apples, planted by a German family, way back. Fankhousers, we think. 'Stone Pippin' called 'Jelly' apples would fall on the ground and still be hard at Christmas. There were six Gravenstein trees amongst it, but they did not have twisted limbs as was the usual case.'

Fred explained further. 'If the Gravenstein is grown on its own stock, the tree branches will gnarl up, twist, break, go corky. So Pop got the idea it was the stock they were grown on. He grafted some and put them on to different roots. It was a yellow striped apple. One tree, Pop found, had very attractive red striped apples on one limb. So that's how we got our red Gravenstein. Pop propagated a lot of them grafting from it.

When Pop started, I was still going to school. Late twenties, early thirties. The stock grown on was very strong. Trees would be twenty feet across and nearly that high. We picked forty-six bushels off one tree one year. Big apples, too. One year we had 1500 cases of these. Don't know where the stock originally came from, perhaps Germany. It was nearly ten years before they bore. Then once they started bearing, they had good crops.'

'Ah,' I said, 'Another riddle solved. The red 'Mock' Gravenstein you grafted for me six years ago has had very few apples on it.'

'It will bear well in just three or four years then.'

'Why isn't it a popular apple now?'

'The cool stores could keep last year's up to Christmas. Didn't like this apple anymore, because it's a soft apple. Keeping quality isn't so good.'

Min had been listening and thinking. Now she said, 'But I do remember during the war people coming into the orchard with bags, and picking up good fruit from the ground, and sometimes not so accidentally from the trees. This was mostly at the weekends.'

A memory of mine! Olfactory. The wafting perfume came first, then the image of stocks planted in the Mock's front garden. The sweetly distinct perfume was especially strong in the evenings. As a child I admired these heavily scented, thickly flowered stems. My favourite hues. They ranged from ruby to amethyst and a soft cream, then a white. This memory had precipitated my planting of stock seedlings this very autumn. I was delighted prior to my departure that they had burst into flower.

It was enjoyable hearing Min elaborating. 'The seeds were planted in seed beds. When four or five inches high, they were transplanted in rows. Then, as they grew up, they spread up and flowered progressively. They were cut and bunched and put in boxes and sold. Same as sweet peas. There were several colours, white, pink, mauve and dark magenta. The mauves were very popular. Prices were about threepence per bunch to florists, as well as those sold in the fruit market. Double and single flowers. They made seed pods like a sweet pea. So the pods when dry were put into a paper bag and kept dry. We eventually shook the seeds out after belting the bag.'

We returned to the subject of war. Fred was particularly emphatic. 'I wanted to join the Air Force. Fly!'

Not surprising, given Fred's adventurous spirit and his mechanical ability with all manner of things, including the building of a lift in their previous home. As he spoke, he wound bandages on an electric self-winder. This was another invention of his, this time for the local geriatric hospital.

There was an aggrieved note in his voice. 'But they wouldn't take me. Got rubbed out! The army examined me and tossed me out because I'd had T.B. I got over it. Never had it back since. I was working in a garage as a motor mechanic and Mum asked me to come home to work on the orchard. She said Dad was wearing out. Also, my brother Tom was called up. He ended up in the Middle East.'

War. Cars. Housing

Min seemed to remember clearly. 'So many things were rationed. We strained any tea which was left in the pot and warmed it up later on. We used animal fat in our cooking instead of butter, that is, except for special cakes and so on. We recut men's half worn-out trousers to make overalls for toddlers or warm skirts for girls. We made our own baby clothes, including the nappies. We made our soap, also our self-raising flour, as self-raising flour was more expensive than plain. We even ground wheat for porridge. Oh, we did a lot of bartering, apples for spuds and so on. When a baby was expected we did get some extra ration cards to get clothes for baby.

We were fortunate to have a car. The car, the V8 Ford, was fitted with a bucket boot, one that had a top opening.'

Fred had been winding bandages all the while. He was spinning the long thick bandages into neat tight rolls. 'One thing I remember most, was the shortage of materials used for car manufacturing. Therefore, the production of cars was limited to war needs, and the second-hand cars were controlled in price. We bought our first car, actually we owned it half with Bert, a second-hand Ford V8 1935 Sedan about 1942-43, for 165 pounds. It was already fitted with a gas producer. The gas system worked by using wood charcoal in an enclosed drum, with a small hole feeding a small fire with air which produced a flammable gas. This took the place of petrol, as petrol was rationed during the war to four gallons per month. The gas producer was bolted on the back-bumper bar of the car, a bit like a small extension. This made the back of the car very heavy.'

'Yes,' agreed Min, 'so the heavy ones, people, had to sit in the front seat. It held three. We were then able to do more trips, like going home to Little Hampton, or to Fred's sister Elsie Trigg at Warrnambool. Any long distance travelled we would carry a spare bag of charcoal, though some garages would sell it on the way. The bag was about the size of a spud bag. We can't remember how much a bag it cost, but it was cheaper than petrol.

Fred's mum had a stroke in August 1942, while Fred and I were on a week break at Rosebud. Fred was recovering from the measles. She was paralysed all down one side and the car was very necessary to carry her around. It also gave me a break to go with Fred to take her to Elsie's, then return to get her in a few weeks' time.'

The window framed Fred as he disappeared behind the double crimson hibiscus on his way to collect the mail. 'What was your main domestic concern during the war, do you think?' I asked Min.

She did not hesitate. She talked again about that momentous event. 'Housing was our main concern.' Min's voice rose with jubilation. 'Eventually at the end of 1945 we had our own house! That for me is the thing that stands out about the war years.'

Looking back on the tapestry of Min's life, there were many threads of different hues. Poverty and plenty, horsepower then mechanical power, war and peace.

'What invention has been the most notable for you during your life?' I asked.

Fred was bending, newspaper under his arm to pick up his glasses. 'The motor car.'

Min silent, pondered. 'For me, it was chloride of gold. This was used in 1934 in the wards of the Mont Park Sanatorium in Melbourne for patients with tuberculosis of the lungs. It was injected into the patient. Fred was the first one to have it in his ward. They were dying around him like flies. This treatment was the beginning of the wipe-out of this terrible disease.'

Min and Rosa. Diphtheria. The Cake Shop

The next day, Rosa, still thickened with cold, had much improved. The morning was cool for Queensland. Companionable tones drifted from the bedroom.

'We're here!' called Min. And there they were. Sitting up in the double bed, cosy, with flower patterned doona, and fat cushions. And laughing. Merriment perhaps engendered by happy memories of their shared childhood, and the sharing back there too of a double bed and many secrets. The subject was the past, and they seemed to be reliving it. Two sisters. A quiet understanding. Concern one for the other—even admiration. Thrown together by destiny, each had found a friend. Yes. They really did like each other.

Their earlier years in the market gardening sand belt at Cheltenham seemed a good place to start. To see what collectively they may recall, Min having voiced concern about a sluggish memory. Perhaps we could blow away some more cobwebs, the dust of at least eighty years.

Childhood illness surfaced for Rosa. 'Remember when we had diphtheria?'

'Yes,' said Min. 'We weren't very old, about eight or nine something like that.'

'Or maybe you were nine, and I was ten, as it was while we were at Cheltenham in Chesterville Road. And Dad had scarlet fever too and was sent off to the Fairfield Hospital later. And we thought we heard Georgie cry when we were in the hospital. And it was him. They'd put George into Fairfield too; we knew his cry. We wanted our little brother with us. And the Sister said we should have told her, but we told her the next morning.'

'Yes. But she wouldn't shift him, would she!'

'I think,' said Rosa. 'They should have put him in our ward. He only had the same as us!'

'He was three years younger than me, about five then. Fred's younger brother had diphtheria and he died. He was very, very young.'

Rosa was animated. 'I was supposed to come home a day after you, and they let me out a day earlier than they should have. I had it worse. They'd let you have a pillow, and they wouldn't let me.'

'What!' I exclaimed when Min shared the next bit.

'We had a phenyl bath, didn't we?'

'Yes. Right at the gate they had a little bath house, and you had to get in this bath before you were allowed out.'

Min was animated too. 'And all our clothes were, I don't know how long they were in this hot cupboard, to make sure that they had no germs on them.'

'And they gave us needles,' remembered Rosa. 'What they didn't do, I don't know. We were too sick to bother, anyway.'

The laughter of kookaburras drifted through the bedroom window. Min and Rosa were laughing too. Perhaps a laugh of relief knowing they had been able to survive this difficult episode in their lives. Diphtheria was not a light matter back then.

'There were a lot of kids wiped out with it.' was Rosa's sobering statement.

'The phenyl bath. Sticky and smelt nasty. Oh, we hated it!'

They were both laughing again. 'Looked like a bathtub of milk didn't it.' said Min.

'I don't remember what it looked like. But the smell!'

We moved to happier subjects. The cake shop. Min was savouring the memory. 'We used to go in there to get our lunch, didn't we, and a piece of rainbow cake for a penny? It was the cake shop in Chesterville Road, Cheltenham, down near our school, right near the railway line on the home side of the railway.'

Rosa was recalling other gastronomic delights. 'It was also a pie shop. It had homemade meat pies and apple pies. We were given threepence each to buy our dinner so we could get a pie and a piece of rainbow cake. Or we'd go right up the street to the Co-op and get a penny's worth of broken biscuits. They'd make a little funnel out of newspaper to put them in. Newspaper was used for a lot of things and we were none the worse for it.'

Min was looking puzzled. 'I'm not sure of the amount of money we were given.'

Rosa was still on her epicurean adventure. 'Whenever Mum would send us up to the Cheltenham shops to buy some flour or whatever she wanted, she'd give us a penny or halfpenny and we'd buy a lolly. We would get for a halfpenny each, little bars of toffee with chocolate around. Oh, they had all sorts of lollies for a halfpenny or a penny. We could always get something nice,'

Somehow this talk about money had triggered another memory, and Rosa strayed in a different direction. 'Well, Mum used to pay for a lady to come to do the washing at Point Nepean Road, Mrs Morris. When we moved to Chesterville Road, Dad bought Little Doll and a jinker, and a cow. Do you remember Mrs Morris?'

'Yes, I remember Mrs Morris.'

'Why have a washerwoman?' Perhaps I sounded trite.

Min's answer was immediate. 'Because Mum had four little kids, and she was also helping in the garden! I know in Chesterville Road she used to wash carrots, and that, didn't she?'

Rosa concurred. 'And money was more plentiful for the family in those days.'

'The irony of it.' I said. 'Olive had a lady to help with the washing when she had four, and when she had twelve, she couldn't afford to have any lady to help.'

Min's answer was again swift. 'Yes, she did. She had Rosa!'

Rosa's response was quiet, 'Yes. Well when I wasn't working. I had to go to work some of the time to get a few bob. She had Minnie too.'

Memories of inviting aromas, freshly baked pies and cakes enticed me back to the cake shop at Cheltenham. Min sighed, she seemed relieved. 'We wander away, don't we! I think it was Mrs Rose in the cake shop. She said, 'I've got two little girls just your size, and we want to measure you to see if the dresses fit.'

'And we'd like you to try them on,' continued Rosa. 'We were about six or seven. We didn't know it was just Mrs Rose's way of giving us a surprise.'

Min continued enthusiastically. 'Mine was mauve! Well, I think it was. And there was a pink one, or was it blue?'

'I must have had the pink one then. I don't know. But they were beautiful. Oh, didn't we think they were lovely? It was crepe I think, wasn't it? A cotton crepe. One you can wash and don't have to iron.'

Min smiled, 'I know they were pretty, that's all I know. But I don't remember what they were like. We wore them to the Sunday School Anniversary. The lady must have gone to the same church. The anniversary was coming up, and she knew it.'

Little Doll

Min was laughing, blue eyes dancing with merriment. 'Little Doll, well she was very high spirited. She was lovely of later years. She was beautiful. A gorgeous little horse!'

'Yes she was, we all loved her,' Rosa's voice was quiet, slower. 'I wasn't there when she died. She lived for a long while. Died of old age. It was a heartbreak for everybody. We had her at Cheltenham right through from when we went to Taradale and Little Hampton.'

'She and Big Doll, both died of old age.'

Rosa's eyes were lively. 'Remember at Cheltenham, Little Doll played up when we were coming home from Sunday School, the anniversary. And we got our pretty dresses dirty. We got thrown out of the jinker right near the gate when we were coming home.'

'I remember Mum used to drive Little Doll in the jinker at Little Hampton,' said Min, not sure.

'She must have endured the cold of Little Hampton too.' I said.

'They always had a stable to go in at night. Always.' was Rosa's quick and spirited reply.

It was clear that both sisters had a special place in their hearts for this horse. Min was thinking back. 'I know Dad bought Little Doll at Cheltenham. Because I remember when he brought her home, she'd had a foal not long before she'd been sold, and he used to have to milk her. He just used to milk straight on to the floor of the stable. And we gave her cooked potato, and she liked it.''

Rosa's voice was adamant, indignant. 'She'd stop whenever she saw a little horse for years. I think that was terrible! Separating her from her foal when it was so young.'

It was clear both Min and Rosa had ridden Little Doll. They must have been quite adept as riders. Min explained. 'We used to hop on her back and ride without a bridle, a saddle, or anything. We'd just hop on, just touch her on the neck and away she'd go. We'd pat her on the left on the neck and she'd go left, or patted her on the right and she'd go right.'

'And Robert used to stand on her back and reckon he was a circus man. He'd do all sorts of things on her back! She didn't mind; just do whatever she was told.'

'Yes.' Then Min remembered something else. 'When we were galloping along the track at the bottom of our place at Little Hampton, there was a creek we had to cross. She used to have great fun jumping across that creek and stopping suddenly.'

'She did that with our cousin Mary Porter. Remember Mary?'

'Yes,' said Min. 'She went straight over Doll's head! And Doll stopped. Mary had fallen in between her feet and, oh, we thought if Doll takes another step, she'll walk right on her! Doll stayed still till we got Mary out of the way. She was half unconscious.'

'No. She didn't take another step.' laughed Rosa. 'Oh. She used to play jokes on us, didn't she? She waited till I had four loaves of bread. Dad said, 'Just look at her eyes, she's in a bad mood.' I said, 'I'm still going on her.' No saddle, had a spud bag. We didn't have a saddle for years. But when I looked, you could see it in her eyes too. Dad said, 'She's going to play up.' And she did too. She tossed me off, then waited for me to get on again. She almost told me to get on again. And she waited for me to get on again, but I wasn't game. I walked! And she walked beside me like a little dog. I'd been to the corner house where Attwoods are now. Because the baker couldn't cart the bread over our boggy rough road and had left it there for us to pick up.'

Min broke the convivial silence this time. 'I remember being in a different accident. I remember being thrown over the front and missing the shaft! We had quite a few accidents on that bush track, didn't we? I remember coming home one day with Dad, when little Bessie was with us. The horse got up a real gallop and I can still hear Bess saying, 'Teddy Doll, Steady Doll.' '

Rosa was excited 'And I jumped out. And I hit the ground hard. Dad said, 'Don't jump out!' My word the ground was hard. I was sorry after. The horse finally stopped in front of a tree. And everybody else was all right. But I wasn't.'

Min was dimpling, laughing again. Now Rosa was laughing too. 'I was just so determined. I wasn't going to be in the accident.'

'Then you made an accident!'

'And Dad was saying, 'Don't jump out. Don't jump out. She'll stop in a minute.''

Min was checking back. 'Yes, that's right, we did. We had Little Doll right through. And Big Doll. I remember Mum used to drive Little Doll in the jinker, and at Cheltenham Little Doll would walk straight up to the electric light pole on the edge of the road and just stay there. She used to shy quite a bit and play up. She used to love eating the flowers of the scotch thistle.'

Grandma Bruton. Cheltenham. School

'When you talk about your years at Cheltenham, it seems there were many happy times. Visiting Grandma Bruton's. You've both talked about this.'

Min and Rosa nodded with vigour. 'Yes.' said Min. 'We loved Grandma, and our times at Cheltenham were very happy. It was for me!'

'It was for me too.'

Rosa interrupted the reflective silence. 'We hated the school at Taradale.'

'At Cheltenham we were so happy.' Min sounded wistful.

'Until I got diphtheria, and I was shoved down into Minnie's class. They didn't examine me. Just told me I'd been away so long I had to go into the lower class. It must have been Miss Squire.'

Min did not remember being in the same class. Rosa continued, 'Oh, I felt awfully demoted. I was pushed down into your class and my schoolwork was good. I felt dreadful. They didn't do that to you.' Rosa's voice quietened. 'They were terribly big classes, and I think they were glad to get rid of some of the kids. Very big classes. Thirty or forty in one class at Cheltenham Primary. There were a terrific lot in my class.'

This I found interesting, having imagined smaller classes in that 1918—1925 era. I wanted to know what they wrote on initially at school. Min was crinkling her brow, trying to remember.

'I've got a feeling we had a slate, and exercise books when we got older. Slate pencils used to break sometimes. But it is a very vague memory. They were like little, long pieces of steel but were made of slate. But if you pressed too hard, they'd break. But if they didn't write very well, you just licked the end. Slate on slate.' She was looking worried. 'I think I tend to forget the things that really should have sunk in sometimes.'

Rosa's voice was reassuring. 'You're just a little bit younger than me.'

'I can't remember my wedding. I can remember being picked up to go. I don't remember a thing about the church, and I can only remember part of the reception. I remember going over to visit you Rosa, while you were in hospital with Joy, and making you cocoa. I said to Fred one day, 'I can't remember our wedding.' He said, 'Can't you. Well, you did all the right things.' '

Rosa turned to me. 'I made Minnie's dress and I couldn't quite finish it. I said to Minnie, 'Bring it into the hospital and I'll finish it.' But she wouldn't! My memory is a bit hazy too, but I do remember that.'

Daisy

Min was remembering Daisy's birth. 'Not far from the school in Charman Road, a few doors down on the same side was Doctor Scantlebury's. We went up from school to visit Mum at Doctor Scantlebury's. He had a private hospital in his home. He was such a lovely man. He wouldn't have had many patients in there.'

'Yes. The doctor didn't mind us calling in to see Mum. He was so nice. I think we were well-behaved children too.'

'I remember the nurse,' said Min. 'She was very nice too.'

'Oh, they were all lovely there. And they said they were going to save Mum whatever happened. And they did! We didn't know how sick she was then. It was later, when we were grown up, that Mum told us. She had to go in a couple of days before she was due, because the doctor wanted to make sure he kept her alive. She was so sick, and they didn't know if she would pull through, and whether the child would live either. So after she came out of hospital Auntie Elsie and Grandma came to help. Probably took turns. And Daisy got the measles. She was only about a fortnight or so old. She was a very delicate little baby. But we made a terrific fuss of Daisy. And of course when Bessie came, we transferred a lot of it to Bessie and that's why Daisy was a bit dissatisfied.' Rosa's voice sounded sad. 'I know I used to feel so proud of Daise, I used to bring her everywhere. Take her over to get the milk, take her all over the place.'

'Well, she was a little girl after four boys,' added Min.

'Oh, we thought she was lovely! And George wanted her to be called Pansy. 'Oh that is a lovely flower, we'll call her Pansy.' '

'George and Robert were as thrilled as anything to have a little girl too, weren't they?' echoed Min. 'Most of the others were born at home, but Daisy wasn't.'

'And didn't Dad get scarlet fever when Mum was expecting Daisy? I think she had the baby while he was away in hospital. Or was it the same time that we got diphtheria?'

Min was definite. 'It couldn't have been exactly at the same time because I had scarlatina and Mum got the doctor to me. I can remember being in the bed and having all the blinds drawn, and the doctor came to see Dad because Dad was so sick and running such a temperature. And the doctor said, 'He's got a fever of some sort,' and Mum said, 'His daughter is in there with scarlatina.' 'Oh,' he said, 'He's got scarlet fever! Well, he'll have to go to hospital. He's not allowed visitors either.' '

'And they cut off his moustache. And when he got home, his mother Grandma Bruton was visiting, and she did not recognise him.' remembered Rosa with excitement.

'We must have moved about twelve months after that to Taradale. Bessie was born there. Mrs Hyde was the midwife in Taradale who attended Mum. And then Percy and Harold were born at Trentham. Mrs Rodda was the midwife.'

'When Daisy was four. Mum said to me, 'Go out and ask Stan to clean Daisy's shoes. Stan was annoyed. He said Daise can clean her own shoes, she's four years old. Did he kick up a fuss? Anyway, Daise tried but she couldn't do it.'

Min was laughing, merry eyes, and that dancing dimple I envied. 'Well, Stan is only three years older than Daise, isn't he? Or three and a half. There is only Allan between them.'

'And who cleaned Daise's shoes in the end?' I asked.

Min looked at Rosa. 'You probably did.'

'I suppose I did.'

Taradale. Bessie. Allan. Bernie

The fateful die had been cast. After Cheltenham, living in Taradale further north and inland, constituted quite a different lifestyle. The Brutons felt like pariahs in a strange parochial and sometimes hostile land. The family was closely identified with the southern sand belt, as had been their forebears. They had contributed to and partaken of the richness of the supportive social fabric around them.

This move was no fairy tale, but immediately and startlingly real. That move from a coastal climate, away from their relatives, away from a comfortable, familiar way of life.

'The fortunes of the family changed after the move, didn't they?' I said.

Rosa answered first. 'I suppose it did, because Dad was making a good living with the gardening at Cheltenham.'

'He was the eldest son too, and the others, when you look back, wound up to be fairly well off. But Harry ended up being poor,' I added.

Rosa's words came fast. Passionate. 'It wasn't that he wanted to move. It was that he had to!'

'For the health of the children,' added Min. 'It wasn't only Tom. Stan too. Dad was told he had to move up to the country because of both of them. It was years before Tom got rid of his cough. Stan always coughed as long as I can remember. He might have been a sick little boy, and we didn't know. We took it for granted, didn't we? We didn't take any notice.'

'Dad wanted to move up there from Cheltenham as soon as possible because they said Tommy could come home then.'

Climate and culture were not the only inescapable challenges.

'Oh,' said Rosa 'Mr Jackel's son, he teased us! 'Oh, there's kangaroos in the bush and watch out for the blackfellows.' Oh cor,' she said laughing, 'What we were looking out for. We didn't know. But we still went exploring, didn't we?'

Minnie was remembering the pine nuts. 'Up Jackel's fence along the side of the creek. Do you remember? Oh yes, they were lovely. Yes, I've never found another tree with them on. There is one at Port Fairy, two or three in a row alongside the road. They were lovely, weren't they?'

'Oh, they were beautiful.' repeated Rosa. 'The house we lived in belonged to old Mr Jackel. Dad met him through the church. Dad was supposed to be buying it, then Mr Jackel said he wanted more. I don't know what happened. Dad didn't know till Mr Jackel had sold it. He treated Dad terribly. Very unfair! And Dad had planted a great big patch of potatoes, and they reckon Mr Jackel made a tremendous amount out of these potatoes. Dad used to water them and all from a big tank. He would drain the water down the hill and then it went into the potato patch.'

The farmhouse was single fronted, grey timbered with an iron roof. Very Australian. When I last viewed it, enroute to the thriving historical gold mining city of Bendigo a couple of hours further north, it had seen better days. It now served as a barn. Defending itself from the wind, leaning to the lea, the house sat quietly alone among the sun-bleached summer grasses. Cows wandered around it. One, a big happy faced brown and white, stood chewing her cud on the worn, weathered timbers of the front verandah.

As I peered from the road that day, I could see no garden. No orchard either. That is, apart from what looked like a fruit bearing tree. Scrawny and old, this lone tree, bent by the prevailing winds, sheltered against the side of the house.

'When we were first bitten by leeches, we hadn't seen them before. Min yelled, 'A snakes got me! A snakes got me!' And Tommy said, 'It's only a leech. It's only a leech.' But Min wouldn't listen. She was heading for home as hard as ever she could! The leeches were about six inches long.'

Min remembered in vivid detail, 'The blood used to run down our legs. Remember we had a leech cemetery in the sand on the side of the creek? We'd put a stick up their tail end and roll the flesh right back. Then leave the stick up in the sand. A cemetery of inside-out leeches.'

Rosa wrinkled her eyes, puzzled. Her face suddenly cleared. 'Because you really couldn't kill them, could you?'

'No. Not without turning them inside out. Oh, they would have died straight away.' said Min, looking at me. 'They were big. We needed long sticks to turn them because they were long.'

'Cruel probably. We didn't know what we were doing.'

But the Bruton children did see snakes. Rosa was excited. 'Remember the tiger snake when we went down for a swim? We had run down to the creek. We were going pretty fast too, and then we raced back home.'

Now Min added more. 'Another snake story too. When Bess was born. Dad met us on the bridge that day and told us not to go home straight away. So we went around the creek and there was a snake just curled up, half asleep I suppose.'

'I remember Daisy saw some snakes. She said, 'Come and look!' And I went with her to see. And there were tiger snakes. May have been mating. A whole lot of them. Daise had wandered around the bush by herself.'

'Remember the fun you had in the old store?' I reminded them. This store story I'd heard before from Rosa. She would tell it with great glee. The disused store had been a drapery. Remaining in small drawers were lengths of ribbon of various hues. Also reels of cotton, buttons, elastic and other items. An exciting place to explore. Apparently Min, being the climber, managed to balance and crawl up over large spools now empty of their former rolls of material. Somehow, she had climbed as high as the ceiling.

Rosa burst out. 'Min called out, 'Rosa! Come and help me down!' She was up high on a shelf. I'm saying, 'Shush shush.' A policeman had just walked in. But Min kept calling 'Rosa! Come and help me down.' 'Rosa turned to Min, laughing. 'You gave us all away. We could have hidden. The policeman said to Min, 'I'll help you down.' Then we got a lecture.'

'I suppose we deserved a lecture.'

'There were others who got through the window too. Not only us. They were enjoying themselves. So why shouldn't we. There were nice things there. We didn't want to steal anything. Guess some might have. Stan told me he ran all the way home. About a mile. 'I never stopped to even look round. All I could think of was getting away from the policeman.' It was a long-time later Mum found out. She was wonderful really—she'd see the funny side.'

As Rosa spoke, Min smiled quietly. She was amused at Rosa's spirited account. I was smiling to myself. Not about this story, but another recollection of climbing. Trees this time. My cousins and myself.

Rosa was saying. 'Min, Tom, Rosa, Bob, Stan. I suppose all of us must have been there.'

However, I was up in the big pine tree near the Mock's in Mahoney's Road, surrounded by the refreshingly piquant aroma. I was remembering too, the less pleasant sticky sap that would cling to one's skin in defiance of any amount of hard soaped-up scrubbing. My cousin Judith and Barry Mock from across the road. Up high we were. Like Min, Judith had a taste for adventure. Barry and I became participants with her in a latest escapade. Well. I think I did. We thought it was fun watching the amber droplets falling like small waterfalls, glistening in the sunlight. I'm not sure what we proved that day. Perhaps that urine falls like anything else. I didn't share this with Min and Rosa. Not today. I didn't want to divert their trains of thought.

Rosa was continuing the shop saga. 'Mum didn't know. If Miss Pruitt had ever known she would have told. She lived up one of the hills on the main Taradale road. Miss Pruitt used to walk down and see Mum with her pet chook on her shoulder. Mum would send us down with a hot meal for her if she hadn't seen her.'

'A little brown chook. Every time we saw her, she'd come out a different door. She was always glad of a dinner.'

It was common in those days for farmers and market gardeners to keep a family cow. Harry brought theirs when they moved and inherited four more which went with the Taradale property.

Min smoothed the quilt slowly, softly, backwards and forwards. 'I don't remember the horses so well at Taradale you know, and yet I can remember the cows. The cows were there when we moved and Dad bought them. I don't think he took much from Cheltenham. He had his own draught horse that he used to take to the Victoria Market from Cheltenham. And then he also took 'Little Doll.'

How was the regular twice a day chore of milking accomplished; given Min was all of ten, and Rosa eleven, when the family moved. Tom, the eldest, was away at the T.B. Sanatorium further north. Mother had a young baby, Bernie, and was soon pregnant with Bessie.

Min continued. 'I don't know, but I seem to think that I always milked a certain one. A Friesian she was.'

'I had Bridget and Cornie or something like that. I was the only one who could milk this one cow. She never kicked me, but she'd kick everyone else. She'd play up like mad, but she didn't play up for me. I don't know why. And I always used to milk her.'

Min was trying to recollect the name of the cow she milked, but nothing came to mind. Rosa didn't remember either. 'Was it Mitzi? I remember Bridget. She was the nicest cow that anyone could have. The little ones used to get on her back and have a ride! Oh, she was lovely. She wouldn't hurt anything.'

Min's voice was calm. Even. 'There are cows and cows aren't there.'

'Yes. Oh, some of them are nasty and this cow was nasty to other people. But why she wasn't to me, I don't know.'

Min's reply was unexpected. 'You were more precious. You had to mind the family.'

That summer day Bess was born. It seemed this had been a notable day in more ways than one. The Bruton kids had been playing on that enormously high, sky reaching railway bridge which spanned a deep gully in Taradale.

Rosa recollected. 'Dad came along and we thought, now we're going to cop it. But he just asked us, asked me to look after — I don't know, it wasn't Tom, always me, to look after all the kids. And to wait up at the plum tree. Because they didn't want us at home for the time being, because Mum was sick. She was going to have a baby, but we didn't know then.'

'Earlier we'd all gone for a lovely walk up the creek.'

'So we stayed right away up the end of the paddock near the plum tree. And Allan wriggled over into the paddock. Remember that? And the big horse was galloping, and he came straight for where Allan was. And we were yelling. And we ran over to the plum tree, and we left Allan sitting there!'

Min was sitting, listening, watching Rosa's expressive eyes and hands. 'I don't remember.'

'Oh, and the big horse slithered. It realised it was going straight for Allan. Slithered right up to Allan and managed to turn! He couldn't turn earlier because he was galloping too hard.'

'I don't remember that.'

'I do! Oh, was I, we were all frightened! Oh, so we took Allan over to the plum tree then.'

Allan with those large brown expressive eyes. Eyes like Rosa's and inherited by my brother. I'd wished I'd been bestowed such eyes, especially after my piano teacher told me when I was about eleven, 'What beautiful eyes your mother and brother have.'

Allan knew how to use those eyes to advantage. They were very persuasive. He needed them as a major tool to cope with his handicap. 'How old was Allan when he caught polio?'

Min's memory was quick this time. 'Age two. Don't remember how long he was in the Children's Hospital. He had the frame his arms were strapped to when we were at Taradale.'

That frame! I'd heard about it. It looked like the crucifixion. The inquisitive little toddler's arms were immobilised. Worse though, this deprivation and cruel restriction was a pathway to nothing. Probably a greater handicap. Subsequent to this treatment, a nurse discovered an effective way of treating polio, or infantile paralysis as it was then called. Mobilisation. Thank goodness Olive's compassion and independent spirit eventually flouted medical direction. Both Min and Rosa were subdued as they remembered their little brother's hardships.

Rosa broke the silence. 'Mum said she was so worried because Allan was so upset. He was in such pain and agony day and night. He suffered terribly. He'd been in it for so long, about six months. So she let him out. He'd crawl around the floor and he was happy then.

When he was older, every now and again he'd go to Grandma Bruton's at Mentone, and Auntie Elsie worked terribly hard on him. She got him on his feet with brooms upside down. She worked terribly hard for Allan.'

As if the woes of moving, of Tom's and Allan's illnesses weren't enough. There was more grief in store. Toddler Bernie, three years younger than Allan, his dark-eyed image, became ill.

Min remembered visiting Bernie at the Children's Hospital with her mother. 'I was with her. Mum and I came down to see Bernie, and we stayed at Grandma's. I remember we were standing at the door. Bernie caught sight of us, called out 'Mum!' He was crying. He was standing up at the sides of his cot. I doubt he was three. And the nurse came along, sat him down without saying anything like 'Poor little boy,' anything like that.'

Rosa exploded. 'Oh, they were real cruel. And he was there such a long while. They told us it wasn't time to visit. That visiting hours were two o'clock, and this was just before two.'

'And we got as far as the door to look in and see him. And he saw Mum. And yet we were not allowed to go in.' Min's voice became very definite. 'The poor little kid, and we had to wait!'

'Probably only one hour's visiting, I suppose.' I was feeling their pain.

'That's right,' said Min. 'I don't know how long the visiting was, but we weren't allowed in till a particular time.'

Rosa's eyes were flashing. 'She got letters from the hospital saying she should be coming to see her little boy more often. She had no hope of coming because she lived so far away and didn't have money to buy even the fare!'

Min's voice was even. 'Nowadays a lot of hospitals supply a little lodging house beside the hospital, don't they? They do in here; the Red Cross supply the place.'

'Oh, it was cruel. Terribly cruel!' remonstrated Rosa. 'And then she was told to go and get him—to collect him—and he was dead and she didn't know.'

'I don't know about that,' said Min.

At this point there was a sudden interruption. We were catapulted into the present. A knock at the front door. Fred was ushering into the lounge room Ted Shelden. Min jumped out of bed to speak with him. Ted, their brother-in-law was going to pick up some of Daisy's, his wife's washing. 'Yes Ted, Daisy has a clean blouse.' Min was saying. Min called on Daise regularly. She was an inmate in the retirement village hospital, ten minutes' walk away. Her affliction with Alzheimer's was a sadness for everyone, and we visited Daise several times during our sojourn in Nambour. A cheery word for us all, and Ted left with neatly folded freshly laundered washing tucked under his arm.

'There was a lovely little orchard alongside the house at Taradale,' said Rosa 'We used to get all the fruit we wanted, didn't we?'

'The almond tree was there too. We used to get lovely almonds off it. All the blossoms. They used to fall like snow. It was right up under the kitchen window.'

'But it didn't snow up there, did it?' I asked.

'No' said Min.

'Yes, it did!' Rosa exclaimed. 'Because I can remember Mum saying, 'That almond blossom! Just look. The petals. All coming down like snow. Then we realised it was snow.'

'Late snow' said Min.

'We'd never seen snow before, because it didn't snow at Cheltenham.'

'Taradale was pretty cold at times.'

Little Hampton

Another unwelcome and unforeseen change was to hit the family heartlessly within two summers. Lamentably, they would be uprooted from the warmer red gum studded plains of Taradale, and relocated to that decidedly inclement hilly pocket, further west near a big state forest, at Little Hampton. This was where the last two Bruton children were born. Percy, then Harold. Rosa, thirteen and a half, left school after they moved from Taradale. Min left nearly two years later.

Min was saying, 'Dad took us in the....'

'Spring cart.' finished Rosa. 'And he had to go over two or three times. Had to get everything. I can still see Mum with Bessie in her arms, seated up in the cart. And they left me with all the kids.'

'And the house was full of fleas.' exclaimed Min.

'And little white grubs and things, and they got into our clothes. They got into everything. It was a dirty place, wasn't it?'

'Yes. Old Ted Isles had been staying there with his dogs, living inside.'

'And we, we were supposed to go in and go to bed. Dreadful! And we blocked the door up so nobody could get in. Because we were so frightened. And then Mum and Dad arrived, and we had a terrible job to move everything away from the door so they could get in. I don't know where they slept that night. There was nothing for them to sleep on. Oh, it was an awful house!'

'And it all had to be cleaned, scrubbed with phenyl and wiped with kerosene. Mum said, 'I'm glad there are no white ants, but there is everything else.''

'And the climate?' I asked.

'It was terrible.' said Rosa.

'I didn't notice the climate. All I remember is the creeping things in our shirts when we first went there.'

These moves, immensely challenging for Olive and the children, must have been extremely arduous for Harry too. For any born and bred market gardener used to the particular planting conditions of his birthplace. A great test for Harry's farming prowess and adaptability. He had to learn quickly. Farming in black sand at coastal Cheltenham to an unfamiliar climate and terrain at inland Taradale. Then, just as he was adjusting to new farming practices, uprooted to begin again. This time, to work the heavy red mountain soil, amid an even more extreme climate, at Little Hampton.

What Min mentioned next was a revelation to me and an indication of Harry's fortitude and courage. And desperation.

'There was a thing he hated doing when we went to Little Hampton. That was, he took on the sanitary collection. He'd go round and collect all the pans and bring them home, and empty them down the furrows in the paddock, and he hated it. We went to a concert at the Little Hampton School shortly afterwards. We were all sitting in a row there, and I heard the kids behind me. 'That girl over there, she belongs to the shit carter.' And we were enjoying it till we heard this.'

'Kids are cruel!' I exclaimed.

'Yeah, they are.' agreed Min. 'Well, they can be. Some kids are not, but most of them are. He brought some home, put it down the back of the pig stye on the slope there. Probably did the ground a lot of good.'

I wanted to know how long Harry had suffered this desperate job. A servile position for an independent farmer.

'As soon as he could make a few bob, he knocked it off.' said Rosa. 'Oh yes. It was very heavy. He used to say when he went to the Trentham Convent that they didn't have enough toilets, and they were always running over.'

'It was Frank Hunt took it on after that.' Min said quietly. 'He had a family of youngsters too, to keep.'

This was during the mid to late twenties, when unemployment and deflation were gathering momentum. Those tough years, leading up to the even more difficult depression of the thirties.

'He had to put some seed in and start literally from scratch, didn't he?' I observed.

Rosa remembered those times vividly. 'Of course he planted potatoes. There were all potatoes around there. Other things too. Carrots, and all kinds of vegetables. Couldn't sell them. Couldn't sell anything. People didn't have the money! And we sent a whole lot of stuff to Bendigo, time and time again. We didn't get paid for the vegetables we sent to market and still had to pay for the train freight. And then they would send it down to the tip because they couldn't sell them. Why they had to take them to the tip when people were so hungry, I don't know. I suppose people would go down to the tip and get them wouldn't they?

But we always used to work all hours to try and pick the peas, because there was a lovely lot of peas. We'd have to get up real early because it was cooler to pick them. We'd work terribly hard. They were sent in big chaff bags full. Then he got a bill for them! Then to think they were just thrown away! Break your heart wouldn't it? And then after Dad ploughing them and looking after them.'

'Mmm, mmm,' agreed Min, leaning back into soft pillows of pink and green, content, even comforted by Rosa's talk. She had repeated several times great concern about a failing memory. She seemed glad Rosa's recollections were triggering her own.

Rosa continued, 'I mean, he worked terribly hard and got nothing for it. But then we didn't either.'

'And picking. It would be back breaking,' I commiserated.

'I know one year when I was about fifteen,' shared Min. 'I was working at Peter Drummond's. I wanted to leave, and I gave the excuse I had to help pick peas.'

'Well, Dad used to tell us to leave and pick peas, didn't he? I was working somewhere. I remember. I was at Uncle Will's because I said to Uncle Will, 'Should I have to go home?   I don't want to go home. But I suppose I have to, because Dad particularly wants me to.' We both had to knock off work to pick peas and got nothing for it. They'd all been planted too and fertilised. What upset us too was there was an orphanage, and to think the peas were just taken down to the tip. We had no say in it. It was dreadful.'

Rosa was the first to break the convivial quiet. 'Oh yes! I was only getting a very small wage, but at least we were getting a few bob. But we didn't when we got home. We got nothing.' She sat silent, thinking. Her voice was sad. 'They just didn't have the money to give anybody anything.'

'So,' said I, 'You'd have thought it would have been better for Harry to encourage his daughters to stay in their jobs because they were making some money.'

Rosa sounded torn, 'It wasn't much. But it was hard for Mum because she needed help with the kids, didn't she?'

'I remember Mum took on the mail.' said Min. 'She used to say, 'if I could only be sure of getting one pound a week, I'd be happy.'

'And when she got the pension, she thought that...'

Min finished Rosa's sentence. 'She had a fortune. At least it was there.'

'She knew it was coming, and it was regular,' added Rosa. 'I did a bit of sewing too. But the trouble was, there were so many things to do in the house. I'd try and do the sewing in the evening, but Dad used to kick up a fuss if I was running the machine in the night. I had to give up the sewing. I couldn't manage because I couldn't leave Mum to everything, and it was the only time I could do it. And I'd get all the fat women who needed special sewing. Oh gosh. I think I only got the fat ones, and those who were expecting babies.'

'What were your favourite dresses when you were growing up?' I asked.

'We had what we could get.' said Rosa.

'Mainly what Rosa made for us.'

I queried as to why Harry did not like Rosa sewing at night. 'Was it because he thought you were too tired, or was it because he didn't like the noise?'

Rosa's voice was sympathetic. 'Oh he was tired; he'd go to bed. He used to get very tired. I was keeping everybody awake if I started sewing, I suppose. I resented it, but I shouldn't have. But in the daytime, I'd think, I'd better do this first, I'd better do that first. Quite apart from that, the light was very bad from the kerosene lamp. I did work for quite a few people, and they were happy with what I made. I had to redo some things that other people had made, because they hadn't done it right. But I couldn't keep it up because there were too many things to do at home. The only way we could make any money, we didn't make much anyway, was going to work.'

Min was nodding 'Mmm, mmm.'

'And we worked hard too in those jobs. Remember Boort? We had to get up early, and to bed late. We worked terribly hard there.'

'And yet Mrs Lacey was very good to us. She made that picnic hamper for my twenty-first. But I don't remember doing very much washing at home,' said Min. 'I remember doing a lot of cleaning. Scrubbing around the place.'

'Mum used to say the washing was too hard for her girls, and she worked real hard so we didn't have to. But it just got too much for her. We had to do some. But we didn't even have a washing machine. We had to do it on the stove in a kerosene tin cut on its side. And we just used to boil a few things and then put it on again and boil some more. We were boiling things all day, weren't we?'

Min's dimple was showing. 'Remember the pot stick we used to poke? Like a broomstick. We used to poke the washing down to keep them boiling.'

'Oh yes. Oh yes.' Rosa remembered alright. 'And I was hurrying out one day with...'

Min was stretching out her arm. 'Walking like this with the stick stuck out in front of her. You ran into the door post!'

'Whanged me in the tummy. Did it hurt! Took my breath away. Only Minnie and I at home. I started laughing like mad, and then I started howling like anything. Min was going to pour something over me, because she thought I was burnt. I was holding the kerosene tin with both hands and didn't realise the stick was pointing at me. I managed to put everything down without being burnt. I had a lot of washing to take out to the line. I don't know perhaps, we had to wash that all over again, too. See, Mum was away with Allan or Bernie, I don't know which.'

'Mum would have been down in Melbourne with Allan at the orthopaedic hospital in Frankston. I remember something else. The day the Daffs, Uncle Moss and Auntie Rose and their youngest, George came, and our pet sheep stood on the bread. Rosa was away working. Four tins of bread and he put two feet, one in each tin! I can just see those loaves of bread resting on the edge of the front verandah, out in the morning sun to rise. And, as well, the wind blew some of the roof off while they were visiting.

Everything went wrong that day. No. We weren't worried about what Mum would say about the bread. She's that kind of person who would say, 'That was an accident. And what are you going to do about it now?''

'The sheep used to come inside. He came in with any kid. The kids used to ride him and he'd go anywhere they wanted.'

Given the large family and small house, I wondered where the children slept. 'Often Minnie and I and Daisy as well, slept in the double bed in the girls' room.'

Min added. 'Mostly there were only us two. Ted used to say, 'Daisy used to lay in bed and listen to her big sisters talking, and she used to hear all sorts of things. Then there was a single bed in our room, that was often double decked, wasn't it? Top and tail.'

'Remember the Easter eggs Auntie Min Bluhm gave us?' Rosa glanced at me, elaborating further. 'She was a lovely lady. Nice to everybody. Pretty eggs. Made of hard icing. A little spray of moulded flowers on the top.' Looking at Min, she added, 'You ate yours.'

Min was laughing. 'That would be right.'

'I'd put mine on top of the wardrobe. I'd look at it, put it back. Think how lovely it was. And the mice ate it. But we were in the bed at one stage down near the kitchen too, weren't we? That's where the cat had the kittens. Must have been really Mum's room. The young ones always slept in cots in Mum's room, two young ones at a time. We sneaked in to make her room nice one day. And oh. She was wild! We were not allowed to touch her room. It was always nice and tidy, and she never got the nits in her hair or anything.'

Olive's hair was long and carefully braided. The plaits were wound around her head like a crown. Hair almost waist length. I remember seeing her sitting up in bed in her faded flannelette nightgown, brushing her hair and then plaiting it before sleep. In youth, her fine hair had a reddish glint to it. When aged, her hair still retained a hint of this richness.

Rosa was continuing. 'Then the young ones went to the back room. Mum made a door through to the little room at the back from their room for Harold, to keep an eye on him. And of course there were the two rooms made for the other boys each end of the front verandah.'

'That was after the cows had gone. Because the shed that was moved for one of the rooms used to be the separator room,' said Min.

'We separated the milk in the wash house after that was built,' said Rosa.

'Oh, so we did, that's right. That was another room. And we had the bath in the washhouse, and the copper and the separator.'

109

'Yes, that's right. It was a lovely big room, wasn't it?'

The other room, the back room, I was thinking about. Small, linked to the parental bedroom with a back-stooping door. I strayed into it many years after Percy, the last to live in the house, had vacated. The walls were carefully patched with various sizes of brown paper here and there. The ceiling bowed in the centre, looked as if it was hanging by a thread. All this reminded me of a brown shrivelled cocoon, its usefulness now gone.

I picked through a pile of debris. A small stack of 1940s Women's Weeklies. Thirties periodicals with tissue dress patterns. The bottles of plum jam, some with rusted lids, still looked good. Gooseberry preserves, too. Olive always had some of these prickly bushes with the yellowy green, strange, flavoured fruit. Not to my taste, but obviously to someone-else's.

The room smelled damp. Delicate lace curtains now rotted, wisped flimsy in strands among the cobwebs at the small window. In the gloomy light I held up a slender blue bottle, half filled with castor oil.

Amongst old papers, wood and general mess, my hands had found something hard. Perhaps a plank of wood. I was jubilant to find a wooden violin case. With excitement I opened it and found the old violin, its bow snug and protected. Perhaps this was the violin that sang with William Bruton's playing or that of sweet natured Eva's, one of his daughters. The youngest child, she remained unmarried and died young with 'creeping paralysis.'

'No, it isn't a Stradivarius!' the leather aproned Mr Samson, the violin maker, upstairs in Elizabeth Street, Melbourne, told me. The romance of the old violin fuelled my determination to have it restrung and repaired. The expensive 140 pounds was worth it.

Before I had found a teacher, a family conflict erupted.

'Left to the person who wanted to play it, Auntie Elsie told me.' Rosa apparently said. But Daisy was adamant, she believed it should be hers. There ends the story of the violin after Rosa's capitulation, and her demand that I relinquish my find.

Cats. Mother. Father. Harold

'You put the cats in a fruit box and nailed it shut when we left Taradale, and also before we left Cheltenham. You were pretty young too. You sneaked them into the cart. I didn't think you'd be game to do it, but you did.'

Rosa turned to me. 'She was only a little girl, but she managed to save her cats.' She added thoughtfully. 'It was cruel that Mum even thought of leaving them behind, really.'

'I wasn't going to leave my cats behind!' Min fell silent, reflecting for a moment. She spoke ever so quietly now, looking down at the soft pastel quilt. 'I suppose Mum had enough kids to worry about, without cats.'

'Remember when the cat had kittens on our bed. You said, 'Leave it alone.''

'That would be Tiger,' said Min. 'They took it to the Black Forest. Poor little thing. It had been used to us all around it.' Min looked down on the floral quilt again, lips tight, sad. 'I've never loved a cat like I loved that cat.'

Rosa was sad too. 'The cat just disappeared. We found out later it was a long, long way away in the forest. We felt very upset with Mum. She'd sent Tiger with Uncle Will in the truck to dump on his way home to East Burwood, in the Black Forest. They thought it would get enough food in the bush. Probably one of the Bluhm kids told us, Joyce or Ron.'

'And did you talk about this with your mother?' I asked.

'No! We were never game, were we?'

'No,' echoed Min. Min was laughing now, 'The mean old mother we had.' Her expression changed, now serious, her voice slow. 'No. Mum had enough worries of her own. It was too late. Tiger was gone.'

'Do you sort of remember getting cuddles from your mother if you were upset?' A question that somehow needed asking.

'No,' said Min 'I don't remember any cuddles.'

'I don't either.' repeated Rosa. 'I remember kneeling alongside of her to say my prayers.'

'I remember that too.' said Min.

Later Rosa recalled Harold sitting on his mother's knee, 'But he'd make sure no one was in the room! If anyone-else came in he'd slip off.'

Now there was another question I felt pressed to ask. I wondered whether Harry their father had been more demonstrative, openly affectionate, than their mother Olive.

'Yes. He gave us cuddles.' said Rosa. Min did not remember sitting on his knee.

'Yes, you did! I remember.' said Rosa.

Min was thinking about this. 'I've got a feeling I sat on Dad's knee, but I can't say for sure. He used to sit all of the babies on his knee. I think we all did. I remember him telling stories about the zoo animals. He took us all to the zoo. He was lovely with little kids. I remember seeing someone sitting on his knee. He was singing, just gently, *Jesus loves me, this I know.*'

This song I remembered quite well, having heard it as a child both from my mother and grandfather. Also, it was one of the main songs sung in Sunday school. Min and Rosa confirmed my recollection.

Now Min recited it.

Jesus loves me, this I know,
For the Bible tells me so,

If I love Him when I die,
He will take me home on high.
Yes! Jesus loves me,
Yes! Jesus loves me,
Yes! Jesus loves me,
The Bible tells me so.

As a toddler, I recall cuddling comfortably on my grandfather's knee as he sat in his big commodious armchair in front of the big blazing fire at the old farmhouse. I'd watch with fascination as he poured steaming hot white tea from cup to carefully balanced saucer. Then, holding each side with large smooth sun-browned hands, he'd sip, placing his lips lightly on the edge, his thick hardly grey moustache barely touching the rim.

His quiet voice recounted stories, recited poetry and sang to me. *Joy Bell* was one of his favourites.

'Joy bells ringing,
Children singing,
Fills the air
With music sweet.
Joyful measure, guileless pleasure,
Makes the chain of song complete.
Joy Bells! Joy Bells!
Never, never cease your ringing!
Children! Children! Never, never cease your singing.
List, list the song that swells,
Joy Bells! Joy Bells'

One poem he recited, *Jerry Joy.* I learned from my mother when knee high, and with childish lisp, recited it at small family celebrations and concerts. I remember the poem to this day.

I loved these quiet intimacies with my grandfather. I soaked them into my very being. Especially, I suppose, since my English father was restricted in this area. But one day. Devastation! My trust died. Shattered forever.

'But he belted me when I was six!' I burst out suddenly. I could feel the anger of betrayal building up in me even now. This sudden change from quiet teddy bear to a frightening monster confused me, and I avoided him after that.

'I became very frightened of him! He got the razor strop to me! Eventually Mum, you stopped him. That was terribly traumatic for me. I have never forgotten.'

One could have heard a pin drop. Neither sister responded. A yawning gap of nothingness. This was an area my mother and myself had not reconciled. Her usually supportive and sympathetic response was always lacking if I mentioned this incident. 'You were giving me cheek.' she would say.

On the day in question, I did not want to go to school. Our stay at Little Hampton had been unexpectedly extended due to my sister Grace's pneumonia. I had to go to the tiny Little Hampton School, which had a dozen other pupils. The mile walk beginning between the crop rows, then the red muddy dirt road held no appeal for me. Especially in the usual nippy conditions of icy wind, sometimes driving hail and sleet. And I tended to be a bit shy. Although some of our relatives attended, especially my special cousin Dorothy, I didn't want to go. A couple of days earlier, I had wagged by hiding in the chaff shed.

Perhaps Min and Rosa's retreat into silence signified a protection of their father against judgement. Whatever! Life had been very hard for him. I changed the subject hastily, endeavouring to spare them discomfort. 'Any stories of Harold when he was younger?'

Harold and I used to enjoy each other's company. He was like a big brother. A kind and generous man. I have kept some of the birthday presents he sent me. Unfortunately, Harold developed the scourge of epilepsy, which proved fatal.

'Oh, replied Rosa, 'He didn't like school. He hated school, didn't he? And he would go right down the paddock to Dad and Dad would say 'Oh let the poor little kid stay home.' And Mum would be trying to make him go to school.'

'I wasn't home very much,' said Min.

'Well, neither of us were. Dad was down at the bottom paddock, quite a walk down the hill, and that was even better. Because Mum would not go down all that way.'

Somehow, I felt some irony. I said nothing. I hadn't fully shaken off the re-visitation of that cataclysmic experience with my grandfather, Harry.

'What do you miss most about the old days?' I asked.

Min's answer was quick 'Running free down the bush.'

Rosa was quiet for a moment. 'The love of the family. Talking together as a family.'

War. Tom

Min and Rosa both married not long after the bloodied, barbaric nightmare of war struck. Min spent most of the war years living at the Mocks and helping to care for a sick mother-in-law. As many died in the slaughter, Min and Rosa gave birth to new life. I was thinking of the many lives in jeopardy.

'Frightening for the young men this business of having to go to war.'

'It was either frightening or adventurous for a lot of them. Some were looking forward to a bit of adventure.' Min commented.

Rosa now quietly contributed. 'I don't know. But they were prayed for every day. Never missed. By the whole family, as well as each one by individuals. And I believe myself that it was prayer that kept them safe. Because there was hardly a family that didn't lose somebody.'

'That's true.' underlined Min.

'Those prayers.' I said, 'Did anyone rebel against them?'

Rosa's reply was definite. 'No. We wanted to!'

'Their names and everything. Dad did the praying. We all knelt in the lounge-room by the fire.'

'Anyone turn up late?' another provocative question on my part.

Rosa was fast off the mark again. 'Nobody. Nobody.'

'Why?'

'Because it was a rule.'

Min added, 'It was just expected and it was done.'

'Had to be there for prayer, whatever happened.'

Now we moved to the women's war effort. Min and Rosa had both contributed.

'We used to make fruit cakes and plum puddings,' said Rosa.

'Special tins. Special Willow tins I bought. You baked it in a tin, put the lid on. They'd be wrapped in unbleached calico and sewn up.'

'And you had to leave it cool first, though.'

'Oh yes. You had to leave it to cool, I suppose. I don't remember.'

Rosa remembered alright. 'Yes we did. Because I sent a plum pudding and...'

'It was rotten!'

'I used to use powdered milk tins. Didn't buy special tins. Stan got one, and it had on it the use-by date for the milk. It was that date he got it, and that made him wonder whether I'd bought it or not. It didn't say milk. He said, 'It tasted as though it was homemade, but how could it?' We used to send parcels to Ern's people in England too.'

'I remember getting a letter from Tom when I was down at Eckie's. Judith was a few weeks old. That garage had burned down where Fred was a mechanic. The parcels Tom received eventually in the war camp, were from the Red Cross. The prisoners of war could only get parcels from the Red Cross.'

'Tom said the army thought he was dead, and they never sent any parcels to him for a long while, so he missed out a lot. He said soldiers looked forward to the Red Cross parcels. You could get something you particularly wanted, especially cigarettes. They'd exchange cigarettes and various things with the sentries.'

'Stalag 18A, Germany, wasn't it? Nazi. Captured in Greece. He and Stan volunteered. We used to have a cutting from a newspaper concerning Tom.'

This period of Tom's 'Missing in Action' and then his subsequent discovery in the prison camp added considerably to the war woes of the Bruton family.

Rosa explained. 'Mum always said he was alive, that she'd know if he was dead. He was in the prisoner of war hospital for a long while with Beriberi, and they sent him home. He was halfway home when the war finished. They sent their very sick one's home, the English did too. So they could die at home. Tom was sent home for the same reason. He wrote while he was a prisoner of war to tell us he was there.'

'It would be interesting to have that first letter, wouldn't it?' I observed.

Min was emphatic. 'Be interesting to have any letters.'

'When Mum got the letter, she told the Red Cross. They said he was a very brave man, didn't they, different ones in the army. I had a lot of Stan's letters Mum got, and some he'd sent to me. I gave them all back to him because he was going to write them up.'

'Tom sent birthday cards and things, and he sent something when baby Judith was born. I don't know if he was in the concentration camp then. Think he was in Syria.'

'And his home coming?' I asked, amid a beeping from the kitchen. The oven was signalling, along with a homely wafting aroma, a new cake creation of Min's.

But Min's mind was elsewhere. 'I don't think there was any fuss made at all. Rosa and I were both busy having babies and looking after the home, weren't we? Robert and Bess were away. Bess was a nurse, wouldn't have been able to get away. Tom was in the same camp as Fred's cousin, Lance Pepperill, who escaped three times, was recaptured, and eventually made it home!'

'You've got a hot oven there.' observed Rosa.

'Didn't I turn it off? No. Fred. Will you turn it off for me please?'

'Mum looked after Tom's two eldest children for two or three years. I used to make real nice dresses for them and overcoats. When Tom was in the Heidelberg Hospital he was rolling on the floor in pain and they thought he was putting it on. But he had cancer. He was never one to act. He must have been in shocking pain. Oh. I think it was terrible.' remonstrated Rosa.

'Blackouts during the war?' I asked.

'Yes,' said Min. 'We had special black paper we had to put over the windows.'

Rosa lived at Avonsleigh, the bushy Dandenong Ranges during the war, and blackout restrictions occurred there too. 'You had to buy blackout paper. The police would come and say, 'Your lights are on. You'd better do something about it straight away or there'll be trouble.' I hadn't been doing it much. But after that and the police saying I wasn't doing it right, and that aeroplanes going over could see my light, I had to change in a hurry.'

'It wasn't my responsibility because we were living with Fred's parents,' said Min.

Having read about special shades for car lights during the war, I wondered what comments Min and Rosa might make.

'No cars anyway.' said Rosa. 'Couldn't have any lights. There was no streetlights. And all the names of the roads were cut off. No names left. But there was hardly anything went on the road at night. There were no men anyway to drive them.'

'Not many people had cars. We got a car after Betty was born at the end of the war. Our first car.'

'You wouldn't want to go out in a car at night, anyway. I don't think anybody drove at night.'

'I don't think so either.'

Min now added more information about their war experiences. 'Even clothing was rationed. You could buy blankets, and a lot of people cut up blankets to make coats.'

'I made two or three, one for each of us. There were some people in the Dandenong Market who used to sell blankets.'

'We didn't have enough coupons.'

'No. Even if we had the money, we didn't have the coupons to buy coats.'

'All the clothing was needed to be sent away.' added Min.

'We used to make some jumpers, mittens and helmets. I was at home and I made a lot of toy dogs and gave them to a lady who sold them for the Red Cross. Things like that, didn't we?'

The note in Min's voice was unsure. 'I don't think I did anything like that. Yeah, oh, I knitted some socks.'

'We knitted a lot of things.'

'Oh. I was with Fred's Mum and was pretty busy.'

Domestic Endeavours

Framed by the door, those two pots of sweet, claret coloured jelly could be seen sitting on the lace tablecloth. I recalled Min's enthusiastic comment that she liked cooking. Another dissimilarity between the sisters. It was never a chore to consume at predictable mealtimes Min's culinary efforts, unlike Rosa's capriciously timed hasty have-to cooking. And not always tasty.

I wondered if Min had photographs of the many wedding cakes she had made for various members of the family. Amazingly spectacular creations they were. Beautifully elaborate with embellishments of fine lace icing. All different.

Rosa, not wanting to miss anything, had emerged momentarily to view the photographs. She noted Min's well organised collection and stated whimsically, 'Min was always tidier and better organised than me.'

It was the black-and-white picture of Beryl Bruton's wedding cake that especially took my eye. Dramatic in its simplicity. A tall structure, there was a large icing flower on the corner of each of the three tiers. The three cakes were sitting square, the top two each balanced on four upturned clear wine glasses. Atop this classically simple design, complimenting and providing even more elegance, was a vase, simply and stylishly arranged with white flowers.

'Judith's was three-tier, so was Betty's. Barbara's was two-tier. The top decoration was a small silver vase with a real frangipani in it. Dorothy Bruton's was one of the first-tier cakes I made, because I know it was the first time I used fondant icing.'

'Looking back, have you been into the sewing?' I asked.

'I played marbles and cricket and so on while Rosa looked after Mum and did the sewing! I'd rather be out playing with the boys.'

Rosa flew to Min's defence. 'You helped. You did the washing up.'

I persisted, feeling Min was short-changing herself. I knew Min had undertaken some hand work. 'When sitting in front of the fire as a child, what did you do then?'

'A little bit of fancy work or reading a book. I liked romping around outside. I preferred to knit. I remember struggling to finish that jumper for the anniversary at Drummond Church. Red with a grey front.'

Rosa commented on a jumper she was knitting at that time. 'I put some gum leaves across the front. Copied some I picked.'

'I wasn't that clever! I had to follow a pattern.'

'Me too' I mumbled.

'Min, you were. I just liked the idea of having something on the front. It wasn't the usual thing. I fancied it.'

Min was still knitting her jumper. 'I was knitting even on a Sunday morning to get this thing finished.'

My mind rubber-banded back. I knew during her marriage Min had sewn on her treadle machine, later modernised with an electric motor by Fred. As a child, I saw her carefully repairing sheets and other items. She made some pretty summer sun tops, bubbly cotton seersucker with shirred elastic in rows. One each for her girls. And me. Thoughtfully included by Min, I unselfconsciously accepted these kindnesses. These important, apparently small gestures. Gestures that make a child feel at home. I think my top was green. I wore it proudly on the Mock family expedition to Phillip Island. Also probably on an outing or two in the Mock family car to Little Hampton.

It was only six months since I received a parcel from Min. A gift of several pairs of hand knitted slippers for some disadvantaged children we know. Also an intricately crocheted bookmark is something valued by me. All crafted by her own fair hand.

The fruit cake was now cold. The pleasant fruity aroma still lingered. Cooked by an expert, it was flat across deftly fringed with grease proof paper. Perfectly browned.

The excitement over and awash with tea, both sisters retreated to Min's greenhouse looking for new buds, admiring another orchid.

As Rosa passed Fred, sitting in the open porch, she asked him, 'Would you have liked living in a different era?'

'No.' Fred was definite. 'If I had, I wouldn't have met Min!'

The day had drawn to a gentle close. The waning but still warm sunshine was soft on Fred's chair. We sat together. Talked about life. And death.

As I re-entered the lounge room, the daffodil gold at the window caught my eye again. Nine days had passed. These precious drops, these brush strokes of cadmium yellow straight from the tube, were now shrunken, almost transparent, paper thin. But like Min and Rosa's relationship, the pure gold remained, gilded with evening glow.

A few days earlier Min had taken a photograph. This, after much deliberation and repositioning of the daffodils. She eventually carefully decided on a spot in front of the white net curtains. She had pressed the shutter several times.

This golden bouquet, the sunshine, still graced the table in front of the window when we departed a few days later.

Percy

The Old Place

The big piece of blue lined writing paper, left conspicuously on the Laminex table just inside the rarely locked kitchen door, read 'Stan and I have gone to Elmore Field Day we should be like the chooks home at dark. Love Percy.'

The year was 1998, July. The place, Little Hampton. The weather? Cold! Of course. True to his word, Percy was home at dark.

He was born in late winter, August 1926. But snowstorms had not faded into spring, not yet, in this chilly region. Little Hampton, four miles or so from Trentham Railway Station, about eighty miles from Melbourne in the Bendigo steam train, or by road, in Percy's green Austin ute. But that was in the forties.

Now, half a century later, it was the same Percy with the ready smile, sense of the ridiculous, and a good story. Still the straight brown hair hardly greyed, combed back from his forehead, with the tendency of a 'cockie's crest.' Observant blue eyes roundly open, as if to see as much of the world as possible. A perceptive and keen mind. I suspect he saw a lot, but like the wise monkey, tempered his words.

Spawned in the icy chill he may have been, but there was nothing wintry about Perce. His sunny personality reflected the shine of summer's warmth, whatever the weather. Even as a younger man, on icy days his trilling, melodic flute-like whistle rivalled the lark. It could be heard from the bottom paddock in the spaces between cold, windy gusts. Sometimes he'd sing or yodel, and always in tune. Unlike some of his siblings, they also sang or whistled, but not always as melodically. He seemed to embody an optimistic spirit, and at the same time, a down-to-earth realism. The various vicissitudes of life he accepted with equanimity.

Today the flickering firelight playfully illumined the dining room walls. Since Percy's marriage in 1959 to Doreen, daughter of a dairy farmer, six children had been reared within the confines of this unprepossessing house. Just half the number who grew up in his parent's household. Percy was their second youngest and older brother to Harold.

The old Bruton farmhouse, now empty, was about three miles from Percy's. Firstly, a turn right from Perce and Doreen's home farm to the road up over Meuser's Hill, bitumen these days. It used to be gravelled and a slidable trap for the unwary. A turn off at the sharp bend near Frankie Attwood's dairy farm, and you were on the road towards the Bruton's simple farm gate. In those earlier days, logs pulled from the state forest, which abutted the Bruton farmland, had worn giant furrows. In wet weather, not infrequently, this long mile would be a quagmire. A test of skill for any jinker or horseman.

But the travesties of time and illness had indelibly marked Percy's once strong body. I lifted Percy's dead heavy legs on to the elevated sofa. No more running and jumping off tractors, hauling bags of freshly dug vermillion earth-covered potatoes. These legs were now stricken with the limitation of a neurological condition. Rosa and I were staying for a week while Doreen had a well-earned break.

It was a variation of motor neurone disease which Percy had been living with these past fifteen years. After talking with a specialist and undergoing exhaustive tests at a Melbourne Hospital, Percy was re-diagnosed as suffering from chronic inflammatory demyelinating polyneuropathy or CIDP. 'I realised that it must have been something different when I was visiting a specialist, and he said to me, 'You're a bit of a mystery. You should have been dead two years ago!' If you were diagnosed with motor neurone disease and died two years later, well and good, but if you lived for five years, they couldn't work out why.'

Percy had been receiving an intravenous substance, gamma globulin. 'I'm not getting any worse. I was horizontal last week after the gamma globulin worn off. I'm usually vertical. I've been right as rain after it for about three weeks. Then I start to feel weak, can't pick up a knife and fork. Then I get a piggy-back to the loo, shower and kitchen. Thank God for two or three strong boys. I got charged up again yesterday, so I hope to walk to bed tonight or tomorrow night, instead of one of the boys lifting me, or Mum with her hoist and me like a big fat pig in the sling. I'm not getting better, but I'm not getting worse and that's something to live for. As long as I can feed myself, I'm happy, and turn over the pages of the telephone directory.'

Percy was glad to turn his mind to more interesting topics. He was never one to moan. I had initiated this subject. This wasn't the first time Percy and I had talked about his condition, or about many other things for that matter. 'I don't worry about a bridge till I come to it,' he'd told me one day.

'What was grown on the farm when you were a boy?' It seemed to be a good place to start.

'Maybe before my time, Dad had peas out the front, but in my time the front paddocks were always spuds or oats or wheat to feed the horses on. Cut with a reaper and binder and stooked and then stacked, then cut into chaff, and put in the chaff shed for feed for the two or three horses and a cow or two. There was very little to sell as the horses ate five ton of chaff each in a year.

The flat paddocks were used to grow peas and spuds, maize for the cows. Dad would move the water from the spring higher up on the hill, down the rows for irrigation. He made one furrow around the side of the hill just below the spring, and then small furrows at right angles from this. He'd divert water by blocking with a log or tufts of grass.

When we dug the spuds and I was a kid, they always had to sell the number one grade and plant the round seed. All the rest were either fed raw to the cows, or boiled in a four-gallon kerosene tin on the open fire, and then mashed up with a lump of timber and a dipper full of pollard or bran, and fed to the pigs. When rabbits were plentiful, they would sell the skins and boil up a tin of rabbits, bones and all, and feed that to the pigs. I just remember someone killing a pig and curing the bacon a couple of times. But later on, we would sell it to the butcher, and he would come with his utility and load it up, or sometimes kill first, then load it up and take it away. They were also fed on vegetable scraps, as everyone had a good garden and plenty of skim milk. Everyone drank whole milk and cream. I suppose if I had a pig now, I'd have to feed it cream and butter, and I'd have the skim milk.' added Percy laughing.

The old Bruton property was no stranger to us kids. Many a time as a child on wonderfully long school holidays, my mother Rosa, sister Grace, brother Keith, and myself stayed there. We walked in the bush and earned some pocket money working on the farm. Sitting around the fire in the lounge room after dinner comes to mind. The weather was cool and the fire would burn. Percy would invariably have forty winks in this comfy warmth while lying on the sofa with the wooden turned legs, which was next to the dresser with the mirrors that reflected the firelight's dance. I remember taking advantage of his somnolence. He woke to the sharp smell of nail polish which had been painted on his fingernails. It was of course good fun, and a run would follow.

There were lots of piggy backs, shoulder carrying and romping when we were younger, and fun chases when we were older and our legs were longer and faster. A particular time stands out for me. My sixteenth birthday in the summer holidays. 'Sweet sixteen and never been kissed!' yelled Percy. The chase was one long shriek. Percy caught up near the horse trough. He grabbed me and held me upside down over the water. I could see my nose mirrored in the watery blue sky one inch below. For a couple of perilous seconds, I hung there. But I knew Percy would not dunk me. I probably got a 'dry shave' on that day too. A rub of Percy's sandpaper cheeks against mine. Not particularly pleasant, and then a faster pink-cheeked run would ensue.

Percy would often go out in the evening. I'd ask, I suspect with a proprietary air, 'Where are you going?' He'd say, 'To see a man about a dog.' It took me years to work that one out. If he went out to Trentham or Kyneton during the day, his homecoming would often be accompanied by a chocolate bar, Violet Crumble or a Polly Waffle. And a whole one each at that.

'The logs in the old fireplace at Little Hampton would be three or four foot long. But I think we could get about a four-foot six inches log in sometimes if we were too lazy to cut it.' said Percy.

My thoughts always seem to be drawn back to that fire. A big fire, like a big warm heart! The house was not large. Somehow it seemed to expand and miraculously accommodate the Bruton brood. It was probably Percy's ingenious mother, Olive, who organised the extensions. Two sleep-outs emerged, one each end of the brooding bull nosed verandah. And there was one fairly small room at the back of the house, entered by a lowish door from the parental bedroom.

Percy explained. 'When I was at school, there were three beds in the left-hand sleep-out, and one in the sleep-out Tommy built on the right-hand side. In the front bedroom, the girls' room, there was one double bed, one single and a cot. In the half closed in sleep-out at the back there were two beds. Then the middle room off the kitchen was Mum and Dad's bedroom with their double bed. Tom was in the one he built, but he left and Bob moved in. George, Stan and Bob, or Allan, or me, were in the bigger sleep-out.

There was no lining to these two sleep-outs on the front verandah, only corrugated iron. Water would drip from the rafters when there was a frost. Harold and I were in the back room first, but as the big boys left the next in line would move into the front, till only Harold and I were left, one each end of the verandah. In one sleep-out there was a curtain across the corner of the room. The other had a chest of drawers, no room for anything else. We put the good suit in the girls' room wardrobe. In the backroom sleep-out near Mum and Dad's room, were kerosene cases on their edge with curtains down the front. They made very good cupboards. No flash wardrobe there. A kerosene case holds two tins of kerosene, four gallons each, or before that, petrol. Super Plume or Atlantic, or some such. These pine boxes were well made and morticed on the corners.

There was a big snow fall about 1939 or '40. We went to bed in the boys' room, the sleep-out, with a cold north wind blowing. In the night I got cold, so I put a big military coat over my bed. Next morning we woke up with two inches of snow all over us! It had drifted in through all the gaps in the door and under the corrugations of the roof. When we opened the door, the snow reached half way up the door right along the verandah! Halfway up the front door too. George had to ride the horse to get the mail because he could not get the jinker through it. Miss Jackson told Mum we had not had such a fall for eighty years. Another time he could not get the motorbike to move to do the mail, so he walked up to Collyer's, and Mr Collyer took him in the car in the afternoon. It didn't matter cause the train was a couple of hours late too, slipping in the snow.'

Percy was certainly stoic. One had to be. 'If you were not healthy, you were dead!'

Transport. Harold

Percy's large, capable hands smoothed the crumpled page of the Weekly Times on the table near him. I saw his thumb, bent back, flexible. Like my mother Rosa's, and his father Harry's I noted. Strong hands. But recently he'd said he had difficulty opening a screw top bottle.

'Yes' Perce was saying, 'My first motorbike I bought at age nineteen after the war, a BSA ex-army bike, 500cc side valve. I learned to ride George's two-stroke when I was thirteen, when he wasn't looking! Then I used to ride his BSA bike and sidecar when I first left school. And after Mum had her accident with her jinker when the horse had bolted, either me or George would cart the mail. And he'd take the bike and sidecar and park near the post office. Actually, before George bought the motorbike and sidecar everyone travelled by jinker. I can just faintly remember our horse-drawn cab, but it was well out of action by the time I started school. I guess my mum would have picked you people up from the train in the pony and jinker. Later on after I bought the utility about 1950, I guess I would pick you up. After Mum shifted to Avonsleigh I might of gone up to see Mum, and brought you back from Emerald, but I don't really remember.

I guess George got married about 1943 or '44 and before that he had the bike and sidecar. He would cart a few people in that. When Bob was at the war, George used to put Freda on the pillion, and Nell and Dorothy and Barry in the sidecar. It was a mighty good bike. The two girls were pretty big and heavy and Meuser's Hill pretty steep and rough.

You could get your licence at sixteen during the war. But I had to have a letter from the teacher and a birth certificate because the police didn't think I looked old enough. Jack Maine had a Matchless motorbike. We'd get around a bit to Omeo, over Mount Hotham, and the Great Ocean Road. Last decent ride, we went to Mainie's sister's place at Portland. We went out spotlighting. Maine and I were supposed to round up the kangaroos on the bikes, a fellow was going to shoot them. The motorbikes were red hot! You see a dozen kangaroos, try and head them off, and then there would be another dozen from the other direction. I don't think I have ridden the bike since. Doreen's brother pulled it to bits when he was sixteen, rode it round the cow yard. Peter Bruton had it at one stage. It's still out in the sheds. A lot of people want to buy it. Don't know who to give it to so it's in the shed, probably rusting. After the motorbike, in 1950 when I was about twenty-four, I bought a brand new green A40 1950 Austin ute.'

Yes, the ute. Remembered well by me and connected with farm holidays. Us three kids loaded into the back, scarves, rugs, gloves and cushions. An image of my sister

Gracie's pink windblown cheeks. Rosa sharing the economical front bench space with Perce. We were cold, but happy.

'Then I traded it in '56, bought a new one with Freddy Bremner, and we went to Darwin. Austin blue Hilux utility nearly the same as the A40 but a little higher geared. It cost me about the value of ten ton of spuds. Spuds were eighty-pound top in July, and when I got back from Darwin, they went up to 150 pound a ton. That would be a fortune now. Fred Bremner was here building me a shed, and we decided to go. We'd pull up on the side of the road, sleep in the back. We went Adelaide, Port Augusta, Kingoonya, Kulgera, Alice Springs, Darwin. Back to Tenant Creek across Mount Isa, Atherton, Cairns, down the coast and home in three weeks. It rained all the way from Port Augusta to Alice Springs. Slipping, sliding and broadsides. A graded track was the road. You'd have to put one wheel up on the side to pass. When it got too boggy or tough, they just moved the track over a few feet. Even the road up the coast to Townsville there wasn't much bitumen.

When we got to Darwin, it was only like a one-horse town. We asked someone where Francis Camp was and out we went. I guess it was old army barracks. Harold was there with hundreds of others working with the Department of Agriculture. They were hoeing in pineapples. Harold picked us a ripe one and I guarantee it was the sweetest one I ever tasted. Harold was working on an experimental farm. All the milk and vegetables and everything else had to come up from Victoria, so you could imagine the cost of everything. Before he was in Darwin, he put bitumen strips on the gravel road between Camooweal and due east of Tennant Creek. And before that, he worked in Mount Isa. Pretty good wages there too, with the lead bonus. He was a very healthy, strong man in those days.

He bought an old ute on the way up, dropped a bit out of the carburettor and lost it. So someone had to sit on the bonnet, lift it, and pour the petrol in to keep it going. Only two or 300 miles. They were halfway across the tablelands from Mount Isa when it happened, as they were heading for Darwin. I suppose they'd only have one pace and that would be flat out! The road wouldn't be sealed, mostly gravel.'

'I bet Harold got a fright the day you turned up out of the blue!'

'Don't remember his reaction. Probably none, being a Bruton.'

Harold, yes. Youngest of the twelve. Kindly and generous. His gift of the pink sewing box I still have. And the piano. Moths have ravished the small, cushioned box, but this symbol of a loving spirit I seem unable to throw out. The piano was a welcome addition for our family, much practiced and played. Harold travelled to England in an attempt to find a cure for his epilepsy. A grand mal fit killed him in the end. Barry, Bob's son, found him suffocated in the cold July mud. The whole town turned out for Harold's funeral. Ironically, Percy's son Mark, also an epileptic, died in the same place as Harold, in front of Percy's spud shed.

A dream told me Percy had a life-threatening illness a couple of years before the bad news. And Harold had dreamed those dreams too. Harold had rung Rosa the week before he died. 'I dreamt I am at the end of my rope,' he told her. Rosa returned from Harold's funeral to find his birthday present to her in the mail. A wooden fruit bowl, with a card and his love.

Today, July and wintry, was thirty-two years after Harold's death to the week. Percy and I revisited the trauma, briefly. We also remembered Harold's owning a motorbike. And how his black and white Jack Russell terrier, predictably called, 'Spot,' rode on the fuel tank, leaning on Harold's chest between his arms.

We moved from Harold's bike to Percy's. 'Then when I got a motorbike, I would go to Kyneton for a ball or two. I think I must have been a bit mad. Frost and rough gravel roads. When I got the ute, I thought it was Christmas. No more snow or rain or frost, and the sheilas all chase you!' Percy was grinning and chuckling. 'Change that subject.' he laughed.

There was another who rode in that green ute sometimes to dances. That was me. During school holidays, Percy frequently took me, gauche, shy and long legged, to the Saturday night dance. I must have been about fifteen. One night we drove a longer distance to Daylesford. That particular dance does not stand out in my memory, but seeing the wombat scurrying across the frosted road lit by our headlights, does.

Typical country dances. Girls sitting on benches along the walls, fellows smoking near the door. Percy loved to dance. My greatest fear was becoming of dubious wall flower status. Thankfully Percy was never too far away, and he didn't worry that I had two left feet. He also introduced me to various others, including potential partners. I recall him saying after one of those evening sorties, 'Jack was wondering who the good sort was with me the other night.'

These memories are somehow precious to me. And those other times when he used to call me 'almond eyes.' I used to sometimes stare curiously at those eyes in the small mirror on the nail next to the kitchen door.

I was surprised that I did not feel like sharing these recollections during our discussion. Not now, anyway. I pressed on.

'And before you had the motorbike?' I asked.

'When I started to go to dances, I would ride the push bike into Trentham on a Saturday night. Doctor Gwen Wisewould, our local doctor, would run them for the Red Cross. Doreen insisted that I tell you about the time I rode the pony into the dance one night, before I had the motorbike. I used to ride the horse into the dances and leave him in the stable behind Scala's the blacksmiths. One night I went to get him and it was snowing and he was gone. He'd opened the door and nicked off! I started to walk, but lucky for me, Fred Thorpe came along on his motorbike and gave me a lift. We must have passed the horse but didn't see him. Next morning he was standing with his head over the door looking into the stable, with a good coat of snow on him and six inches of snow on the ground.'

Horses

Percy had mentioned the magic word. Now I wanted to follow through that strand. I wanted to hear about the Bruton draught horses. Percy remembered the horses well. He'd had quite a deal to do with them. He told me a horse worked ten hours a day. The routine of a working horse was new and interesting to me.

'The horses had breakfast at about 5am, dinner, tea, then supper about 10pm. We didn't always give our horses supper, but the Rothe's always did. Each horse would have three big drinks and four feeds of chaff a day. After breakfast, before they went to the paddock, we'd give a drink of water, give a drink before dinner, and teatime a drink before going into the stable for the night. Our stable had four stalls. The horses worked a six-day week with Sundays off.'

'A normal working day?' I asked.

'Lunchtimes I'd drive the horse up to the yard, unhook him. He would walk down to have a drink down at the dam, then come back to his stall. While they were down at the dam, I'd open the stable panel, put a kero tin full of chaff in the manger, and by that time they'd be back. The horse would be partially unharnessed, you'd take off the blinkers and the chains, leave the collar and hames on. At night-time he would be completely unharnessed. Next morning, I'd give the horses a rub down, they'd be caked in white salt.'

I had to ask a ridiculously simple question. 'Do the horses lie down in their stalls to sleep?'

Smiling at my ignorance was not Percy's style. He answered as clearly and honestly as he could. 'Some horses don't like to lie down. Some lay down and can't get up! John Rothe had to pull a horse up with a rope once, using another horse. Sometimes a horse would almost fall with going to sleep—he'd give a stagger.'

Obviously, working with horses was very different to using a tractor. I could imagine the tiring nature of this work; a man would have walked many miles in one day. A good wash must have been welcomed at the end of a hard and dusty day's work. There was not the luxury of a shower in the Bruton household. A weekly bath sufficed.

'It was very peaceful working with the horses. They did three miles of ploughing per hour. Sometimes there would be a three-furrow plough with four horses in harness. There was one at Rothe's. The Brutons didn't have one. A four or five furrow plough would have more horses, up to eight. We had a single furrow plough with two horses.'

'And how many miles per hour of ploughing would the tractor do?' I asked.

'Four or five or six. If you go too fast, they say you put too much air in the soil, spoil the texture of it. Whether it's true, I don't know. The horses had to stop every so often.'

Percy's eyes smiled. 'Those days you had to knock off because the horses had to knock off. The tractor could keep going half the night, which is what us young fellas did.'

I wondered about the use of bits and reins. This, in view of Percy's father's attitude of not liking to place bits in the mouths of his horses.

'With ploughing, you don't need to use reins. The horse would do just what you told him. The horse soon wakes up you go up and down between the rows, after a few weeks. We could scuffle spuds without reins too. We used to skite about this. But I would never yoke a horse up without a bit in his mouth. It's just there in case you need it. Doesn't hurt. You don't jerk on the reins. Scuffling is scratching the ground between the rows. A cross between a harrow and plough, like a tine implement, when the spuds are about three inches high. The horse would pull it. Do one row at a time. The rows need to be planted straight too—otherwise you scuffle out your spuds. When they are eight inches high, you do the same thing. Have a moulder plough to throw the dirt up around the spuds.

Most horses do as they are told with instructions. 'Gee orf, come 'ere.' Means 'Go to that row,' and 'Come to this one.' But when the foundry whistle blew at midday the horse would head for home. It was amazing. We could hear it four miles away at Trentham. We'd listen for it—that's the time to knock off. And the horse would learn it, and they take a bit of stopping when its knock-off time. I remember planting spuds one day. Mum and Nell Bruton were cutting spuds for seed—Bob and she had been married two or three years then—he must have been in the army. We pulled up at the house for lunch. Someone said, 'What are you doing home! It's only eleven o'clock.' But the whistle had blown at eleven, one hour early, being Armistice Day. The eleventh hour. Even during the war. We went back and planted some more spuds for an hour. We didn't have a watch in them days. We generally used to look at the sun, see where it was.

How much did they eat? You'd have three-ton chaff for every horse you had. Working horses five ton. Our chaff shed took about twelve ton, and it didn't do three horses for the year.'

That repository for the horse feed, the weathered old grey chaff shed with its two doors, one above the other, is no longer there. At age six I hid in that shed amongst the sweet pungent golden warmth. What better place to wag school! This was that month visited upon me, at the pint-sized Little Hampton School, due to Grace's unfortunate sickness prolonging our stay. My mother soon discovered me, who being the gentle person she is, probably spoke firmly to me and that was that. I know it took a concerted effort on my part to pick all the prickles off my socks and jumper.

Percy explained about the construction of this shed. He assisted me to understand why the chaff was kept so beautifully dry and mouse proof.

'The chaff shed was lined with tongue and groove pine, and weatherboard on the outside. This kept the chaff in and the mice out. Filling the shed involved gradually placing one board above the other inside the doorway, as the shed was filled. The door would then be closed, providing an extra barrier. To complete the filling of the shed, a sheet would be pulled off the roof. As the chaff was used, the boards inside the door would be taken off one by one, until eventually you could walk into the shed.

Have to cut enough hay in February. The chaff cutter would come around and go house to house, cut the hay, and fill it up for a year. It was the kids' job to tramp it down to pack it. Would be very hot! You'd take your boots off, only trousers, or you'd tie your trousers around your boots so the chaff wouldn't get in. Sink in a foot at the start, then it packs down, and you'd go down another six inches. When you take out the boards, you can have a wall of chaff, because when it's tramped down it sticks together. After six months, it would be pretty tight. When we were kids, we'd tunnel in a little way. We always put the chaff in loose. If you had bags, you'd have a thousand mice in there. But if you did want to store some full bags, you'd put them on the floor and cover them with chaff, so there were no spaces for the mice to live in.'

Crackles of warm fire filled the quiet as Percy and I sat, each engrossed in thought. There had been many happenings on the farm I had taken for granted as a child. Now, I was learning that careful techniques underpinned the deceptively simple.

Percy broke the silence.

'That old reaper and binder you asked me about out the back of the old house. George bought it for ten shillings at a clearing sale to fix it up, and it's sat there ever since. There is also the old spring cart and the remains of the buggy and old dray too.'

Chaff Cutting

Although us kids often spent our Christmas holidays at the Bruton farm, I did not recall the chaff cutting. Perhaps it was done after we had reluctantly returned home to school. Percy ably filled me in about what seemed to be quite an event. It involved a number of men. The women of the farms fed them. It was hot and dusty work.

'Jack Gillies owned the local chaff cutter. He was the only man who could take a bag off, sew it, stack it, and then get back before the other bag was full. Old Jack could do it. Not many men could. If you did have men who could do it these days, you'd have trouble with the union for working them too hard. The cutter cut about twenty ton per day, and there was a production line to achieve this. There would be a horse and dray waiting, which would take a dozen bags or so. These would be stood up in the dray, not sewn. The two men on the horse and dray would be kept flat-out, just keeping up with the chaff cutter. There would be a boy in the shed tramping, and one man on the haystack forking it, and one man on the chaff cutter, cutting the bands around the sheaves, one man putting it in the chaff cutter, one man taking it off.'

It was quite a community effort. 'Two or three neighbours work together to get it away from the chaff cutter. And there are usually four men following the cutter. The bags were sewn and put in a big stack, if the intention was to sell the chaff. Nowadays there is a chaff cutting mill. The mill buys a whole paddock of hay during the summer, puts it in the shed, and cuts it up, and sells it. Yes, there are some chaff cutters about still. But they are just antiques. But come to think of it, I do remember there is a chaff cutter still in operation in Ballarat. Racehorses still eat chaff. A lot of people cut their chaff even now. But most people feed their horses grass hay. Chaff seems a bit better. You can't expect a horse to work all day on ordinary hay—it would probably get too skinny and not able to work.'

Crisis

Percy seemed to have enjoyed his various farming activities, and grape picking in his teens was no exception. A particular delight was hearing yarns of various people he met. Our discussions had stimulated his memory of another story, and after breakfast he shared it with me.

'When George and I sometimes Bessie, used to pick grapes at Nyah, up north Victoria, an old fellow Bill Evans, used to sit in the shade and tell stories about the early days. He was one of the first settlers at Chinkapook. He said at Tin Tinda Swan Hill, there is a grave at an historic homestead. Apparently, the aborigines speared a fellow, a bloke from Tin Tinda homestead. The missus would make twenty to thirty loaves of bread for the abos. But her husband would go to the abo camp and play up with the abo women. The aborigine men speared him. She didn't like it. She put strychnine in the bread, and laid out aborigines, about thirty, in all directions.'

The two-way radio was making another spluttering noise. It was Ray asking whether a recalcitrant cow had been seen. Our discussion was often interrupted by some communication, either via this mode, or via the telephone on Percy's small mobile tray-table next to his right arm. These were Percy's links with the workings of the Bruton farms. His boys, Ray and Karl's important communications with him, and Percy's with them. At any moment Percy knew which of their big transport trucks had left, how many tonnes of spuds, and its destination. Just as he knew that one of the shorthorns had escaped and from which fence, and who was chasing it up. 'Ray's going to Warrnambool today and Glenn goes to Boundary Bend—up past Swan Hill tonight. Be there about five o'clock in the morning. Karl's ploughing.'

Then there were the welcome interruptions of Rosa's cheerful meal calls, she having taken on the role of chief cook. Other breaks occurred when Percy regularly throughout the day, laboriously and with great determination, exercised on his walking frame. At these times I helped him swing his legs from the sofa and put his frame in ready reach. He reminded me each time to press his knees in 'hard.' This was to lock them in place, otherwise, as he said, he would fall down like a sack of potatoes.

'I get off my chair and walk up and down the kitchen every hour or two, helps keep the legs going.' he said.

Sometimes as I walked and talked a bit with Percy as he exercised, my eyes would be drawn to the long view through the kitchen window. A view along the fence line, uncluttered by the vehicle sheds and the hay shed further up on the left; or on the right, the dark but welcome windbreak of big pine trees, planted by Percy fifty years previously. My eyes would travel along this fence line through the newly ploughed red furrows of the front paddock, to the mauve misted distance. Strong brush strokes of big gums were silhouetted against this softness and the blue of Mount Macedon beyond. The mood was always changing, and always beautiful.

Invariably my surveillance would be completed with a short view of Doreen's garden not far from the kitchen window, inside the house fence. The big bushy crimson grevillea on the right, bent by prevailing winds, was a preferred food of the honeyeaters. It always amazed me to see so much activity. These diminutive, brightly coloured, long-beaked birds seemed to feed every day on the small spider shaped flowers. An eye-catching streak of colour as they flitted here and there. I made a mental note to grow some cuttings from this magnificent bush.

One night is etched on my memory. Hovering above Mount Macedon was the glowing golden embellishment of a full moon. The softest pink behind the mountains melted into a breath of lemon, then green. A fitting accompaniment for the royal orb. A reverence seemed to pervade the early evening, as I stood silent at the kitchen sink. It was always hard to tear myself away from this expansive view, whatever the time of day.

Through the lounge room window where Percy and I usually conversed, there was another bush which often caught my eye. I had seen its umbrella shape clothed in various seasonal garments. A shady green canopy in summer. The kiss of the sun in spring and it became festooned with the thickest, softest, pink blossom. Now, it was completely bare. Its many branches looked vulnerable, but it held firm, strong, against the sudden winter blasts.

Somehow the weeping cherry was to become a metaphor for me that day, two days after our arrival. The weeping cherry wept. And so did I.

The day began well. As usual, in part due to Percy's high spirits. Mine too, for I enjoyed my uncle's company. Always did. The radio had spluttered its messages. Sue, Karl's wife was heard reminding us, Percy, Rosa and me, of our invitation to lunch. The tall chimneyed elegance of their eighty-year-old house, built by Martin Rothe in his heyday, could be seen from the kitchen window past the front paddock at the end of the big pine windbreak. Behind this house, the greyed green of the raggedy bush gradually blended into that familiar blue mountain mist.

It was seeing Percy fall! That's what did it. He fell backwards on the concrete ramp. Big man, I could not hold him, 'I'm going down!' he called. The back of his head slammed brutally into cruel hardness. He appeared unshaken. Made some sort of quip. I don't remember. Wiping my tears with hurried fingers, I was fighting to gain some composure.

But a good lunch was had by all. Ray came over quickly, picked Percy up and transported him to lunch in his ute. Karl, amazingly, carried him from the ute on his back, and deposited Percy's heavy weight on a chair at the big solid wood dining room table. All this amid further humour and a smile from Percy. Sue's roasted dinner was delicious, the conversation enjoyable. At times we all split our sides laughing. Rosa and Percy surpassed themselves with funny, interesting vignettes from the past. At one stage quiet Ray must have nearly choked with mirth. He fell about laughing when he heard Rosa's story of a horse which would not cross the creek. How she and George took the horse out of the shafts of the jinker and pulled the jinker over the creek themselves.

Somehow though, I was not entirely present. I felt catapulted into a different place, still feeling the shock of Percy's fall. I was standing back, watching him and feeling his vulnerability. And my own. Anguished inside. And I was aware too of the lion heart within him, his spirit of courage and acceptance.

During that night it snowed. A silent, thick blanket lay over the farm. The weeping cherry etched white against the pewter sky. It always snowed near his birthday, Percy said.

Spuds. Moloneys. Rothes

The planning, the preparation of paddocks for planting the seed. The nurturing of the new. Yet more steps in the cultivation process. All critical for successful outcomes. This, mundane to Percy, interested me. We talked about spuds. Of course.

'In July or August, we plough the ground. Leave it a month or two, then we work it up and start planting spuds about the end of October. You hope you don't get a frost in November, sometimes you do. The spuds are just coming up then.'

Memories concerning my own childhood experiences in the spud paddock were easy to recall. When I was about twelve, picking up spuds was an important source of revenue for me. I even steeled myself to rise early in the freezing mornings, as the lure of gold was great. On a good day, I'd pick up about twenty-five bags. Bought that first woollen coat and a wristwatch from this bounty. Although the work was hard, Percy's humour always provided a lightness. His method of waking me was sometimes novel. As the sleep haze cleared, I'd see a hand holding a gently dripping face washer, and above it, peering down at me, Percy's wicked grin. He wasn't beyond playing a joke on the spud field either. 'Catch this!' he said urgently one day. A rotten, syrupy, foul-smelling potato splattered over my hands, messing my jumper and leaving a stinking slag on my cheek. But I wasn't caught twice!

Percy would dig the spuds by hand, Harold too, when he was at home. A few years later Percy had bought a mechanical spud digger, pulled by his new Fergie tractor, and I used to pick up behind this as well. But before this, I picked up while Percy dug. He was lithe and fit as a mallee bull. And fast! Sometimes he threw his sharp fork like a well-aimed javelin, and the prongs sank in behind the dried brown stalks in just the right spot. He did not spear many. Before long, he would have dug a long row of brown nuggets.

The smell of the earth. I loved it all. Sometimes I was allowed to brand the new bags. Usually on a wet day. A tin stencil was placed flat over the empty bag, and a couple of deft swipes with a full brush of deep rose-coloured liquid would do the trick. Percy's hessian bags, light beige, would appear magically with 'P.C. Bruton, Little Hampton' emblazoned across in red. Percy told me the colour was made from a powder called Rosene mixed with water. Sometimes us kids would make houses with the new bags out in the big open shed. We'd hang the bags on wire and make various rooms.

It was out in the paddock, enjoyed myself the most. When younger, I picked up half bags called 'butts.' Percy would add two butts together, dumping the bags up and down deftly to ensure they were properly filled. Hanging from his leather belt were pieces of twine all cut to the right length, together with his big shiny steel bag needle. Sewing was a quick art, completed with a triumphant jerk, breaking the string on the side of the needle.

The sight of the strings hanging laconically from Percy's flexible waist, swaying as he moved, somehow engendered the feeling of a primitive dance. But I could never have imagined him in the New Guinea Highlands, resplendent in native head feathers. His kindly and good-natured countenance did not look fierce enough.

It would often be almost dark when we finished, me driving the tractor, while Percy loaded the spuds on the trailer. Before the loading commenced, I would gain a great sense of satisfaction to see, in the fading light, plump bags standing like statues along the furrows, sometimes gradually disappearing over a rise.

Percy's body had always been strong and supple. His six foot would be a match for any rebellious sheep or calf. He used his sure footedness to advantage, sometimes taking risks. I saw him jump off his moving tractor sometimes and allow it to creep along slowly as he loaded bags of spuds on the trailer. In later years this reliance on balance and quick reflexes almost cost him his life. In 1985, the sinister beginnings of disease were secretly under-mining Percy's finely tuned leg power. He made his customary leap and fell under the tractor.

'The wheel caught my foot and ran right up my leg, over my ribs, and the tread on the tyre must of caught the skin above my left eye. It looked like a peeled tomato. I knew I wasn't going to die, but I gave other people a heck of a fright! I woke up halfway to hospital. I was in hospital ten days. Then I came home, had three cracked ribs. When I went back to the doctor I said, 'You better send me to a specialist' and that's how I came to find out.'

Now, as I looked through the window in the morning light, the weeping cherry still sported a little sprinkling of white. Bullets of sleet seemed to be hitting the window. 'Remember the time you were renting Bridgee and Maimie's paddock and we were working in the sleet?' I asked Percy. No, he didn't. But he did remember very clearly buying the Moloney's property.

'I don't know why Bridgee and Maimie never married. Perhaps old Jim wanted them to live at home to milk the cows as he had no sons. Vera never married either. They were three daughters of Jim Moloney who was the son of William Moloney who came out from Ireland and selected forty acres of bush. Bridgee was born around 1900, then Maimie. Then Vera, the same day as Dave Rothe. The midwife came and delivered Vera, then walked across the paddock to deliver Dave. So Bridgee told me once. Then walked back to Trentham. When Vera left school, she worked up at her grandmother's and two bachelor uncles Con and John Moloney. Her grandpa William died but grandma lived to ninety-nine, I think. When she died Vera stayed and looked after the two bachelors and milked the cows etcetera, as good Irish girls are supposed to do. For the love of it. No money. Then one day she found out the farm was left in their will to Bill Moloney, Vera's cousin. She up and left after working for fifteen or twenty years for nix! So the girls had a set on Bill ever after.

She got a job up in Bendigo in the Tea Rooms, then as housekeeper for a catholic priest. When she got old, she came home to Bridgee and Maimie. The old priest used to come and see her every year or two. But not good enough to get their money when they all died. Tommy got most of it after a couple of charities. I paid Vera 240 thousand dollars not long before she died, so Tommy got a good heap. But it did him no good. He lost his pension because of it and he didn't really want to give it to his kids. Then his wife died and now he's in a hospital with Alzheimer's. So I guess the Government are the winners.

When Bridgee died, Doreen went up and helped Maimie and Vera sort out the funeral, then they got it all fixed up. And then Maimie went to bed and died! So, they put the funeral off a couple of days and had a double one. Then Tommy the cousin and his wife came and lived with Vera for a few years. Then Vera sold it to us and Tommy and his wife lived there and looked after Vera for a while.'

Intriguing to me was Percy's later acquisition of land that he used to rent, like the Moloneys. He also now owns Dave Rothe's old farm and Fred Rothe's too. The Rothe's were members of the wealthier German descended family who had considerable land holdings in the district. Fred was a sort of mentor to Percy for whom he worked from time to time. Fred's two daughters, Nell and Freda, married two of Percy's older brothers, Bob and George.

'As you know, we bought Rothe's original farm one year ago. The original stone fireplace is still there 8'6" by 4'3". So June, Dave Rothe's eldest stirred up a few relations, and her husband and sons put up a nice steel fence. And out around it a nice brick and concrete thing, with a plaque on it, and all the family had a picnic there on Anzac Day. 'This site selected in 1867 by John Gottlieb and Anna Rosina, Martin Rothe etcetera, then, 'the original home built on forty-one acres which was owned by the Rothe family from 1867 to 1996.'

After staring into the fire, then standing with the warmth to my back, my thoughts moved to a different tangent. 'We haven't talked about school.'

'Oh, school was alright.' A hint of a smile was beginning at the corners of Percy's mouth. He spoke the words slowly, savouring each syllable. 'Fred Rothe said, 'Give a man an education, and he will be no good to you thereafter!''

As Percy told me this, I noticed his keen glance, as he knew obviously, we disagreed on this point. I remember sometimes over the years he would look wickedly at me and say, tongue in cheek 'Now. You're an educated woman. What do you think about the business of butter verses margarine?' The word educated, he would roll out slowly like spuds on a sorting belt. I expect he also said 'heducated' too, pretending stupidity. This self-deprecating element was, in my estimation, a smoke screen. Percy didn't really have a low opinion of himself. Rather this pretence, coupled with a relaxed smile and sudden slitted eyes, hid his hand and the shrewdness therein.

School

'Why did you stay so long at school if you were not interested in education?'

Percy's answer was straight and simple. 'I stayed at school till sixteen because my mum was determined to have one educated one out of a dozen. But then I reckoned it was too hard, and I decided to be a spud grower.'

Percy's eyes betrayed a twinkle. 'Not a digger. I wasn't interested in going to school. Mum wanted me to learn carpentry. I'd see Fred Rothe with his new car and think there must be more money in farming than building.

After I left school in the December—was during the war, I helped George, Mum and Nellie, Bob's wife, plant spuds. Then in February went to Nyah near Swan Hill picking grapes. The Manpower Authorities instructed George to go picking, so I went on the pillion seat of his 500cc BSA motorbike 220 miles along the pretty rough Calder Highway. We run the bike mostly on power kerosene, as petrol was scarce as hen's teeth. Then when I was nineteen, I bought an army motorbike, BSA, and it never stopped going.'

'Did you actually dislike school?' I persisted.

'I didn't particularly like or dislike school.' He added with a wry grin, 'I reckoned only bludgers stayed at school and everyone should be working!' Percy broke the short silence. 'I'm not like Stan, who always likes to study something. I'm not interested in study. I just like staring into space.'

'But you have a retentive memory and you are an expert in your field,' I said.

'Oh. I don't think so.'

Perce's earliest memory was of walking home from school in the snow. 'I used to love the snow and I still do. You're frozen stiff when you get home. Your hands are frozen. Some people said to put them in warm water, but this is very painful. You either put them in your pocket, or cold water. We don't get as much snow now compared to them days.'

'So what about a pair of gloves?'

'We wouldn't admit it. We didn't wear gloves. Only sissies wear gloves. We were flat out to wear boots. Used to run around in the snow without. Our boots always had a hole in them. We'd have cardboard or rabbit skin in the bottom. If we went in the water, we'd get wet socks. You'd put them in front of the fire, otherwise you'd put your feet into wet socks next morning.'

'So what do you like about the snow?'

'Oh I don't know, just nice. Everything nice and white and peaceful. I don't like it when the wind is blowing because it's freezing then. But it is generally calm after the snow.'

Percy attended the small school at Little Hampton, as did most of his siblings. 'I didn't have any particular friend at school, but I seem to remember half a dozen or so that I played with. I was at the State School till grade seven. I walked a bit over half a mile or three quarters, except Monday, Wednesday and Friday. These days Mum drove the pony and jinker into Trentham with the Little Hampton mailbag. On those days we rode in the jinker to school and walked home. Then I went to the Daylesford Technical School.'

'Which sisters and brothers went to Little Hampton School during your time there?'

'Harold and Bessie went to school with me, but we didn't play together much. Daisy was there for a while. Allan for a while. I presume Allan went with Mum in the jinker when she went for the mail. Otherwise, I remember him going in the box cart. Bessie and Daisy pushed, I think. I don't remember pushing it. Think I was too shrewd for that. I remember the old bloke who used to cart the logs. Dick Kanty. He gave Daise an apple because she was pushing Allan in the box cart.'

A routine school day, when Perce was a ten-year-old, exemplified the characteristics of country living.

'I was up about seven. Sometimes milked the cow, sometimes not. If it was a hot day and I was hungry, I'd squirt some milk into my mouth. I'd get on our pony Little Doll if I was tired, she'd take me down to the paddock to get the cow if she hadn't come up. I'd jump on Doll's back. We always rode bareback, no bridle. Then I'd follow the cow back. We usually had one cow, milked once a day. Old Brownie. Min bought her at Gilmore's sale, George bought a dray there too. Before that, it was Beauty. We had a black poll milker, 'Pet' we'd call her. Pest instead. She'd jump the fence. If we argued the point—the more we'd rouse at the cow, the more she'd kick! Pop would milk later on. But he'd only get half the milk. We wouldn't let him do it much, because this would dry them off. Mucked about till half past eight or quarter to nine and wandered off to school.

After school sometimes I'd pick up some chats, the small potatoes for my brothers. Usually not. Sometimes I'd try and catch a rabbit in a trap, sometimes a little homework. Very little. Wind up water from the well. I'd cart stable manure for Mum's garden in the wheelbarrow sometimes. Maybe dig the garden. Argue with Bess about who washes the dishes and who will dry them after tea. Then I might read a bit of a comic in front of the fire and then into bed soon after eight o'clock. I usually took lunch to school, but I never cut my lunch. My mother usually cut it unless I had a sister handy, which was not very often.'

'What about pocket money?' This was tongue in cheek. I knew I was pushing it.

'We took it for granted there was no money about and that was all about it. When I went to Tech, my mum used to cut my lunch. No one had any money—except Jack Orr, a spud grower's son. He'd put his hands in his pockets and rattle it. He always had something. When Stan was on leave, he'd give me two shillings to buy my dinner. Then there was the man who lived halfway to school before we got on the bus. He was a World War I fellow, he was gassed. He married a girl from the Justice family. He would give me two bob to buy a Herald and the Sun Sporting Globe at Daylesford, which cost threepence each paper, and he would tell me to keep the one shilling and sixpence change. I did too. Actually, I think that it might of been two-and-six that Stan gave me, because we had to pay two shillings per week for the bus fare, and the Government paid two shillings, so the bus owner got four shillings. The Government just started the two-shilling subsidy about when I started Tech. Before that, the kids had to pay the lot.'

The Brutons didn't own a saddle for many years. Riding bareback fascinated me. I wished that I'd had the experience of knowing a horse, of galloping, feeling the wind in my hair. Percy's answer was not exactly poetic.

'If you wanted Little Doll to go to the left, you'd put your hand over her right eye. The opposite to go to the right. The only thing wrong with that is you're not hanging on, just as likely to fall off. If you fall off, she may stand there, or she might head for home! She was as cunning as a hat full of monkeys.

I couldn't have been that old when I rode her up to Tom's wedding. Robert had the flash horse and jinker. I got halfway up there and she wanted to go one way and I wanted to go the other. So we parted company. I'd get up on the fence to get on and she'd move away. They came along in the pony and jinker and Bob gave me a leg up on Little Doll, and of course they were faster than me. I suppose I was frightened I'd fall off again. I remember Sally's brother Ned throwing the rice over, I thought 'What a waste.' I got there when the bride was coming out.'

We returned to the subject of primary school. Percy made sure his face was really bland. This usually meant he had another story with some humorous twist up his sleeve. 'Ginger Rothe told me that Charlie Hourigan, who used to go to the Little Hampton School, had a pipe. As soon as he came out of the school gate, he lit his pipe. The schoolteacher threw it into the fire! The next day, Charlie's father turned up in his buggy and confronted the teacher. 'You took Charlie's pipe.' 'Yes.' said the teacher. 'Was he in school?' 'No.' said the teacher. 'The minute that he steps outside the gate, he can do whatever he likes. And if he doesn't have a new pipe by tomorrow night, you'll be in big trouble!'

Jimmy Dunell was one of the teachers at school. He was a real disciplinarian, but he had a lovely wife. We used to get the strap. Rather that than being kept in though. Then there was Mr Fulton. He would lecture and not give the strap. We thought he was a bit of an old woman. He threatened and would not act. We had more time for the teacher who gave us the strap, than the one who didn't.

Philip Collyer was the teacher when I left Little Hampton. He was a little man and had a solid wife. He would not hit anyone and could not control the kids, but he could get them to learn. I don't know how, but he was what I call a good teacher. He would dig spuds before school and then again after school. Reg was his oldest son. He had four more sons. Their mother died just last year. Reg was one year younger than me. We were mates at Little Hampton, but not at Tech school. I thought that he thought he was pretty good, but don't suppose that was right. I think in those days I had an oversized inferiority complex.

When I first went to Primary School there were about only twelve kids, then it came down to about five. Then went up to thirty, just a year before it closed. They even brought two portable classrooms, then it dropped to twenty-two and closed in the early nineties. In my class there was Bessie Swaby, Bessie Bruton, Harold Bruton, John Barrow, Reg Collyer, Fred Thorpe and Ernie Rainey. I remember playing rounders, and I hit the ball and also Ernie Rainey just above the eye. The teacher raced him off to the doctor with blood going everywhere.'

Percy was not to know that eventually his big sister Rosa would marry Ernie Rainey's father, Ernest Rainey. Ern, an expatriate Englishman, had become a widower. His wife, one of the Rothe girls, also named Rose, died tragically along with their new baby, with complications of childbirth. Fairly common in those days. The original farmhouse still sits on the crest of the hill, is now owned by Freda, daughter of Fred Rothe, and still referred to as Rainey's.

'No. I did not particularly like or dislike school. When I was at State School, we had a once a year 'Bird Day.' We would walk down the bush and name every bird we saw. That was good fun.

When I was about thirteen, I went to Daylesford Technical School on the old Reo bus. Bernie O'Flaherty was the driver. He was a good driver on a very rough windy metal road. He would come out of the pub at night and he would drive better after a bit of grog.' added Percy, joking.

There was another Bruton boy who may have attended the school at Daylesford. I was thinking of Harold and his harsh burden of seizures which could strike at any time. Distressing too for his parents and siblings. When he was a young man, this sudden cruel malevolence threw him into the gutter in busy Swanston Street, Melbourne. The pitilessness of passers-by who believed him to be drunk was assuaged by the timely assistance of a Salvation Army man. When I heard this story, it impacted upon me deeply. Ever since I wonder about the circumstances of anyone I see in similar degrading situations and try to act. Ironically, the smell, the sickening sweet staleness of numbing amber liquid, is usually present.

'How did Harold's epilepsy impact on his schooling, and yours?'

'He'd have fits at school, or going to or from school. He might of went to Daylesford Tech one year. I went one year, and Harold went the next year with me. The third year Harold went back to the State School. That was the year I left Tech. Mum didn't want him going up to Daylesford by himself because he might have a fit. He took one going through the bush to the bus one morning. He was lying on the ground in some chopped off wattle trees. They were sharp. Seemed all right, though. I'd take him home.'

For the three years Percy was there, he rode a push bike about a mile along a bush track to meet the bus on the Daylesford road. 'I'd chuck the bike in the ferns. Just expected it would still be there when I was dropped off at night. In the summer Reg Collyer and I would sometimes ride our bikes all the way. We would leave Little Hampton the same time as the bus and get to school the same time. Going up hills we would pass the bus and going down he would pass us. On the flats or a bit of good road we often hung on the back and were towed. It was about fourteen miles to Daylesford. It was war time, and the teachers were old fellows. Too old for the army, I guess.

I think it was Mr Cogel who used to give us the cuts with a leather strap at Tech. He would fold it over so it looked worse, but it was actually not as bad, because when it came down it made a loud whack. I only ever got one or two, but Teddy Dobell was a big kid and would swear at Mr Cogel so he would get six of the best. Then he'd sit down and swear at him again, then get more, till the teacher got tired of it. The teacher had to give up, as Teddy certainly would not. He was a big kid. He could play the mouth organ and smoked Log Cabin tobacco. Roll your own.

He went to school with us in the bus, and when the bus would stop at the pub at Lyonville, he was the only kid game enough to pelt stones on the roof of the pub. He reckoned he was safe because he reckoned the driver shouldn't be in the pub. He left school and joined the army and went to New Guinea. The bosses found out he was sixteen and sent him back. Twenty years later he was on TV selling cars, but I heard he died a long time ago. His brother went up the education ladder and was principal at Daylesford, then up to boss of the whole area. Whatever they call that. He has since retired.

Sometimes we were supposed to go up to the showgrounds to play footy or cricket. But me and a couple of other mug players spent most of the time watching and waiting, so we'd say, 'What a waste of time!' And next time, instead of turning into the sports ground, we'd keep walking for home and catch the bus halfway home or hitch a ride on a truck. A couple of times we would hop on the back of a cab. An old man ran a cab with two horses from the Daylesford railway station to Hepburn, sometimes passengers, but most times just mail and newspapers and small things. He didn't mind if we hitched a ride. He would make out he didn't see us. We would just walk around and look at things for half an hour or so and then walk back and hope to catch him going back.

I don't think we ever played the wag from swimming. Sometimes we used to nick down to the lake at dinner time. Sometimes we'd pick some apples in a place near the high school, then we'd hop over the fence into the high school instead of going straight back to the Tech. And the high school kids would get the blame.' Percy was smiling roguishly. 'We weren't silly.'

'What was the best fun of your school days?' I asked.

Percy was laughing. 'On the bus annoying the passengers. Old Mag Plant. Tom's mother-in-law. She would go to Daylesford every week or two and we would tease her and she would go mad. Some passengers were good, and some were mad. Sometimes the bus would conk out and we would walk! The driver would ring up his father, if he could get to a phone. We'd walk a mile or two or three, and by that time his father would turn up with a big hire car. It would fit about twenty kids in it. If there wasn't room for the big kids, we'd have to walk five or six miles. The bus usually broke down going to school.'

'Very fortuitous,' I muttered, not having been a lover of school myself.

'We didn't walk too fast. Didn't want to get to school too quick.'

War

Yes, of course. While Percy was in his second year at Tech, the Second World War was just beginning. Stan ended up in the Middle East, Tom in Greece and a prisoner of war, and Bob in New Guinea. Thankfully, George was there to run the farm. Allan was away in Melbourne, handicapped with polio and valiantly struggling to make a living by selling newspapers from his wheelchair. Harold, the youngest, was still at school.

'The war did not worry me in those days,' said Percy. 'I just 'knew' we would win and when I get eighteen, I'll join up. But when I got eighteen, I was busy growing spuds, and my brothers in the army convinced me that growing food was more important. I think Stan was a lance corporal at one stage, and Bob an acting sergeant. My mate Eric Martin worked for John Rothe. Come over one day, and said, 'I'm going to join up, are you coming?' I said, 'You're mad. The war is nearly over and you will spend your time marching up and down and obeying orders.' I'm glad I didn't go too.

He just marched up and down and obeyed orders for a few months, then went to Japan in occupation forces and came back a drunkie. I think he died since.

Everybody else was in the army, and you felt as though you should be yourself. And then find they bludged and you feel you worked! I was fourteen when the war started. It was a relief after the war had finished. Though I never felt worried about the outcome. Bob got malaria, he drank beer and never worked as well after. Tom was a wreck! You'd either be wounded or a wreck or an alcoholic. Stan came home more normal, though he had a hand off. I think it was a hand grenade that went off before it should have. It was handmade; they had to make their own from soft drink bottles. Stan and Ted Shelden came back from Syria. They were in Queensland, Yandina, at the training camp. Stan was on leave. Had a few bullets. First time I'd seen an army rifle— a 303 fired. Went through a tree about eight inches in diameter, and out the other side.

Bob didn't speak about the war. He'd say, 'We're getting a bit sick of this sitting under the palm tree, swimming in the water.' When George used to think about joining the army Bob would say, 'Don't you, it's a waste of time! It's just staged. All you do is dull, play soldiers. You do far more good growing spuds.' If you could have gone overseas straight off it would have been okay. But going down to Melbourne and marching up and down. No! Bob wasn't able to fire a shot for six months.

It was '42 or perhaps '43 when Bob was conscripted. He was digging spuds and cutting wood down the bush for burning, to turn it into charcoal for charcoal gas. As the war got worse, they'd come to the foundry etcetera. and ask, 'What are you doing? What's your job? Can the family do without you? We want you.' Charcoal was an essential industry like primary production and they thought fairly seriously before they'd take you off the farm too. But if your wife could run it or it wasn't a paying proposition, they'd tell you. Bob was working at John Rothe's and cutting wood at the time and told he had to go—report for medical check-up, and then, if he was okay, into the army. To begin with they didn't send the conscripts overseas, but after they had been in the Militia for a while, they were pressured to join the A.I.F. Australian Imperial Forces. These were the ones that went overseas. And they were not allowed to go overseas till they were twenty-one. We didn't get the vote until we were twenty-one in those days either. Bessie joined up in the army; she wasn't allowed to go interstate because she wasn't twenty-one.

The Manpower Authority had control over everybody during the war. Fred Mock had a gas burner on the back of his car. The charcoal gives off the gas for the car fuel. It's dangerous. The charcoal can let off sparks and cause bushfires. George was working from home, growing spuds, so they didn't call him up. But in the summertime, while waiting for the spuds to grow, the Manpower would send him to pick grapes etcetera at Mildura. They told people where they could go—he was sent off between jobs.

Ted Shelden and Stan were both in Syria. Both joined up together, both went over together. They reckoned it was good. They were issued with one blanket each and got under the two blankets together to keep warm in the cold desert. When they discovered they were sailing for overseas Ted, who was writing to Daise, sent her a secret sign they'd prearranged, something like 'We went to the Maoris' farewell.'

Ted's sister went to the movies and recognised Ted going up the ramp of the ship. So she took Pop Shelden to see it. He stood up and called out in the picture theatre, 'Hey Ted!'

Stan and Ted both married during the war. I remember Stan was given a tin kettling when he was back from service. He jumped about three feet in the air, and his hair stood on end. They were making all this noise.'

Percy responded to my questioning eyes and raised eyebrows. 'Tin kettling. In the old days when anyone got married, all the neighbours would come and bang on kero tins after dark. There'd be supper. The Irish would open a keg of beer and have a very good time. The protestants did tin kettling too. Basically it was to welcome the couple to the district.

Clever Hutton told me when John Rothe got married, he was given a tin kettling and he wouldn't come out. And Dave Rothe hopped up on the roof and put a wet bag over the chimney to smoke him out.'

After we'd had a good laugh, we returned to the subject of the war.

'Under the Manpower Act you had to have an identity card and ration book and tickets for petrol, butter, sugar and clothes. Four gallons petrol per month for a motor car, one gallon per month for a motorbike. Kerosene wasn't on it, because we needed kerosene for tractors. We'd buy a couple of four-gallon tins of kerosene, and shellite at the store to run the lamps on. We'd mix the kerosene and shellite to run the bike on. Not very safe and not very good for the bike either. Shellite is only petrol with some of the explosive taken out. When we went to Swan Hill fruit picking, we'd run the BSA motorbike on pure kero, and George would carry a soft drink bottle of shellite in his pocket. We'd put a bit in to give it a kick to start it, then switch over to power kerosene. Mr Collyer the schoolteacher had a Chevrolet car, but with only four gallons of petrol a month it wasn't driven much.

The Civil Construction Corporation, they come here where Freddie Bremner was working in the quarry. Manpower told them to put the machines and the drivers on the train and have them up to Albury in two or three days to put the road in. I remember when the Manpower Authority sent a man to Trewella's Foundry in Trentham. 'We'll have this and that machine and the men who drive it.' They'd be put on the train with the machine off to work on the road Alice to Darwin. They put that road in, in a big hurry, 1000 mile long. There was no road from Port Augusta to Alice Springs then, only a graded dirt track.

They sent you a form when you turned eighteen, I must have gone to a JP. He wrote a note saying that I had three brothers and a sister in the army and I was needed at home to run the farm. The war was nearly over by then, not as desperate. George felt he should be there too. He felt a bit guilty because he wasn't at war. And then he thought he should be home. He felt a bit torn. George roared like a bull when he thought that I might be a bit interested. 'By crikey if you, if you do! I'll join!"

During the war, the Bruton family shrank considerably. Even before. Two of the three boys at war. Bob and Tom were already married. Min and Rosa too, had set up their own nests. Allan was in Melbourne. As war gathered momentum, Bess joined the medical corps. Daise, working as a housemaid in Melbourne, came home intermittently, before and after her marriage to Ted Shelden. Stan married Audrey Burtt, and George, Freda Rothe. The two youngest of the brood, Percy and Harold and their parents, constituted the sum total inhabitants of the Bruton farmhouse.

'Which of your brothers and sisters did you admire the most?' I asked.

'My brothers Bob and George. Because they let me work with them, or maybe for them, and treated me like an equal instead of a kid.

I remember George and I used to go down to Ted's old paddock to clear it of stumps. In the old days, they cleared all the bush, just left the stumps. They'd grow oats, spuds around the stumps. After about fifty years, the stumps would get rotten and you could pull them out. We had old Dickie, a whopping big horse. A very good horse. I had to have a box to stand on to fix his collar and straps. He'd step forward and feel the chain and pull. He'd pull two feet at a time, sometimes churn up the earth with the effort. You'd dig a bit more out of the stump. He'd know if he could pull it out. He used to pull out wattle trees too. Some horses would jib, refuse to pull. Most of the horses we had would try very hard, dig their toes in, bend their knees, and their knees would nearly be touching the ground.'

An image was before me. Not of jagged stumps but of graceful lifeless trees. The trees which had dotted those big wind-swept paddocks. Tall, ring-barked, their limbs stretched to the sky in seeming supplication. Silenced by axemen for a century or more and sacrificed for farmland. Grey and naked they stood, these once majestic monarchs of the forest.

'There aren't as many of those enormous dead trees in the paddocks now,' I said.

'They hadn't been properly cleared. There were some very big trees about—and they became those big stumps George and I worked on.

We had a mortgage to Moss Daff who married one of Dad's sisters. They owned a market garden at Moorabbin. Every so often Mum would take the interest down on the train. What ever happened she would pay the interest. George told Dad that if he put the place in Mum's name too, he'd pay it off. 800 pound. He was worried that Dad might sell the place one day when he went down to visit Mentone. So the farm ended up 'O.M. and T.H. Bruton.' I remember Uncle Moss told Mum she shouldn't be carrying so much money. So then she'd go to Bill Donnan, the draper, in Trentham. She'd pay him the cash, and he'd write a cheque out. When it was time to pay, she'd go around our family collecting interest. George did quite well during the war with spuds.

I remember the first year I left school, George did particularly well. He planted forty acres of spuds, some at home, some at Wickham's up the road, and some Belyea's across the road. At that time, spuds were a good price. There was a Government guaranteed price of eight pounds per ton. It was the main staple food. The Government wanted to encourage farmers to grow more spuds so paid the subsidy. But the storekeeper only had one or two pennies or so per pound weight profit.

Just before I left school George had a patch and put spuds in it—he used to dig for Fred Rothe. We'd clear an acre or two when he wasn't busy and he made quite a lot. About three shillings per bag, fifteen bags to the ton. You had a lot of forms to fill in, plant so many acres and that. Sign a contract with the Government.

One year, towards the end of the war, the Government had more spuds signed up than what they wanted. This is the last district to plant—so they cut everybody in the district back twenty-five per cent. They paid us for the fertiliser we'd bought and the seed, and the value of the rent of the paddock. But they wouldn't let us plant. Had to nominate where the paddock was. A fellow would come measuring the paddock with a pushbike wheel and a handle on it. Nine turns of the pushbike wheel was a chain, and he'd have a map and write down the size. We had to get rid of about a quarter of our seed. We made sure we had good seed in one heap and got rid of the poor seed. Cockies aren't properly stupid.

A year or two later during the war George bought Dagg's off Ted Shelden. Ted paid thirty bob an acre for it and George bought it for four pound an acre. So George bought it about the same time he paid off the farm at home. The anticipation was to build a house down there. They went to Jack Talbot's place later on. George asked Jack if he thought of selling it. George bought it for twelve hundred pound which is twenty pound an acre. In those days you would buy it for what you could afford to borrow. You'd think to yourself you could put so many spuds on it and pay it off the next year. Nowadays people only pay interest and they run into a draft and then they run into trouble. George started renting a house off Dave Rothe, I had my twenty-first birthday there. Then he moved to the old house Jack Talbot had. When Jack sold his farm, he built a two-room hut across the road. The banks didn't lend much in those days. My first dealing with them was when I said, 'A bloke wants to sell me a tractor.' The manager said I'll lend you so much. I sold some spuds, paid for the tractor and didn't need the overdraft.'

Later, I wanted a loan to buy some land. When he came back from the war, Bob Bruton rented the Hunt's place. Fred Rothe's wife was a Hunt, Charlie Hunt was going to sell it, seven pound an acre. I went to the bank and wanted a loan. 'We'll lend you thirty percent of the value, and the value of the ground in this district is twenty pound an acre and its overvalued at the present.' The war was finished and things were booming but it was only seven pound an acre. I said to the bank manager, 'I was here six months ago and I was going to borrow money to buy a tractor. I didn't have to, because I sold spuds and paid for it. But you'd lend me for a tractor.' He said, 'You'll earn more with a tractor—you can go contracting with the tractor.' I said, 'In fifty years' time the tractor will be in the tip not worth two bob. They're not making any more dirt. A farm you'll always have!'

Wicker bought it then—Dorrie Rothe lent him the money. Old Fred used to say, 'I could help George and Bob more than I do. It doesn't do any good to help. They have to learn.' But I think it is important to help. Young people need to get the first start. In those days it was the men who inherited. Ernie Rainey inherited fifty pound from his grandfather's estate. The girls didn't get much. And Dave inherited the property.'

Now another story, a different story emerged. 'One day George was ploughing with four horses in the three furrowed plough, down where he lived at Talbot's. It was springtime and a bit stormy. I was leaning against the fence, standing on one leg with the other one bent against the post, and George's border collie dog sitting under it near me out of the rain. The lightning must of struck the fence away up the hill. I guess the electricity ran down every post being a bit wet. When it got to me, I got a whack behind the shoulders where I touched the top wire, and a whack on the bottom where I touched the post, and on the soles of the feet. I jumped about six foot and George wondered what hit me! The dog moved just as fast as the lightning down to the house and into the cowshed where Freda was milking the cow. The dog Laddie shot under the cow, knocked over the bucket, and nearly knocked Freda off the stool. The poor old dog was scared stiff of thunder ever after.'

Percy's chuckles and smiles had turned to outright open-mouthed laughter. My eyes were fixed on his teeth! He'd had false teeth as long as I could remember. He was laughing heartily on that day too. We were all at Mentone Beach, various cousins and families. Us kids were cavorting in the water, and Percy, Rosa, Bessie and Fred swimming. The sunshine was like small, golden fish darting through the curling waves. Laughing uproariously, Perce was standing waist deep in the water, lightly bronzed, thoroughly enjoying himself. Suddenly his top denture shot out! Frantic groping and diving failed to elicit the errant teeth. We now digressed for a moment.

'No! I never found them. I got new ones. There used to be a mate of Frankie Attwood's, Jack French. Be about 1956. He was a dental mechanic. He had a big Indian bike and side car. He was digging spuds and making false teeth for everybody round the place. He'd be sitting down on wet days in front of the fire making these false teeth.

He returned to Melbourne and I looked him up to get some. He said, 'You'd better get the three or four teeth on the bottom out. Come to Dandenong, I have a mate there.' So we hopped in the car and went to Dandenong. There was half a dozen people sitting in the waiting room and we just walked straight through to the dentist. He had three or four dental chairs. He'd give you an injection, then he'd pull out someone else's teeth while waiting. And the dentist comes along. 'Are you a farmer? I like getting into these tough farmers!'

Anyway he fixed me up and pulled the teeth out. And he put the false teeth on the top of where the others were taken out. Told me to leave them in for a few weeks.'

Percy saw me gasp. 'It worked out alright. Then I was telling Sib, Uncle Reub's daughter about losing my teeth at Mentone. She said, 'I remember about that time there was a notice in the paper. 'Found, a set of dentures at the beach!''

There's no teeth like your own, I always believed. 'How old were you when you had the top ones out?'

'About seventeen. They were rotten! I've never had one filled in my life. Harold got his filled. And I guess I was too chicken. I couldn't stand the idea of a drill in my mouth. I'd say, 'Pull it out!' I had about fourteen or something out and Charlie Hunt said, 'You shouldn't be carting.' I said, 'I'm alright.' We were down at Price's; I remember Phyllis gave me a bowl of soup.

My teeth were plain, ordinary rotten. I never cleaned mine. Old blokes before me used to clean their teeth with charcoal. They say they did. Freddie Bremner never cleaned his teeth. Still had them age eighty-five. We would have cleaned ours with salt and teeth paste. We had plenty of sugar. Yes. Fred Rothe was into lollies and fizzy drinks all his life. Still had his teeth when he died.'

George

After our welcome tea-break, my mind turned to George again. It had become clear that Percy particularly enjoyed working with George. This relationship, I suspect, blossomed during the war when George was in charge of the farm. My thoughts were sombre. George was the second to die, toddler Bernie having preceded many years before. The Brutons were greatly saddened at George's untimely death.

I wanted to know about the day George died. I knew he had been with Percy on that fateful day.

'George was the stack builder on the top of the haystack. He got a pain in the guts. I was on the lorry taking the sheaves off and throwing them up. Fred Rothe was turning the sheaves. Freda took George to the doctor's. He opened the car door, stepped out, and dropped dead. Strange. Him and Freda had been to the pictures the night before and saw this picture about this woman having to bring up the kids by herself and pay the farm off and get it going, because her husband died. George was telling us about this film and died an hour afterwards. Strange coincidence. Another thing, a couple of months before he died, he went into the insurance people and took out a life policy.'

Percy was thoughtful. He gazed through the window. 'But if he knew he had a heart problem, he would have had to sit down for the rest of his life. Could you imagine him doing that? Yes, on that day he walked to the car, 'You'd better take me home.' Didn't say anymore. We had morning lunch—I got up the top of the stack in George's place. Fred said, 'You get up.' He showed me how to build it. Teddy Winn came over about 11am he said, 'I just met Freda and George heading for Woodend—they were flying.' I got a shock when Doreen said George dropped dead. Ray was two years old then.'

A most traumatic time. George's death at forty-four in the summer of 1960, had left his young wife, Freda, Fred Rothe's youngest, bereft and with a farm to run. The lives of Freda and their three young boys were now changed for ever. Bobbie the eldest was thirteen, the youngest Ken, six, Max in between.

'It was January or February, when George died. Bobbie didn't turn fourteen till March or April. He didn't go back to school anymore. He stopped home and worked.'

I was thinking of Percy's loss too. 'It must have taken you years to get over it.'

Percy answered slowly, his tone unusually cheerless. 'Yes it did.'

Quiet for a moment, he broke his reverie. 'George could crack a joke, a good ordinary sort of fellow. A real Bruton! Easy going, reliable, conscientious and he'd stick to his word. He used to sing a lot in the paddock, and at church he and Freda would sing. Bob was into the beer and chasing the women. George was more into working. Bob was into working too. He was tough, but he took up smoking. I think Mum knew Bob would have a drink, I don't think Pop did though. Bob and Tom. They both rebelled. George was more content to go along with the intention of getting somewhere. I thought George was as fit as a trout! After he was married, Freda tried to get him not to work so hard. George had a fair bit of responsibility and I looked up to him. He'd fix things up and not make a song and dance. With Stan he was always trying to teach you something. Show you a bird nest or something or other.'

'And you helped George's family out!'

'Oh, we got on well, Freda and I. Oh well yes, a little bit. Oh, Freda did a lot of work. She still works. In her eighties she still gets on the tractor, gets Maxie to hook it up, harrows and mows. She's been barred from sitting on the spud digger by Maxie and Irene now. She was only seventy-nine at the time when she was tipped off the digger and hurt her back.'

The Old Farmhouse. Siblings. Father

My thoughts strayed back to the old Bruton farmhouse a mile or three away from Percy's. The many school holidays spent there. Evenings spent in the hospitable, warmly comfortable armchairs, the walls alive with the dance of flickering firelight and shadows. Pictures etched upon my memory. Most of this time was during the later war years, and the ensuing ten years or so. These years spanned Percy's early adulthood through his early twenties until marriage at age thirty-two in 1959. After he married Doreen, they moved to their present house, a property which Percy purchased in 1953 or '54. Percy has continued to work the original property. Harold batched in the house earlier, between his forays up north and living in the spud diggers' hut at Percy's. We stayed in the empty old house too sometimes, after Perce had left, but it never felt the same without Percy's cheery magic.

My memories are crystal clear, especially of those evenings, those enjoyable times spent in what the Brutons called the sitting room of that homely house. The firelight. The lamplight. The companionable creak as the wind caught the blades of the windmill seen through the small window on the left of the fireplace. This window had been cut by my practical grandmother to provide more light into this gloomy room behind the front verandah. One day, in mid-winter as I sat in warm cosiness on the wooden couch with the intricate wooden beading, I looked up at this small window. The windmill, framed within it, was now blurred into soft greyness. This time, it was standing very still, enclosed in a soft thistledown blanket of gently falling snow.

Today, over the usual cup of tea, Percy talked about the windmill. 'The windmill was the first thing I did! Put it up as soon as I saved up after I left school about 1942. I can't remember how much money, but I got the feeling it was forty pound for the mill, a tank and pipes, taps for the wash house and garden. We even ended up having a nice cold shower over the bath in the wash house. Was it cold! Harold used to like a cold shower. I don't know if he liked it or he was making out he was tough. I don't know.

I asked Fred Rothe who was the best man to put up the windmill. Doug Price. He was a church man, too. There was a tree in the way, so we then jacked the mill up five foot higher. Before that, we used to wind up the bucket from the well, and put the water into a drum. It was our job to carry over the water and tip it into the drum, so Mum had water in the kitchen. We must have carried it ten to fifteen years before Uncle Will brought up a much bigger drum—forty-four gallons—and someone built a stand for it from the bush and a tap through the wall to the kitchen. Mum would sometimes carry the water to the drum too.' Percy paused, added laughing, 'The reason I put up the windmill was because I didn't like carrying the water.'

A kaleidoscope of memories flashed before me. I was back in the sitting room by the big fire. I used to enjoy dreaming into it. To go nowhere in particular, but become part of its flickering and unpredictable light. Sometimes my reverie would be suddenly interrupted by what seemed like an explosion. The culprit coal would be caught red-handed as it were and returned to its place over the black iron of the surrounding fender and wire screen. I used to admire my mother's nimble ability in fielding these glowing coals. She would quickly dampen her thumb and a couple of fingertips with her tongue, then, in one quick movement, pick up the coal and haul it back into the fire.

We also did a lot by the soft lamp light in the evenings. At the heavy dark table, us kids played fiddlesticks, jacks and various board games. Knitted, too. But to me, the ambience of this mysterious shadowy room lent itself more to losing oneself in one's thoughts, one's imagination, or a book.

There were many books in the floor to ceiling bookshelf on the right of the fireplace. Some of these were very old. A collection of stories from Sunday at Home

1868, with fine black and white drawings, sometimes entertained me. But I especially enjoyed reading a book, a Sunday school Prize which had been awarded in 1935 to Harold. Whiskers at the Zoo. Many of Whisker's adventures were read in bed holding a candle in the draughty old sleep-out.

Given Percy's dislike of books, it surprised me that he had in fact been the builder of the bookcase. 'Made by me as soon as I left school. I think I got some boards and planed them up, but I can't remember where the boards came from.'

'It was your mother who motivated you to build it?' I asked.

'No. I don't think so. I wouldn't read a book from one New Year's end to another. Just somewhere to put the books and rubbish. Mum would be knitting and mending. She didn't do it on a Sunday. Only feed the kids and read something. You'd never see her knitting or mending on a Sunday. Whether it was because her husband didn't believe in it, or she didn't, I don't know.

There was never electricity at Little Hampton. We always had kerosene lamps in the house and candles in the bedroom. A common request was 'Get out of my light!' About 1945 or '46 or '7, I bought a Coleman Shellite lamp, like a petrol lantern. It had a mantle made of a sort of cotton. You put it on the lamp and burnt it and then it became fragile, then it would glow very bright. You had to pump the lamp up for pressure to make it go. It had a plunger in the side of the tank. It only held about two litres of shellite and was a very good light. You could take it out in the wind or rain and it would not blow out. Before that, if you went out in the dark, we had a kerosene lantern. They were okay, but not bright enough in the house. We would tie it on the back of the jinker if going out after dark. Showed others where we were. It would not show the horse where to go. It just threw shadows everywhere and disoriented the horse. When we got off the main road, we would put the light out and let the horse find his own way, and it would do it even in the pitch dark.'

Yes! The Coleman lamp I remember. It was always a worrying time for me when the lamp was being pumped up. I feared it would explode with the pressure. There were however two other lamps which I considered special. One was kept in pride of place on the heavy dining room table. The other lived on a rough shelf in the parental bedroom near my grandmother's tall chest of drawers. The chest was a lovingly cared for antique, crafted from cedar, with a soft burgundy patina and candy twirling embellishments up each side. The lamp kept nearby on the shelf, Rosa told me, had been used by her mother Olive when tending sick children. A pretty lamp. I asked Grandma if I might have it. It is still as attractive as when I first set eyes on it. Opaque milk glass, sky-blue. Small, raised flowers and a fan shape on each side. It sports a clear, slightly deeper blue, finely ridged glass handle, the usual wick, and a funnel chimney with a scalloped top.

The other lamp in the dining room was larger, more dramatic. An iron base with intricate holes through which one could see the white damask tablecloth. It was heavy and tall. Kerosene would be poured into a white squarish china container atop this heavy pedestal. This was attractively decorated with what looked like hand painted green leaved pink fuchsias. Above and encasing the double wick was a clear glass chimney. This was in turn surrounded by a magnificent glass orb. Like a large balloon, it floated above the lamp. Some of the glass shone clear pale green, a fuchsia pattern frosted and opaque within it. It shone like a gentle moon, weaving a mysterious circle of light below it on the table. At least two generations would have been grateful for the soft glow of this old lamp.

Percy continued to describe some cameos from his experience living in the Harry and Olive Bruton family. He recalled Christmas times as some of the most enjoyable. 'Everyone came home and Mum fed the lot! I remember twenty-seven one Christmas day.'

Another highlight was when his mother's brother Uncle Will and Auntie Min Bluhm came to stay, and brought various fruits from their orchard at East Burwood in their big truck with the covered-in back. This truck was also used to take crates of apples, pears, peaches and cherries to the Victoria Market.

'Joyce, Ron, Dorothy and Allan came. There would be people sleeping everywhere. They'd bring four or five cases of fruit. We'd put the pears in the chaff. They'd ripen in the chaff. I suppose you'd get an even temperature. I don't know. They'd bring up small apples. We always had apples. Apple pie.' Percy recounted with some relish.

'Lollies?'

'Occasionally we'd have a 'Cure-em-Quick,' a tiny liquorice. Mum used to have aniseed balls. Black on the outside, white inside. Only lollies we ever saw.'

Another scene flashed into Percy's mind. The family on their knees in the dining room. 'In the mornings there would be prayers. I used to be looking at the clock while on hands and knees. Dad had no set time. Nine times out of ten, I reckoned it was when we were rushing and tearing to go to school. I opened my eyes, and I caught Harold red handed reading the paper! We had a fight over it. I got into trouble.' Percy added quietly, 'I think Harold was favoured by his father.

I was scared stiff of my father! I kept away from him most of the time. The only ones who had time for Pop were the ones who rebelled on him. I think Tom got on better with him later when he came home after clearing out. Rosa still sticks up for her father all the time. Rosa and her father had a row one day. Pop said, 'It says in the Bible you should love your father and mother!' It stumped Rosa for a while. Then she went into the bedroom and came out and said, 'It says, do not provoke your children to wrath!' Percy's voice had taken on a staccato clipped definite tone. Now he returned to his usual slow, relaxed drawl, 'I wouldn't be bothered. I'd think 'you silly old thing.' I'd go down the paddock.'

This subject was probably difficult for Percy. He had rarely mentioned his father during our conversations. That is, apart from my infernal questioning and his searching within himself for an honest answer. 'I don't remember much about Pop. Just blacked him out. I don't know why.' Percy added philosophically 'Probably over nothing much.'

Further comments he made were enlightening. 'I used to get wild with Pop. For years I'd think I'll wait my chance to tell him off, but I didn't. I got one belting from him. He'd threaten a lot by taking his belt off. It hurt our dignity more. He'd bellow and roar! Stan and I were having an argument. Pop grabbed his belt. He kicked me and Stan out of the door. Stan got to cutting wood in the moonlight. I bawled on the front step for a good while. I was told by Mum, 'Come in if you're good.' Stan would use his frustration for benefit, I'd use mine to bawl and bellow.'

'But Stan was seven years older than you.' I said.

Percy changed direction suddenly. 'Bob used to make the bread. I used to think Bob got his muscles through making the bread. Though, I didn't do any. We'd have homemade bread at school. The other kids thought homemade bread was lovely, and we thought their bought bread was lovely. Bess, Harold and I used to fight over the washing and drying up. The only thing I remember about Daisy was she played the mouth organ, otherwise she didn't do much. I remember slinging off at Bessie for being slow. My playmates were Bess and Harold. I don't remember much about Daisy; she was three or four years older than me. I don't remember playing with Daisy at all. Don't remember what we played at. We took it for granted that Bess could do anything we could do. Daise would be inside reading a book.'

Percy and Harold were the only children to be born in this locality. Unlike the older members of the family being born at Mentone, and Bess at Taradale. 'Harold and I were delivered by a mid-wife, a Mrs Rodda, at her home in Trentham. Mrs Rodda was apparently concerned that the building of the new hospital would take her customers, which it did! Soon after Harold was born, the hospital at Trentham was built.'

Perhaps Harold, Percy's junior by two years, may have been Percy's confidant and playmate for him. Especially, I thought, since Percy had provided a home for Harold after his marriage. Also employment for him. 'We didn't work together much. We didn't get on together very well.' Percy's tone softened 'He sort of had a sense of humour, April fool stuff and so on. He had a bad temper, bit unpredictable. He used to get sick of me being the boss. I took it for granted I had more brains than him. He'd get sick of it, and then there'd be a row. He went away to work up north. I cleared some of the ground down at George's at Dagg's, cleared the bracken fern and blackberries and sowed spuds. Harold would do the same, then he would go off to Sydney or Mount Isa. He sold me the spuds for the price of the work he'd put into them. Nine times out of ten, I'd make some money from them. I probably robbed him.'

Harold's first epileptic fit had been a shock to Percy, and during our discussions he mentioned it on at least three occasions. 'I was about nine at the time, and Harold about seven. We were out in the sleep-out and we were supposed to be putting Allan's boots on. We were arguing about who was to do it. Suddenly Harold turned around three times and went head over turkey and kicked.'

Recreation

Percy did not remember any sorts of games he played. But some pranks stood out in his mind. This one was not his. 'Clever Hutton told me, that when he was a boy, must have been around the turn of the century, 'We'd chase Mrs Plant's cows down near Wickham's, into the creek where they'd get bogged. Then we'd tell Mrs Plant her cows were bogged, and that we could get them out. She'd say, 'Good boys.' And give us a biscuit.'

'How did your family amuse themselves?'

Percy's knee jerk response was 'Work, mostly.' He reflected on this for a moment. 'I enjoyed riding the push bike or walking through the forest near the farm, to Ord's Mill or to the Lyonville mineral springs or to the Sugar Loaf. The Sugar Loaf is a steep little hill covered with rocks and trees, a couple of mile down the bush, maybe eighty or a hundred foot high. Maybe it's a part of an old volcano or some such thing. We just used to take a walk there for something to do, perhaps on a Sunday afternoon. A lot of us kids used to go for long walks in the bush.

Later on, Harold and I used to play tennis at the courts near the church. We used to paint our sandshoes with white clay. The women used to paint the inside of the fireplace and we used to paint the inside of the chook coop with it too. The clay would last for a long while, called pipe clay. You'd put the clay on with a wet rag. Min and Rosa used it; I don't remember Bessie and Daise doing it. Harold and I used it sometimes. Otherwise we'd buy this white stuff in a tube, paint it over our shoes. We'd have to do it every Saturday, too. There was a patch of white clay on the side of the metal road near Trentham Falls, and one behind Price's on the back road at Little Hampton. You'd just go and scratch a little rabbit burrow with a shovel and put it in a bucket.'

'Rabbits?' I asked.

'Shot rabbits and parrots!'

'Parrots?' I queried with bated breath on the edge of disillusionment concerning Percy's apparent benign attitude to the world.

'Well,' Percy justified 'They were eating our apples. If one was shot, the others would go away.'

In those days, the humble push bike was an essential mode of travel. 'I used to ride the five miles to the picture theatre at Trentham, but not often. Harold did not go very often. I was two years older than Harold. He didn't go out much at night because then he'd take a fit the next day. 'Tarzan and the Apes' or 'Gene Autry' or 'Destry Rides Again!' I think Deanna Durbin might of been a favourite, but I forget what pictures she was in.'

At Little Hampton there were three main structures which attracted community participation. The school and the tennis courts. And the weatherboard Methodist church with the plaque on the wall to Rosina and John Rothe. The electric organ, before this the reed treadle organ, has been played for probably the last fifty years by Freda, Rosina's grandchild, who became the widow of George. The Brutons were all regular attenders at the church. Most locals had attended the pocket-sized school and some of them played tennis on the courts next to the church.

Percy recalled an elderly gentleman who had attended the church.

'Old Steve Stephens had a big white beard and hair which would get mixed up. When I was a school kid, he used to wheel his barrow up the road with a crosscut saw every day to get wood from the roadside. He'd go to church and sit in the second row from the front. Nell or Freda, or their mother Hannah would be playing the organ. The organist always had to give him a piece of paper with the hymn numbers on it. 'What numbers did he say, Nell?' he'd say during the service. Us kids sat up the back. We'd think it was a great joke. He'd fish in his pocket for a packet of peppermints. 'Here, have one Nellie!' '

Percy continued on a more serious note. 'There used to be houses on about eight acres down the bottom behind Frankie Attwood's at Thrum's Saw Mill. Thrum donated the timber to build the church and school—Ginger Rothe told me at this time the government did not own the schools. He paid a one-year wage to the teacher. A few years later,

the government took over the schools. In the early days the teacher used to write and complain it was too cold, the snow was coming through cracks in the wall, and they needed a floor in it.'

Siblings and Father again.

'Rosa would come home and look after us when Mum was away, don't know why she was away, when I was six or ten years old. I didn't think Rose had the authority; she made us clean our teeth, wash and so on. You'd get away with anything with Mum. We'd go to bed without a wash and pretend to be asleep, and she'd tuck you in. But we didn't get away with Rose. Rose used to bath us. She'd scrub you up more than Mum would, and then we'd stand in front of the fire. Rosa would say, 'You should eat your green vegies! Don't waste toast, you've gone to a lot of trouble to make the toast and don't waste it.' Mum would have just put it aside quietly.' There was a rebellious note in Percy's voice. He was quite open in his negativity. 'Harold and I resented Rose a bit, and Minnie too. You could put it over Minnie a bit though. Minnie would trick us into thinking we had made the decision, whereas Rose was more confrontational.'

'And Tom?'

'He left home when I was just born. Then he came back when I was about five or six-year-old. I just said, 'There's a strange man out there.' Or so they tell me, I don't know. I was a bit afraid of him, because I did not know him, did not have anything to do with him. When he got married, I was only nine. I rode the pony up to the wedding at Lyonville. Everyone else was in the jinker.'

Percy had obviously carefully studied Tom's diary, written at about fourteen or so, after leaving home suddenly, due to that altercation with his father. 'Rose found it and I've given it to one of Tom's sons, Bernie. Tom took off on his push bike and he had eight punctures.'

'Punctures! Puncture repair would have been critical, especially when one was on a lonely road miles from anywhere.' I said.

'You always had a puncture outfit in a little tool bag under the seat. It had a little spanner that would fit all the nuts, two or three tyre levers, about as big as a teaspoon. Half a dozen or so patches, some as big as your little fingernail, or as big as your thumb. Nine times out of ten, the small patch would mend it. Then there was a little tube with a solution that consisted of glue for rubber which would stick the patch on. You'd just undo and lever the tyre, mend the puncture, then put a bit of chalk over the mend to dry the solution. You don't want it to stick to the tyre! Put it back on again and pump it up and away you'd go.

But I wouldn't have liked Tom's job of riding up there to NSW. Was all dirt road, bit of metal through the towns. On the open plains there would just be a graded track. He went up through Echuca, across the river, past Deniliquin and up to West Wyalong, which is way up in New South Wales. Then he headed up to Ungarie. I said to Doreen when we were going to Queensland, 'Let's go look.' It was a very tiny place. Tom spent a lot of time picking up sticks and roots from land clearing. When it got pay time, the man apologised and said he didn't have any money. Tom left after about four years or so. Finished up, he never got paid. Would have been long hours because there'd be horses to feed too. So he got well and truly robbed! Not many young farmers had any money at all in them days. They always anticipated getting some next year. Tom had three kids when he went to the war, Jean, Irene and Tommy.'

'Had it tough' I said.

'My oath he had it tough. I said to Tom later on one day, 'Diesels are okay, but too complicated.' Tom said, 'No they're not, everyone will have diesel one day.' With the kerosene tractor—if you had rain tonight, rain tomorrow night, then it wouldn't go. Then you'd buy canvas and cover it up for the night. Old Tom Thorpe used to. Even then a misty night can still be a problem. With the diesel you turn the key and away she goes. Old Lloyd Lang used to come down from Melbourne and fix my diesel. He said, 'We'll convert to gas one day.' I said, 'You think so?' 'I know so!' he said.'

However, it was George's name that Percy mentioned the most.

'I'd follow George around as a kid, do a bit of work with him. Later, when Bob married, I deferred to George as the eldest. I felt secure with George; he fixed things up, he didn't make a song and dance. Reliable. He had a fair bit of responsibility. I looked to him instead of Pop.'

Percy and George spent quite a lot of time working for and with Fred Rothe. It seemed like an easy working relationship. 'We had an agreement; we'd cart his hay, and he'd cart ours.' Percy acknowledged Fred's influence on his life, too. Perhaps George himself may also have related to his eventual father-in-law as the father he would have liked.

'I'd look at Dave Rothe, he inherited his farm. John Rothe was too bossy, I didn't take notice of him. Fred was a gentleman. I'd watch what he did. Then later in life, I found out he was rigid, and the other two more broadminded.'

But according to Percy, he was not the only one to depend on George. 'Sally was a worry when Tom was in the army, and George sort of, had to be Mum's spokesman. George was the only one Mum would talk to. I don't think anyone talked to Pop about it.'

'Did you talk to anyone about your inner-most thoughts when growing up?'

'No, I don't think so. Not at all!'

Later in our conversation, Percy returned to the subject of his older brother George. 'If I talked to anyone, it was George.' As well as speaking highly of George's strong work ethic, he seemed to find him easier going. 'Stan had his ideas, for example, when clearing out the stable, he'd tell you to put it on the poorest part of the paddock. George would say, 'Cart it where you like, put it somewhere.' Percy's smile had not reached his eyes. 'Stan would be more trying to teach. You'd walk across the paddock with Stan once, and he'd say, 'Look at this! There's a ground lark's nest.' And so on. Funny, he's always spent his life learning. He wants to do everything thorough. Near enough is good enough. George Daff said at the Bruton reunion, 'You can always tell a Bruton, but you can't tell him much!' '

Percy brushed his hand across his forehead. 'P'raps Stan was more a farmer than anyone else. He would be trying to conserve the soil, to plant trees. But a farmer's got to be prepared to make short cuts and make money. You had to make some money and George had to make every shilling count. Stan would be more inclined to study up what you should be doing. He would make a good farm manager, I suppose.'

He was silent for a moment. 'The trouble with my boys is they won't go to the field days because they reckon they haven't got time. Stan. I used to say he has the seven-year itch. After seven years he'd change his job, his house. He is a Bruton but different than the Brutons.'

It was while I was kneeling, pushing in Percy's knee caps to a more stable locked position as he leant on his walking frame, that he raised the subject of his brother Allan, who was so severely handicapped all his life. Percy's own painful struggle had stirred up his sympathy for Allan. He had gained a greater respect and admiration for

Allan's stoicism. 'Us kids used to argue the point about who was to help Allan with his leg irons. Now I think what a thing to argue about.'

On the other hand, Percy never really warmed to him. He reflected on this. 'Perhaps it could be the similarity of Allan to my father, which is the reason why I did not get on with either of them. I just kept out of their road. I did not understand what Allan was about and I still can't. I remember one day when we were kids, I asked Allan if when he died, he wanted to be buried or burned. Allan said, 'I don't care what they do with it—throw it down the back garden.' 'Percy spoke quietly, 'That stuck in my mind ever since.

Harold said to me once, 'Allan was trying to tell me how to make money.' Harold said, 'There's plenty of ways of making money, but there's only one honest way.' And Allan said, 'What's that?' And Harold said, 'I didn't think you'd know' Had Allan stumped!'

The complexities of families. Different birth order, different experiences, different perceptions and different responsibilities. Different views of one's parents. I ushered Percy back to that compelling and difficult subject. His father. Percy hesitated and then flowed on.

'My father was forty-six years older than me. He was about sixty-six when I started work. If we wanted to plant spuds, George and I would be a man short. We might ask Pop to handle the single furrowed plough which he was good at. He'd do it for one day and next day he'd have his good suit on. Off to Mentone. He'd get on a train and off he'd go. We'd say, 'Where's Pop?' 'Oh, he's gone.' Sometimes when we were ploughing, we'd do a bit of swearing, and he'd just huff off and turn his back. We'd have to use psychology to get him to keep working. He was a funny old fellow.

After I left school, Dad was head cook and bottle washer when Mum went to Melbourne. He'd get the lunches and bring them out to the paddock, bring out a billy of tea. No. I don't remember doing anything with him when I was a kid.'

It was later that Perce remembered he had gone with his father to Glenlyon to a saw mill to get some timber. 'Pop made stone drains to make the bottom paddock's swampy areas usable. He made big ditches and put logs in. He'd get a shock if he saw it as it is today, a big dam now filled with water.'

Percy looked into the distance. 'There was a big kangaroo in the dam- standing in about two foot of water. The dogs were jumping and barking. I put them in the ute cabin. Then the kangaroo got out, was sunning himself on the bank. I picked up a stick, self-preservation.'

Percy was drawing himself up, eyes big. 'The closer I got, the higher he stood up on his hind legs, bigger and bigger!

He reached out as if he was taking my stick. I back-peddled!' he said, laughing.

Now serious he added, 'When a kangaroo is chased, it will grab a dog and hold it under the water and drown it.'

This enormous dam was one of the first Percy created.

'It can water about fourteen acres of spuds. It is fed from the spring, but I don't think the spring is as good as it was sixty years ago. The dam fills in the winter from rainfall runoff and the spring.'

The size of this dam was eclipsed later by an even larger one Percy constructed in the front paddock adjacent to the very long straight driveway that leads to his house. I omitted to ask if he'd stocked the first dam also with fish. I remember sitting on the bank of the old dam in the sun one day and suddenly discovering a coiled black tube next to me. It started to wake up, raising its head. I thought I was telling Percy a dramatic story when I recounted this. But he was not concerned. Snakes were commonplace to Percy. Sometimes while he was swimming in the creek, a snake would be seen gliding from one bank to the other. Percy's mind was on more practical subjects.

'Pop made a hut out of bark from the bush. Called it a hut. He wanted to put chaff in it. It wasn't steep enough for the water to run off. We used to keep the jinker in it. Better than nothing. We used to throw dead rabbits up on top of the roof, and Harold was up there one day and threw one at me. Hit me on the side of the face.

I remember I was going to set some rabbit traps one day. I was trying to fix them, bashing away on the front verandah. Pop roused at me for doing it on Sunday. Mum said, 'Well, it's not a good place on the verandah. If you want to do it, do it in the shed where he can't hear.' I was just about old enough to believe I knew more than my old man. I was probably hammering and saying a few words. The front verandah was the only 'shed' we had for a long time. Everything happened there. Pop made that bark hut, but he didn't put enough bark on! It would drip on a wet day. I think it kept everything out, save the rain. I pulled it down and put a tin one where the bark hut stood. Expanded this shed three times. Then made a garage at the end of the shed, eventually. I must of done a lot of things when I first left school. Put up the windmill, put pipes round the garden. Mum thought it was Christmas! Then I got the carpenter to put up the shed.'

There was a remarkable contrast between Percy and his father. Unlike Harry, Percy became good mates with his kids, as he was with us. I suppose my sympathies were with Percy and his siblings, those who were afraid of their father. I also shared a fear of Harry, my grandfather. That day he hit me a number of times with his heavy leather razor strop I have never forgotten. I was about six and totally unused to such treatment.

Still, Perce concluded his remarks about his father with a peace-making statement. 'Then when I had kids, I thought he wasn't that silly, as I thought he was. Pop was a quiet man until he got mad.'

Percy commented on his father's handling of horses. 'Pop was too gentle to be an animal man. He would not put the bit in the horse's mouth. No way! Sometimes a horse would be frightened of a steam engine at the side of the road. Pop would cope with a situation like this by putting a bag over his eyes and lead him past whatever he was frightened of. I saw Pop doing it two or three times. Pop would put the bag over the horse's eyes and hold it, and lead the horse a few steps, then take off the bag, and the horse would continue walking.

I bought a pony and jinker when I was about eighteen. The pony was very frisky and would stand up on his hind legs. When you told him to go, he'd ignore you. He had a habit of it. He'd just stand, or lift his two front feet up about two foot high. I took Pop over in it to George's when he was first married. This day, Dave Rothe was there. The Rothe's had half a dozen draught horses and a pretty good jinker horse. He knew a fair bit about everything. They were getting into trotters. Dave said, 'You hop in the jinker and tell him to go. And when he rears up, I'll give him a wallop with a piece of timber.' So me and Pop got in the jinker and I told the horse to go, and he reared up a foot or so and Dave gave him a hit. So he reared up about six foot to his full height and fell over backward. So Dave just sat on his head, and George unharnessed him and then harnessed him again in the jinker. Pop was disgusted. Just got out of the jinker, didn't say boo, and went home. The horse reared up. Dave gave him another wallop. He took off like a rocket! So I drove him home. I passed Pop halfway along. I asked him if he wanted a ride and he wouldn't. I took him for a gallop to Lyonville after that.'

'How would your father have handled this situation?' I asked.

'He would have put a chaff bag over his eyes and get him by the bridle and lead him forward, and had someone in the jinker. And he only had to take about a dozen steps and drop the sugar bag off and step back. The horse would continue walking. He'd do this when a horse was frisky and difficult. He did it with my horse at home to get him moving.'

I knew I was putting him on the spot. 'Why didn't you do it on that day?'

'We always thought we was too smart.'

Gold Miners' Shafts. Property

Times past. The ebb and flow of life. Pondering our discussions the following morning, I picked my way through soft, muddy tracks. These lead to the enormous outbuildings with semi-trailers, various tractors and equipment. As I strolled to the back paddock past the big hay shed, red Hereford steers quietly grazed in front of Mount Macedon blue. Further along, green paddocks became burgundy, the tilled earth silently awaiting seed. All attesting to life's transience.

I crossed from the lee of the hill to the paddock, which sloped down to the bush, the wind biting my back. Along the ridge was a long strip fenced off from the sheep. I climbed over this fence and kneeled down on the partially damp earth to better see the tiny beginnings of a eucalyptus wind break. Percy told me later that his boys Ray and Karl had ploughed two rough furrows and sprinkled these with eucalyptus seed.

There, unexpectedly, in the distance at the bottom of the hill, was a small patch of daffodils, their gold vibrant against the red furrows. Double old fashioned. Perce told me later there had been a house in this area, burned down in the bushfires in 1942. 'I'd just left school. I was carting hay next door in Martin Rothe's at the time.'

The raggedy disused track through the bush on the other side of the fence attracted me. It was impossible to open the old, rusted gate silhouetted in front of the typically dry olive-green Australian bush. The gate was firm under my weight as I jumped down on the crackly leaf litter. This, amid the shrieking cacophony of perhaps a hundred white cockatoos over-head. The old track was no wider than a small car, furrowed in places where there was less clay. A wattle or two, and every so often, a sapling had grown in the middle. I ambled along; I suppose about a kilometre. As I stared into this typical bush, the greyness seemed to gradually disappear. The scene became transformed. A myriad of colours. Blue greens, dark amber, the occasional golden glow of an early wattle. A banquet of aromas too. The refreshing clarity of the eucalypt. The nose-tickling mustiness of small dogwood flowers, along with wattle's heavy polony sweetness. The dampness of rotting leaves underfoot added an earthiness to this cornucopia.

The bush beckoned, but I did not stray far from the track. The heaps of clay here and there near the periphery seemed sinister and menacing. They harboured half hidden holes square and pitch-black inside. Partially obscured by bushes, these old mine shafts were relics from the gold fever days and had lain silent and crumbling for over a century.

After my climb up the hill, then over the back paddock and return to the house, Percy and I talked more about these holes. Perce had cleared part of his own bush paddock. The holes had been filled in with a bulldozer.

'There were dozens of shafts in the front paddock and the adjoining paddock in the flat halfway between our house and road right up to the state forest. There was a big open cut about twenty-five metres square and four or five metres deep. We use it as a tip. The Wombat State Forest next door still has lots of shafts. The old shafts would be fifty or sixty foot deep. By the time you'd hit the bottom, you'd find out! Some would have water in the winter. Stan gave me a little booklet from the Mines Department. Were three or four reefs. The book was written about the turn of the century, was about 1890 when the holes were dug.

Ray called and called his dog one day. After a couple of days, he took the torch and went up the bush. He heard a small whimper and there was the dog ten foot down at the bottom of a hole! Ray went home and got the ladder and carried him out. Why the dog didn't bark, I don't know.'

This wasn't Ray's first foray into one of these dangerous places. I shuddered to think if the floor of the mine had given way, plunging Ray even further into a black abyss.

'One day Ray lost an Appaloosa foal. He hunted for a couple of days, then found it in a hole twenty-foot-deep in the paddock. Got a lump of rope and the forklift. The foal was covered with clay. The mare was watching from the top but wouldn't take it, so we raised it on a bottle. Sometimes now, after a wet year, a hole appears in the grass, four foot by about three, about five or ten foot, or even twenty foot deep. When we filled in the holes in Meuser's paddock there were a lot of them, about six or so acres. They were joined with tunnels, which also joined the open cut.'

'Oh!' I said. I didn't like those holes.

Percy was unperturbed, 'A great place for foxes.' he added.

'Have any of the dogs been lost and never found?' I ventured.

'Only one. We lost him a couple of times and found him in a shaft, then lost him altogether.' Percy seemed to note my sad expression, my ever hoping for happy outcomes. 'Evidently the kangaroo can negotiate the hole and the dog goes straight in.

One time when Barry Bruton was working with me, we'd sown a paddock of oats. When you were ploughing, you'd drive the tractor over some holes just covered up with sticks. One wheel could drop in about six feet. The oats were about two foot high. I said to Barry, 'You go and have a look.' The earth had caved in, a hole about thirty feet. When you looked down, there were the oats growing at the bottom. Barry's eyes nearly fell out.'

Percy tackled each subject with an enthusiasm and openness which was refreshing. Truly a man of the land. Perce started off with mixed farming, spuds, sheep, cattle and growing oats and hay. I asked him more about his various land acquisitions. He had certainly built up his holdings. 'Pop bought the old property for about 700 pounds about 1925. Later on, when Pop was in his late seventies, he wanted to buy the house at Avonsleigh. So I bought his half for 1,000 pounds, and Mum said, 'You can buy my share when I die for the same 1,000 pounds' and I did. I bought 180 acres overgrown with rabbits and blackberries where we are now, for 3,000 pounds just before I was married about 1953—54. Then sixty acres with bush and dozens of mine shafts for 240 pounds, about the same time, then seventy-five acres at Meuser's Hill, then fifty acres down the back, then 120 in front of my house.'

The subject of money stirred my memory. A couple of Percy's many generous acts. Perce was never mean. A maker of money, he was also a sharer of it. This included the lending of money to various relatives. One loan includes my family. On the deaths of my grandparents, we decided to buy back the house at Avonsleigh, which my parents had originally owned. Percy had not demanded, perhaps even expected interest. I do recall my mother insisting at the conclusion of the loan that interest be paid.

Another story sticks in my mind. Apparently, Percy returned home from Daylesford one evening in his socks. He had stepped out of his valued, strong, comfortable farmer's boots, and given them to a bare-footed pyjama-clad man, as he helplessly watched his house burn down.

Eventually, after acquiring a couple more farms in 1996, he bought with his boys another of the Rothe farms. 'Land's too dear now.' asserted Perce. 'So I'd better stop.' Then he added with panache, 'Till we pay this one off.' There was a note of pride in Percy's voice as he talked about his purchases. But the jewels in his crown were probably the old Rothe properties, for they in their hey-day used to employ the Bruton boys.

I asked, 'What year did you finish consolidating?'

'According to Karl and all the experts, you have to get bigger, get smarter, or get out. Looks like I'll have to keep getting bigger for the next twenty years.'

Spuds

Invariably our conversation returned to those nuggets of brown gold, the mainstay of the Bruton family. Percy had employed many a man, occasionally a girl.

'I think when you were a kid you used to pick up twenty or twenty-five bags a day or maybe thirty. They were big bags those days too. Fifteen to the ton. There are none of those about now. The biggest bag you see now is twenty to the ton, about fifty kilograms. I think I used to pay four shillings to a man to pick up spuds. But being a relation who I could rob, I think I paid you three bob.' Percy was teasing, his face crinkled with fun. 'But I had to lug them and sew them up.

I had one girl later on and she picked up thirty-four, but her father Sam Gamble dug and picked up and sewed the bags. Forty-seven for Bill Moloney one day. How about that? He was a champion. Fred Drummond was picking for me that day. He will remember. I used to sneak into Fred's bedroom and strike a match and wake him up at six o'clock. The poor old bloke thought I had just gone to bed. I was a real slave driver I think.'

Yes, I well-remembered Fred Drummond, the grocer husband of Bess who used to also enjoy holiday work on Percy's farm. Much fun would be had by us all when the two families stayed together at the old house 'Planting the spuds. How did you do that in the horse era?'

'I remember one time planting some spuds, working with George and Pop. I had this pony and jinker and I took Pop down to where George was living in one of Dave Rothe's houses. He had spuds on shares. We put Pop on one single furrow plough and George on the other, and I was planting the spuds. We had a four-gallon kero tin hanging around our necks with the seed in. The kero tin opened on the side. Each step you drop the spud. Push it with the side of your foot against the side of the furrow, and then the horse doesn't put his foot on it, because he's walking in the furrow. The rows of spuds have to be straight, otherwise when you come along with the scuffler you'll scuffle them out. Have to keep up with the horses. And you have a manure sower thing on the plough. A thing with a wheel on it. As the wheel goes round, it dribbles manure from the manure box. About five gallons it holds. You didn't put much on in

160

those days. One bag to the acre—superphosphate and ammonia. Now you have about ten bags to an acre.'

The spud farmer uses more fertiliser now, fifty years on. 'Why?'

'You've got to grow twenty—twenty-five ton to an acre now. In those days five ton would be a good crop. If you did that now, you'd go broke. Just to make it profitable.'

'Is it alright to pick up spuds in the wet?' I asked Perce.

'We can't pick up wet spuds because the delicate housewife don't like it. Sometimes if we got caught in the rain, they got very wet and muddy, we would have to pick them up. Or we might get a big frost and if they were still out on the ground, they would get frosted and go rotten. In those days, every load of spuds had to be inspected by an agriculture inspector. If he found anything wrong, he would just say 'No. Pick them over.' And then he would have another look to see if it was done right. Some smart farmers would put rubbish in the bottom of the bag or in the bottom of the load, but the inspector was smarter than that and he would be stricter next time.'

Perce was galloping on enthusiastically about his favourite topic.

'You can't gamble with spuds as you used to. In 1956 spuds were up to eighty pound a ton! Then they went to a hundred and 150 pound per ton. George sold a load for 175 pound a ton. Four ton of spuds bought the ute I went to Darwin with. Bought Fergies—a lot! Put it down on expenses for the taxman. Now you can only claim ten or eighteen percent for new equipment. The Italian spud buyers would pay cash.

In those days if you got a good thunderstorm in January, and you got five tons to the acre, that was wonderful. Now, if we can't get fifteen tons, we'd go broke.'

I wondered at the apparent big jump in production. Percy's answer was quick. 'Irrigation. It was a major factor. There was no irrigation in the early days, you just looked at the heavens, and hoped it would rain. And when the potatoes were grown dry, you could not put so much manure on.'

My stock question again! 'Why?'

'Because they could burn. If you irrigate, you can put more manure on because it dissolves in the water. We used to plant one third ton per acre, now, a ton and a half. With irrigation, we produce four or five times more. Ten years ago, the size of spuds they wanted was smaller. Now the fish and chip fella wants bigger ones for chips. We are planting wider this year—to get big ones. Big demand for ready cut chips! At Bordertown in the Mallee, up near the Murray, they have 200-acre paddocks of spuds, where you wouldn't think of it thirty years ago.'

That day over lunch Ray had mentioned some substance they sprayed on spuds. I wanted to understand more about this. Percy addressed the subject after the news that night.

'We used to spray blackberries with 245T, and for thistles 24D, or it might be the other way round. Then once in a while when you got a dry year—I suppose 1955 was pretty dry, we sprayed the spuds with DDT while they were growing, about February,

March. No irrigation in them days. When it was dry, grubs would get in the bushes, then go down into the spud. Used to be bad in Gippsland. Then we'd dig them and sell the number one grade, then we'd leave the chats in a pit for seed, and sprinkle them with DDT and water, from a watering can.

No. We wouldn't use gloves. Nothing! We didn't use the DDT very often. Only once in a blue moon. The Horticultural Department recommended it as a good thing. Was the answer to everybody's prayer in those days. Might have been the summer of 1956. The winter was very wet all over Australia.

The grubs were sprayed only once about every ten years. But once you started irrigating, about 1957, the cold water kills the grubs or just heals up the cracks in the ground so the grubs can't get at the spuds.'

It sounded as though irrigation must have cured the spud-grower's woes. That is, apart from having to get out of bed several times on a hot night to move sprinklers and heavy pipes. But on talking with Percy further, these moist conditions gave rise to another danger. A fungal problem called 'early blight.'

'The blight may be worse now because the spuds aren't as dry with the irrigation. We use fungicides now. Not in the early days. Started about eight years ago. You have to spray three times altogether—once every ten days when the crop is half-finished growing. The spuds stay green and you get the extra growth. Get an extra ten ton to the acre. The fungicide is 800 dollars for a three-litre tin. As expensive as gold. If you don't spray, you'd only get half the crop. When there was no irrigation, you'd get four ton to the acre—if you got ten you were very happy. Now, the fungicides help to get a bigger yield. You need it to make a farm viable. This year it was very hot, dry weather. Had twenty—twenty-five average to the acre. Fresh ground. We'd bought Billy Moloney's farm and it didn't have spuds on it for twenty years. Put a terrific lot of water on them.

In the old times when you dug the spuds with the fork, there would often be a lot of grass too. Be three times as hard work. You don't have to work the ground as much now. Before we had to plough, then harrow it, and then a few weeks later plough again to get rid of the weeds that had come up. These days you spray the weeds with Roundup, leave for two weeks. By then the weeds have shrivelled up and you plough it. If you have a paddock of twitch grass, some call it 'couch,' you have to knock the daylights out of it!'

Percy sat quietly for a moment, reflective.

'George would say, 'Old John Rothe said you shouldn't plant spuds unless the dust has blown.' We proved it a couple of years. When I was a young fellow, we planted whether it was wet or dry. They used to say, 'If you can't get oats planted by April don't do it.' Now they do it in September alright. So who knows?' Percy was philosophical.

'I get my own idea of what is right. You try and tell your kids. Then I think so-and-so told me that, and he was wrong. So I try to keep quiet. Just because I did it that way, it is not necessarily true it's dead right. Let them do it their own way.'

Batching. Local Personalities. Cows

We returned again to the old house where Percy had lived by himself for a while.

'I was a bachelor for a long time. I think I might of been thirty-two when I married, but I did not batch much. My mum or dad was there till I got to about twenty-six, I think. I have an idea Dad went to Avonsleigh about 1954 or there about and Mum soon after. That means I might of been on my own or with Harold for about four years. I'm not too sure.

When I was batching, I would always cook bacon and eggs. Chops and eggs. Steak and eggs. Or for a change, I'd have sausages and eggs and toast. Now and then I'd cook a chunk of corned beef and eat it for a few days. Then my good old sister Rosa or Bessie would come and feed me my vegetables for a while, or I would sometimes jump in the ute on a wet day and nick into Trentham. Three shillings for a three-course dinner at the Cosy Corner Café. Then Mrs Hammond got too old and retired. So then I'd sometimes go to the pub for a three-course dinner. Five shillings. Mrs Hammond died last year, aged 104, I think.

Most days I'd make sure I was working down at Freda and George's at dinner time and even teatime. Freda would feed me up. Even a couple of years ago when I could walk, Freda would say, 'It must be tucker time.'' Percy grinned.

Percy's bachelor diet contrasted sharply with the fare of his youth. He'd told me earlier, 'We usually had boiled mashed potatoes, cabbage or pumpkin or another vegetable, and a little meat, like mutton or corn beef, or plenty of rabbit. Pretty often roast potatoes, pumpkin etcetera and always pudding. For breakfast we had porridge of oatmeal or wheat meal and eggs on toast. The chats, small potatoes, boiled up over the fire in a kero tin were pretty good with butter and salt. My mother always did the cooking except when she was visiting in Melbourne. Then my father could cook a good meal. Sometimes my sister would be home and do it.

I often knocked off at 9pm. Mum used to growl, then later, my wife did. Now my boys do the same thing. You try and get in before the weather. But I did have morning and afternoon cuppa which my boys often don't.'

Percy, Rosa and myself were having a cup of tea by the fire. Percy was enjoying himself. I think we all were. Now, Percy shared some stories, small glowing coals plucked from the fire of local lore.

'Down near Dagg's, George's farm, Clever Hutton lived in a hut. He was an old gold fossicker, used the cradle. He was born about 1887, I think. Died about 1960.

George and Bobby Bruton went to feed the sheep or something, and Clever was dead in Dagg's yard between the shed and his hut. He had a heart attack and dropped. He'd come up from the creek where he lived and worked by digging spuds or cutting wood. He'd say, 'There's more money in gold than spuds.' He originally came from Glenlyon Shire, and his old house still stands. He woke up one night and sparks were falling from the ceiling! He just had time to grab his trousers and run. The next day Dave, John and Fred Rothe, and Jack Talbot, he was head carpenter, and George Bruton, built him a one-room hut on the road at the edge of the bush and got him some clothes. The hut is still there.

After the war Clever had got disused bits of aluminium from aircraft and made a lean-to. He kept dogs, birds and so on, in it.

He was always an argumentative old drunk when I knew him. But I saw a photo of him in uniform the other day, and he was a very handsome young soldier twenty-five years before I knew him. He was at Gallipoli, but that's all I know. He used to tell us about Egypt, and the girls when on leave, but I forgot all he told me now. He told us he was married and had a son, but his missus cleared off with another bloke while he was at war. He would only tell us that when he was drunk. Every Saturday he would either ride the bike or walk into Trentham and get drunk, and someone would bring him home to his hut.

His father had a store where the Prices used to live, halfway between Price's and the school, on the lane there, a hundred years ago, and was very religious and a preacher. His two sons were the opposite. I think Frankie Attwood owns it now. Bridgee Moloney used to tell us that her father and his brother would go to the store on a Sunday and buy sixpence worth of lollies. Mr Hutton would give him the lollies but he would not take the money as that was trading on the sabbath. So the kids had to take the money after school the next day. I thought my old man was the only man like that.

I did not know till that day I was talking to Billy Moloney. But Justices lived next door to Clever, and they had six kids, two rooms, and a lean-to at the back made out of spud bags. They lived there a long time.'

Obviously old Clever amused Percy, who went on to tell another story about him with some relish and a carefully nonsmiling face.

'Old Clever was a bit full one day, and Paddy Cohen was drinking beer with him. Clever was standing there. He'd grabbed his gun and was brandishing it. He looked down the barrel, no cartridge in it. Paddy said, 'I'm going!' Half an hour later Paddy heard a bang. He thought it must be the end of old Clever! He visited him, and there was a hole in the roof.' Percy smiled as he reached the punch line. 'Clever had banged the gun, and the bullet passed by his ear!

They had a do in Trentham this time last year. They were cleaning up the cemetery, and the committee had about a hundred working bees. Came across this patch, the pauper's part of the cemetery. Clever Hutton was one of them, a few returned soldiers. They didn't think that's right, so cleaned it up and made a real good job of it! Someone thought of the idea of having a celebration for Old Clever. They found he was over in Egypt in the First World War. They also found he had been AWOL and that sort of thing. Even traced some of Clever's relatives.'

Jack Talbot was a name I had heard mentioned over the years. I knew he was an old bachelor who lived in the vicinity of Percy's farm. He lived in a hut, simply, as had Clever Hutton.

Percy recalled. 'I think Jack Talbot was courting Rose Rothe. I'm not sure if he was engaged or not when Ern Rainey came along and cut him out. He stayed a bachelor till he died about eighty-five years old, I think. He was a great old-time dancer and he would ride his bike into Trentham dances and be MC. Ern used to play his mandolin and accordion at some dances too. In the First World War Jack was in the Cavalry or Light horse in Egypt and I think he was at Gallipoli, but I was too stupid to ask. The only thing he ever told me was that when they sailed out on the ship everyone was seasick, except him and two other blokes. And I think he said they had to look after 1400 horses. I'm not sure of the number. Jack always walked like a soldier marching.

About 1950—52, when we put the bore down, Jack Talbot brought his gold panning dish. Bill Close used to work in the mine which was under this paddock. While they were looking for the gold seams, they struck water and then ran out of money. Jack was hoping we were putting the bore down on the gold seam. He was there working as the bore went in. A long bucket, about ten-foot-long would fill with water and slurry. We found water but no gold. The bore is still going but the windmill conked out. It's pretty hard to find someone to fix a windmill these days.'

It was the next afternoon, after I had brought home the geese, two I'd caught at the back dam, that we continued our discussion. Beautiful plump birds, soft feathered bundles with knowing blue eyes which looked straight at me. I'd been told they should not be there; they had escaped from their run from somewhere over the paddock and would foul the dam. The foxes had caught some. These two were left. I baled each up against the fence in the corner and carried them back in my jumper. Now they were safe from the fox, ensconced in Doreen's chook coop. Or so I believed. Unwittingly I had contributed to their ultimate betrayal. A few weeks later Doreen said, 'They were a lot of trouble. Karl got rid of them.' I remonstrated with myself, my lack of insight into the pragmatics of farming.

The Brutons in the early years used to have a cow or two. I wondered if Percy had ever owned a milking cow himself. 'We had a cow for fifteen years or so after we were married. I milked it till the kids grew up a bit, then Doreen. When I left school, everyone milked six to eight cows. Two butter factory trucks would come and pick up the cream on the side of the road. Now there is no butter factory and the nearest one is at Ballarat. Fewer people with cows now, only Frankie Attwood down the road and he's selling his. The Brutons had two cows usually. When I left school, I used to milk them. If we had too much milk, we'd separate off the cream, save it up, and take it to

Frankie's corner in a stainless-steel billy. The butter factory would pick it up. We'd get one pound per cow for cream. If we got that now, you'd make a mint! You don't see the cows as skinny these days as when I was a kid. They'd put a bag sheet, like a blanket over the cow, and they'd say it was to keep the cow warm. I think it was to cover over the ribs. We never used to. We had enough sheds for the cows to go in.'

I suddenly recalled an image, reminiscent of an oil painting. Percy on the small wooden milking stool, head cushioned against the side of old Beauty the Jersey cow. Beauty's head was lowered in the manger. All were silhouetted against the dark of the slightly rusted galvanised iron milking shed. That noisily ringing tin bucket would be filled in no time. The strong and quick squirts from Percy's practised and nimble hands left a two or three-inch-thick froth, like a big cappuccino. A deft squirt sideways and the black and white cat had a whisker wetting, paw licking drink.

I don't recall Percy talking to Beauty. I used to chat to her, when I tried, always unsuccessfully, to milk my slow and torturous way to a full bucket. Beauty would answer me with a soft moo. I loved the pleasantly pungent fragrance of the cow and fresh milk, and the subtly pervasive aroma of the hay Beauty chewed in the manger. Percy filled a cup for me one day straight from the cow. I found the warmth of it repugnant. Perhaps it was still too intimately, too personally, hers.

Later that evening, after a meal of chops, mashed potato, carrots and silver beet fresh from Doreen's garden, we retreated to the lounge room again. Percy settled himself in his mechanised armchair, which at the press of a button would change position, then we chatted. Books in Percy's household were few in number, but one of them caught my eye. It was a book written by Doctor Gwen Wisewould, a medical practitioner who became legendary in the district. Percy remembered her.

'She was a bit of a wizard really. One Saturday Harold and I were digging spuds and we heard a bloke sing out down in Cam Andrew's bush. We went down and Cam had fell a tree and hit his back and he could not move. We rang Doctor Gwen and she came within half a mile of him in her large utility. We got her stretcher and took her down to him, then carried him up to the utility and put the stretcher in the back, and hopped on the back with him. No room in the front with two or three sausage dogs and all her gear! We carried him into the hospital, then waited till she fixed him up and hopped in the back again and came home. She always had sausage dogs with her. I think they were as important as the patient.

I don't know what she lived on, as she would never tell her patient how much. If you poked the money at her, she would take it, but if you did not argue she would say, 'I will send an account when I get around to it.' And never, ever did. I think she was about eighty-four or eighty-five when she died. She worked right up to a few days before. Doctor Gwenny was what you would call nocturnal; she would visit her patients out in the country any time of the night. I don't know when she slept, if ever! She used to run Red Cross dances during the war on a Saturday night. She'd organise the ladies to do the supper and so on. Also ran concerts about once a year, I think. A Miss Bell used to live with Doctor Gwen, and they would organise those concerts, using mostly local talent, and they'd be in the concert themselves. Those 'Doctor's Concerts' were very popular. Both these and the dances were held in the Trentham Mechanics Hall.'

I made a quantum leap to another subject. Absolutely unrelated. 'What are your saddest memories?'

There was a silence. Percy racked his brains. 'Don't remember any!' was his eventual verdict. 'Perhaps I was sheltered, the second youngest.' A few days earlier he had commented, 'I think being one of the youngest kids had its advantages. Now and then, not often, I could get a few bob or something out of the big ones. But the trouble is, the older ones thought they were the boss. But I soon woke up they were not, and I could soon put it over Mum and Dad.'

'And who do you think had the least fun in the family?'

'I don't think Dad had any fun at all and Mum seemed pretty happy all the time. I think that the mail trip to Trentham three times a week wet or dry, kept her happy. I think walking to church at Drummond every Sunday, twelve mile, was Dad's fun. I think Rosa had the least fun as she worried about everyone.

No. I don't think I would change much of my childhood even if I could!' was his answer to my question.

As had the Bruton children before our time, we kids and our cousins also enjoyed walks in the forest which abutted two fences of the old farm. Usually with Harold or my mother, Rosa. When alone, we were not confident about venturing any distance along the old logging tracks, and we'd never explore far from them as the Bruton kids did. These tracks seemed to our unfamiliar eyes almost invisible. We had to be very observant not to miss the tell-tale indentations on the bush floor. 'What do you know about the era of the bullock teams?' I asked Percy, realising they were probably operant well before his time.

'I know bullock teams did work in the bush hauling logs to the saw mills early in the piece, but for the last hundred years all that work was done with horses or the odd steam engine. Well! Come to think of it, I think Rosa had some photos of bullock teams.

When I was about eight-year-old there were two teams of horses carting logs past our farm. Sometimes one big log, more often four or five. They'd be stacked then chained. Mostly bigger logs than they are now. There'd be Jack Kayes with six horses, and Dick Kanty with six horses, with a load of big mill logs on each four-wheeled wagon. When they got the load on the wagons, all with horses, they would leave two horses in the shafts of the one wagon, and put the other four in front of the other team of six, making a total of ten horses, to pull the big load out of the Glenlyon bush.

It is a fair hill coming up from the bush on our road. They needed that extra horsepower to pull the logs over the hill and through the mud, to the metal road near Frankie's at the corner. Then they'd take four down the bush again just yoked together and leave the wagon already pulled out with the shafters in it up the metal road.

When both wagons were on the metal road, they would put six horses on each wagon and head for the mill at Lyonville about eight kilometres up the road. Imagine the mud along the road at the front of our driveway. The whole road, at least a kilometre from down past our way up to Frankie's, was a quagmire.

The horses learned to work as a team and were mostly driven by voice. They'd call the two horses in the shafts 'shafters.' Often heavier, stronger horses, they had a pretty rough life, the shafters. Coming up past our gate there'd be a pothole or two, a big strain on the shafts. The shafters have to hold against the wheel when it goes into a hole and basically have to steer the four-wheeled wagon attached behind them with the big logs on it. They get a bit of a spell when waiting for the other wagon to be pulled up with the extra horses.

Eventually round about the end of the forties, they closed the mill down and shifted it to Daylesford. The motto was to close all the mills in the state forest. Think it was something to do with the electricity coming and steam engines causing bush fires.

Old Dick Kanty was a great old horseman! A lot of the time he did not use reins to drive the horses. He had a horse named Pilot out the front of the team. He would do exactly as Dick told him. Dick was a fat old bloke with a voice like three fog horns, loud and clear! I used to love to get out and hear his vocabulary of swear words away down the state forest. I dared not let Pop know I was out there listening.

When I left school Dick was working for Bill Ogden. They had a mill down the bush about six kilometres from home. Where Mr Ord had a mill fifty years before. I used to go down sometimes and ride Dick's pony and lead a horse or two into the blacksmith in Trentham to get shoes on. The horses had a bar across the toe of the shoe so as to give him a chance to get a grip in the mud. The horses lived and worked in mud two feet deep day and night, but he always had them as fat as him.'

Percy was looking a bit self-conscious. He was apologetic. 'When I start on Dick I can't stop! He lived in a hut in the bush with his horses and didn't have a tooth in his head. He lived on steak. He had a wife and eight kids over near Ballarat at Gordon. He always had a lovely pony and jinker, and would go home through the bush country, shortcut, on a lot of Saturdays and come back Sunday. I don't know how far, but I reckon it would be forty or fifty kilometres. One day he was on his way home and stopped at the Lyonville pub. He stepped out of the jig and dropped dead!'

Mail

It seemed amazing how word would get around of the various types of happenings. No telephones, and few people owned radios. Percy's mother's mail round, when she drove the four miles to Trentham in her jinker, was an important contribution to the communication network in those days. She would deliver the mail to the tiny post office at Little Hampton. Sadie Price, a single lady, was the post mistress for about forty years. I remember as a child noticing her efficient and kindly manner. Even more noticeable was her hair! Neatly waved, I admired the carroty colour. Rich and deep, it glinted orange fire in the sunshine. The post office next to the school was the size of a telephone box or a country dunny.

'When she was bringing the mail, Mum used to throw the newspaper over the Enders' gate. These were two old maids who lived down near the bridge,' said Percy. 'Mum did the mail run for a long time; I don't remember how long. The Little Hampton Post Office was inside the school at that stage.

Mum got on well with everybody in Trentham. She was in there three times a week with the mail run and had to fill in a couple of hours. She was in at the draper's one day when a Rigby girl was in there. Mum said, 'Sorry your husband has just died.' The girl said, 'oh well. I'll just have to keep my eyes open for another one!' Mum thought that was a great joke.'

'Why did she give up the mail run?' I wondered.

'Mum finished when I was about seventeen, in 1943. She had an accident. We were having dinner and the horse came back with the harness and no jinker! Pop jumped up and headed off up the road to meet her. The horse had pulled back, pulled off the blinkers. They hit a bump about two feet deep and Mum fell out on the ground. Phillip Collyer the schoolteacher saw it happen. He took her to the doctor. She had a bad back. I think she always suffered after that.'

This pint-sized post office was an important place of contact for the locals. Probably many chin wags occurred there. Percy remembered the mail system clearly. 'Years ago the mail was sent to Little Hampton. The schoolteacher's wife or Prices would sort it. Everyone in the district would walk up and get it at lunch time three times a week. Then about thirty-five years ago they sent it to Little Hampton and Sadie would sort it, and the mail carrier would take it and put it in everyone's box. Then twenty-five years ago they closed the post office and sorted it in Trentham and delivered it all around to everyone, RMB numbers, every day. Sadie got the sack! I bet she missed the job too. It was her social life. Three times a week for years, then to church on Sunday. Now she is the last of the Prices. She lives in the hostel in Kyneton. Aged about ninety-three. Her birthday was last Sunday. I think she is happy in there and I think she will live forever!'

'The Little Hampton School shared the same fate of closure, didn't it?' I asked.

'It closed about three years ago. About Christmas 1994 or '5. The reason everyone thought it closed was that the politician Jeff Kennett said it had to. But later on it turned out the teacher had a choice but no one knew that. Actually with the cost of computers and all the jazz the schools have to have these days, it might be just as well it closed, and the kids bus it to Trentham. No matter what political party we have, it would close. Now the problem. What to do with it. It's supposed to be sold last

Christmas. I talked to the bloke and his wife who bought it. But now the rumour is he can't build on it or something to do with National Trust.'

The subject of buildings attracted my mind's eye. I was looking at a different one. A square house encompassed by a verandah. Typically Australian, with traditional corrugated iron roof, it was rubicund painted with tall gables. Reminiscent of a tall hat, I used to think. This was the house of the Bruton's neighbour, Frankie Attwood. It sat at the corner of the main road, thankfully metalled, and that awful red gluey wheel gobbler track. That red track, a quagmire in winter, which passed the Bruton's a mile or so further on, before snaking into the Wombat State Forest. Still there, the house on the corner remains a home and looks just the same to me. Frankie and his wife, Chris, whose red hair echoes that of Frankie's Aunt Sadie, have long raised their children. Frankie still has a cow or two.

I mentioned this house to Percy and asked who had owned it earlier.

'Mrs. Cam Andrews, Phyllis, lived next door and they sold out to Frankie Attwood. They had a son the same age as Barry Bruton. Cam used to trap rabbits and dig spuds etcetera. Then he started cutting and carting wood. Then he started getting the wood down at Drummond and Malmsbury. Good box wood. But then he would only come home every week or two and Phyllis did not want to shift to Malmsbury, but she did eventually. Sadie and Myrtle her sister went to see her Friday and sat up worrying all night about her. Next day she went missing. They found her shoes first on top of the well and then found her in the well. I think the water was close to the top. Cam got married again later and I think it was a good match too.'

I did recall now having met Jimmy, Cam's son, as a child, when playing at the Bruton farmhouse. My major memory of Jimmy was that his ears were red! Knobbly at the edges. No wonder in that inhospitable ear chilling, chilblain making climate!

Harvesting

'When the oat crop is finished growing about Christmas, the stems of the oats change colour from a green to a sort of gold colour. It is ready to cut with the reaper and binder. If it's two feet high it's not a bad crop, if three feet it's a pretty good crop. A series of knives go backwards and forwards through 'fingers' and cuts the hay off about three inches from the ground. Beaters lay the hay on a platform of canvas which carries it up through two more canvasses, and then every time an armful comes out, it pulls a trigger, and an arm comes out with twine, and goes right around to the knotter which ties a knot and cuts the string and pops out the sheaf of hay.' Percy paused. 'The bloke that invented that sure had some brains.'

This harvesting was another notable activity with a community flavour. Big pressure to get summer's bounty cut and stored while the dry weather held. Too terrible if it suddenly blew up rain. Or so I thought.

Percy sounded unperturbed. 'Everyone goes and sits under a bag, under the shed or the haystack. If it rains, I don't touch the stooks just leave them as they are. If your stack was half done, what you do is you stack your sheaves up. Make sure the sheaves are tipped so the rain runs off. Next day, you'd take the top layer off to dry and stack the rest. If it rains three days, three weeks, could be a disaster. Just have two choices. You can growl about the weather, or can say like they do in England, 'Let it rain!'

A big bag sheet was good to protect the stack from the wet. You'd let the horses down the paddock and stitch the bag sheet up in the stable, the only dry place. The size of the sheet would depend on how many empty bags you had. You didn't buy new ones, just used the old super phosphate bags. Farms generally only had a stable, barn, and a shed for the jinker. Our jinker shed Dad made with a bark roof leaked.

In those days the hay was sheaved and standing in stooks in the paddock. If the weather was dry, we had to leave it in the stook for ten days or fourteen to dry out. Then cart it into a stack, the hay stack. If you cart it in too soon or a bit damp it goes mouldy, and gets hot, and may even get spontaneous combustion and catch on fire!'

'How did you make a stook?' I wanted to know.

'A man comes and picks up a sheaf in each hand and stands it up like this.' Percy put his fingers together and made the shape of a tepee. 'Then gets two and stand them against the sides to block the gap. That leaves four little gaps so you put four against these gaps. Some farmers, John Rothe used to put eight sheaves in a stook, dries out quick. But I used to put another row around it, and make it a dozen or fourteen, doesn't blow over as easily. If the weather is very hot, the big stook holds the moisture better, but if it got very wet, it would not dry out as well. So then of course the smaller one is better.

The first year we came to Little Hampton, Pop said it rained the day they came and didn't fine up for twelve months. Fellow next door would go and turn the damp sheaves to the sun, it would rain and he'd get sick of it. He put them on the dray and hurled them over the fence into the blackberries. Before he got to them to set fire, the cows had eaten them!'

Percy's earlier comment, that he used more sheaves for a stook because it held the moisture better, was a puzzle to me. It seemed a contradiction to desire moisture in what should be dry hay. I wanted to revisit that comment before it slipped away. 'What do you mean holds the moisture?' I asked.

'When it's hot and dry with the sun beating down, the sheaves get pretty dry. The middle not as much as the outside. But then if the weather stays damp, they don't dry out as well either. If you're making a haystack, the very dry sheaves are harder to handle, they are dry and slippery. It's like trying to stand on a bit of soap. If there is a little moisture, not damp, it holds together better. It's tougher.' Percy tried to illustrate his point. 'If you take a handful of grain and clover on a hot day, it's like tea leaves. Dry. But if you take a handful just after the sun has gone, and you squeeze it, it makes a nice ball. Hay's good dry, but not bone dry. Bone dry, you squeeze it and it breaks into a thousand bits. Just a cold day will make it tough.'

I like a good stook. If it rains, you only have to let it stand another day or two and it would dry out. And you generally don't cart them in when you should. Could have to stand there a few days. Then pretty well before you load them into the haystack, lay them out in the paddock for three or four hours. If you re- stooked it, you can bet your life it will rain again. Have to get it dry before piling. Otherwise—that spontaneous combustion!

A fellow, Peter White at Sidonia, now my son-in-law, got some hay up in the morning, big one-ton bales, pretty tight. He put them into the shed, a real big shed with doors on it and everything. Had the hay one end, and machinery the other end.

About three months after, it went up! I was talking to a fellow, I said, 'Was it insured?' 'Nothing was insured.' I was suspicious with other fires that a box of matches may be involved. Not now.'

Threshing

The harvest, having been sown, reaped and stored, was still not won. Not yet. The grain had to be separated from the long stalks of straw. Feed for the farmer, his animals, the farm chooks. Perhaps some grain to sell. And warm straw for bedding in the stable. Not all grain crops were threshed. Earlier Percy had explained about chaff cutting.

'You make up your mind before you plant what you will thrash. A paddock for each, and each's own haystack. Sometimes the same grain, say, oats in each paddock.

They are cut at different times. Only a matter of a few days, maybe a week between. You'd do the chaff paddock first. For chaff, you cut it with more moisture, more colour, more vitamins in it. Use the heads, grain and everything. Draught horses are fed on this. We'd add a dipper of oat grain to the horse's oaten chaff if the horse was working hard.

The paddock for thrashing you'd let get a bit drier before you cut it. Most of the grain we thrashed would be sold.'

I asked Percy about the word 'thrasher.' 'Is it thrasher or thresher?'

'We always called it thrasher. But when you look at the dictionary it says 'thresher'. After the war thrashers went out, and headers came in. Nowadays they use a big header—go across the paddock, take the heads off it and thrash it into a bulk bin. The stalks stay there—can mow it and bale it or sell it as straw, or turn cattle on to it. It took eighteen men to work a thrasher, headers one or two.

Percy particularly remembered the excitement of threshing.

172

'Eighteen men would start work before daylight about 4.30, have breakfast seven o'clock for half an hour. Then the whistle would blow about 9.30 for morning lunch, which lasted a quarter of an hour. Then at twelve, they'd stop for about one hour for dinner, three o'clock afternoon lunch. Then would go till it was pitch dark. As there was often men from ten mile away, they'd stay the night, find a nest somewhere, curl up in the chaff. You'd hear the steam engine whistle, like a steam train, early morning, then again when they finished. The thrasher was quite noisy. You'd hear the whine and hum, because the beaters would be racing around pretty fast. They didn't get much spare time for sleeping, and they wouldn't have their tea till it was too dark to work.

The women would all get together; Miss Barrow, Rothes etcetera, would have a large washing basket full of sandwiches, sometimes cakes. They'd make the tea in the house and bring it out in three big milk cans. These won't spill. When you put the lid on, will hold the heat alright. Probably use a dipper or a jug.

The men with the thrashing equipment visited a number of farms. If you had a couple of haystacks and you wanted the thrasher to come and thrash it, you'd have to get a heap of wood and water for the steam engine. There was no tractors. In those days there were steam trains, also chaff cutting and thrashing machines powered by steam engines. You'd fill up with wood and water. Used to be steamrollers on the road. They'd put rock on the road and roll over it with the roller. They'd go 'clang, clang' pushing steam and smoke. Frighten the living daylights out of a horse!

Yes, it was a long day usually. Fellows would be paid by the hour or the bag. They would chug away to the next farm. The boss of the machine would have to organise the setting up and dismantling. For travelling they would fold back the benches alongside the thrasher on which the man feeding it would stand, also the belts which drove it. When it went out the gate, it would go flat out, about half a mile per hour! See them moving and that's about all. Rough roads. The men would walk alongside, or climb on top of the thrasher and have a snooze. Some of the men were locals; some of them would travel with the machine. If you lived three mile away, it would be too far to go home. Have to walk or go on pushbike, may as well curl up and stay there! Little pay.'

After hearing all this, I was surprised at Percy's next comment. 'I never really worked on one. Watched them. Worked half day with a local one when I was about twenty. It would come through Glenlyon, through the bush. Don't know where it came from. Probably started up past Bendigo and worked its way down because this district is about two months later than up there. We only had the thrasher once or twice in my life. Only once, really. We didn't have a big enough farm to warrant it. We'd grow some hay and cut it into chaff for our own horses. Whereas, others grew enough to sell, and for their horses. I did work on the chaff cutter a few times filling the shed, but I didn't work around much. Mainly on my own property. Just as I left school, they stopped using the big steam engines. We would power it with the tractor.'

'How did the thresher work?' I asked.

'It would stand near the haystack; you'd put the sheaves into it. A lot of little bars going about a hundred miles an hour and it belts the daylight out of the hay. The grain, oats, wheat any sort, falls through little holes into the bottom. A fan blows off the cockie chaff or the shavings. A lot of farmers didn't bother bagging it, it would just go through the bottom into a heap. Some people used to feed the cows on it. It was as light as a feather, no weight in it. What doesn't fatten will fill, I suppose!

A bloke with a horse would put a bar of wood across and a horse chain each end and drag this light chaff into a heap. Could leave the heap in the paddock and let the cows help themselves. The heavy straw would go along the elevator, there'd be two or three men building a straw stack. Usually give the cows some of this heavier straw. Need a certain amount to tickle the rumen. We'd fork some into the stables too.

There'd be a fellow with an oil can. He'd squirt a bit of oil on the bearings. An oil can in one hand, and a bit of wire in the other. He'd clean out the oil hole on the bearings with the wire and squirt it. It's pretty hot weather when they do the thrashing. Can't afford to let the bearings get too hot, otherwise it would catch on fire. The bloke with the horse dragging the cockie chaff out was called a 'chaffie,' fellow with the oil, a 'mousie.''

Having seen a relic of a Furphy water carrier on a farmer's paddock in Gippsland, I now asked Percy about these. 'The Furphy water cart was hooked behind the thrasher steam engine. The local farm would supply a horse and they would take the cart to a dam or somewhere, and take a bucket and fill it up. Well,' Percy scratched his head, pondering. 'How would they fill it? Unless they had a windmill. These water carriers were a bit before my time.'

The sturdy water carrier I saw had a circular motto raised on the cast iron at the back end. I recall straining my head to read the message. Perhaps it was for the draught horses who pulled the heavy load!

> Good, better best
> Never let it rest.
> Until your good is better,
> And your better best.

The subject of the threshing had provided a further spark for Percy's yarn telling ability. 'There was another story Bill Evans told us when we used to pick grapes up at Nyah. He'd thrashed his wheat, and it was ready to put on the wagon the next day to take to the railhead, probably Bendigo. And at 4am the next morning, the emus got to it and scattered it everywhere! The same fellow, in the 1890s drought, had to go to the Murray River with the horse and dray, to get a drum load of water. You'd think the horse in the dray would drink all the water before he could get the forty miles back to the house! The Murray River would have been almost dry too because there were no weirs in those days.'

Haystacks

Now the storing of the precious harvest. Those golden sheaves. These seed topped stalks, glinting and shimmering, carefully gathered and placed in skilfully engineered stacks, could hold nutrition for ten to twenty years, Percy told me. Pity help the farmer when thirsty earth turns to dust, the dreaded devastation of drought, and he has no lifesaving storage stacks!

'I've been noticing my rain gauge since 1940,' Percy had said. 'There's a drought at least every fourteen years. One thing up here you'd always get a crop, be kept mainly for horse feed.'

Stack-making, a centuries old practice, has only recently given way to shed shelter. The making of a haystack fascinated me.

'To make a haystack, you cart the hay in from the paddock. We used a dray with a wooden frame on it to make it twice as big, or a two-horse lorry or a two-horse wagon, both with a frame around. To start a stack, you work out how much hay is in the paddock so as to know how big to make the stack. I think about eight metres by four metres would hold about twenty or twenty-five ton. You have to be very careful to get the foundation right and square. On the first layer you put a few sheaves along the middle, and then lay the next row against it, with the grain top of the sheaf on top of the other sheafs, and that leaves the bottom of the sheaf on the ground. And the next row and so on till it's the right size, keeping the grain head off the ground, as the ground is damp, and the hay on the ground draws the moisture. Next you start on the outside row, and work your way in, keeping the bottom of the sheaves pointing out. You do this with every layer until about ten foot high. When you are up about ten or eight foot you put the eave row on. In other words, put the outside row out about fifteen centimetres or six inches, to run the water off. Then every row, bring it in six inches until you come to the top. Then put a stook along the top and do it so it won't blow off.

If it is built right, the top of the stack will run water off all winter, if it's left. If it's not built right, it will try to fall over and the farmer will have to prop it up with posts, as the stack settles down over weeks, and will sit on the posts and straighten up a bit. The bottom of the stack gets bigger as it goes up to halfway then gets smaller. On a hot day it's a hell of a long way up to throw a sheaf.'

Percy placed his fingers firmly on the table. He was emphasising an important point. 'The top half or roof must slope all the way, to shed rain or it will soak in and ruin the lot!'

Percy drew a small picture for me of a stack. There was a stick figure on the top. 'That's George.' At the bottom there was a wagon. He pointed to the figure on the wagon. 'That's me. There would be two men at the top. The sheaf turner provides a sheaf for the stack builder who is the boss. The sheaf turner can be very young, or very old. He just lays the sheaf at the feet of the stack builder, who puts a sheaf down and stands on it. Then you have a man on each wagon. One man up the paddock getting a load on, while the other fellows are with the other wagon taking the load off.

We always had a fellow who is a sheaf turner to turn the sheaf exactly the right way. So the stack builder stands on the previous sheaf and just puts the next one exactly right. Anybody who goes too close to the edge of the stack gets roared at very smartly, as does the man on the wagon, if he does not put the sheaf right in the middle of the stack or knocks out a sheaf near the edge.'

My eye wandered to the cherry tree through the window. No longer burdened by snow, the branches, twisted brown, had taken on a tortured quality. Yet, overall there was symmetry, shapeliness, a harmony. Percy asked me to reach for a cutting from the Weekly Times. It was about a new cow feed. I then adjusted his right leg, which was laying precipitously close to the edge of the sofa.

The Old House Revisited

The next morning was the day before Doreen was due home, and two days before we were leaving. It was on this day that we made that necessary pilgrimage to the old house. In the afternoon. Earlier I had collected a big hessian bag of pinecones. For fire starters, I reasoned, as I dragged it back to join the split eucalypt wood already stacked on the verandah, just outside from Percy's hungry fire.

Not so wet under foot now. Amid pale slivers of sun, Vickie, Percy's eldest daughter, accompanied Rosa and myself as we walked around the deteriorated building, a stone's throw from Vickie's new home. My perception of the size of the old house had shrunk since my youth. It seemed amazing that the commodious wings of the house had sheltered all.

Now free of adornment, apart from green lichen almost iridescent, covering the grey weather-beaten timbers, and the old deep green laurel tree at the front, the house looked stark. It seemed the old cottage with its hooded verandah eyes had given up. No longer loved. Not appreciated. That is, save by various sheep who had wandered in through the front door, blown open. I looked through the gap where the big chimney once stood. The bricks had been harvested by Vickie to construct a feature wall in their new home.

Rosa was walking about outside, her quietness broken by Vickie's bubbling conversation. 'There were a lot of old bottles here! I told the school they could come and help themselves.'

As I stared at that fireplace, a sense of sadness swept over me. Times past. Never to be repeated. Suddenly I realised that the warm hearth and fire was the most important aspect of the house for me. This symbol, this reminder of happier times, was now dismembered and sinking into the earth. Some scenes flashed through my mind briefly. It seemed too painful to take hold of them properly right now. Long, home-fashioned wire toasting forks. The inviting aroma of crisp browned toast. Toast spread thick with homemade butter and one's choice of various jams. Red plum, blackberry, pink quince or marmalade with lemon. Even melon jam, with melons from the Bruton market garden at Mentone. Sometimes salty vegemite.

The black iron bar had gone. Its ends had been embedded in the bricks each side of the fire, stretched across a couple of feet above the blazing wood. This bar must have been strong, for on it had hung my grandmother's 'fountain,' an enormous black iron pot with a lid, and a tap in the side. This supplied ready hot water. I learned to be careful lifting this lid, to hold the special flat handle attached to it. Otherwise, the hot steam could painfully sear one's wrist or hand. Then there was the sooty iron kettle. It would comfortably sit on the less active part of the fire, singing contentedly, providing cups of tea aplenty. The iron fender with the vertical patterned border around it, the protector of the floorboards and non-descript lino, had long since disappeared. The ceiling pasted over many times with brown paper was hanging down dismally in the corner near the front door.

We gathered a few rosy apples still clinging to the old, gnarled tree at the fence. Not far from it were some native trees and shrubs, some walnuts and chestnuts recently planted by Stan. On the way home, we crunched a sweet apple, but my thoughts were a melancholy ode to the demise of the old house.

We were well entertained. Percy was his jovial self. The flavoursome dinner, cooked by Rosa, an inveterate roast maker, enhanced the scene. Naturally, it included potatoes. Richly browned, crisp and tasty. Also carrots and silver beet, vibrant and fresh from the garden. And thick, brown, full-flavoured gravy made from the meat juices. Doreen returned after we were replete and quite jolly. We were pleased she had enjoyed herself.

Another of Percy's jokes surfaced. Doreen took it in her stride, considering the topic. 'This wife rang up her husband. She was having a lovely time on her holiday. 'I wonder if you mind if I stay another week—I'm feeling a new woman!' Her husband said, 'I don't mind. Stay as long as you like. I am too!'

Later on in the evening, amidst family talk and hearing about Doreen's trip, Perce shared a couple of pub jokes. This, in spite of the fact he himself is a teetotaller and had only frequented the pub to buy an occasional meal—and this was a rarity. 'Chris Ryan used to skite in the pub about his son. A real Irishman. He had a son when he was pretty old, 'Leo.' He said each hair on his head was worth 1,000 pound! The local blacksmith said, 'Why don't you cash-in the little bugger.' Another time he said his son 'Gallops along with every foot out the stirrup save one.' Yes. Chris Ryan used to say, 'People are dying who never died before; it's getting unsafe to be alive!'

Bernie O'Connor was in the pub one day, and there was a police raid. They were taking down people's names. Bernie went up and said to the police, 'You haven't got my name.' He was asked later why he said this. 'Good enough for everyone else, good enough for me!' Another Irish man said to John Rothe when he at eighty gave up spud digging 'Don't do that. Give up spud growing. They all end up dying when they do this!' John lived ten years after that. And Bernie used to say, 'Keep out of hospital, it's the last place to go or you'll die!' He was dead right. Ten years later he had to go to hospital, and he died within two days.'

The next morning we headed off, but not before visiting the patch of ginseng which Doreen was proudly and patiently growing. I had mentioned earlier to Percy I thought the old house looked very sad. 'Doesn't worry me.' he said. 'All the windows are busted and the laurel leaves and the berries get in there. And Stan would spend half a day or so cleaning it up, and the next time, the sheep would be in. I just think what's the good of cleaning it up. No one's going to live there. The wind blows the door open. The catch was never much good. The house is as old as Methuselah.'

A few spuds in the car boot later from Doreen for Rosa, and we backed past the grevillea with the busy honeyeaters. I called out to Percy, 'Don't catch the flu.'

He was laughing. 'No, I'm too slow.'

Brutons, Mentone

It was a few weeks later that we conferred by telephone. I wanted to ask Percy whether he remembered his Bruton grandparent's market garden at Mentone, east of Melbourne. But first I heard about Percy's latest trauma, which he recounted as an adventure. 'I fell off the chair in the kitchen—must of gone straight over frontwards—hit my head on the floor again. Anyway, mum rolled me over and covered me up and left me there until someone came along. I didn't have specs on. It would be alright, but I generally wreck my specs and get a black eye out of it. Better than last time. Last time I had to get stitched.'

Percy was chuckling, 'The floor comes up pretty quick! On my way down I'm thinking 'I wonder if there's a way for a soft landing?' and then I'm thinking 'when my nose hits the floor it will flatten, I'd better turn my head.' So I turned my head to one side a bit'

I expressed my shock and horror. 'When you don't have that strength to be able to stop yourself, it's too terrible. An awful feeling of helplessness, I'd reckon.' Percy changed the subject.

'Did you hear about our other bloke sticking his foot in the harvester? He's alright, he's home working again. He's got all his bits and pieces. He thought he was going to lose two or three. They opened him up, cleaned the spud dirt out.

He was away in hospital for three weeks. He had a skin graft. Came home on Friday morning and he was driving around in the ute Friday afternoon, and Saturday he was in the tractor and went spud digging. The district nurse come out to dress it. He said he'd go into Trentham every day, save her coming out. I think Peter and Ray got a bigger fright than Karl did.'

Yes. Percy clearly recalled spending time at his paternal grandparent's market garden. His mother's parents, the Bluhms, had deceased before his birth. William Bruton, his paternal grandfather, died when he was a toddler. Memories of Grandmother Elizabeth Bruton were crystal clear.

'I went down there to Mentone with Pop one time on the train. We slept in the bungalow at the back. It was Auntie Elsie's knitting machine room. Grandma Bruton would give me sixpence to fix her chook house so her bantam didn't get out. Dead spit of Minnie Mock. She'd give you threepence, a 'trissie.' I'd buy an ice-cream for her, me and Auntie Eva. A penny each. I'd buy the ice cream from a man who came along with his cart ringing the bell, and you'd run out get the ice cream. It was packed in drums with dry ice around them.'

Now, a question I had delayed asking, a diversion from the topic, but the answer of which I felt I had to know. I blurted it out slowly, as though it didn't matter. 'What happened to the horses at Little Hampton when the tractors came in?'

Percy's voice was matter of fact. Maybe purposefully nonchalant, I don't know. 'Old Dickie was taken down the bush and shot, he was the last one we had left.'

'Who was the one to do that?'

'Me. If you had a crook horse, you'd just go and shoot it. They get skinny. When they're in the Melbourne sales, if the farmers don't buy them, the blood and bone, Fitzgerald's would.'

'Must have been rather hard to shoot them.'

'No. It doesn't worry me! When Ray was a little bloke, we went walking in the bush. Ray said, 'Here's a big lot of bones with a big head.' I looked, and it had a bullet through it. Probably Dickie. Ray brought it home and set it on a stump for a few years.'

'When did Dickie go?'

'A couple of years after I got my Fergie, about '57, '58, I suppose. Bob got a Fergie as well, in '56. Spuds were worth ten pound a bat then. Old Tom Swaby, he went into Melbourne with a fist full of money and bought a Holden ute. Was five ton of spuds. It was the same when I bought the Fergie. I think it was about 800 pound, being about six ton of spuds then, in '56.'

'Your father. When did he and your mother move from the old house?' I was silently wondering whether Harry had known about old Dickie's fate.

'He had moved to Avonsleigh about '52, '53.'

A change of topic was a relief. There was still the subject of Percy's grandparents, the Bruton market garden to pursue.

'I don't remember Grandpa apart from hearing him. He had a pet song he'd sing. Uncle Ted and Uncle Joe would argue the point all day. I liked being with Joe more than Ted. Harold went to Melbourne with Mum, I never went. I didn't want to go. Harold would tell me about Uncle Ted and so on. After the war, I went with Tom sometimes; he'd drop me on the way to his farm at Redhill. I'd come home on the train. I only went down once or twice in a blue moon.'

Percy remembered staying on the Reuben Bruton property at Heatherton further east from Mentone. 'I used to stay at Uncle Reuben's a few weeks. I remember being over there when the big bush fires were on, 1939. Must of been '39 when Gippsland got burnt out, because I remember Clarry Bruton and them were washing carrots at the trough. They had a big trough, about ten-foot-long and about three foot wide. Concrete. I was there helping them wash them. I said something about the colour of the sun. It was just a little red blob up in the smoky clouds. And Clarry, who was always making jokes, giggled and said. 'That's not the sun, that's the moon.' Uncle Reuben was reading in the paper the next day. He said. 'Drummond isn't far from your place, is it?' I said 'No.' 'Well' he said, 'Drummond was burnt out.' He was reading where the fire had been. I'd be about thirteen then, I was born in 1926.

And Auntie Nell, Reub's wife, used to cook for all the blokes and the kids. She went away for a few days' holiday. I don't know where she went or anything about it. But she asked me to milk the cow. I was a champion cow-milker, so I milked the cow every day while she was away. And when she came back, she bought me a brand new shirt. Oh, she was a good old stick as far as we were concerned. They were different. Instead of up our way where you were supposed to sing hymns. Silly wasn't it? You weren't supposed to be singing dance tunes and that sort of thing. Yes. Never heard anyone singing round here unless it was a hymn! One day Auntie Nell was doing a bit of a jig. It was to the music 'Doing the Lambert Walk.' You don't know it?' Percy began to sing, 'Once you get down Lambert's way...!' I thought you'd know it.'

No, I didn't. 'I heard your whistle on the wind, singing too. All sorts of songs from the paddock. I used to marvel, you were always in tune and joyful, like a song-bird. 'Tra la twiddle, dee dee, dee, it gives me a thrill to wake up in the morning to the mockingbird trill.' Do you remember that?' Percy was surprised at my recollection. It wasn't however part of his repository of memories.

'Maxie Bruton was playing golf with a bloke. I think he came from Bacchus Marsh or somewhere, and he said his name was Burgess. The fellow said, 'I used to have an uncle or some relation down Heatherton way and they knew a Reuben Bruton.' And Max asked me, 'Is there a Bruton market garden over at Heatherton? The fellow said after Reuben died some of the Burgess's or somebody bought it. And he said they were digging up bathtubs full of money!''

I said, 'I remember it was in the paper where someone dug up a kerosene tin full of money, and this was just before I was married and I was down at Hoopell's, and old Hoopell, Doreen's father, was saying 'Oh look at this! I betcha this is a relation. Old Bertie Bruton. He had a tin full of money dug into a hole!' Evidently when they sold out, somebody dug up this tin of money and they didn't know what to do with it. Whether to put it in their pocket and say nothing, or give it to the relations who used to own the property. I think they should of just put it in their pockets and told nobody. But I was telling Max that, and Max said, 'This bloke said it was tubs full of money. Not buckets full.' '

'Perhaps this may be exaggerated.' I said.

'Yeah, that's right. I remember Uncle Joe saying when it came in the paper about the tin full of money. Uncle Joe said, 'Yeah, that would be Turk alright.' That's Reub's nickname. Joe said, 'When I was a kid, he had a plant down in the stable. He didn't think I knew where it was, but I knew where it was alright. When I was running a bit short any time, I knew where it was!' 'Percy was laughing. 'Two bob pieces, I'd say. It wouldn't be much good stashing paper money away; it would go rotten.'

'He had a lot of children, didn't he? Would have had a lot of mouths to feed,' I said.

'Yeah. It finished up not very good because oh well, the oldest one Alf sort of reckoned he should have inherited it, and he should have been entitled to buy it at a discount, and he'd worked there for nothing while Reub was raising the kids. The others reckoned they were entitled to it. And they had big arguments about who shouldn't and who should of got it, and some of them never spoke to one another since.'

I observed that all of Reuben's children, Percy's cousins, were now no longer alive. Percy continued, 'I don't remember doing any work there. I remember Uncle Reub used to get out of bed at four o'clock in the morning and used to shift his sprinklers, and his sons went to market. Alfie or Clarry. The sprinklers would be going all night, and he'd go and shift them and it wouldn't be worth going back to bed, and he'd get down on his hands and knees weeding carrots 'til about seven o'clock. Then he'd have breakfast, and then he'd be still down there weeding carrots when it got dark. I suppose he had to go down the paddock to shift the sprinklers and it wasn't worthwhile walking back home. So he'd only get down on his hands and knees and weed carrots for an hour or two. By God he used to work long hours.'

'He ended up with diabetes?'

'Yes. They chopped his toes off, then they chopped his foot off, and then chopped the leg off. Then I think he got sick of it and died!'

Diabetes and a similar trauma had been visited upon Harry, Percy's father. In his old age, both legs were amputated. But we were talking about Harry's brother Reuben.

'What was Reuben like as a person?'

'I reckon he was a great old fella. When I was a kid, I must of went there fairly often. When it was time to come home, he'd say, 'Now come out here to the shed!' and he'd get some seeds. He'd get down his box of carrot seeds, beetroots. 'Oh here's

181

a few turnips, a few radishes and here's something else.' And he'd have a little packet of this, a little packet of that. I'd have enough seed to plant the whole garden when I got home.

Uncle Reub came to visit us once when we were chaff cutting. He worked like a slave all day. He'd never seen a chaff cutter before. He'd light up his pipe at lunch time. He really enjoyed it. My Dad didn't do much when we were chaff cutting in my day. Reub would come up home and sleep in the sleep-out with us boys. We'd wake up at seven o'clock, and he'd be gone. He'd come in and say, 'Who lives in that house two miles away?' He'd be up at four o'clock in the morning at home and he'd do the same at our place. You'd see him puffing along with his pipe—like a steam engine.'

I had heard that Reuben played a musical instrument.

'Never heard him play anything. He used to sit at the table as though he was half asleep, and would be rubbing his eyes with his hands. Don't know if he had sore eyes or what, or whether it was just lack of sleep.

I think all of Reub's boys worked on the farm. They seemed to get on well till after Reub died. Clarry, Uncle Reub and Auntie Nell would come up home in an old market gardening truck. Chev, I think.

This is another sad part of it. When we were down there, Uncle Reub was saying, 'They've got the green belt—they've got all this planning business. You can have factories here and houses there, and this part here is going to stay a green belt.' And he was in the green belt. It had to stay a market garden. So when he died, they sold out. Whoever bought it had to use it as a market garden. So he only got half as much money as what it was worth. You know, if you live ten kilometres away or something you could have sold it for building blocks, and made a lot of money.

So it's still a market garden, though it does have a house or two on it. At the junction of Kingston Road and Old Dandenong Road, that's where the store is. Uncle Reub was right next to that. Last time I was there I reckon the old weather board house was still there—another house was next door to it. I went past the joint about five or ten years ago. I looked in the gate and I thought the old shed is still standing even though everything else is different.'

'Someone told me that Uncle Reub used to back load with pig manure on his way home from market,' I said.

'Clarry's the bloke I used to like to go to market with. He'd buy you more ice creams and that sort of thing! We'd go to market at four, three o'clock in the morning. He'd get me out of bed and I'd hop in the truck with him, and he'd sell the vegetables and that, and then we'd go round to the railway yards and we'd fork up the straw out of the railway trucks. The railway trucks see, were packed. There was none of these cardboard cartons then, things were stacked in straw and you'd get a truck load of straw. And then we'd take the truckload of straw round to Peter's Piggery at Heatherton, and we'd fork the straw off into a heap. Then we'd back up to the pig manure heap, and we'd shovel all the pig manure on to the truck, take it home, then shovel it off into Uncle Reub's manure heap. Then we'd have to go and get the hose and wash the truck out ready for the next load of vegetables.

Uncle Reub would turn this manure heap over two or three times, you know, to make manure out of it. And a heck of a lot of straw in with the pig manure. And Uncle Reub used to get the pig manure for nothing and supply them with the straw. And I think he'd get the straw for nothing. I don't know. Looking back on it, I think he would have, either from the railways or the shipyards. I think most of, or all of it came out of the railways. Everything came by train those days, and a lot of it would be packed with straw so it wouldn't get knocked about. Carriages were open at the top and they put a tarp over them.'

'Produce he grew?'

'Uncle Reub used to grow a lot of beetroot for the raspberry jam factory. They put beetroots in the raspberry jam to give it a bit of colour. You'd be put in jail now, I suppose, if they caught you doing it. It would bulk it up too. I suppose beetroots would be cheaper than raspberries, wouldn't they?

He grew a few potatoes too. I remember I got some seed spuds off him one time, went down in the A40. He got them from a pit. He'd store some potatoes this way, sell them off before they sprouted, before about September, October. He'd build the sides up a foot with a log each side, the width of the dray. You'd just back the dray into it, tip the spuds off the dray. They'd sit up like a pyramid about four foot high. He'd dig a gutter along the side, put straw over, then sand. Uncle Reub and Dad would put earth over them. George and I found it was hard work for nothing. Worked just as well to put a foot of straw on it. We found actually, about six inches of straw was just enough to keep the daylight and water out. Make sure the straw is matted, so the water will run off. Nowadays we'd take them to a cool store to keep them.'

I recalled a comment I heard one day. 'Someone said when Reub took his vegies to Gartside's canning factory, he'd pile up his truck and put water on them to keep them fresh. He gave a liberal dosing of water which would put the weight on.'

'I suppose it would too. I know as we were washing the vegetables, we would stack them on the truck, throw them up. And somebody would be on the truck and catch them and stack them. And then you'd have to give them a squirt of water. All the time you were putting them on, you had to put the water on them to keep them fresh, water them well down. Then pull the cover over them and away we'd go.

Uncle Reub used to say, 'I wouldn't mind buying a spud farm.' I used to say, 'You must be joking! He's thinking about buying a spud farm when he has a good job like this.'

It was just plain ordinary sand, and the only reason it grew vegetables was because he put all of this pig manure into it and watered it. And over at Uncle Joe's they didn't grow a quarter as much stuff. Uncle Reub had a dozen men doing things, well half a dozen. Every time you looked up, had a dozen or two sprinklers going. He'd have a heck of a great big water bill. The water came from the Yan Yean Reservoir. I think he might have had only about eighteen acres. It wasn't much. He was a real good gardener.

Mum used to say Reub had a knack of growing. Well he'd have everything. Whereas when my dad was a market-gardener he'd say, 'Oh lettuces are pretty dear.'

And he'd plant a lot of lettuces. Of course, so did everybody else. And then he'd plant a lot of beetroots, and then the beetroots are no good. He was on the wrong end of the stick all the time. But Uncle Reub did the same thing all the time and had a variety, and had good stuff and did well out of it. I knew he drank a bit. You'd see a bottle of beer sitting on the table once in a while. A lot of beer in those days would only be chicken feed now.'

'Your father, Harry and Reuben, both had market gardens in the sand belt, didn't they? Joe and Ted market-gardened at the family property, and Albert was a carpenter.'

'Dad rented over where the Kingston Golf Course is now. Someone said he had lettuces growing there when they shifted up to Taradale. But that was before my time, I don't know. I remember more about Uncle Reub, Joe and all them, than I do about my own father! I can't say I got on with him, it's just that I didn't have anything to do with him! Perhaps that's why I have blacked it out of my memory.'

'We often remember times we've enjoyed. You enjoyed going to Reub's, and Joe was fun to be with. Do you remember Allan and Bob being at Grandma Bruton's?' I asked, recalling that Bob and Allan had stayed at their grandparent's property at Mentone quite a lot due to regular hospital visitation.

'No. Allan would be five or six years older than me. Was before my time. Now when I think about it, riding the bike. I must of rode the bike from Uncle Reub's across to Grandma Bruton's. I'd be staying at Uncle Reub's. I'd ride to Grandma's then down to the Mentone beach, then back to Grandma's and then on to Uncle Reub's. Probably borrowed the bike from them. Clarry had a stiff leg, one leg six inches shorter than the other. Had polio or something when he was a kid. And he had a fixed wheel bike. The pedal goes round and round and by cripes he'd keep up with the other blokes, Just with one leg! One leg stuck out sideways and the other one peddling.

I used to walk through the back gate at Grandma's, over to the railway line and up to Cheltenham and buy a comic and ice-cream, and walk back home again. Sometimes Uncle Ted used to flush the rats out. He'd turn the hose into the rat holes under the shed, and when the rats ran out, one of the dogs would pounce on them.

When Grandma used to get me to climb up on the chook yard and fix the roof, she'd give me that sixpence. Gee. I reckoned it was Christmas when I got the sixpence. Grandma used to have a fernery. She'd spray them every night, I still remember that. I think it was a paddock of daffodils between the house and the road—or jonquils. When you look at it now, it's only about ten foot wide. Uncle Joe used to fork up the old, dried tops into heaps and then we'd see him burn them when we were sitting on the verandah. And there was that big fig tree in their driveway. The footpath along the railway line to Cheltenham used to be sand. It's concrete now. It was a short cut to Mentone Station too. I remember going down to the beach one day with Auntie Min Tudor then, once with Dad. He swam a long way out. It seemed as though it was to the horizon.'

Percy was silent. He shared his thoughts. 'It's a funny thing. Dad always used to get on well with Uncle Reub, and I could never figure out why. They were as different as chalk and cheese. I thought, 'He's a heathen, drinking beer and smoking a pipe.' But Pop never used to say a word against Uncle Reub. For that matter, he never used to say a word against anyone much when I think about it.'

Percy's voice was beginning to slur, as it did these days when he was becoming tired. 'Sorry about your black eye,' I said.

'Well, that's my trademark! A good talking point!'

Rosa

Little Hampton. The Depression

Flowers festooning the front. Flower filled vases inside.

Rosa's sparkling dark eyes beamed welcome. So did her namesake, in the elegant, clear glass vase upon the small timber table with the hand crocheted doily. A large rose of the softest pink, a surprise of warmer tones, tinges of tangerine deep at the base of the petals. The strong green sweep of the leaves, a classic accompaniment. Such a beauty at this time of the year was unusual. Now in late autumn, the bite of winter was already here in the cool Dandenong Ranges, east of Melbourne. As I touched the velvet petal, Rosa said, 'Grace brought that from her garden. It's lovely isn't it?'

Rosa's smile was not quite as vivacious as usual. 'You tired?' I queried, as I noted the new haircut, probably trimmed by her own hand. Grey hair slightly waved. Soft darks around her face and nape of neck hinted at the thick jet-black twirls of her youth.

She nodded slowly, reluctantly. 'Yes I suppose I am a bit. Been digging daffodil bulbs. They're overcrowded. I want to thin them out before the winter. Thought I'd have a loaf yesterday and not go to church. I was going real slow having my breakfast. There was a special lunch, and I suddenly remembered I was to bring the bread rolls! So I hurried up and got there, just as they were singing the first hymn.'

Since in Rosa's household, most activities were prefaced with cups of tea from her cosied commodious teapot, this day was no exception. As we talked and imbibed white tea, I glanced around the room. The cataclysmic clutter reflected Rosa's diverse interests and activities. Even here, the garden intruded. A green leaved plant with long dancing arms seemed happy to have never seen any pruning secateurs in its life, jostled with two horse figurines on the cabinet. At the other side of the room, on a cedar chest, sat a fine maiden-hair fern, fronds cascading over the carved wooden edge. It had been carefully kept moist for at least a decade. One of Bob's he'd given her. Perhaps this they had gathered together from a special spot in a gully near Kyneton.

A bowerbird Rosa! If one needed anything, Rosa would find that special needle in her haystack of collections. An eye for the unusual, for beauty. And the practical. The spade and hammer propped just inside the front door attested to this. When something that needed to be thrown out—chips on a vase, Rosa's acquisitive instinct prevailed. 'It might come in handy.' would be her adage. And no amount of persuasion would change her mind.

My thoughts drifted to the privations of poverty endured by the Brutons way back there at Little Hampton. Recycling was a way of life. Inventiveness generated by necessity. Lean years, leading up to the even leaner of the thirties depression. Then the war.

Rosa didn't mind talking about these hard times. These times when they had to make do, to courageously cope. Times long past, but the pinch of poverty had left an indelible pain. She was proud of how they had managed.

'The walls were in poor condition and we had to paste hessian from sugar bags on them and then put paper over that. Either brown paper or sometimes Mum would cut out a picture and put on it. We utilised everything we could. The flour bags, I made into pillow slips. Robert was pretty smart. He made a chest of drawers with fruit cases and you could pull out the drawers. It didn't look very flash, but it worked. We had a homemade robe behind the door of our room—across the corner, a piece of wood to hang things on, and a curtain in the front.

Mum made the concrete paths. Anything like that she did. We carried some bricks up from down the bush. A fallen chimney from Ord's Mill.'

'Why did the family move to Little Hampton, that cold place!' I asked Rosa. I felt indignant. It had to be one of the most inhospitable locations in Victoria! Colder than Taradale, it was a far cry from their beginnings at Cheltenham on the temperate coast, where there was only an occasional frost.

Rosa spoke with passion. 'Because Dad could buy it! He had to get out of Taradale. Didn't know what he was going to do. Dad had rented the place with the intention of buying, and Mr Jackel suddenly sold the place over his head. And there were acres of potatoes he'd sown ready to dig too, which he had to leave behind. We were very short of money when we moved. Dad should have stuck up for himself. His mother bought the acre he owned at Cheltenham to help finance Little Hampton, and he added a bit more. He didn't want to sell it, really. Then later on, the Daffs loaned him the mortgage. I know Mum was terribly worried about the money. I sent every penny I could home when I was working to help pay it off.'

Passion had turned to pain, and now her voice seemed to take on an acceptance, even pride. 'We ate mostly vegies we grew ourselves. Rabbit sometimes. Occasionally if Mum could get enough money, she'd buy a shin bone and she would make soup or stew with it. I got sick of rabbit! Mum would boil it with an onion. I would roast it, stuff it and stitch it up, serve with roast potatoes and vegetables. We often had plum pudding or apple dumpling for sweets. The boys would trap rabbits along the fence. You'd see dozens of rabbits playing on the top of the hill. Dad didn't like it. He said trapping was cruel. And it is really. I could never stand it. Killing rabbits. Minnie could wring their necks! I'd run away. 'I don't want to see. I don't want to!'

If meat was going off, we'd wash it with salt and vinegar. We usually had a pig, sometimes two, and every year Robert would kill one. He didn't like doing it, but he had to. Dad couldn't do it.

I never knew the butcher to come, couldn't afford a butcher. Robert would be helped by Wick to do it.'

Rosa read my widened eyes.

'I'd go and hide. Put my head in something. You could still hear it. Didn't worry Minnie. The squeal . . . oh..!'

Rosa squiggled up her eyes with pain, left hand over her left ear.

'Oh. Deafen the noise with an old overcoat. Anything! Pillows, anything you could find.'

Anguished, her face momentarily twisted, she added louder, 'That's something that I didn't like. It was dreadful. At least I thought it was.'

She drew a heavy breath, willing herself to forget.

'The pig would be preserved. We had bacon. Mum preserved the pig in brown sugar. Rubbed it over until it really impregnated. She also used another way, of rubbing salt on, or soaking it in brine. Anyway Mum rubbed it over every day for a couple of weeks. Then it would be hung up in a big safe at the back verandah. I did it on my own a lot.

When Uncle Will came, he would bring some fruit from his orchard in East Burwood, and take home some potatoes. Before we lived at Little Hampton there were apparently cherry trees, but a man chopped them down. In the early days before Uncle Will got his truck, he and his wife Auntie Min, would come up in a covered wagon pulled by a heavy horse. It took a couple of days. They'd pull into a big dam and sleep, he made a bed in the wagon. If he had the boys, Ron and Allan, he'd have a tent for them. We'd been there about thirteen years I think, then Uncle Will brought up a forty-four-gallon drum. It was high enough to run a pipe out of it through the wall. So, we had some water in the kitchen.

We had our own cow, a very good one, our own butter. Milk was scalded as soon as it was brought in. We'd skim the cream off and make the butter. If we had plenty, we'd have bread, jam and cream. The milk was put in a bowl in the big safe with the fly wire sides on the back verandah. We all had to have a turn making the butter. So many rounds on the old cherry churn. We'd make scones with the leftover whey. I don't remember the young ones helping. I think us older ones did more than we should have. We sort of protected the younger ones. The washing up, the boys had to take turns. Mum said, 'I think the boys should do as much as the girls.'

Robert used to make the bread sometimes. He'd say to Mum when she was doing it, 'Come on Mum and sit down.' He was very helpful. Mum used to say Robert reminded her of her father. I was going to see my friend Hazel one day and was going hard to get the bread made. We had to make three loaves a day, and Robert said, 'Come on Rose, you go. I'll finish this off.' Another day, I hadn't made the scones yet, so he said, 'I'll do them. Don't you think I can make scones!'

Mum made a lot of melon jam. Grandma Bruton used to send up melons. I remember once when I was thirteen or fourteen; she sent such an enormous melon up on the train. The biggest I've ever seen. Mum said, 'I can't understand it. Grandma always sends a lot of melons, this time it's only one.' It took two boys and the station master to lift it on to the dray. All us kids had to get the seeds out for Mum. She also made blackcurrant and strawberry jam. Some blackberry. There weren't as many blackberries around as there are now.

She'd paste over the tops of the bottles with brown paper, using paste made from Silver Star starch. We'd pick up the bottles for the jam or be given them. Mum had a round ring, maybe of iron, with a little handle. We'd heat it to very hot, then drop it over the top of the bottle and the top would fall off. Mum then used these for jam jars. I think sometimes Mum pasted newspaper on the tops to seal the jam, but not often. Not sure if we had much newspaper, usually brown paper, I think. The shop gave us the Leader free, because Mum carted the papers.

Mum used to save dripping too, to make the soap, and she would boil this up, I think, with caustic soda, I don't know what else. She'd let it half dry before cutting it. We used to think it was horrible stuff, didn't smell very good. I never made it. She used to make it. Maybe she bought the dripping, it was very cheap, because we didn't have much meat. Rabbits were the main meat we had.

Dad couldn't eat rabbits, they upset him. Mum wasn't home, and we all had some cold rabbit. I heard funny noises from his room, and I said to Robert, 'Go in. There might be something wrong.' I was scared to, thought I might be in trouble being a girl, but one of the boys would be alright. I had trouble persuading Robert, but when he came out, he was shocked. Dad was unconscious. Soon after, he came to, and asked Robert to 'Get me a pen and some paper and I'll write a will. I haven't written a will!' He wrote a will, leaving everything to Mum.

George hopped on the horse and went to get the doctor. Just as the doctor came, Dad started to get better. Mum said she remembered afterwards, when we were little, he'd had cold rabbit, and when she'd got home, he was unconscious on the floor.

Dad didn't have any rabbit at all after that. Something Mum did used to buy was a shin bone. One and sixpence it was. She'd make stew with a lot of vegetables. There was a lot of fat in that meat, which Mum saved for dripping and roasting. The scraps that were left on the bone after cutting meat for the stew, she'd make potted meat with onion, and a little bit of broth. After this, she'd use the bones for soup. We always had lots of vegetables. I think that's what saved us during the depression. There were a lot of rabbits around then. I think the rabbits saved a great many people too. There were tents everywhere up near us. People who had lost their houses.

Something else we made do with were paper doilies. Min and I made them sometimes. We did have crochet ones elsewhere, but she and I made paper ones to go across the mantelpiece to decorate it. We'd fold paper and cut designs in it, then open it out. We'd sometimes hang it over the edge, that is, the pattern. It was plain on the top. The paper we used was mainly the white paper the butcher would put around the meat.

Every Saturday we had large tins filled with cakes. Big tins. Queen cakes, sometimes with sultanas, occasionally icing, not often. With our own eggs, we'd make a couple of large fruit cakes per week. I don't remember Mum ever being without fruit cake. The boys always had a big wedge in their lunches. We made eight loaves of white high-tin bread twice a week. There were four double tins, each would take two loaves, and all could fit in the oven at once. We also made a lot of scones.

We'd buy flour by the bag. It was white. We didn't know about wholemeal flour in those days. Uncle Reub brought up a drum which had a steel lid top. This was very good for keeping the flour in. Mum would put suet in her cakes, but if she had plenty of butter, she would use that. Min loved cooking, did more than me. I did more sewing. But Min and I took turns whatever the job was. Whoever went for a walk down to the mineral springs would take a few bottles and fill them with mineral water. We used to enjoy that, particularly in summer.

After we moved to Little Hampton, we went to the Drummond Church. It was about fourteen miles along tracks through the bush. No one else except us used these tracks. Dad cleared it a bit better to make it a bit safer against branches. We went in the cab. I think Dad must have bought it at Cheltenham to fit us all in. This was a covered vehicle, two seats each side and two steps at the back to get in. We used to cross shallow creeks. Mum didn't go very often. The youngest kids stayed home with her, and the rest went. In later years Dad would walk. It must have been when we didn't have a pony. I don't know, because Dad still had the horses he ploughed with.

One day we were in church singing, and evidently Min must have felt funny. And all at once the Minister came down and grabbed Minnie just as she fell. He carried her outside, laid her down on the grass. And then different ones came out, and we tried to bring her round. I was so upset about Minnie; I stayed outside. Min would faint now and again, especially if she got some sort of a shock. I used to wish I could, but couldn't! Actually, she suffered with anaemia and we didn't know that till much later.'

'But you suffered with anaemia too, and I remember as a child you fainting.'

'But I could not have had it as bad as Minnie. I never went out to it.'

'Why would you have wanted to faint like Min, anyway?'

'Oh! When you're feeling crook people would know, you'd get some sympathy!' Rosa laughed.

My thoughts were on a different tangent. Sounded romantic to me, being carried out by the Minister! Especially, as I subsequently discovered, he was a young theology student.

'The Drummond people at the church wanted to give us some clothes. They gave us one lot, but Mum didn't want to accept any more. She was proud. She was very upset and cried. Told us, 'We're not on charity, we've been able to pay for everything until now, and will keep paying!''

The quiet strength in Rosa's voice was familiar. 'Oh! To take charity! That was a terrible thing to do. To even think that she needed it. And they thought they were doing us a good turn, and so they were. And she wouldn't let us wear the clothes to church. Us kids didn't care, we were real glad.'

Rosa pondered a minute. 'And yet, at Cheltenham she was glad of the things from the Folletts when their girl died, and she had some beautiful clothes. Perhaps it was a bit different, because the girl died and they couldn't use the clothes again.

Mum always made our clothes when we were children. I don't remember her ever buying anything. She was clever, and she could use both hands equally well. When cutting out a dress pattern, she'd just switch to the other hand to cut around a corner. Dad would stand with his back to the fire sometimes. I can still smell his scorching pants. Mum would mend them. Her mending was almost invisible.

Yes, all our pots were heavy black cast iron, and also the irons for pressing the clothes. We'd put them in front of the fire to heat, as there would be too many pots on the stove. We'd put a blanket and sheet over the kitchen table and iron on that. Clean the bottom of the iron with a little bee's wax. If we didn't have that, oil or fat. We'd rub it on then scrub it off. We did have at one stage an iron you put coals in. Mum gave it to Auntie Elsie because she was doing knitting to earn some money and had no iron. Mum used to think of people like that, she'd go without so other people could have it. She thought Auntie Elsie needed it more than her.

Everybody including the girls had to wear grey woollen flannel singlets with short sleeves, about three buttons in the front. Mum made them. You always had two. We always had to wear them,' Rosa emphasised.

'Worn under our other clothes next to the skin. Was the correct thing to do. Oh we couldn't wait... Oh my goodness! We all thought we can't grow up fast enough to stop wearing those flannel shirts. But we didn't say that in front of Mum. But I thought it. Saved us getting colds all the same. We really needed them because it was cold weather.

It was a great help when Mum got the tender for the mail run. A lot of people would have liked this job. The person who offered the lowest quote got it. Applications were through the post office. Mum had it for years. It was hard in winter; you had to always be there. No excuse. One day it snowed a lot. We didn't think we could get the jinker going, so George went on the horse. When I was at home I used to go for the mail in the horse and jinker. Mum did it mostly and I think she enjoyed it. It was an outing for her. We were paid ten bob a month.

The mail came in on the train to the post office at Trentham. You would have to leave Little Hampton about nine into Trentham and give the mail in before ten, then wait for the incoming mail to be sorted and bring the bag to Little Hampton Post Office. Sometimes it wouldn't be sorted until after eleven. It took half a day. This was three times a week on Mondays, Wednesdays and Fridays. People would also send notes up asking Mum to buy them a pound of tea and so on, and she would be quite busy. She would never charge for doing these things.

Rosa's body suddenly seemed at odds with her tranquillity. She shrank, her lean frame hunched over, face contracted. A gauntness. 'Even some days now, when I'm in the car and it's raining, I remember about the jinker. Being in the cold. There was no cover. The Trentham grocer said one day, 'My, it must have been a cold ride today. I can see you wiping the dewdrops on your nose.'

I remember putting a heated stone on the floor of the jinker one cold day. Covered it with the horse chaff. I put my feet on it on the way to get the mail. When I got to Trentham, suddenly the stone fell out! It had been too hot, burnt a hole in the boards. I had the cart tied, brought out the mail. Must have just smouldered and dropped.'

The needle cold of night came to mind. Trying to gain comfort. Chilblained feet in a cold bed. No luxury of fleecy covered rubber hot water bags in those days. Rosa tackled this topic with her usual enthusiasm.

'We'd grab every glass bottle we could find, and we'd use, not bricks, we couldn't find bricks, big stones. We'd put them at the fire edge to heat up. Big ones, because they keep warm a lot longer. We'd put around the bottles and stones any old rags we could find. Even a bit of paper, but it wasn't that plentiful.'

'When we were kids, you used a lemonade bottle in a sock.' I remembered.

'We did use socks for bottles. We didn't put the water in too hot because we knew it would break. Sometimes we'd put it in hot and tip it out and then put the hotter water in. We never threw the water out, we always saved it for something. You'd do something with the water, you wouldn't waste it.'

The depression was difficult for many, and the Brutons were no exception. Already rendered vulnerable by their move from Cheltenham, they worked hard for meagre return.

'When I worked away, I sent home all the money I could, never felt I could afford anything. The younger ones seemed to afford things I couldn't. We'd have starved if it had not been for the garden! The only clothes we got were given, and I used to alter them so that they fitted nicely.' Rosa was quiet for a moment. Her eyes flashed. 'But there were a lot worse off than us! They used to camp in tents and you used to see where they had grubbed out our potatoes. Dad would say, 'Poor things, they probably don't have much to eat.' He never went crook about it. He was never mean with anything he had. When people came and asked Mum for something to eat, she never refused. She said, 'That could be my boy.'

For that matter, Mum was always helpful to people. Do all sorts of nice things for people that we did not know about. We used to take dinners to Miss Pruitt at Taradale because she couldn't cook for herself. Mum would put out an extra plate and say, 'Come on you kids and take it to Miss Pruitt.' She saved up a lot of tiger lily bulbs and gave them to the man down the road later on when she lived at Avonsleigh, so he could sell them because he was out of work. It was when she was older, in her eighties, and when she had a little money to buy bulbs herself. Never made any song and dance about it. Then she would send spuds and so on to Trentham to Mrs Hunt. Take them in the jinker for her because she was hard up.

There were so many people, so poor. Even Dunkling the diamond people were poor, there were some of them wandering around. All sorts of people. You couldn't get the pension as you do now! People died with hunger. The Dunkling's man lived in a tent. A brother from the jeweller family, he existed by fixing peoples' clocks.'

Rosa was animated, 'However bad you were off, there were others worse! A man with a young wife pregnant. He was told to go away from home and work under the sustenance scheme. He tried to get odd jobs, but in the end, he had to leave to look for work. His wife was ailing, had the baby, and went mad. They had her in an asylum and he had to look after the baby. I left the Sallmanns to honour a promise to Ada Holt, Ted Shelden's sister, to look after her kids while she went to hospital. They only paid me ten bob. They knew my previous wage. I had to leave the Sallmanns job, I couldn't get it back. After Min and I were married, the Sallmanns wanted Bess to work for them because Min and I had worked so hard. We told Mum not to send her. She was slow, and we didn't think she could manage to get through so much work. Now I think perhaps it might have been better if she had.

One day during the depression Mum was in bed. She'd had the baby, and I had to put hot poultices on her breasts to help her. A man came to the door and asked if he could mend something. I said, 'Mum is sick. I am looking after her, I don't have anything to mend. Dad is in the back paddock, but I can give you something to eat.' When I turned round, I saw his foot was in the door! I was really scared. Then Dad just happened to come in that moment! The man never, ever came back.

The text hanging in our bedroom was always a comfort to me. If I was scared, I would repeat it. 'Whenever I am afraid, I will trust in Thee.' Every two or three days in the depression someone would come. Whatever we had, we gave them. If Dad was not home, Mum would not ask them in. When Dad was home, he would frequently ask them, and they would come and have dinner with us. Then sometimes he'd sit at the fire with them and have a chat. These swaggies, a lot of them, were very good people.'

Rosa looked down, then up, eyes and voice definite. 'Bess said she was ashamed we were poor'. Now her voice lifted, almost sang, 'I was proud of how we managed!'

Water! There was the well at Little Hampton, and I remember the creak of the windmill as it drew water. However, in those early days there was no windmill. The deep, cold waters of the well had to be drawn up with a bucket on a chain.

Rosa explained. 'You'd have to put your hand on the swivel as it unwinds, otherwise it would go too fast and the bucket would bump on to the sides of the well and knock dirt in, and the bucket would only fall on its side. If you went slow, then it would go straight into the clean water. The well was thirty feet deep. The water down below was from a spring. It never went dry. Beautiful water. The well had a high bucket which held quite a lot of water, more than two ordinary buckets full. Mum said, 'I'm not ever going to touch that; other people can do the winding up. Once I start doing that, I'll be expected to keep it up.'

It was hard work. I used to get both hands on it and pull hard. Dad and Tom and Robert, I remember, used to do quite a bit of winding. There were no taps. We'd put the water in kero tins mostly, not make them too full as they had to be carried inside. We always carried them inside for our washing. The washing was put on the kitchen stove in a kero tin on its side. We always seemed to be washing. The tin would only take one big sheet or two small ones at a time. We carried all the water in, and we carried it out too. Did for years. My word, those kerosene tins were handy. We used them for the washing for a long time.

That well was very handy to set jellies in the summer. We'd just put the jelly in the bucket and lower it down. Dad tried to dig a cellar not far from the well, but it started to cave in. We used it to a certain extent, but we'd hoped to put milk and cream in it.'

Those intrepid kero tins! Very important equipment in those days. I recollected as a little girl, Olive asking me to go into the small back room where the plaits of garlic were hanging, and ladle some honey from a kerosene tin. This was put into a pretty floral honey container for the table. I reminded Rosa of this. 'Another use for a kerosene tin.' I said.

'Yes. We had honey. We used to eat a lot of it. Mum captured two or three hives. She put them in apple boxes. They didn't have specially made frames for their comb; the bees just made their own. She had learnt about bees from her father. He had them all through her growing up years. She reckoned she used to look after them and help him.'

It was only in the last few years that there was no bee keeping in our family. Rosa herself had kept them, and I had inherited them.

Rosa was now contemplating the bees. 'There are no bees around here! My tomatoes didn't come on properly, nor the nectarine. I want to get a hive and put in the garden in the corner.'

She returned to that heterogeneous helper. 'We used those kerosene tins for lots of things. They were cut in half and a handle was put on them. We cut across, and a handle put on the corners, and you had two dust pans to sweep your dirt into. People even flattened them out for roofs, or walls.

Before we got the washhouse, I used to bath the kids in the kitchen. The kerosene tins lying on their sides, with the top side cut out, were boiled up on the stove. We had a tin bath which I carried in for them. Usually it was by candlelight.

Tom built the washhouse out of reject wood. Mum told him how to construct it. She knew more about that sort of thing than Dad did. When she was growing up, she made a shade house at Chesterville Road. Made a sort of verandah at the side of the house and planted a grapevine. Mum told me that one day when the butcher or baker was calling, they heard the cart, but couldn't understand why he was taking so long to come to the door. He was having a feed of grapes! My word, we missed those grapes when we moved from Cheltenham.

Eventually, when we had a washhouse, we had a tap with water, troughs, a wringer you'd wind, and a washing board to rub against. Especially with the boys' trousers. Washing day was a full day's work. When Mum wasn't at home, I had to do the washing. Mum did it other times, because she said, 'It's hard for the girls to do.' She was very considerate and helpful. When I did it, Min would be doing the housework. Making beds in those days—you really had to make the bed every day. You had to fluff up the kapok, otherwise there would be lumps. Double beds weren't big like now. They used to be more three-quarter beds. We used to sleep three kids together in one.

Mum saved everything she could. Everything! She said, 'You never know when you might want it.' She saved the fine wire you used to get threaded around kerosene boxes, or the string if there was no wire.'

It seemed that the Brutons were creative with their limited resources.

Rosa's voice was heavy with feeling, 'And Dad had a bad time too looking back. He was the bread winner, and he did his best. He'd send stuff to Bendigo and sometimes he'd get a bill for cartage because the produce didn't sell. It was very hard for him. He'd work very hard.'

Cheltenham

Another day. Another cup of tea. The peace punctuated by a cockatoo's sudden shriek. 'They eat my walnuts.' exclaimed Rosa. Sometimes the resonant trumpeting of the 'Puffing Billy' could be heard from over the ridge. This was a narrow-gauge steam train which huffed, puffed its way over bridges spanning the lacy delicacy of verdant fern gullies. It stopped at Emerald on its way to Gembrook via the popular tourist attraction of the Emerald Lake.

Seated on her comfortable biscuit coloured chair, Rosa rested her left hand on the worn woollen arm. She reached for her crochet hook among a pile of woollen balls of various hues and sizes. She had been ploughing through this mountain, vibrant against the emerald green carpet, with her usual resoluteness. The night before had been a late one. She had crocheted well past her bedtime.

'But I wanted to finish it. It's nice and warm. It will go over a single bed.'

Now she was standing. 'Come, I'll show you.' She crinkled her big dark eyes up small. 'Hope Claire likes the colours; hope they are alright.'

The blanket had magically evolved from her busy crochet hook, soft stripes with purple. The previous one had been bright and bold, with gold and orange salubriously contrasted with black. I had been the happy recipient of that.

Today, as Rosa's nimble hands crocheted warm pink along with purple, her favourite colours, we returned to the beginning. The very beginning. To Cheltenham. Rosa's eyes shone, her voice light and happy. We were talking of sunnier, happier times.

'We used to enjoy Dad's coming home from market. You'd hear the crunch of the wheels on the gravel, the roads were gravel mostly. The bigger roads had gravel, otherwise they were dirt. The road into the house was dirt. We'd hear the crunch of the wheels and the clip clop of the horse. There was a little seat on the lorry and I think a little canopy over it made of canvas. Dad would often come back with horse manure, but when the lorry was clean and he didn't have manure on board, he used to stop and pick us up. As soon as we learnt to walk, we'd run out, and we'd be looking to see what he had brought home! Sometimes he'd bring big bunches of bananas and pineapples, all kinds of vegetables we didn't grow. He always liked to try something if it was different. We used to love the grapes too. Dad was late one time, and we walked all the way to Moorabbin to meet him. He didn't come home until late that day, because he had a bad sale. We didn't tell Mum when we went. She was real upset; she didn't know where we'd gone.

Dad would leave well after we were asleep, about midnight. The lorry would be piled high with rows upon rows of vegetables; each row was of the same vegetable. If he sold well, he would arrive home early in the afternoon of the next day. One day when Dad came home from market, he raced in to say hello to Mum. Min and I clambered up on to the lorry, because he used to bring things home for us, and the horse moved. We were halfway up or down and she fell and so did I. Min hurt her hip or something. She was sick in bed for a long while. We didn't get into trouble, we were too upset. They sent away to a missionary up the road who was at home, to see if she would bandage and help. They got the doctor to Min. I hurt my leg too, but no one would believe me, not even the doctor. I had a lump on it for years. At that stage we were living at Point Nepean Road in the house on the property Dad was renting.

I loved going with Dad to church. The others didn't want to go. There used to be missions, preachers from America. Dad used to like going, and so did I. I was only about ten or so.

Rosa was thinking. Now she smiled, another recollection.

'One day when I went to get the milk, I was only a little kid too. It was the dairy farm, almost opposite where we lived in Chesterville Road. I'd cut across the paddock. The dairy workers were waving their arms. I looked round and wondered what was going on. There was a big red bull after me! I put Daisy under one arm, and the bucket of milk in the other and raced across as hard as I could. I got through the fence alright and didn't spill the milk!

Wherever I went, getting milk or whatever, I took Daise. But after Bess was born, I may have given her more preference because she was the baby. Poor Daise had a hard time. She caught measles when she was two weeks old, then got chicken pox.'

'Did you have any dolls?'

'I had a doll, small china doll. I'd dress my doll up, loved it. I'm pretty sure Min would have had one because they'd do the same for her as for me. But when I was about four or five, I'd play with Auntie Eva's doll. It was as big as a baby. I particularly liked that one. I was heartbroken when I discovered the doll had gone and Auntie Eva had given it away to our cousin Eva Clayton.'

'And who encouraged you?'

'Mum did a bit, I think. I'd ask Mum all sorts of questions and she'd always answer them. We shared a lot. When I was growing up, she was the main encourager. 'Well, you try,' she'd say. She'd never forbid things we would have liked. She'd say, if I asked, 'Should I do this?' 'You do what you think is right, you've got enough sense to know.' I don't remember her saying no. I don't remember her criticising, going crook about anything. She was a wonderful mother, really. If I made something, she'd admire it.'

Rosa looked down at the mat in front of the gas fire, her expression rueful, 'I used to wish I was pretty. 'Am I?' I said to Mum. She said, 'Never mind! You are in your heart.'

My plea, 'But Audrey told me you were beautiful!' fell on deaf ears.

Enjoyable Times

'We used to have a fire on the sand at Rickett's Point, near Mentone. Dad would swim off a long way out somewhere, with a bag on his shoulder, and come back with big periwinkles and mussels.' Rosa indicated a large, rounded space between her thumb and mid finger. 'That big! Bigger than we gathered off the rocks on the beach.' I said to Dad once. 'Did you ever see a shark?' He said, 'Yes I did, and I never swam so hard in all my life as I did that day.' Mum always took a ready supply of pins to wiggle the periwinkles out, and matches and something to boil them in. Wonder she wasn't frightened we'd swallow them, but no one ever did, anyway.'

My memory flipped back. Rosa used to take us three kids to our great grandparent's Mentone market garden and the Mentone beach. We'd swim, collect big green snail shaped periwinkles, and return with red lobster faces. One day Rosa nearly fainted with sunburn. We too, like the Bruton kids, wiggled the worm-like shapes from their protective shells with pins. One day Auntie Elsie kindly fried a small bird egg I'd found in Booker's paddock, nearby. I remember picking a bunch of flowers for her from the beautiful bounty of gums and wildflowers. And I discovered subsequently that Rosa had picked flowers for her grandmother from the very same paddock.

'Remember you told me once how Allan collected some sand from Mentone beach?'

Rosa laughed. 'He loved it so much that he took some sand home in a matchbox. He was so much younger than us, only about two when we left there, and probably in the Children's Hospital at that stage. He thought he'd take some for the younger ones to show them what sand looked like. We all loved the beach. I remember the fun we had there.'

Rosa had put down her crochet. Now in the kitchen, she filled the kettle with water. For the inevitable. Through the open sliding doors, I noticed the pumpkins I'd brought on the bench.

'Those pumpkins. Might be hard to cut,' I said.

'It doesn't matter. If I can't cut with the knife, I'll put them down. Use me axe!'

Suddenly there seemed to be an eye blink of a movement in front of the bookcase. Like a small brown leaf flying in the wind. Had I imagined it, I asked Rosa. 'Don't worry about those!' she said as she carried in two cups of tea. 'They're two little birds that fly in, they have a look, and they know their way out.'

As we sipped Rosa's favourite beverage, I mused that we were never short of a subject to discuss. Now though, it seemed important to usher her back to these halcyon days on the coast.

'You were born there.' I announced.

'Initially we lived in Patty Street, Mentone. That's where Min, I, and I think Robert was born. A nice new house. Later we lived in Nepean Highway. Mum used to have a lady come to do the washing. Mrs Morris. She was a lot better off then. Dad grew vegetables in Point Nepean Road. He rented it and he bought an acre over the road from Grandma Bruton's next to the railway line. He grew vegetables there. We moved from our rented house in Point Nepean Road to Grandma and Grandpa Bluhm's property, after Grandpa Bluhm died. The house was old, pretty, on the corner of Bernard Street and Chesterville Road. Grandma Bluhm had gone to live with Uncle Will on his orchard at Mahoney's Road East Burwood. Mum grew up in this house at Chesterville Road. I think we left Point Nepean Road when I was about six.

Oh, this old fellow. He lived at the asylum, now called Kingston Centre, for the elderly. People would go to Kingston from the station in the cab. Horse drawn. The people in the cab would call out 'Whip behind!' but he didn't always do it. We'd have a free ride to Bernard Street from the station sometimes. Cars were a real novelty in those days. Be five or six years during the First World War.

Anyway, there was an old man used to come to Mum's. She always gave him something to eat, he'd come there drunk and go to the kitchen and smell 'That's nice.' Oh Jack Green. And Dad got absolutely fed up. He was always poking around. One night he put him outside two or three times to go home and he still didn't go. So Dad stood out on the verandah. He never even had a stick. And he called out, 'Jack Green. You come inside this gate and I'll shoot yer!''

Rosa was laughing, her eyes dancing. 'He never came again! He went away muttering, 'What a shame. Didn't think he would. Good man too.'

At Point Nepean Road, the Folletts were our neighbours. They were a very nice family. I think it was their daughter who died, and they gave Mum some of her clothes and Mum cut them down for us. And I had a beautiful ruby coloured silk dress! Best dress I ever had. And a full skirt. We went to school in Cheltenham with the two youngest Folletts. There was a boy, and Lucy was the youngest one. They were older than us. Was about half an hour with a few shortcuts to get there. I used to try and dodge Lucy, because she wanted to walk to school briskly, and I wanted to look at the flowers.

But I did love that silk dress. Mum made it beautifully. I felt very good in that. I remember when we lived in Chesterfield Road, we always dressed up in our very best for Sunday school anniversaries at the Cheltenham Church of Christ. But one day as Little Doll was getting out the gate with the jinker, we got tipped out, all in the mud, our nice dresses were spoilt, my one had a lovely big sash on it. I was so proud of this. Auntie Elsie Bruton made it for me. Blue sash! She used to do a lot of things for us.

At the church I had Mrs Judd for my Sunday schoolteacher. She was the loveliest teacher we ever had. I remember Daisy Tuck used to go. She showed me how to play 'callings!' The names of the others I don't remember. After the service Mr Robert Tuck, a lovely old fellow, used to hand out a little text each at the door.

Sunday school picnics to Mordialloc Beach were fun! We'd have lolly scrambles. They'd throw lollies, and you'd have to pick them up. When we first got there, we'd be given a round bread bun, raisins and currants in it. We'd all sit down in a circle on the grass for lunch, have sandwiches, cakes. Games were hopscotch, hopping races, ordinary races, Siamese races—two tied together, all sorts. All got prizes. The Sunday school superintendent and teachers all went. We looked forward to it from one year to another.

Transport to the picnics? People came with their lorries, we sat on them. Pulled by one horse, usually. I didn't go to market gardener picnics, but Mum and Dad used to go before they married.

Before we moved, Dad used to take us on the Sunday school picnics and that. He'd look after us. We couldn't get anything out of Mum, but we could wiggle Dad into giving us threepence or something. We always could if he had the money. Often when we were going somewhere, we'd count the white horses, and who counted the most won. Mum didn't have time to go to many of the picnics because she was usually nursing a baby.'

'Remember any fun times with your mother?'

'She was always busy.'

Cheltenham School

'I started school when I was five. I used to enjoy going to Cheltenham Primary School, in Charman road. There was a big block at the back with tea-trees on it and beautiful flowers there. We were allowed to pick the flowers. There were little bushes with white flowers that had honey in the flowers and we would just drink it. We used to get these along Chesterville Road too, small white flowers. We used to call them honey pots. At the school they had an old wash house. We used to pick all the flowers we wanted, then we would put them in a couple of troughs in this old room. Each one would know their own flowers. The teachers would tell us, 'You can go and pick the white flowers.' They'd blow the whistle when it was time to come back.

Also, there were a lot of pine trees along both sides of the school. They were real big, and they used to drop a lot of pine needles. Some of us would make playhouses, and if anyone touched our playhouse, there would be quite a to-do. Three or four would have the same playhouse, and there would be about five playhouses there at a time.

At school we all had to learn poetry and Min and I both used to learn it a lot. I don't know why they don't teach it now, because it teaches people rhyme, doesn't it? There were two classes in the same room. I would learn the poetry from the other class too. I could repeat it as easy as anything. We also used to do a lot of singing at school. A song I liked was 'John John the Grey Goose has Gone and the Fox is off to his Den O.' Also one called 'Old Mother Slipper Slopper'.

My favourite subject was geography. I loved learning about other places. I used to like the teachers, felt sorry for one, Miss Squires. I didn't like her because she came down and slapped my arm so hard, it was terribly sore for a long while. So of course, I disliked her. A girl had banged me on the back to draw my attention, she wanted my ruler. But later on, Miss Squires seemed to be a great favourite, so she must have got over that bit. She probably was a very good teacher, but I didn't go for her because of that. I was about nine.

In class we used to have to paint wildflowers and sometimes geraniums. We used crayons.

You know that school photo somewhere? Wilma Woff with the long hair, is in it. In my class. Oh, she had beautiful hair! I'm the one with pigtails. Tilleys and Stayners went to the school, I remember. Also, a couple of Marriott girls. They were older and lovely. The kids from the local children's home used to come too. Later on, I think they had teachers at the home. I think it was wrong. Should have all been treated the same, at the same school.

I remember George was a very little boy, and he had messed his pants at school. And I had to clean him up and take him home. Auntie Rose Daff loved George as a baby. She looked after Robert and George when Stan was born. They fell in love with George, and that's how their son got his name.

Rosa laughed. 'Oh, we used to tease the kids whose parents, the Gleesons, were the gatekeepers at the Latrobe Street Railway Crossing at Mentone. We'd climb the mulberry tree in Grandma's and yell over their fence. 'Catholic dogs jump like frogs.' And the others would yell back, 'Protestant dogs,' etcetera. But one of them was a bit older than us, he came to teach our class as a student teacher. He didn't like us and he kept me down. This was after Min and I both caught diphtheria and were sent to Fairfield Infectious Diseases Hospital for about a month.

There was no canteen, but the shop across the road sold a lot of things. We used to love having threepence to buy our lunch. The pies cost two pence, and we had one penny left to buy broken biscuits with. They'd put them in newspaper screwed in the shape of a cone. Same with lollies.

On the way to school in Chesterville Road, I remember we used to pass an apricot tree hanging over a fence near Jellicoe Street. Oh my. We used to have a good feed. There was an orange orchard just over where Southland is now. We never pinched the oranges. But someone else had. We found a big packet left near the fence, and we had a lovely feed.

People who lived opposite our place had a dairy farm. Chesterville Road. They had two adopted children, Mervin and Gladys. Oh dear. They did get Tom and Min into some mishaps and mischief!

Also not far from our house in Chesterville Road was Mr Tuck's. There were two huge dams there. We were always told not to go near them because we'd be drowned!

We used to play with our cousins, the two Clayton families in Wickham Road. Auntie Bess and Auntie Ethel both married two Clayton brothers, Sam and George. Ellis was just little; she was Auntie Bess's daughter. Auntie Ethel's kids, Pearson, was a lovely boy, and so was Mavis. We'd play together with them, Min and I, and Tom and Bob. They had a big, fixed wheel, flat, a foot or two above the ground for us kids to play on. We really enjoyed it. We'd just walk across the paddocks to their place. I took lots of photos, gave them to them and the negatives. All gone now. Wish I hadn't given them all away.

The Teagles lived the other side of the line. 'Wakool' was the name of their market garden. They were Elizabeth's, Grandma's people. There was a daughter, Nora Teagle, two or three years older than me. She had a playhouse in the trees where the branches came down to the ground, and I loved playing there with her.

Hawkers? Yes, they came quite frequently, selling mainly clothing and household linen. I remember gypsies in brightly coloured clothes calling too, with clothes pegs they had made. One day a gypsy came to the front door. Mum answered and Min and I, we were quite little, were hanging on her skirts one each side, peering. Mum told me when I was older that the gypsy had pointed to us two and said, 'One of them has more spirituality in her little finger than the other in her whole body.' Mum said she couldn't remember which. I think she was glad not to remember.'

'What do you make of it?'

'I don't make anything of it. You can't depend on gypsies!'

Extended Family

'When we were quite little, Min and I used to enjoy going to see Auntie Ruby. She was quite young. Her name was Ruby Anderson before she married Uncle Will Bluhm. We used to have picnics at her place in Chesterville Road. She died when her baby was born. She was a very lovely person. She gave Min a very pretty teapot, I forget what she gave me, but Min treasured it. I think she still has it. No. I don't recall anything about her funeral. Certainly, children never went to funerals in those days, and very often the women did not attend either. Auntie Ruby, Uncle Will's first wife, was the sister of Everest Le Page's wife; they lived on their market garden up the road from us. We have another connection too, with the Le Page's. Mum's mother Harriett Moore was the only child of Betsy Susan Le Page.

The Tucks also lived along Chesterville Road. Mr Robert Tuck and his wife were good friends with the Bluhm family, and when Mum got married in 1910, they gave her a dining room sideboard.'

At this point, I made a mental note to record Rosa's information concerning that graceful piece of pine furniture, stained dark. This was the sideboard which I had recently rather expensively restored. Originally in the old Bruton farmhouse, its three bevelled mirrors used to reflect the firelights dance.

'The Plumridges were other neighbours, not far from Grandma Bluhm in Chesterville Road. But I especially remember Auntie Eva Bruton, always bright and happy. She had a nurse of you when you were a baby. She said, 'I'll never be able to have a little girl like this.' She had creeping paralysis. Grandma looked after her till she died, and goodness! She was busy enough on the farm.

Grandpa Bruton and the boys used to take the lorries down to the Mentone Beach and fill them with seaweed to fertilise the gardens. Grandma had a bathing box on the beach, I think Uncle Albert built it. She always kept the key. We all used to enjoy going down there. We all loved the water, and the Brutons seemed to be pretty strong swimmers. I remember Auntie Elsie used to swim a mile or so out into the bay. One day she said she got cramp, and that seemed to cure her of going out as far again. The boys, my Uncle Albert and Joe and I think Dad used to climb the lamp posts at the end of the Mentone pier and dive from them.'

Olive, Rosa's mother, was the seamstress of the Bluhm family, her mother Harriet did not sew.

'Grandma Bluhm looked just like Daise. Grandpa Bernard Bluhm had been a seaman. He sailed on sailing ships, grew up in Germany near the Black Forest area. Anyway, he decided he would leave the ship in Australia and that's how he came to be here. He married Grandma Harriet, the only child of Betsy Susan, and Thomas Moore. He was a ticket-of-leave man. All our other relatives were free settlers.

Mum's father used to keep his sewing bag on a hook behind the door. He gave Mum her first sewing machine. It was the first of that type that was made. He paid a lot for it because it was the first model. He was very proud of Mum. He told my father, 'You have the best one of all my children!' That treadle Singer sewing machine. Carefully treasured by my grandmother and by my mother, and in perfect condition even ten years ago. Carved drawer doors on the front, the receipt for that machine had been kept perfectly preserved and in one of those drawers for nearly a century. The date I recall was 1900. Olive would have been aged sixteen. The receipt is now missing, and I have no recollection of the amount Olive's father would have paid for it.'

Rosa was continuing, 'Mum told me once there were some bush rangers in Cheltenham and they held up her family, either her mother or grandmother. Tied all the men to trees. And the women too, except for one, who they told to get them a meal. They stole everything Mum said, even their little stove, which I think was probably a sort of iron pot which goes over the fire. And when one of them cried and said, 'You've taken our stove and what will we do!' He gave it back to her. Might have been 'Black Beard.' I don't remember.

Almost opposite Mr Tuck's house were a lot of wildflowers on scrubby land. Little bells full of honey, green, you could see almost through them. We used to pick and eat them. I have never seen them since. There was that little white flower you could eat too. There was heath, a cream colour, little orchids and various other orchids, bushes with white flowers called 'wedding bush' I think. Beautiful flowers. We used to wander around and pick them. There used to be a lot of wildflowers alongside the railway too. When we walked to Grandma Bruton's house in Latrobe Street, we'd walk through the paddocks, take her a bunch. The Booker's paddock next to theirs had a lot of wildflowers too.

We used to love going there to Grandma's. She was always so lovely to us. She never, ever grumbled at us, and there was always a lolly too. I was expecting Keith when she died. They didn't tell me because they thought it would upset me. Told me after he was born. I was about seven months pregnant. They said she was lying in bed and a neighbour was visiting her and Grandma said, 'Why are you crying? We all have to die! It's time for me to go.' She was eighty-six years old. Everybody loved her. Everybody.

Grandpa William Bruton died before Grandma. He was a very clever man. He used to sing and make up poems about us. 'Rosie rode the roan cow around the rascal's hall,' and then he'd make up that I'd been tipped off and so on. Minnie was like Mrs Judd, he said, because she talked all the time. He never used to talk a lot, just a nice person. He used to have oatmeal porridge and mix dark treacle with it. He played the violin, and we always knew how he was feeling by the way he played. He taught two of his children to play it. Auntie Ethel and Auntie Eva. They used to play in concerts. He loved horses and was known as a very good horse doctor. He treated them with homoeopathic medicines. He was also known for his good asparagus. When he was old and almost blind, he dictated a book to Auntie Eva. I think this was the first time a history of the area had been written.'

'And your birthday 13th of July, same date as his.' I contributed.

It was now over twenty years since I had found this small, dog-eared book in the bottom of a dented tin trunk at my parental home. These were William's recollections put together in the 1920s before his death in 1930. A man of many facets, musical, jocular and charismatic. He learned through correspondence to become a veterinary surgeon. He also treated people during an epidemic of measles with homoeopathic medicine. His large box of Martin and Pleasance homoeopathic medicines was familiar to many of William's grandchildren. On this box was an inscription by the people who had collectively bought the box and presented it to him as a gift, 'of gratitude for services, often rendered free.'

'He was a very clever man,' repeated Rosa. 'The people around the district were sick with measles and other illnesses, and there was no medical doctor in the district to look after them. He did it for nothing. Auntie Elsie told me the people he treated said he saved their lives.'

He also played many a merry tune at the Royal Oak, a short walk from their property, having developed a taste for a drink or two in later life. Rosa said on his return he would sit in the front room, and Grandma would shut the door, ensuring in those times that the grandchildren and he did not mix. 'Grandma must have adored Grandpa. I never heard her say one thing against him. Ever!' said Rosa.

'When he became old and blind, coming home from the hotel, apparently, he would go on hands and knees to get over the small land bridge which crossed the deep drain, along the side of the road past his property. On this day someone's pet kangaroo came up to him and put his paws on his shoulders. Grandpa got a real fright!'

Mum told me Grandma had remarked, in the early days when Grandma was a girl, she would run out to the front of their Teagle property when the milkman came, leading his cow. He would milk straight into her jug. She also remembered the Aboriginals—there were a lot of them, she said. She and the other children wanted to play with them, but the parents would not allow it. Grandma came out from England, age two.

One day when Grandma was becoming older, she said, 'Rosa, you peep out of the window and be very quiet.' She went out and sat quietly, and a lizard came out. A blue tongue. She then stroked it with her stick. It was a real friend of hers. She liked to make friends with everything, even a mouse,' said Rosa. She looked at me intently and added unexpectedly, 'Like you.'

All my Bruton aunts and uncles had nicknames. 'Uncle Turk was always referred to as Turk, I never knew his real name was Reuben until I grew up. When he was a toddler, Reuben liked playing with the turks or pumpkins. They were like his dolls, and he would race everywhere with them on a string saying, 'Come on my turkey, come on!''

The genesis of nicknames always intrigued me, but Rosa had no other explanations for the various titles bestowed on each one. 'Auntie Elsie was called Wigbert or Wig. Uncle Joe, his real name was Joseph. He was called Snake's Head sometimes by Ted.'

'What a name.' I said. 'Doesn't sound as though he trusted him!'

I remember Uncle Joe from my early childhood. A smooth voiced charmer, he took me to a local carnival when I was about four. Bright lights. Excitement. If you could throw a penny on top of a fixed coin, you would win it. The merry-go-round. The magic! But as I was enjoying this wonderful time, consternation apparently reigned in my absence. Uncle Joe had whisked me off without Rosa's knowledge.

After grandmother Elizabeth's death, the property was sold. Ted, Joe and Elsie moved to Joe's property at Heatherton. Elsie kept house for the two men who worked the property. When Joe died, Elsie found his will. She decided to hand it in. He'd left all to the Institute of the Blind.

'They took everything. Even took Ted's things. And his horse! Uncle Ted was heartbroken,' exclaimed Rosa. 'They had to find a place to live. Auntie Elsie found the will in the house. She shouldn't have taken it to the jolly solicitor. I wouldn't have! She should have just kept quiet!' She added passionately.

I tried to maintain a focus; it was nicknames we were talking about. I didn't feel comfortable discussing another injustice. There had been too many.

Rosa listed the nicknames of her other eight Bruton aunts and uncles.

'Dad, Thomas Henry was known as Harry, but he was called 'Boy' when he was younger, and then later on 'Tar Face!' Uncle Ted was 'Chook,' Eva was 'Puss,' 'Biddy' was Auntie Ethel's nickname, 'Besbert' Auntie Bess's. Uncle Albert called himself 'George' because he didn't have a nickname and he wanted one. Rose who married Moss Daff was known as 'Sis.' But I never heard Grandma called any nickname. Grandpa used to call her, 'My dear Mrs Bruton!'

Taradale. Tom

Rosa's eyes flamed fire. 'I hated the school at Taradale. Hated it! The chap, Mr McMillan. He was the headmaster. Yes. And he was examining us. 'You go back and write properly.' I tried the best I could, and I kept taking it to him. It was dinner time, and I was supposed to have gone home to dinner. And I'd keep writing and writing. And anyway, I thought 'Blow him!' And I just scrawled it. And blow me down if he didn't pass me!' Rosa was laughing. 'I suppose he was sick of it too.

There was a lady teacher who taught sewing. The only teacher not hard on me. She praised me. I just adored her. She encouraged me to put a petticoat in the Bendigo Show. It was white linen with a flounce and embroidery around it. Best petticoat I've ever had. Won a First for it. Then the next year, she said to put my doily in. Got a First for that too. It was round with cut-out flowers and edged with embroidery, all pale. Oh, Mum showed me how to dress up small celluloid dolls and make into pin cushions, I'd send them to Grandma and Auntie Eva. My mother was very, very clever, she could do all sorts of things. Showed me a lot. Later on, I'd buy the little china ladies and men dolls to decorate the centres of pin cushions. You'd buy these figurines anywhere they sold gifts. Mostly I'd buy them at Coles. Threepence or sixpence each. Sometimes I made an oval pin cushion and put a man and lady doll on top, which I dressed as a bride and groom.

When I was about twelve or thirteen Mum showed me how to knit stockings. I knitted most of the stockings Mum wore. Black wool, never any other colour. I was still doing them when I was married. No. Not exactly like socks. You knitted them wider.'

Rosa returned from this momentary diversion to the sad school saga.

'Oh, we were so unhappy at Taradale School. Min and I were, anyway. The kids teased us. We'd go to the toilet and lock the door. The school was on the right before you cross the creek. There would have been Tom, Min, Bob, Stan, George and me at the school. Allan was probably in the Children's Hospital, Daise was just little. Bernie was the baby. I was about eleven when we moved to this old gold mining town, about 1923. Tom, of course, was further north at the T.B. Sanitorium at Amhurst. Sent there when he was twelve. He was away for what seemed like many months, so long that he sort of got away from being with the family a bit.

Mum used to say he got T.B. because he wagged school and stayed out all night with one of the local boys. This boy wasn't a good influence on Tom. I think Mum thought, well at least moving from Cheltenham will get Tom away from that boy.

We usually came home from school at lunchtimes. We'd run a lot of the way. Tom, Min, Robert, George. If one came, we all did! Sometimes we took our dinner. We used to leave home with our shoes and socks on and hide them along the fence! Mum never knew. The Taradale kids were different. They didn't mind you going with no shoes.

Apart from school, we had great fun. The Hyde boys, their mother was the local midwife, knew how to pan for gold and I used to go and learn. Got a bit, some flecks of gold in a little bottle, don't know what happened to it. We'd all go for walks along the creek and all over the place and catch yabbies. We were real townies when we first went. Min and I saw a snake in the creek one day, we jumped out and ran hard to get home! Dad went down but couldn't get it. Taught ourselves to swim in the creek. Tom, Min and I did. We always swam in the nude. That is until we started getting breasts and then we'd have to wear something.'

'The cooking of the yabbies.' I asked.

Rosa suddenly threw her hands towards her ears. She looked in pain. Agitated, 'Don't ask me, I can't bear it!'

I decided I could not bear it either. The subject of catching them rather than the killing was safer for both of us. 'You'd grab them across the back. Have to be fast. There were none in the creek at Little Hampton. The water was colder there.' Rosa added, looking sad, 'And no sand either.

Grapes grew along the stone fence from the creek to the property. Beautiful black grapes, and we used to get all we wanted of them. And we had three apple trees, plums and almonds. The almond tree would be laden. It was beautiful. When we left there, we left an orchard.

There was the railway bridge, we'd play on that.'

That imposing expanse, seemingly reaching to the heavens. I'd seen this chiselled bluestone and iron five span bridge etched clearly against the sky, from the main road at Taradale. It had been built to bring goods to the goldfields more cheaply at the height of the gold rush in the early 1880s.

'Yes, it was very high,' agreed Rosa.

'The day Bessie was born, Dad came and found us there. I thought, now we'll be in for it. But we weren't. That was the day he told me to keep the kids down at the plum tree, and not to come till I call you. We found out later it was because Mum was having Bessie. The kids used to love climbing the plum tree, anyway. And we had Allan down the bottom and the horse bolted. Oh dear. Goodness. Thankfully, the horse skidded to a stop just before it got to Allan! Earlier, Tom had tried to get Bob to jump with an umbrella from that bridge! I was climbing up, and when I got there, Tom had almost persuaded Robert to jump. I said, 'No, he's not going to! You leave Robert alone. Good heavens, he'll kill himself!' Tom was always experimenting. He'd drop a cotton reel from the top of the tank stand, or the loft in the shed, to see how high it was. A cotton reel would never have measured the height of the bridge, though.

We used to love going up to that loft area. Dad would store straw, and things like that there. If we wanted to keep a secret from Mum, a present, we'd always hide it up there. I hid some oranges up there once—saving them for Mum's birthday. And Tom got to them and ate them! An orange was very special.

I remember when we went to the Taradale church, Auntie Elsie was staying with us, helping out with Allan. She told Dad, 'Instead of giving money to the church, you should think of your family more, put it towards the boys—training for something they want to do.' She turned to Robert, 'And here's a boy who should be going to college!' There was a big row. Dad said he didn't have enough money to train them. But I got into trouble. Us kids, Min, Robert and George went to the dairy, and I was churning the milk and telling them all about it. I was there taking Dad off, repeating what Auntie Elsie said, and what Dad said. I was waving my arms and turned round. And there's Dad behind me! I raced down to the creek and ran along it to the shopping centre. I was scared, he had such a temper, but I had to go home. He'd got over it by the time I went back.

Dad had water laid on at Taradale. There was a big tank, and water came alongside the road. It would flow by gravity into spouting from the gutter to the tank down the slope. You had to order so much from the water authority, and it would come along the gutter. And you had to have a block to stop it going any further than the gutter. And then it would go along the spouting, fill the tank up. And then he'd let the tank go and have it drain just down the hill. There was a water channel, water race, we called it. We'd swim in it and float down through a long tunnel. We wouldn't let George. We worried he couldn't swim well enough.'

'Harry's vegetables. Where did he sell them?' I asked.

'He used to take vegetables up to the Castlemaine Market from Taradale. Tommy and I used to too. Sometimes Kyneton, sometimes Castlemaine.'

Rosa now lifted her hands, about to recount a drama. 'I remember this day. Fruit, plums. Eggs, roosters, vegetables! We had all sorts of things Mum had saved up so we could get a few bob. What Mum thought people might buy. Dad was busy so Mum said Tom and I had to go, and we could please ourselves which market we went to, Castlemaine or Kyneton. They were about the same distance.

We had a bad accident on the bridge at Piper's Street on the way to the Kyneton Market. Balley Rogers. He came along on his horse from the opposite direction. Was drunk. He tried to get between us and the bridge. He had a horse, a bit savage, and it kicked our horse, Little Doll. She was a good little horse. He was a cruel man. We got tipped out; the jinker was broken. The roosters in the little crates were yelling, plums everywhere! Apples, vegies all tipped out over the ground. The trace broke around the horse's girdle. She was very upset, was running out of control. We were scared.'

Rosa raised her voice, her face and hands animated, reliving the distress. 'He rode off on his horse! He did it deliberately. Both the horses were frightened. We were so terrified we tried to get over the fence to a house. The sheep proof fence was difficult to get through, and we eventually made it to the door. The people took us in and gave us a drink of tea and milk and a biscuit. There was a court case over it. The police came. Dad said if he pays and repairs all damage he'd done, he'd let him off. He would have been put into prison. The police gave him a warning. He never paid a cent. It was a terrible job to repair the old jinker. All the produce gone!'

Rosa paused, eyes large. 'Dad just let him off! No. Dad wasn't cross with us; he knew it was an accident.'

Rosa's voice, excited, was in run-away mode as she revisited another trauma.

'And we were waiting at Kyneton station to go from the train and he came up on the horse. He kept edging the horse towards us too. I don't know what he had against us; we were only a couple of kids. Oh, we had to keep dodging.

A jinker? One long seat in the front, and like a little boot at the back, which was full. I was thinking of all the plums and everything and what will Dad say! And the poor jinker and... dreadful! We mostly used the jinker for transport. Didn't get the bigger cab till we moved to Little Hampton.'

Rosa and Tom also drove the jinker at other times too.

'A neighbour used to give us two bob for taking her to the station. The steam train took about two hours to get to Melbourne. Tommy and I used to run and see who could grab the horse first to harness it up.'

'What did you like doing the most at Taradale?' I wondered.

Rosa's answer was unequivocal. 'Swimming down the creek. I loved the house and the creek. A pretty creek, with trees along the sides. It had real sand we could walk on. Just like the beach. We loved swimming. I know all the Brutons loved swimming. The Bluhms didn't. Mum couldn't swim, never had time to learn, probably. Grandma Bluhm would just put her feet in the water at Mentone because it was 'good for my feet.' Her father was a seaman, but he wasn't able to swim either.'

I was reminded of Rosa teaching us to swim. And our friends. Cousins as well. Now in her early nineties she was still taking her swimming trunks on holidays, hopeful of a dip.

Rosa was looking serious. Staring into the distance. 'I remember when Grandma Bluhm died. Oh. She was visiting us at Taradale. She came up to see Bess the baby, two or three weeks old. Was in January. She'd come up in the train and we'd pick her up in the jinker. Caught pneumonia and died. Reckon she got it on the train. They couldn't pick up her body for a week to take her to the Cheltenham Cemetery. And she was in the house for about a week. Oh, the smell! Mum didn't know where to put us to sleep or anything. We slept in the honey room outside. A big room like a shed, all lined. Dreadful. Oh, it was dreadful!

I've never seen Mum so upset. Crumpled up, crying in the corner, when I came home from school. The doctor said Grandma would have to have some brandy. Dad wouldn't go because he said he didn't want to be seen at the hotel. Mum asked me if I'd go. And I got the brandy and took it home. And Grandma wouldn't have a sign of it.

'I'm not going to touch anything like that. I won't have it!' The doctor told Mum to give it to her and she wouldn't take it, she wouldn't swallow it.'

'That small chest of drawers I've seen in your bedroom all my life, miniature, about a foot high, in warm burgundy cedar. Where did that come from?' I asked.

'Oh! Old Mr Jackel at Taradale. He made it and gave it to me as a present because I helped my mother.'

Suddenly Rosa burst out, 'We thought we were going to be at Taradale forever.'

Little Hampton

Rosa's big eyes looked sad. 'Bernie was sick, and it seemed everything went wrong after we went to Little Hampton.

Dad brought us over there in a dray, not covered. We sat on top of the furniture, the draught horse pulling it. Then he went back to get Mum and the baby. The house was really old with hessian walls. Not nearly as nice as the houses we'd lived in. An old lady up there told us later she had known the house as a child. But my word, we were scared. It was getting dark, and we piled mattresses and all sort of things against the doors, until Dad came with Mum and the baby. Then we discovered there were fleas in the house. So we had to clean and scrub and scrub. It was terrible.'

The standard of accommodation wasn't the only dissimilarity.

'Little Hampton was cold. Bitter! It can be snowing in Little Hampton and at Trentham four miles away, no sign of snow. And in the spring, there are days when the frost doesn't melt.'

Rose was slowly, deliberately smoothing the wood on the arm of her chair with the flat of her hand.

'I pleaded with Mum. Persuaded her to write a letter to the school saying I was needed at home. Well, I was. But that wasn't the reason. I hated school. I was terrified of going to a new one. Later, I felt sorry, because the teacher and kids were so much nicer at Little Hampton.

Dad grew a lot of potatoes, turnips, swedes and peas too. He had all the front block in peas one time. But oh. We'd go to a whole lot of trouble to pick them, and they wouldn't be sold at the market and Dad still had to pay cartage. It was terrible. This was in the depression.'

The Bruton children, inveterate explorers and ramblers, soon had discovered Ord's Mill, and the mineral springs, several miles into the Wombat State Forest which abutted their land on the west.

'We used to enjoy walking in the bush. Used to go quite a few miles into the bush to the mineral springs, also to Ord's Mill, where we used to play on the big sawdust heaps. We used to always be able to find our way. Save for once, I remember. And that was when Min and her friend Connie and some girls, and me and the boys, went down to the mineral springs. On the way back Min and Connie believed it was a different way home than the boys and I thought. Anyway, they got lost. But fortunately, eventually made their way home.'

'Bushfires?'

'When I was thirteen or so, I remember a fire coming right through the bush, to the paddock between it and the house. The paddock probably had green potatoes. Dad was up on the roof putting out the sparks.'

'The bullockies. Did you ever see these teams?'

'Yes, quite a number of times. There were a lot. They'd come past our front gate, a long row of them. Pulling great long logs, real big. You'd hear a man yelling, and a dragging noise. He had a whip, didn't seem to use it much though. Mainly red bullocks, two rows of them pulling a log. I was about thirteen or fourteen.'

'Any photos?' I said holding my breath, hoping, as I knew full well that Rosa, with her simple box camera, had been the photographer of the family.

'Yes! Yes, I did.' But suddenly Rosa's expression changed. She crinkled her brow, looked down, her right hand tapping the wood on the armchair gently with her steel crochet hook. Voice uneven, she said, 'Well, I did. I had a box full of photos and negatives not even printed yet. I kept them under my bed. But while I was away, Daise threw them in the fire! Oh dear—how could she? Allan was sitting there; he gave me a couple he grabbed while Daise was destroying them. So many photos.' Rosa's voice was slow with sadness. 'I had some at Avonsleigh too, years later. And when Daise stayed, she did the same thing. Old letters and photos.'

'Why?' I asked.

'Maybe she didn't like the photos. I was away working. I took photos of her and Bess, and Bess would be smiling, and Daise would be frowning. She did have a hard time; she was a poor little girl. The kids at school teased her, made it hard for her.'

'Did you say anything to her about it?'

'I didn't know until years later that she'd done it. I'd just lost the box, and when I went to find them, they weren't there. No one knew anything about it, they reckoned. I guess they did, but nobody was telling. It was when Allan gave me the photos and told me that I knew.'

Now, we returned from that difficult diversion with dragging feet to an easier subject. The old bullocky tracks were helpful markings when the Brutons drove in their jinker or cab the fourteen miles through the bush to church.

'Sundays we headed off. Took sandwiches. We went to church in the jinker or the cab. The jinker could fit three or four only, the cab we could all fit in. It was covered. One day Con the horse bolted. Dad called out, 'Everyone keep in your places!' But I jumped out. My word did I hit the ground.

There were several families, Blackwoods, Gilmores, who went to the Drummond Church of Christ. Altogether twenty or thirty people apart from us. A lot of people had lunch at the church. They'd light the fire and boil the kettle for cups of tea. Now and then we went to Gilmore's or some other family for lunch. We went along a bullock track a few miles, halfway to Glenlyon. If we had the cab, we'd pick up Elsie Dickson and her brother. Then we turned right after a few miles along another logging track that we then followed. This was marked by a teapot hanging up high in a tree. We'd leave at nine, take a cut lunch and have it after the eleven o'clock service, and then after lunch, there was Sunday school. Sometimes there was a night service too. Mrs Thomas always used to make us welcome to stay the night after the evening service. She lived by herself but had adopted a girl. But the girl hated being there because Mrs Thomas was pretty hard on her.

If we didn't go to church, Dad would hold a church service at home. We weren't allowed to knit or sew on Sundays. The animals had to be fed of course. Dad was always very, very particular about his horses. They were always fed before he himself had his breakfast. He was very kind to his horses, and he often drove them without bits in their mouths as he considered bits were cruel.

We got mushrooms coming home from church. A lot more at Drummond than at Little Hampton. Much warmer at Drummond. The paddocks there were used for sheep and didn't get fertilisers on them. No good trying to get mushrooms where they've manured the ground with commercial fertiliser.

Sometimes in the winter we'd be coming home in the dark. The horses knew their way. That is, if we went the ordinary way along the track that Dad kept cleared, not the shortcut going over the creek.

Eventually we decided to go to the Methodist Church at Little Hampton, which was much closer. Dad used to still go to Drummond. He'd walk and stay the night with Miss Stephenson and her father, and come home the next day.

Mrs Parker used to play the church organ at Drummond. She also used to invite us to stay at her place if there was something on. I remember one day I asked her for the key to the organ so that we could play it in the afternoon. We were wanting to have a singsong. She said no, we couldn't have it. So I thought we jolly well will! I had a good look at the key, and I got a key from a sardine tin, and I scraped it and shaped it on the grinding wheel we used to sharpen knives and spades, and I made the key by guess. So next time we were staying there the afternoon for the evening service, I had a key. I made a key so we could play it as much as we liked. The cheek of her. I reckoned she's not getting away with that. It really gets on my nerves, that sort of thing. Other people would accept it, but I can't accept it! We couldn't have a singsong. There wasn't much for us to do at all. I would have been over eighteen then,' said Rosa passionately, face sparkling with indignation.

'On the way to Church one day I lost my little black purse. I was very worried. I didn't have much in it, but it was a fair bit to me. But on the way home there was a note attached to one of the gum trees. 'Miss Bruton your purse is here,' and someone had found it and hung it in the tree for me.'

My mind was focused on Rosa's strong determination to have access to the church organ. How she loved music. I recalled another occasion when Rosa was steamed up about an organ. But that was later, many years after she'd bought one for herself. An attractive wood, probably oak organ, with small, dainty hinged folding top and intricately carved music stand.

'I scrimped and saved and bought a lovely old Hamlin organ when I was about twenty. Miss Stephenson's father had it sent out many years before from Denmark. It cost me, I think, seventy-eight pounds. But then I'm not sure. I know old Mr Stephenson said he sold it to me cheaper.'

'At ten shillings per week wages. ....!'

'It was a lot of money. It was hard work. I only paid a bit at a time. Earlier on, when I was about fourteen, George and I bought an instrument together. A man came round selling them and played all sorts of things on it. Like a flat harp with strings. It was called, I think, a piano-banjo-mandolin. I learned a few songs on it. I wouldn't be able to play them now.

George used to sing beautifully, you could always hear him in the church. He had a lovely voice.'

Momentarily, we had been diverted from the organ. I knew this would become a hard subject. Before tackling Rosa's organ ordeal, I allowed myself to follow an image emerging in my mind. Obviously, George had enjoyed music. Music entered his life later too, through another avenue. His wife Freda played the pedal organ for church services. Still does.

The memory, however, is of rollicking music. Like beams of sunshine, this bravura would lighten and brighten the small lounge room at George and Freda's. And Freda's round face I still see, shining like the sun, beaming, as her nimble fingers skipped over the notes of her fairly large piano accordion decorated with mother-of-pearl. Perhaps this picture is particularly imprinted on my mind because of Ernest, my father's interest in music. He also enjoyed playing various instruments. The squeeze box and mandolin were his great favourites, and his face would shine with happiness too, when he played them.

My thoughts returned to Rosa's much-loved organ. Eventually, after her marriage, it took pride of place in our small lounge room, carefully placed against an inner wall. This position was important, Rosa said, to guard against dampness. She loved playing it. So did I.

An elderly gentleman was teaching me. That was until Rosa heard the same tune being played over and over. It was a bit much to find a comic on the music stand. The teacher apparently remonstrated, but Rosa now felt that age six was too young. 'We'll start you later on,' she said, and did. Another trick I recall was playing a particular bass note. Poor Teddy, our Samoyed dog, never failed to throw back his head, point to the heavens, then accompany with long crescendos of doom-like wails.

In later years when Allan, severely handicapped, was holding religious services at his home, Rosa loaned him her crown jewel. One day, to her chagrin and numbing shock, she discovered that Allan's wife had sold it. To this day Rosa mourns this loss. Every second-hand shop is an invitation to explore the possibility of her organ lurking under cobwebs in a dark recess.

Now impassioned, Rosa burst out, thirty years seeming like yesterday.

'Allan later offered me the twenty pounds he got for it. I said, 'You give me that Allan. And I'll throw it on the floor and I'll twist on it and twist on it and grind it with my foot until its powder!' He put it back in his pocket and she said, 'Your brother said I should say I'm sorry.' 'Rosa's voice rose an octave. 'Your brother said I should. Nothing contrite about that!'

I silently recalled Allan had dug deeply into his pocket again in later years on his wife's behalf. They had separated. She was probably fleeing the difficulties of their situation and flew home to Yugoslavia. She never did return to our knowledge, and Allan regularly sent her money for several years.

Rosa was really fired up. We'd talked about this catastrophe many times, including Rosa's futile attempts to trace her organ. I threw some water, hoping to quench the flames, and introduced a new topic. She readily diverted her attention to other dramatic episodes. It seemed that accidents with horse–drawn vehicles were not uncommon in her youth. Already some of the Bruton experiences had been mentioned. Now Rosa shared a more serious one. This time George was unconscious.

'We were coming home from Drummond Church, about a hundred yards further on when you turn off the Glenlyon Road. Min and George and I. Don't know if George or I was driving. Suddenly the belly strap broke, and the jinker tipped over backwards and George hit his head. I was fourteen or fifteen. George was knocked out. Min and I were so worried. And it started to rain. We put our coats over him to keep him warm. Had an umbrella. Put it over him. We didn't know how we were going to let Dad know.

The horse evidently ran home. Dad got a fright, and he came straight away in the spring cart. We were so worried. George wasn't able to walk. Then Dad turned up! Were we glad to see him. I think George was just coming round by then, but he was unconscious for a while. They put George to bed when we got home.

Oh, we had a few accidents one way and another. Another time, George and I, and Daisy. In the cart. We had a dreadful horse, a creamy colour, Con. He used to play up. Get to the creeks and he wouldn't cross. George used to tie the horse up, pull the jinker over, then put the horse back. We got up the back of Dagg's. We were afraid of an accident because he was really playing up. So we told Daise to go home, cut up the back. She was really mad about having to walk across the paddock. Was she mad! We'd tipped her out, and she had to walk. We didn't want her to be injured.

We needed two of us when the horse played up. I had to hold the reins, and George would wallop the horse to make it go and then jump on the back of the jinker.

Dad would never blame a horse for an accident. We never saw him lose his temper with horses. He was very good with the horses. So was his father. They loved their horses. The horses were always stabled at night. Little Doll was old when we were at Little Hampton. She died of old age, about thirty. I think the stabling helped them survive the cold.

We had Little Doll for riding, and we'd hop on her back without bridle or saddle. Only for fun, not to go long distances. Just had a spud bag over the horse. Was bumpy. Can't rise and fall, nowhere to put your feet. Robert would stand on her back; pretend he was a circus clown. It wasn't until I was in my twenties that we could afford a saddle.

I was going for the mail one day. I left the horse harnessed because Mum had made a drink. While I was having my drink, the horse kicked and kicked and broke the running board, the bit across the front of the jinker. We had to get the mail another way that day. Dad sold him in the end. Said 'We can't stand it any longer.'

Another day I was in the jinker and the horse was Bonny, and George and I were trying to make her go. Mum said, 'I don't want my girls having to cope with difficult horses.' Rosa's voice now rang resonant with pleasurable recollection. 'George said, 'Rose is as good as any boy!' Quite unexpectedly.

I remember another day with that dark brown horse, Bonny. I was in my twenties. I saddled her and went inside. I was probably changing. I'd pinch Robert's pants if I wanted to go on the horse. When I came out, Dad had unsaddled her. I was as mad as could be with him. He replied. 'I don't want to risk losing my daughter.'

Family Fun

Rosa's eyes were dancing, 'I remember a joke I played. Robert was the accomplice. Dad had employed two young men to dig spuds. They slept in one of the front verandah rooms, it had a double bed. I attached string to their bedclothes and brought it to the lounge through a small hole in the wall. Also put another string in the bed and attached it to a brick over a bucket. When the boys went to bed, the brick hit into the bucket making a big noise! Robert pulled the string hard. They were in the dark and their bedclothes came off. The boys woke up that something had been done to them, so we got chased.

Mum and Dad would usually be in bed before I went. I would sit up sewing or mending, sometimes reading by the kerosene lamp. We didn't have a Tilley lamp until later years. Dad often went to bed very early; he'd get very tired. Mum liked listening to 'Dad and Dave' on the wireless. She'd sit and nurse the baby and mend the socks. I would sometimes do knitting too or crochet by the fire.

Sometimes we'd all have a concert and Dad enjoyed this. We all did something. I remember Robert falling off a chair. He was reciting and he demonstrated so hard he fell off! He used to like impersonating. He liked getting dressed up, putting on an act in ladies' clothes too. Dad would sing funny songs and recite. He used to recite something about a mosquito who would sit on a tree and bark. He'd laugh like anything, and everybody else would be laughing too!

The doctors had been fighting long.
This protects, and that,
And on this point, you'll all agree,

> *To laugh will make you fat,*
> *Ha Ha Ha Ha Ha!*

He taught us older kids when we used to sit on his knee as littlies, a poem—Jerry Joy. Everyone did something. Well, except Mum, who'd be nursing the baby. But she enjoyed it.

> *Perhaps you've heard of Jerry Joy,*
> *Well, Jerry Joy was a naughty little boy*
> *Although his mother had said no*
> *One day he would a fishing go,*
> *He took with him,*
> *A fishing line, a rod, a hook,*
> *And off he went down to the brook.*
> *A light wind blew, the morn was fine,*
> *Baiting the hook, he cast the line*
> *He waited, hour by hour went by,*
> *And not a single fish came nigh.*
> *At last he thought he had a bite!*
> *He pulled and tugged with all his might,*
> *And to the bank he slowly drew*
> *A fish! Oh no, a worn-out shoe.*
> *When once again the line he cast,*
> *He caught his trousers firm and fast*
> *And when trying to undo the hook,*
> *He slipped and fell into the brook!*
> *He was not drowned I'm glad to say,*
> *But no more sport for him that day,*
> *When he got home, all in a mess*
> *He caught a something. You can guess.*

Another thing we enjoyed were 'sing songs' on Sunday nights at various local homes where there was an organ or piano. Nell and Freda Rothe would play the organ at our place. Sheldens, Millers, Rothes, us. All together about twenty. Mostly those who went to the Little Hampton Church. A young man came too, one of the workers. He loved me. I think I should have married him, because he did. He really did love me,' added Rosa wistfully. 'We'd sing hymns, have supper. Then of course earlier in the day we might have had a walk in the bush or to the mineral springs.

We used to recite at church concerts. I did. Sometimes Min.'

'This poem I found in your diary, with various keywords underlined. Is this one of them?' I asked. It was. And Rosa remembered some of it. The rest I copied from her pencilled script, still fresh.

> Smoothing the Road
>
> Ragged uncomely, old and grey
> A woman walked in a Northern town
> And through the crowd as she wound her way,
> One saw her loiter and stoop down
> Putting something away in her old torn gown
> 'You are hiding a jewel' the watcher said
> Ah that was her heart, had the truth been read
> 'What have you stolen?' he asked again
> Then the dim eyes filled with sudden pain
> And under the flickering light of the gas,
> She showed him her gleaning. It was broken glass.
> 'I have lifted it frae the street,
> To be out oh the road oh the bairnies feet'
> That was a royal heart that beat
> Would that the world had more like her,
> Smoothing the road for the bairnies' feet.

'There was another poem. A funny one. About someone kissing in the parlour. Are you able to recall it?' I asked Rosa. She chuckled, eyes merry. 'Yes. That was the cook! I used to recite it a lot.'

I was imagining the audience holding their midriffs quivering with mirth as Rosa delivered the punch line. Unfortunately, she couldn't remember the words. Not surprising, as some seventy years had now elapsed since her oratory heyday.

'How did you get interested in reciting?'

'Auntie Min Bluhm asked me what I'd like to learn. I chose sewing. She paid for me to go to the Boxhill Technical School and sit in with some classes to learn sewing and drafting patterns. And so she said, 'I want to teach Minnie something.' Minnie chose elocution. Fred Mock's sister used to teach it. Minnie would tell me what she'd learned. In the end I think I did the most reciting. I recited that poem Smoothing the Road at Boort and Little Hampton Churches.'

We returned to that perennial pleasure.

'Walking through the bush we enjoyed. We'd take Allan too, in his box cart. We had our own tracks to Ord's mill. This mill was defunct for many years. Lots of old tracks where they had pulled the timber from the bush. There are still some tracks there. Was a mineral springs there. When the creek was low at certain times of the year, you'd see the mineral bubbling up. We used to swim there, but it was pretty cold.

There was a big hill of sawdust. We'd slide on bags, one would pull. We also used to go to Lyonville mineral springs about two miles through the bush. Used to love looking at the flowers in the bush. We never went straight there; we'd hide behind trees and ferns. We'd cross the river, on the stones, to pick maiden-hair fern growing on the other side.

There used to be lots of mills through the bush around Lyonville. The trees had to be a certain size—had to leave the smaller ones. Gradually they cut them smaller and smaller—terrible the wood chipping business now.

At one stage we had some silkworms. Mum showed us what to do with the cocoons. We'd put them in hot water, then peel the silk off.

Different cousins would come and stay a week or two in the summer holidays. Hazel Bruton, one of Uncle Turk's children, came up quite a lot because she suffered with asthma at home. Uncle Will, Auntie Min, Joyce, Ron and Allan, Auntie Eadie and her family. Ted Tudor and Jean.

We had lots of visitors. Even though we were poor, they were always fed well and had somewhere to sleep. People could visit and have tea with us—whatever we had. We were encouraged to bring our friends whether Mum knew them or not. We enjoyed ourselves. There was always plenty of family around to do things with, like bush walks. When Uncle Will and family came, our boys would sleep in the chaff shed. They liked it. It was warm. It was a business picking the chaff out of their clothes.'

'And who picked the chaff out?'

'We all had a go, probably.'

A Girl's Lot

Rosa stared into space. She was looking straight ahead, and not at the varied rock collection in her line of vision. These rocks spilled out from mantelpiece to basket then hearth. There was one large, standing alone, irregular brown with a dark seam, particularly treasured. 'Wouldn't geology be interesting!' Rosa had said one day.

The books, always in every room, bulging from the bookshelves and piled one upon the other, hadn't drawn her eyes either. Rather she was looking within, sorting through her repository of memories. 'Robert was always very helpful if he was around when I was making the bread. George helped in his own way too. Oh, but generally women were not taken any notice of in those days. They have a better say now. Mum used to try hard and Dad wouldn't listen to her.'

Now she set her lips firmly. 'Oh, I used to envy the boys. They were free. They could go to work, come home, then go out! I would have liked to play tennis. The boys all did. But Saturday was Mum's baking day, baking cakes. One of the boys asked me, 'Would you iron those pants for me?' I said, 'What's wrong with you doing it. You're going to tennis, I'm not!' He said, 'Don't worry. I'll wear them as they are!'

The girls had to be at home or had to be at work! People would say—do you know so and so? Golly! I hardly got to know people. So it's no wonder that I'm shy!' Rosa sounded aggrieved.

'And when working outside the home, Min and I got ten bob a week. If it had been a boy, he'd have got more.'

She was in full gallop. 'And then they can go to bed when they're sick. I could when home, not when working. The boys would be brought home. I've envied the boys all my life!

I can remember Min telling me, a lady we were working for said to her, 'Isn't it dreadful how the domestic employed girls behave, they get into trouble a lot.' Min said 'Yes.' I said to Min 'Why did you agree with her? Those girls don't have a chance! They don't finish work till late, they're not able to go to anything!' '

Rosa's voice reached a higher note, a tone of incredulity. 'Min used to agree with everybody. She didn't believe it in her heart. If I was told, I'd say it. Didn't matter how poor we were! Min should have said.

I got a sore thumb. The doctor thought it was due to milking the cow. That was my job. When I stopped, it got better. The boys thought I was putting it on. Milking the cow was not liked. Everyone fought over not doing it. Robert or George had to when I couldn't. I think Min was away working.

The boys had their jobs, we had ours. We thought they had it easier. The boys probably thought we did.'

Siblings

'Us children had conferences between ourselves about anything. So anyone who wanted a conference would call it. Mum was often the go-between us and Dad. But sometimes she'd say, 'You ask him yourself.' We had a conference one day because we wanted to go to a picture show, Uncle Tom's Cabin. We'd read the books two or three times, so they picked me to ask him. He said no at first. Then I told him we'd all read the book. So he let us all go.

Dad would not allow us to go to dances or the pictures. He certainly didn't agree with dances. Our conferences were really just get-togethers, talks. Perhaps it might be about getting permission to take the horses and deciding the one to speak to Dad. Different ones were given the task. It was more likely the older ones, but it wasn't Tom because he was away a lot. When Dad was old and had diabetes, we had a conference about his having his leg off. We were all very worried. All of us went to the Royal Melbourne Hospital. I remember Robert saying, 'You'd think we were all Italians, wouldn't you?' If we were worried, we'd run to Mum. Before Robert met Nell, he'd say he wanted to be a preacher! 'If only I could go to college.'

The person I spoke to most was Minnie. Min and I shared all our secrets. George and I were pretty good pals and would stick up for each other, and so were Robert and Min. But I had to be out at work a lot and on my own a fair bit. Because you can't talk to people you work for. Walking home from Little Hampton Church, Min would walk with Bob, me with George and Stan with Daise.

George was always a doer. A worker. He and I understood each other. When we were kids at Taradale, we built a stile, the two of us, to get over the fence. We'd do things together, talk about problems. Chat over them and decide what we could do. Robert killed a wombat because it was eating all our vegetables. I cooked it. Made soup and rissoles with most of it. When Min found out, she wouldn't eat it. When Ted Shelden came back from the war, George, who had been his friend, said he was upset with Ted's bossing the boys around. He said, 'You were a lieutenant in the army, you're not in the army now!'

'Who liked reading the most?' I wondered, recalling that whenever Rosa read a book her engrossment was so total, she heard nothing.

'I was the worst one. I was reading one of Tom's books, he'd finished it, a boys' book, a Nelson-Lee. A boy called 'Fatty.' Mum ripped the little book up in pieces because I was supposed to be doing the dishes. I had hid behind the haystack and was reading instead. I tried to find the pages afterwards to put it together, but they were too small.'

I was glad Rosa had never done that to me, also an avid reader. She saw my shock.

'I felt I deserved it; I knew I did! I knew Mum had so much to do, and I sneaked away and hid. That was dreadful.'

Rosa's face lightened. Her chiding turned to chuckling. 'It wasn't the first time I'd hidden away either. Never thought she'd find me behind the haystack.' Now she returned to her earlier empathy. 'Must have been terrible for Mum.'

'Must have been terrible for you, all that work.'

Twenty-first birthdays. Made such a fuss of these days. I wondered what was the norm in the Bruton family.

'Tom wouldn't have had one. I was at home on my twenty-first, and nothing happened at all. And no one wished me happy birthday, except Robert. He gave me a little vase.

So after that I made sure everyone had a watch for their twenty-first. I'd collect money from the rest of the family. When I found out how much, everyone clubbed in. Uncle Norm Tudor told me where there was a watch maker upstairs in Melbourne— the National Mutual Building, and I would go there. They all got a watch after that. I thought I don't want them disappointed like I was.'

Perhaps it is the fact that I am an eldest, which motivated me for a moment to silently muse about the vagaries of this aspect of destiny, which place a child in his or her birth order. Both advantages and disadvantages. Rosa the eldest girl was second born of twelve. Rosa's parents Olive and Harry were both first born, both carried heavy responsibilities in their youth. Elizabeth and William Bruton, Rosa's grandparents, were each the eldest of large families.

Rosa's voice was soft and sad. 'But I felt so upset because Mrs Dunell had said she'd give me a do at the church. I asked Mum before she went to see Mrs Dunell, to remind her about my birthday. But Mum forgot! No wonder. She had so many things to think of, but to me it was a tragedy. And Mrs Dunell said later, 'How didn't I know?' I was so disappointed with Mum. Would have been nice if they'd all got together and got me something.

Both Percy and Harold were born after we moved to Little Hampton, each delivered by Mrs Rodda. Mum went to her little house not far from the Trentham Cemetery. She'd stay ten days. Mrs Rodda lived on her own, seemed old to me, a very nice capable lady.

I remember Percy used to run along behind Robert and say 'Lobbit, why do you do this and that.' Whatever Robert was doing, he'd have Percy running behind him. Robert did not mind. He loved having the kids. He didn't mind at all, and he'd keep an eye on them to see they didn't get hurt.

Min and I taught Percy to read and write before he started school. He was always a lovely little boy. Always.'

Rosa's tone was light, laughing. 'Oh, it was funny. There were the younger ones, toddlers, three or four of them, Percy, Harold, Bessie probably, also Allan, sitting on the floor in the kitchen having a wonderful time. They'd emptied a twelve-pound bag of sugar, pots of jam, everything. A big heap. They were all eating it.'

Now I was laughing too.

'Mum said, 'You're all naughty and you're all going to get whacked. And I'm going to whack Allan because he's naughty too.'

Allan would tell the younger ones something to get up to. Then he'd yell out. 'Hey! Look what they're doing!' Mum used to tell him not to tell tales. He got a few whacks. Bessie would tell tales too, 'How will people know if I don't tell them.' She'd get out of jobs in a subtle way. Like putting all the hot water in the wash-up dish, then go to the toilet.

Daise got out of things too. Always had to keep at her and at her to get her to do something. Then you'd do it yourself. When Auntie Elsie was so sick, she had a big tumour removed, Daise was sent to help Grandma. Initially Eva Clayton went but wasn't any good. Anyway, Grandma reckoned Daise was a wonderful worker. I think while there, she must have gone on the push bike to Uncle Reuben's. She kept in touch with them somehow. Anyway, Grandma Bruton couldn't speak more highly of her.'

Bedtimes. 'Who put the kids to bed?' I asked.

'I did. Put the young ones to bed, bathed them. I taught them their prayers. I didn't want them to kneel down, it was too cold. At least I thought it was. They'd say them in bed. Oh. I always used to refer to them as 'our' kids. Mostly when talking to Mum or Dad.'

Now I wanted to sort out a puzzle. 'I thought Harry was totally against a wireless. You said earlier Olive listened to it.'

'We never had a wireless for quite a while until Tom built one himself. He was very clever. Dad was against wirelesses, and so we'd listen to it in Tom's room. At one stage Dad pulled out the wireless, was going to throw it in the fire! A few years later Mum wanted to listen to the serials, Blue Hills, Dad and Dave and so on. Dad relented for this. In the early days Tom would try his wireless out when Dad wasn't around. I'd help him sometimes. He'd say, 'Your fingers are smaller than mine.' I remember a wire called a 'cat's whisker' and a crystal. He made radios for two different men. Went to the trouble to make them, bought parts. He was about twenty. And they didn't pay him. He ended up being a signal man during the war. He was very good at inventing things. It was awful he caught T.B. He had to leave school early at twelve or maybe thirteen.

One day when Daise was being very difficult, she'd listen to no-one and taunt, Dad lost his temper and grabbed her and threw her. Tom got between them and yelled at Dad, 'If that's being a Christian, I don't want to be one!' One day there was a disagreement between Dad and Tom out in the paddock. I think Dad heard Tom swear at the horses or something. Dad told him to go! And Tom got on his bike and just cleared off. Didn't even say goodbye to Mum. She was very upset. Mum was dreadfully worried. She used to cry. Nothing made her cry much, but that did. She got letters later. Tom was about fourteen then.

Tom almost starved and his bike got punctures and so on. Very hard economic conditions. It was very difficult to get work. A woman gave him a leg of lamb, it probably saved him. He ended up in New South Wales working on a grain farm. They were unkind to him, didn't give him proper wages. He slept in the shed. There was a rat plague, and they chewed his nails. Yes, that's true! He used to write to me, because he knew he'd get a reply. I kept in touch with him all the time. The only one, I think. He wasn't sure if he'd be welcome at home. I said, 'You'll be very welcome. You come home; it's dreadful staying there.'

He came home, then later on left again. He was about twenty-one, twenty-two when he came back for good, then he fell in with Sally. So, he felt he had to marry her. Then there were more upsets. It wasn't that he didn't want to come home, he just didn't have the money.

I remember when he came home the second time. I must have been eighteen or nineteen, must have been home from work. It was fairly late. Mum and Dad were in bed. Everyone had gone to bed, and I was supposed to have but hadn't. The fire had gone out. I was sitting under the lamp reading a ghost mystery story. It was scary! Just got my blood boiling.'

Rosa's eyes were round like saucers. 'Then I heard footsteps at the door and the blind was wide open. I raced into Mum and Dad's bedroom and said, 'Someone's at the door.' Dad said, 'You go. I'm ready.' I just touched the handle, and it pushed open. Oh. My heart was racing! Oh boy, did I get a fright! All I could gasp was 'It's Tom!' He had seen me through the window deep in my book and decided to give me a fright. He did!

No. We never, ever locked our door. Didn't even have a key.

I think Tom was very frustrated with the lack of opportunity to learn. He was very good with sums and things. But then, if he had a teacher, he probably would do things his way. But he did used to get very frustrated. I remember Mum saying to him when he was a young boy, 'When I wake up in the morning, I don't want to see you've smashed it up!' He'd get angry fixing something if it didn't go right, and smash it up.

He ended up living at Red Hill on his orchard near the sea. Yet the doctors said years before when he had T.B. he shouldn't. He was quite okay. I think he ended up having a very unhappy life, his marriage and that. A frustrated life. When we were kids, I felt I had to keep an eye on him 'What are you going to do now?' Wasn't always practical.

He was very cheeky to Mum, 'You can't catch me!' And Mum had a dipper of water, ran after him, and threw it over him. This was at Taradale just after we moved. Perhaps Tom had been a bit spoilt. He was a sick baby; he couldn't stand cow's milk. Mum had to get a lamb shank and boil that up every day and give him the broth.

Stan was a nervy little boy, he cried a lot. He was quite studious in his way. He'd notice nature, even as a schoolboy. He'd say, 'It's going to rain, the ants are busy, or the rabbits are out early.' I remember one day when getting ready for school he couldn't find his hat. He kept saying, 'The rat's got it! The rat's got it!'

What was Rosa's saddest memory?

'Allan having to be in that frame! He used to cry and cry. Eventually Mum said, 'I'm not going to let him be in this forever.' At home George and Robert did a lot of carrying of Allan on their backs. His arms and legs were all strapped. Later on Robert would take him to the hospital. I went too sometimes. Even if Mum went, not often, Robert went. Robert would carry Allan to the toilet and so on. Carry him on to the train and tram and up to the Children's Hospital. Allan had a lot of operations. I wish they had not stiffened his legs.

When we were there one day the doctor said. 'That leg should not have been operated on! Who did it?' Rosa paused, eyes wide, lively. 'I said, 'You did it!' He never said any more after that! We had been hoping we could get Allan to ride a horse, he could have been a lot more independent. He didn't start to be able to walk till his teens. And even then, still needed help with almost everything. He was very limited. Auntie Elise used to rub his legs, try to get them going. She worked real hard on Allan. Before he caught the polio, he was a very active little two-year-old. Real good. As he became older, he became more and more religious. Eventually he trained as a pastor and an estate agent. Mum said to me once. 'There's a letter from Allan on the table. I'm not even fussy about opening it. He's always preaching. I don't want a sermon. I can open the Bible if I want to read it! I want to know how he is, not a sermon.'

We'd take Allan for walks in the bush a lot in his box cart. We always took him with us. We knew just where we could get through the fence, had our own tracks to Ord's old sawmill, we'd take him there. He wasn't left out. Used to be mineral springs there too, you'd see the mineral bubbling up.

Allan missed out on a lot of home life because of being in the hospital, or staying at Grandma's in Mentone because of having to go as an out-patient.

Everyone had to help each other in the old days! There was no social service. Now people can do what they want. When Allan was sick, we had to pay everything.

Allan used to reckon he'd like to be a politician. He used to listen to Tom's wireless too. The school of the air, political and news commentaries.

Oh dear. I remember I teased him once. He was sitting under the verandah. I got a wooden stick and wiggled it like a snake at the end of the verandah. Allan called out, 'M..M..Mum!' He was very frightened. I felt awful. But oh. He turned out selfish! I've had to suffer through Allan.'

Yet, it seemed to me in later years, that Stan and Rosa, Bess and her husband Fred, stood by Allan in spite of his preaching and various eccentricities. They likely saw, with compassionate eyes, the struggle within the man. Every step difficult. Completely dependent on others for dressing, putting on his leg irons, meals, transport, and various activities of living, usually taken for granted. He frequently had to cajole or manipulate others into doing for him. This was his survival. Sometimes he'd have plenty. Other days he'd be impoverished, depending on his boarders and their generosity of spirit. Also his 'real estate ventures'.

'He'd trust people he should not trust,' said Rosa. 'And he himself had the same failing. He never considered other people's feelings and you couldn't trust him. At one time I discovered he'd been charging this lady a very high rent, left her only two pounds for food. She couldn't manage. I went mad at Allan and he put the fee down.

There was that day, I cooked and stuffed a leg of lamb for us, a smaller one for Allan. I made a mistake and took the big one over. When I got there, there were five chickens in the fridge. So I didn't know what he did with them all!'

'Didn't Allan have a whole cooked chicken in his bed once?' I said.

'Was at Christmas! He was sick, his legs had given way. So he couldn't come over. When I took a chicken for him, he hardly ate any of it and put the rest under the blankets. I said, 'It won't be any good. It will go off!' 'It will be alright.' he reckoned. I said, 'Give it to me and I'll take it out to the fridge.' But he said, 'How am I going to get it?' He was sometimes left by the boarders, I think. He wanted to read a passage from the Bible to me. I said, 'I know that by heart' and he shut up.'

It was around about this time I recall stumbling over a sizable roll of non-slip carpet near Rosa's hallway. 'I'm putting that down along here for Allan so his crutches can get a grip.'

Rosa was thinking about another sibling. 'And my little brother Bernie. We used to try and feed him and he'd be real sick! It was awful. He was sent to hospital. He was there for quite a while. Mum got a telegram from the Children's Hospital asking for her to come and pick him up. Never said anything else! And we took his clothes and went to the hospital on the train. She took me too, because I had to stay in the park with the baby.

And when she came back, she was on her own, and she'd been crying. And she said, 'The reason they have asked me to come and get him is because he's died.' And they'd never even told her!'

I sat in stunned silence. Rosa looked down. A trembling hand wiped the tears from her cheek. Soft drops. Sadness revisited. One from a long string of sadness's suffered. Like raindrops suspended on a green twig suddenly caught by the light. This moment now passed as I sat with my arm around my mother.

We'd imbibed a few cuppas this day. It was time for another. 'Have you talked about this before?' I asked Rosa as she sipped the warm comfort of tea.

Her voice was very quiet, tight. 'No, I haven't.'

'Thank you for talking about it with me.' I said.

'We found out later that Bernie had been suffering from coeliac disease. He was all right while breast fed, but when he was weaned, he would retch and retch. He used to eat the fruit outside. Perhaps this didn't upset him as much as the food he was having. And when we moved from Taradale, we didn't have all that fruit. His stomach stuck out, he grizzled a lot, you could hear the misery in his voice. He'd have porridge. Wheatmeal.' Rosa's eyes looked bleak. 'And we didn't know, we didn't know at all! We didn't know he couldn't have wheat or gluten. He was a bright little child, big dark eyes like Allan. The hospital had doctors from everywhere to him and they could not work it out.

He was in the hospital for a long time. Mum was very pleased because a nurse used to carry him around and talk to him. There was someone there who went crook at Mum because she didn't come and see the child. As though her heart wasn't breaking! There was just no money for fares. Dad was so worried about the little boy and wrote to the church to pray for him. I don't remember the funeral. Bernie was buried in the Cheltenham Cemetery. I was eleven when he was born, and fifteen when he died in 1927.

Minnie had a granddaughter, Betty's daughter Tracey. She was retching all the time, and they didn't know what was wrong with her. Then the doctors said it seemed like coeliac disease. Asked if anyone in the family had it, and Betty said, 'Oh no.' But then Minnie told her. So, she was put on a gluten-free diet and she became a really strong little girl.'

Now I was seeing in my mind's eye, newborn Daisy. The family was excited to have a third girl after five boys. But it was a difficult start. A very sick mother. An ailing baby. In the three years between the births of Allan and Bernie, Daise born in 1921, horribly wedged. An unfair fate sandwiched between two seriously ill siblings. When she was about twelve months old, Allan developed polio. Then when she was eighteen months old, Bernie was born. Add another twelve months or so, and Bernie was desperately ill. And Daise? How was her tired, preoccupied mother going to provide the mothering for this vulnerable child? Another needy toddler. The best given by an older sibling, a child-mother, was a poor substitute for a nurturing mother's constancy and closeness.

'Daisy,' I said. 'Bernie and Allan's illnesses could have taken a lot of care away from her.'

Rosa stared into the green carpet, her voice soft, quivering. I had heard her speak like this whenever she spied a vulnerable person or creature. 'Poor little Daisy. She really wasn't a well child at all. I suppose that's why I took her everywhere with me, because she needed somebody and I was around. But I was only a little girl! I didn't realise that I might hurt Daisy by including Bess.

She said I never made her anything, and I made all her clothes. Just about everything she wore I made. Oh. She was jealous. And I suppose she had good reason to be.

I didn't want to hurt Daisy!' Rosa burst out again, a tortured note in her voice.

Compelled to address this, it was my turn. 'You're blaming yourself for not being the perfect parent, and you were a child yourself!'

Rosa was continuing. Upset. 'I must have done something wrong!' She looked very sad. 'Used to go and help her with her housework too, when they lived at Gembrook. I'd go up in the bus. We were short of money. I decided to ask Daise if she'd pay my fare. Then she said she didn't want me to come.'

That bus journey to Gembrook I remember well. Rosa had sent her eldest daughter aged about ten or eleven to assist Daise. The twenty minutes or so journey from our home at Avonsleigh, a stop at Cockatoo, then on through the rolling green velvet of farmlands, was exhilarating. Mirrored dams at the apex of the gullies were special gems to be gazed at through the bus window. The bitumen eventually snaked along a ridge. Then there was an enjoyable walk along the usually soft red earthed road belonging to the Shelden's. This led to their new weatherboard home which I considered to be very smart. Smart as Daisy's dress sense I much admired.

Sometimes Daise gave me a valuable two shillings for helping her. In the main, my jobs consisted of sweeping and washing dishes. Also using her sparkling new washing machine, an appliance quite unfamiliar to me. At that time washing usually graced the long propped up line most days, as Bernie was a toddler. Jan and Dawn were probably not of school age.

Daise used to know exactly where her mouth organ was, and she would play it sometimes. This small inexpensive instrument seemed to be part of her. It was frequently seen protruding from her apron pocket. Other times she'd whistle. In perfect pitch, too.

Daisy was the proud owner of a small basic record player, and had several much played records. Now and then we'd listen to Beethoven, Brahms and the various music masters. Daisy's enthusiasm at these times was catching. 'Isn't that lovely?' she'd say with glowing eyes, a gentle smile, and almost breathless wonder.

Looking back, I am indebted to Daisy, not for the two shillings, but for something more lasting. I am grateful to her for introducing me to orchestral music.

Medications

There were more questions concerning the practicalities of everyday life. Remedies for sickness, being one of them. It wasn't surprising to hear they were simple and affordable. Rosa still preferred the simple. 'The reason I've lived so long is because I've kept away from doctors!' she would declare with vigour.

'Castor oil was one of the main ones. You had castor oil for a tummy ache. It tasted awful, but we had to have it. Some families had it every Saturday morning to keep their bowels open. We only got it when we were sick. You'd put castor oil on a bad sore! The cow knocked its eye out and there were maggots in it, and I'm pretty sure Mum filled the eyeball with castor oil. She made it quite well again. We'd wash cuts with plenty of soap and tie them up with a bandage. Put Vaseline on them when the cuts were feeling better to keep them moist. In those days we used boracic acid a lot too, for various things like washing out eyes, and disinfectant for sores. I remember Robert getting a fly in his ear. And pher! He had a terrible earache, and Mum poured some warm olive oil into his ear, and the fly came out. Robert said it didn't get washed out, it crawled out.

Once when Percy and Harold were very small, still in cots, they had very bad diarrhoea. The ordinary medicine from the doctor didn't do any good. Nell Shelden was a nurse. She said, 'Go to the chemist and get some glucose syrup.' We gave one teaspoon now and again. Think it saved their lives.

George was an extremely hard worker and he would take Clement's Tonic regularly. I'm not sure how much that would have helped him, because years after he'd died with that sudden heart attack, we discovered that Clement's Tonic actually had something like arsenic in it.

At one stage George had very bad eczema. We found that boiling up dock roots and drinking this was wonderful. It actually cured his eczema. He went to doctor after

227

doctor to get treatment, but they couldn't do him any good at all. Something else we found useful as a tonic was the black molasses.

I remember about the dock root. I went to do some sewing for some people in Trentham, and the lady Mrs Bransky told me her son had eczema very bad, and they boiled the dock root and gave it to him, and it got better. If George started to rub his arm it would come, and so he'd have to have a bit more dock.

Gee. It was terribly bitter. But my word, he was glad to take it just the same.

If you had a boil, anything like that, you'd mix up sugar and soap. Mix it all up and put that on. It helped the boil to come to a head. S'pose you put it on lint first, I don't know, I'm not sure. George used to get boils too, when he was a teenager. Arms and neck, everywhere. He had a bad trot. But he wouldn't eat his vegetables, and the doctor told him that he should. He would pick the carrots and things out of the stew. We all ate our vegies but he didn't. In the end, he was glad to eat anything that would help him.

Gosh. I remember our minister coming, and he had a boil right on the tip of his nose! Mr Hunting. But he stood up and preached just the same. Boy. Must have been awful for him!'

Father

It seemed we had discussed a plethora of painful subjects. Fortunately, this was gradual over a period of time. When I visited, I'd ask Rosa something else. On this morning it was nearly summer. The green hills blending into distant sapphire, were snoozing in the sun. Already, as was her habit, Rosa had clambered down the steep slope of her Emerald property first thing, observant eyes revelling in each new bud.

Today, no exception, she had gathered some flowers to grace one of her many vases. 'Look at this.' she said, sharing delight in a white lilium. The front door had been left open. No exception, no matter what the weather, inclement or not. It seemed she hardly noticed the breeze. Bracing, I thought, for this time of year.

Now, we tackled a somewhat bracing subject. Rosa's father.

'There was a letter that I haven't been able to find,' said Rosa. 'It was from Dad's teacher at the Moorabbin School. He said he had taught Dad all he could when he left school age twelve. Dad was always well read, he always carefully studied things.

He was the eldest. Used to do the marketing, drive the horse and lorry with the vegetables to the Victoria Market because his father's eyes were bad. I don't know what else. This was done in the night. He was aged twelve then. Dad worked a terrific lot. He worked very hard there.

He used to tell us that he had made friends with a Chinaman at the market. He had a stall next to his. Dad said the Chinese man would tell him, 'Don't lower your price! You stick to it.' He'd tell Dad how much to charge. Dad was a great supporter of the Chinese.

I can remember Dad telling us about himself and the other schoolboys. They used to go down to the gardens, and they'd pull up the carrots. And some of the kids used to, with their pocketknives, scrape the carrot and put dirt in and then eat it. And he said one boy was terrible, he was doing it a lot. He was always skiting that he could eat it. And he died.

One story I remember clearly. When we lived at Little Hampton. This man was real mad with Dad because he was helping Miss Stephie. This man thought Dad was doing him out of a job, and he abused Dad. He said, 'You Italians are all the same!' 'I'm not an Italian.' 'What are you then?' 'I'm descended from the aristocracy of England!'

I said to Dad coming home, 'But why did you say that Dad?' 'Well I am! Well Grandma told me!' 'What did she tell you?' 'We're descended from Lord Monteagle!'

And I don't know what he did wrong, but he was the youngest son of Lord Monteagle and he came out to Australia. And he dropped the name Monteagle and called himself Teagle. But Grandma said Lord Monteagle sent his son to Australia because he was a naughty boy. He didn't want to spoil the family name! Lord Monteagle was involved with stopping the Guy Fawkes plot, Grandma Elizabeth Bruton, who was a Teagle, told Dad.'

As well as a strong church man, Harry was a strict teetotaller. A Grand Master of the Rechabites. Perhaps his father's liking of a drink or two at the Royal Oak in Mentone put Harry against alcohol. Perhaps it was just as well. Given that Harry seemed to build up anger and frustration and then explode.

'Dad had difficulty in controlling himself when in a rage,' said Rosa, 'but I think I was the only one who could stand up to him. I'd answer him back! I always did if I objected. He'd quote scripture, and I'd answer him back. Perhaps I was a favourite. He never belted me or anything, but he didn't hit the others either. But he sometimes hit things like the walls or chairs. He would disappear down the paddock. But his moods would upset everybody, including Mum. I think he might not have been well.

He was diagnosed with diabetes when he was older. In fact, he had to have both legs off because of diabetes. He still did the gardening, though, and grew a lot of boronias when he moved to Avonsleigh in his late seventies. He would wiggle along on his bottom on top of a bag with his hoe. Now I think he probably had coeliac disease. It's connected with diabetes. He used to get so very tired and lie down in the paddock.

If Harold didn't want to go to school, he'd go down to Dad in the paddock. Dad would always stick up for him, 'Oh the poor little kid, let him stay home.' One night I asked Harold to wash his legs. Dad said, 'Oh, he doesn't have to!' I said, 'You don't have to wash the sheets. I do!' Dad didn't believe in washing. The more you wash your skin he said the more you wash away the protective barrier. But he did have a bath once a week. When I would go crook at Dad, he didn't hold it against me. He was always nice to me.

Dad said one day 'Respect your father and mother!' over something or other, which wasn't quite fair I thought. Whatever it was I said, 'Provoke not your children to wrath!' Dad went into his room. Each time he'd get mad with me, I'd have the answer from the Bible. He went to bed; he'd withdraw into his bedroom. He'd suddenly remember something and call it out and I'd answer it back!

Dad would bellow at everyone. Then he'd go to his room. He'd act next day as though nothing had happened.

One day, when I was in my late teens, Dad was kicking up a shine. Usually happened on a Saturday. And Mum ran out into the dark, ran down the road. Robert got on the horse and went up and down, yelling out 'Mum! Mum!' She showed herself, eventually.'

Rosa's voice trembled. 'I think she'd just had it then. She told me in later years that she was going to kill herself. She said she couldn't stand it anymore and off she went. Robert said he wasn't going to let anything happen to her. Think Dad got a bad fright. Don't remember when it was.

I remember Dad used to chop things down. At Little Hampton there was a greengage plum on the fence line between our place and Barthelson's. Was only a little tree, but it had a lot of fruit. We depended on it. Mum would state what she thought. He'd tend to be the opposite. Contrary! If she didn't want a tree cut down, that's what he would do! Mum bottled things in—talked to me a lot.

Dad planted some black currants. We had a lot. Had them for years. Then all at once they were chopped down! There were two very big gum trees at the top of the hill, they were beautiful. He chopped them down! No reason at all. It was a heartache to Mum as she liked the trees as we do.

But Stan likes to chop things too! Not as destructive as his father. Sure as eggs Mum said, when Stan did her garden, he'd get rid of something. Mine too. And yet Stan is so helpful in other ways. He got a tap put on in my front and back garden. He paid for it, got the man to come.'

Rosa quietly broke a momentary silence. 'There was this local farmer, went to our church. He used to bring some beautiful wildflowers when he visited us. I never liked him. He wanted to marry me and tried to get Dad to persuade me. Dad said he'd leave me to make my own decisions. Even if Dad had tried, I still wouldn't have married him.

When Dad got in a rage, Mum would say nothing. It's something Mum didn't have any experience of. She said if she said anything it would become worse. Nothing would stop him. He tended to bottle in his feelings, then, there'd be a big bang. But there had to be something to start it off. Dad said he didn't believe in hitting children.

Mum would just sit and cry sometimes. When I was small, I used to hide behind the chest of drawers. Get out of the way if he was in a bad mood. Mum knew she couldn't do anything. Then she'd try and repair things with Dad and the others after it had happened.'

Rosa quietly looked into the distance, recovering perhaps from painful recollections. 'Come to think of it, Mum was very methodical. She always had everything ready on time, cakes ready, something to eat. It must have been terribly hard to manage with such a big family. She grew things as well. Onions, carrots, parsnips. Garlic! She'd sell it, and we used it too, in the sauce.

And she was very tidy for somebody who had a large family. And the things she did to get rid of the bugs and what have you. Some people would have given up. She never, ever got the nits. Kept her comb really separate.

'If anybody's going to do the growling, it's me, and don't you start!' We weren't allowed to row with each other, and we didn't. I think that's what made our family different. We all got on.'

Rosa's voice was feeling her words. Empathic, tortured even. 'A baby every year just about! And even when she'd been told if she had another baby she would die, he still had babies.'

It was exceedingly rare for Rosa to criticise her father. And if so, somehow, she balanced this with some positive, supportive remark. This next outburst was therefore notable.

Rosa paused only to take breath, her voice now heavy, anguished. 'How could he? How could he?

She had a terrible life! She told me one day that she wished she'd never got married. I said, 'But you'd never have had us!' She said, 'But I wouldn't have known, would I!'

She loved each one of us, as if we were the only one.'

Employment

'When I got my first job, I was thirteen or fourteen. About 1925. Mrs Alexander who lived at Little Hampton came to Mum and asked if Mum would let me go. Said she'd pay me ten bob a week, and she'd treat me like a daughter. The old cow! I would cut through the paddocks and stay there. I had half a day a week off.

On this day I had to wipe the floor over, wash the dishes. Then I could go home for lunch and come back. I was only a little kid and worked hard.

When I was there, Mrs Alexander boiled up the copper, put caustic soda in it to kill the weeds. I had to carry it over. Spilt it on my foot. I sat in the kitchen with my foot in water and the baker came, and Mrs Alexander told me to get up and go and see him. I had to hop out, get the bread, and then put my foot back. I still had to cook the breakfast and so on. My foot was too swollen for me to go home for my afternoon off. Her son gave me his slipper to put on because it was so swollen. I wasn't there very long, about six months.'

Rosa's eyes sparkled. 'Anyway, Mrs Alexander had the eggs and bacon in a big baking dish. I'd probably cooked them. It was like a frying pan with no handle. I was ordered to serve it up. It was very heavy and very hot. I dropped it. Did she rouse! She ranted and raved, as if I had done it on purpose. I thought to myself, if I had done it at home Mum would say, 'My that was an accident,' and help me clean it up. I was thinking to myself she won't hit me, she would not be game enough, because the men were there, anyway she told Mum she'd look after me like a daughter. It was only an accident.'

Rosa was enacting the drama, waving her arms. 'But she had no concern for me! I was amused and thought to myself what a funny woman, she can see it's an accident. She went on and on. Then she went over to me. She must have just about danced. 'How dare you laugh at me.' I wasn't laughing. I was thinking what a stupid woman. She must have seen the amusement in my eyes. Fancy going crook about this. I could not help it. She said, 'You can go home if you like!' I said, 'Thank you. I will.' Then she quietened down, said she'd be wanting me for the harvest. But I decided to go home. Mum was upset when she saw my foot. There was no way of letting her know it was crook. How far I hobbled home? About three miles.

Another job I had was Mum used to send me to Uncle Will Bluhm's at East Burwood. I used to help Auntie Minnie with the kids and the cooking and the washing. I was there when I caught rheumatic fever. I was eighteen, was July, about the time of my birthday, 1930. I didn't know immediately what it was. Although I felt terrible, I was still expected to work. My legs swelled up bigger and bigger, they were so sore. I'd been sick for a while. Eventually I was told to stay in bed. Auntie Min Tudor said she'd have me, but Auntie Min Bluhm said to stay. The preacher came to see me; I was in bed one month. My wage was ten shillings a week if they had the money, and if they didn't, I worked for nothing.

I was working all the time one way or the other, either at home or outside of home. One job I had was at Boort at the Lacey's. The church would put ads in some paper or other for us, and the minister heard there was this job. I got to know the Burtt family at the church and used to bring their daughter Audrey home to our place at Little Hampton for a holiday. She got to know Daise, and they became good friends. She eventually married Stan. She was a fair bit younger than me.

Other jobs I had were in Melbourne as a maid. I came home one day, I was giving Percy a kiss, and he ran to Mum and said, 'That lady kissed me!'

It was very upsetting. I wasn't allowed to come home those days. Had to keep working. Called it one day off per week, but you had to wash up and wash the floor after the midday lunch! By half-past two or so you'd be finished, so it would be just part of an afternoon off. I couldn't possibly come home on that day. You'd go somewhere for tea like Auntie Minnie Tudor's, do some shopping, and the day was gone. It was impossible to get out in the evening when you were working. You didn't make friends with the people you worked for; they were a step above you. You couldn't meet the men you'd like to meet, the men you'd like to marry.! If I'd been able to mix around more, I'd have got a different man. No holidays at all. A little wage, ten bob a week, and that was for being a cook. The only way we could get away was for Min and me to swap jobs. We were overworked.'

This was during those devilish depression years, I reminded myself. Rosa and Min, country girls, did exceedingly well to obtain jobs in the big city, a competitive market at any time.

'The best job I ever had was at Sallmanns, Louis, in Toorak for twenty-five or thirty shillings a week. More than anybody else. I was only getting ten before. They were both very nice. Had a son and daughter, and a child carer, a nurse, to look after their eleven-year-old son. I remember I was working there when there were the bad bush fires, on 'Black Friday,' 1939. We were even worried they might be getting too close; the smoke was so bad. In the morning at seven, I would have to make a cup of tea and get the paper. Then there was cleaning and cooking. No time off during the day. Tea was at seven o'clock. I didn't stay very long as Ern wanted me to hurry up and get married. I told him, 'I'm going to buy a sewing machine before I marry, and a hammer!'

I hated housework! Still hate it. When you are a servant, you are not a person with needs. There is a rigid routine. Clean the dining room and sweep the fireplace, were jobs you did before you cooked the breakfast. Then they didn't have dinner till seven o'clock, you had to do the dishes and the floor. Finish about half past eight or nine. I especially hated the ironing. My legs ached so much I didn't know where to put them.

You couldn't even get off to go to the pictures. Then you would go to your room and be quiet. Silence. No one to talk to.' Rosa was silent now. Remembering. Suddenly the silence burst with sound. A memory indelibly imprinted on her mind. She'd told it before. A need to repeat it was clear. Perhaps someone to understand the privations suffered. Seared upon her.

'What really annoyed me once, was a woman we were working for, told Min that the workers ended up to be prostitutes. Min said she nodded some sort of agreement.' There was fire in Rosa's eyes. She spoke with force and indignation. I said to Min, 'You didn't agree with that? Why didn't you tell her? You don't finish until it's too late at night to go to a picture or anything, and the work is too long.' I'm so different to Minnie, she'd take it. And I would say, 'Why should we? Why should we?'

While I was at Boort Mrs Lacey lent me her sewing machine and I made some dresses for Daise and Bess and some pyjamas for the boys, Perce and Harold. Their first pyjamas. Before this they used their shirt tails. I remember I made Daise a beautiful flannel dress with scallops all around the hem and fancy work at the top. It looked lovely on her.'

Rosa was looking into the distance, into the past again. 'I tried to do things for Bess and Daise, but I always seemed to do the wrong thing. Daise didn't think I made any dresses for her. We have photos in the dresses I made for her. I also used to make dresses for her children when they were little, do all sorts of things.'

War

'Dad always had prayers at home and a Bible reading every night after tea, which everybody had to attend. During the war, he always had special prayers for the boys. Every day! Never missed! When Tom went missing, Mum never ever believed he was dead. 'If he was dead, I'd know,' she said.

Stan and Tom were in the Civilian's Militia before the war started. They automatically went into the army then, when men were called up. Most of the Militia were eighteen to twenty-year-old's. Robert was more like Percy. He didn't want to go. He had young children, had Dorothy then. It was a very hard time for the boys. Robert had to dive into holes where there were dead rats and snakes, half full of water. Tom was a prisoner of war. He hadn't been listed to get the Red Cross parcels because they thought he was dead. He could have escaped in a boat from Greece before he was captured. But he was helping the wounded. He was so worried about them he stayed behind.'

George worked hard; he was now the mainstay of the family.

'He was always a very conscientious worker,' said Rosa. 'George had to have a certificate for the army that Dad had an enlarged heart. We needed someone at home to help.

Whenever Mum hadn't heard from Stan, she'd race off and ask Mrs Shelden if she'd heard from Ted, because of course they were together in the same army unit.'

In 1939, the world was on the brink of war. Rosa married Ern in April. She was twenty-six, he thirteen years her senior. Also during this year Min became engaged to Fred. Rosa became stepmother to Ern's twelve-year-old son, Ernie. She went with Ern to live at Avonsleigh in the fern-gullied eucalypt forests of the Dandenong Ranges, east of Melbourne. Too far away from the precious home fires to visit often. And then only via three modes of tedious time-consuming transport.

The bus, after a journey of nearly an hour, met the red electric train at Ferntree Gully. This arrived at Spencer Street, Melbourne, after another hour or so. From here it was the steam train for another eternity, probably a couple of hours. A Bruton would be there at Trentham with the horse and jinker. This meeting was pre-arranged by letter—the major communication in those days. Later, in post-war years, Perce would drive down the ninety, hundred miles and pick Rosa and her brood up.

Ern stayed home, happy to tinker in his workshop. A mechanical whiz, he invented and fixed, astounding various people with his abilities. A particular creation from his workshop comes to mind. Something he made for Grace and me not mechanical, but which must have taken a great deal of dexterity and patience. A small silver heart each, made from carefully filing and shaping a threepence. He'd carefully decorated them with our initials in script on one side, and the date 1946, on the other. Atop this was the further fine detail of a tiny hole which fitted the heart to a bracelet. The bracelet has long since gone and I don't recall what it looked like. The little heart though, I kept in a matchbox during my later childhood. Now this special gift resides in pride of place in a small jewel box.

Memories of the train journeys are vivid. The electric red rattlers jogged along at a somewhat uneven pace. White glass appendages hung from the ceiling, reminiscent of chandeliers. I remember how these rather grand looking carriage lights danced and swayed to the staccato rhythm. Sometimes at night when there was a particularly abrupt jolt, they would suddenly blink, even dim. It wasn't unusual for one or two to extinguish, leaving many a newspaper frustratingly unfinished.

In the absence of a book or conversation, one would usually stare at the large framed black and white or sepia photographs of the Australian countryside, which adorned the walls. Perhaps a thoughtful attempt to beautify a somewhat uninspiring journey.

Rosa frequently found someone to greet and make some form of conversation, albeit short. As she never wished to intrude, there would be long periods of silence. She told me once, when on the red rattler, that a woman leaned over Rosa's then baby, myself, commenting 'What beautiful eyes your baby has. Just like a rabbit.'

On alighting at Spencer Street Railway Station, Melbourne, Rosa would push my brother in the stroller, flanked by us two older girls, each with one hand on the handle. Platform number two was our destination. Here the big black engine-powered Bendigo train waited, snorting imperiously, straining to gallop on with the journey.

We would carefully clamber over what seemed to be a large step and enter a long passageway. This, edged with windows on one side, extended the length of each carriage. On the other side, running at right angles from this passage, were the cubicles in which we'd sit. Usually there were other passengers who also sat on the shiny brown leather-looking bench seats. Usually there was the luxury of foot warmers under the seats.

Mostly I enjoyed standing, holding the shiny rail in the long passageway, watching, amid lurching and shaking, the gradually unfolding scenes of sheep country. This flatter terrain was in sharp contrast with the hilly forests to which I was accustomed. My sense of adventure had the better of me one day, and I opened the window and put my head out. The smell of acrid soot hit me. This was one thing, but a face full of black and painful grit in the eye, another.

Of course, this would have been after the war, Keith having been born in January 1945 near its conclusion. Though a young mother and managing on a shoestring, Rosa, like so many others, found time to contribute to the war effort. The subject of letters came to her mind.

'I've saved all the letters the boys wrote me when they were overseas. Yes, I made cakes, knitted and so on. Sent food parcels to Ern's relatives in England. They were finding it hard.

We were supposed to block out the light from our windows at night-time. I didn't bother. There didn't seem to be any need for it. There was the rationing, butter and so on. Ern was away for weeks at a time. He was in charge of an internment camp deep in the bush. Young Ern joined the RAAF. Wanted to fly. He did part of the training, but his eyesight was too poor. Because he was so good with wireless, he ended up in that section. I was alone. I did feel very lonely being so isolated from my family, so far away from them up in the Dandenongs.

Everybody in the city had to arrange for somewhere to go in the event of an attack. We were asked to take someone. The Mathiesons, Min and I used to work for at the East Burwood shop and post office, wanted to come. But we said we had so many relatives we wouldn't be able to fit them in. But told them if they wanted to come and stay in a tent, that would be fine. Fortunately, none of that had to happen. Mrs Mathieson used to keep in touch with me. She'd always send Christmas presents for you kids. The last time, she sent them in the winter. She said, 'I've got a feeling I'll be dying before Christmas,' and she did.

'Did she keep in touch with both you and Min?'

'No.'

I wondered what Harry's attitude was towards war.

'He did not believe in it. He was a pacifist. Someone sent him a white feather during the First World War at Cheltenham. He was very upset. He had a big family to support but anyway he didn't approve of war.'

'How did you know this?' I queried.

'Mum told me. Mum was my source of information about almost everything. The feather signified that you were afraid. Some silly person sent it.

But we were afraid! We were afraid for the boys' lives of course.'

Now. And then

'Your happiest memories?'

'Auntie Minnie Tudor, Mum's youngest sister, used to ask if she could curl my hair. She used to put water on it and twist it around her fingers, and it would be very pretty. Auntie Min made a fuss of me, she made dresses for me. She'd stand me on a chair while she measured the hem. I was about three. Mum said I should not ask her to do my hair if she comes to see us. 'She is coming to see everyone.'

But I remember my very first memory. I felt the wind on my face! I was so excited. I ran round and round saying, 'Isn't it lovely. Isn't it lovely?'

The cry of a true child of nature. 'I hate cages!' Rosa said one day 'It's wrong.' When she moved from East Burwood back to the colder Dandenongs and had no safe area for her bantams, she gave them to me. She said as she surveyed the cage for transport. 'Poor things—they don't have any say in it.' Then there's that photograph of Rosa and her white duck. Its beautiful sleek neck draped around Rosa's.

A story Grace told me one day flits past. Another feathered friend. 'I called into Mum's at lunchtime. Mum was crying. She said she'd put a tiny sick chick up her sleeve to keep it warm. But then she couldn't find it. Thought she'd squashed it. But then... she found it up near her armpit.'

Rosa would never eat her friends. She does however find supermarket cooked chicken irresistible. Her first thought when visiting is 'I'll take a cooked chicken.'

One day Rosa gently warned me that Kate, my cat, special to me, would die soon. I was aghast and unconvinced. But she did die a few months after that. 'How did you know?'

'She told me. Just the way she looked at me She definitely told me!'

There were times I 'knew' things too about Rosa, but mainly health issues.

'What would you have changed if you could about your growing up years?' I asked.

'I would have liked a few pretty dresses, learnt how to dance. I hated going out to work. I wouldn't have minded nursing. I always thought I would love a picture of the sea. Got them now. And I painted them myself!'

She stared at the cream wall. 'Ern was a good dancer. After we married, I asked him to teach me, but he didn't want to.'

'And what would you say to the younger generation?'

'I would say, 'Make sure you discipline your children!'

Rosa's complexion was especially fair as the light lingered on the wall above her. I gazed through the window and tracery of jade, my eyes following the long view beyond over the gum treed gully. The sky was big, with pearly chariots racing against the silvered light. The passage of time. It was over thirty years since Rosa had become widowed.

We sometimes teased her, saying she might remarry as she did have some admirers. 'No. No!' she'd say with the laugh of certainty.

We took Ern home from hospital to die. Not the first to die in our house. He died in the same bed as did Olive. Harry didn't. He died on the eve of his eighty-sixth birthday, sitting in his chair on the front verandah at Avonsleigh. Rosa was the one to discover him and break the news to her mother. 'Mum was in the kitchen. I told her, after I'd suggested to Grace that she and her friend went for a walk. I heard him. He just gave a great big sigh and you could tell it was his last. I knew what it was.'

When Olive died, Rosa was on a fold-up bed next to her. After the funeral, the usually very active Rosa took to her bed for several days, heartbroken. She told me later. 'As Mum was dying, she couldn't talk. Her eyes watched my face.'

Auntie Elsie was the next. After the deaths of Joe and Ted, though stoic, she became very lonely. Crippled with arthritis, she had suffered a couple of heart attacks. She died suddenly in my old bed with a third heart attack. Calling out to me to help her. I felt powerless, not knowing what to do. This spectre haunts me to this day.

After this, there was Miss Carr. She was discovered by Rosa incarcerated in an elderly persons' home. This was during Rosa's visitations for the church. Miss Carr's only brother entreated Rosa to give his sister, suffering with dementia, a home. Rosa regularly drove with her friend Amy Miles to visit sick, dying and shut in church members. 'I used to know; I'd get the feeling if they weren't home. Amy would say, 'Are they home?' as we were driving there.'

And then Rosa, in her sixties, took on a foster child. 'It would be terrible for him to go into a home,' she said against Ern's remonstrations. Rosa's car is not as busy these days, but still taking her to the little Avonsleigh Church five or so kilometres away, and the big Fountain Gate shopping centre. Sometimes she drives to Mentone to see Bessie, about an hour's journey.

My mind flipped back to happier times. The mêlée of motherhood suited Rosa. She revelled in school holidays, and so did we. These were made special too by friends staying, like Eric and Brian Price, cousins Dorothy, sometimes Judith and others. The chartreuse creek resplendently decorated with gums, tree ferns and flitting small birds was one special playground. This shallow stream gurgled softly at the base of the gully, then through a tunnel under the road. We used to straddle this tunnel, walking to the circle of sunshine where the stream emerged, continuing its murmuring meander. In later years I was amazed at how low and small this slippery underpass really was.

Rosa would take us further afield. A walk along the 'Puffing Billy' track, from Wright Station, Emerald or Gembrook. Picnics. A favourite was the Emerald Lake. And she taught many a child to swim. Usually Rosa was accompanied by her veteran box camera. Under her guidance, we'd develop films in the kitchen.

All in all, there was much fun in those early years, punctuated by extra fun at Christmas. If we didn't celebrate on the farm at Little Hampton with our Bruton grandparents and big extended family, we'd spend it at home. The traditional roast fare with chicken. Rosa happily cooked our Christmas feast in the black wood-fired iron stove, whatever the weather. The plum pudding, wrapped in an old cloth, boiled for several hours. This was my favourite. I suspect that an added impetus for my greed were the threepences and sixpences in it. Fortunes increased according to one's indulgence. There was however one person whose mastication did not result in wealth.

Rosa would say, 'I made sure young Ernie got some threepences, but he can't find them. He bolts his food too much.'

Nowadays Rosa regularly provides this 'piéce de resistance' for the Christmas luncheon at the little historic Avonsleigh Church. Various members of the family are grateful recipients of other festive puddings, also generously large.

Odd things stand out in my memory. Rosa never wore lipstick, said her mouth was too big. Apart from a light quick swish of perfumed face powder, she used no creams or makeup. 'Minnie's the beautiful one,' she'd say with admiration. She said I could use lipstick when I turned sixteen. Seemed surprised when I pressed my claim.

And that day Rosa sat on the bull-ant nest. It was school summer holidays. Several of us had been sitting on the bank at the roadside awaiting the bus, with togs and picnic, all going to the lake. Rosa was jumping, scratching frantically in the bus. How she managed not to throw off her clothes in front of the driver, Mr Casey, and his passengers, I don't know. When we alighted and pulled up her cotton singlet, at least half a dozen ferocious culprits emerged amid many fiery stinging bites.

Gardens and Rosa were synonymous. Languidly hovering butterflies, bustling bees and tiny birds, would be seen amid Rosa's large rambling floriferous scented abundance. There was a small orchard, and Ern too had a garden, and he provided the vegetables for our family's simple cuisine. We consumed lots of silver beet, carrots, peas and pumpkins. Turnips, too. And we ate the turnip tops. Reluctantly.

Meat was not plentiful. In the summer any meat was placed in the coolgardie safe under the cool dense shade of a spreading buddleia at the side of the house. A particular occasion comes to mind. Jackels, neighbours a mile or so along the rough earth track at the back, had given us a gift of some lamb. This, in return for some assistance given by Ern. A fox pulled the safe to pieces and made off with a carefully cooked prize, replete with gravy.

Rosa coped with other inhabitants of the bush too. Mosquitoes, flying ants, march flies. She contended with a still born and a miscarriage, marriage, and making ends meet. Optimistic and enthusiastic, industrious, creative. Even as a young child I was aware that her simple sincere warmth was bestowed without fear or favour. And sometimes I didn't like it. I felt embarrassed when she spoke and smiled with warmth at a ragged, unkempt young mother in the bumpy red Melbourne train. There was that time I remember, in later years—perhaps it was some criticism I'd made about someone. Rosa was often subtle in the ways she taught us. She quietly said, 'There was this lady. She was lonely, so I took her to meet my friends. She picked out all their faults! Of course they had faults. I knew that! If I'd focussed on their faults, I'd have no friends at all.'

The Cockatoo Country Women's Association with Miss Yapp and others. They put on amateur theatre and Rosa enjoyed acting. Even roped me into play some naughty girl or other. I enthusiastically learned my lines, throwing myself into it with great abandon. Perhaps the role was not entirely foreign.

Then there was the annual Cockatoo Show. Grace and I were amply rewarded with certificates for flower displays in eggcups, our scones and sponges. All cake creations of course cooked on the wood-fed stove; the sponges beaten laboriously by hand. 'I won a prize for best handwriting.' I told Rosa recently. 'You wouldn't now.' was her cryptic reply.

Church. Ern wouldn't go. Rosa said in later years, 'He did promise me before we married that he would!' We others went. Too often, I think, looking back. This included Nig, our black Labrador, who would creep through the bushes on the side of the slippery red dirt road as we walked to the Avonsleigh Church.

This church, an old weatherboard building in its heyday, was called East Emerald. There were half a dozen or so, who attended. This included Miss Ruby Nightingale and her sister Mrs Hanson. They lived next door to each other and Miss Nightingale shared her fence with the church. She grew tall clumps of creamy coloured pampas grass along her wire fence, and kept several peacocks, and us kids prized the feathers. True to her name, her operatic voice would soar above all others. And Nig's snores punctuated many a sermon.

Grace and I always sported a beautiful new dress for each Sunday School Anniversary. These were run by Mr and Mrs Boys, a sister of Miss Nightingale and later, Vera and John Jackson, who still drove a jinker from their farm at Macclesfield. We believed that every mother was endowed with the ability to run up a dress, sometimes drawn and designed by ourselves, at a moment's notice. No trouble either to come home and find me with a long length of plain cotton, decorating it with fabric paints. Climbing trees and mud pies were fine, too. Just wash the mud off!

Rosa made baskets from flax gathered from the Emerald lake, also from 'cut grass' she found in the bush. She carefully hand-moulded flowers from fresh white bread and painted them with water colours. Pretty hats from plaited crepe paper. Always a garden flower, whatever the season, and a bunch for someone. I was given a small patch of garden to work too. Then there was the soup she'd ask me to take over to a neighbour Uncle Bert Arnott when his wife Daisy was away, and flowers for Mrs Biggart up the back.

Amid all of this, Rosa wrote letters. Especially to Min.

'I've always especially loved Minnie. Kept all her letters.' She thought for a moment, now more quietly, 'Don't know if she's kept mine.'

That basket of hand moulded flowers I see in my mind's eye. Small pink roses, a sprinkle of green leaves. Each somehow fixed to long thin wire stems covered with green crepe paper. Many roses, a small basketful, standing upright, the wire ends anchored into a cake of soap.

'That pretty basket of bread flowers, what happened to them?' I asked Rosa.

'Auntie Min Tudor admired it. I gave it to her.'

Another picture is percolating, now with the flavour of embarrassment. The scene. The evening bus, Rosa and her three small children aboard, travelling from the Ferntree Gully railway station home to Avonsleigh. The bus bulging, slowly negotiating the many twists and turns of the road through the Dandenong Ranges. Some passengers, not lucky enough to gain a seat, fairly common then, were standing in the aisle clutching leather straps which hung from the roof.

The seat in front of me was occupied by Rosa and Grace. Keith, a toddler, dressed in his smocked cotton suit made by Rosa, sat on her knee at the window. Nose almost against the glass behind, I watched the round moon. Light luminescent topaz. According to my fantasy, that of a seven-year-old, it was cheekily playing hide and seek behind the dark silent gums. The bus was subdued with tired travellers, quiescence inside and out. Suddenly, a thin piping voice, staccato, the singing of a young child, broke the silence. Mortified, I realised it was my brother. He was singing and proud of it. A song learned from Sunday school. 'Jesus loves me.'

'Shush up.' I whispered, pulse racing. I leaned forward and hissed urgently in Rosa's ear. 'Shush him up!' All this frustration and chagrin was to no avail. 'Let him sing!' Rosa replied, and Keith was more than happy to oblige.

A sensation, now olfactory, surfaces. The sweet smell of ripe blackberries. In my mind's eye I see a tapestry of fruit and leaves. These are adorned with the delicacy of tiny cobwebs outlined with crystal droplets shimmering in the soft mid-morning sun. A tiny jade beetle tentatively ventures from under a leaf. The movement of a white moth. A butterfly with painted wings of black, red dots and dash of yellow. They float gently on the windless spaces. The scene completes with the hint of another aroma. Distinctive and unmistakable, it is soft, musky, primevally peat-like. The earthy rotting of leaves, a testament to transience. Autumn's autographs. Slower than summer, this, my favourite season. Somehow, at this time, I always feel closer to nature's heartbeat.

Blackberries. Picking. This was after we moved the three miles to Emerald during my earlier teen years. Rosa's trim body would be encased in khaki overalls, with a string around her waist on which to tie her bucket. This was to free both hands for grasping the prickly clusters and hence hastening the picking process. Rosa gathered great quantities, kerosene tins full. These enormous bowers of blackberry lusciousness tumbled over many a fence or gully. They were so high that Rosa threw a plank across the canopy to walk on. I felt worried that day when she crashed through dry stalks to the leaf littered light-starved bottom. Looking down, I saw the top of her head. 'Be careful of snakes!' I shouted. Snakes were not on Rosa's mind. She clambered out proudly, holding her bucket, having spilt not a shiny black drop.

Recently I found a receipt from Rosa's blackberry picking days. Issued by D. Camm & Sons, Jam Factory, Monbulk, dated March 1957. She had picked the weight of 1375 pounds, earning seventy-four pounds, nine and seven pence, just over one shilling per pound. 'I earned enough to pay for a new room,' Rosa told me proudly.

Us kids used to pick sometimes, too. So did Nig, our Labrador. He'd carefully place his lips around low-lying fruit and savour the succulence. There now in my memory is Grace. She is standing still, bucket half full. 'Look' said she whizzing her bucket around fast, like a cartwheel. 'They don't fall out.' The next part of the circus caught me unawares, me always being a sucker for a joke. Grace proffered her hand, asking me to take it. Mystified, I did. A hard thump ensued; I was spread-eagled on red earth. Nig stared. I steamed. Grace split her sides. A bit smugly, I thought. Clearly, she had benefited far more from the Emerald Youth Club judo classes than me.

That warm, often balmy blackberry weather, when driven by a scorching north wind, became foreboding.

Bushfires spelt disaster. A cruel desecration of the beautiful bush and its inhabitants. I remember at Avonsleigh, blackened eucalypt leaves sometimes burning, floating from the sooty sky, the sun red blurred through the smoke. The local men, including Ern, would face this malevolence with heavy knapsacks of water strapped to their backs. They'd also use hessian bags to beat out those flames from hell.

The soft screen of night would mask the smoky star starved opacity. Respite from the heat, not necessarily the fire. Sometimes we could see the glow of the bushfire's baleful eyes. We'd smell the penetrating pungency of burning bushland on the night wind.

On one such occasion Grace and I, about six and eight or younger, took destiny into our own hands. We packed our little travel cases quietly in the bedroom. We were frightened, going to escape the nightmare. Somewhere. But nowhere was the only place we could have gone.

Rosa was unperturbed, as she usually was in a crisis. We probably ended up sitting in our tin baths on the bare timbered floor of the washhouse cooled by precious tank water.

Later, in 1956, we moved to Mahoney's Road East Burwood. Rosa and Ern bought the home previously owned by Uncle Will Bluhm. Uncle Will, genteel and kindly, had died, and we lived on the orchard, now worked by his son Ron. Rosa, having gained her driving licence in her forties, was a willing taxi. Her car would fairly bulge with passengers for Sunday church. There were many trips to hospitals and shopping. She regularly drove to Ernie's at Oakleigh and looked after his four energetic shed-climbing boys.

Then came her era of self-imposed nursing duties. I used to feel guilty sometimes for viewing these house guests as intruders. Ern, sheltered in his workshop, tended his veggie garden. Sometimes he drew us small pictures, often of horses. Sometimes, with great gusto, he'd play his mandolin, or piano accordion. He would smile, laugh more then. Occasionally he'd sing. I tried to accompany him on the piano but there was some difficulty harmonising. I think this was about the time Grace moved further afield to work. Keith was probably still at school.

My eyes now strayed across the room to the low side board with the glass front, with Rosa's pretty china cups and saucers, and some drinking glasses decorated by Bob with shells on plaster of Paris. Here also sat a few evidences of Rosa's latest handiwork—several clay pots with flowing eucalyptus leaves and flowers. On the left, in the corner atop this, among a jumble of framed family photographs, were piled several photograph albums. Rosa's very first camera, a square black box, was still in the hall cupboard among her many vases.

'How did you start off with photography in the first place?' I asked.

'Uncle Joe gave me my camera, when I was ten or eleven. Grandma got him to, I think. She knew I was saving up for one. The old lady over the road from us used to ask one of us to do something, and each time she'd give us two bob. We used to cut through their place to go to Cheltenham School. I was saving up mine for a camera.'

How Rosa had learned to develop her own films intrigued me.

'Eddy Tudor, Auntie Min Tudor's stepson, told me how to do it. It was after he'd been for a holiday to Little Hampton when I was about thirteen. He sent some materials to start off with.

Sometimes I'd develop the film and I wouldn't have enough to pay for the paper to print them. Used to develop and print Minnie's photos, too. Some of the pictures Daisy got into hadn't ever been printed. I never knew what happened to them till years later.'

Lunch times always arrived too quickly during our discussions. Today we'd partaken of a salad lunch embellished with one of Rosa's favourites, her fried potato chips. 'Don't throw your chicken bones in the garden.' I called as Rosa took aim from her balcony. 'The foxes might get them.'

Rosa was unperturbed. 'Oh well, they can't help being foxes, can they!' But she hadn't been as magnanimous about that fox which tried to catch her broody chook. Rosa was still somewhat surprised about the outcomes of this incident. 'He had his head in her box. All I could see was his tail. I grabbed it, whirled it round my head and banged it down hard. Oh dear.' added Rosa, 'I don't know what came over me! Anyway, she just had a little bit of blood on her wing.'

Now, in her ninety-second year, Rosa was still claiming she would have liked to train as a nurse. 'Min used to say she would have liked to be a schoolteacher. I wanted to be a nurse. Not a domestic.

Sorry,' she said to me one day, soft eyed, contrite with self-reproach, 'Sorry about your nursing. Very sorry. I don't think I listened well enough to you about you're hating it.'

'I should have rebelled.' I said.

'What do you think is the most notable invention during your life?' I asked.

She was enthusiastic. 'I could never imagine anything like TV!'

Those clouds again. I stared at them. Ever moving. Willy-nilly. Willed by the wind. The tricks of fate. At times during our discussions, I felt horrified. I had never seen quite the extent of Rosa's pain before, her privations. Her strong, rebellious instinct. Strong emotions hidden under a quiet voice, the sunny smile. Only hinted at sometimes by fire in her eyes, and the occasional impassioned speech.

It was the next morning. I'd awakened earlier, to the happy heralding laugh of kookaburras drifting from the gully. A new sound reached my ears as I walked sleepily into the kitchen.

Rosa was smiling. Fully dressed in her dark, velvety pants and deep fuchsia jumper.

'I'm practising! Getting my whistle back now my teeth have been fixed. Something I miss about the old days. You don't hear people whistling anymore!'

Bessie

That Photo

Sparkling with effervescence. The girl probably not yet twenty. Her hair softly waved, wisped whimsically around her face. Dark eyes. They beamed sunniness in keeping with her expansive smile. The photograph spoke of a carefree contentedness.

This monochrome image of Bess was familiar. I had seen it several times in Rosa's and Min's collections. Printed on strong photographic paper, it was the only enlarged photo I had seen from that era. Apart that is from wedding memorabilia. Enlargements were uncommon during the penny-pinching depression. This, the third decade of the century, when the flower of Bessie's girlhood was just beginning to tentatively bloom.

On this day in 1996, as I sat sipping the inevitable cup of tea at Bessie's, I asked her about the photograph. Not before, of course, a walk around her prolific pretty garden and fruit trees recently pruned by Fred. 'I'm not sure a man with a saw always knows when to stop' she'd commented, laughing. That laugh! It seemed the same as that of the young girl of the picture, taken at least sixty years previously.

Bessie had agreed to talk with me about her life on the farm at Little Hampton. The youngest of the four Bruton girls and sandwiched between two boys, she was the tenth child of Olive and Harry. Percy was the younger by two years, and Bernie older by another two. Older still was Daisy, and then Allan. Harold after Percy was the last child to be born.

'That old black and white photo! You in the dark dress with the tie at the neck. What are your memories about this? How old were you? What was lifelike for you at that time?'

Bess was tapping her third finger. It resonated sharp against the wood on the arm of the sofa as she sat next to me. She tapped as she talked. She looked perplexed.

'No. No memory. No. No idea. No. Because I can't remember a dark blouse. I can only think of light colours and bright colours.'

Her fingers were now smoothing the satin wood as she glanced at the carpet, patterned in shades of earth brown and gold. 'Might be the brown woollen dress I had. That was the photograph that Ted and Ada Shelden's friend took. He was into photography a bit. I was aged sixteen. I used to baby sit. I don't think babysitting meant the same as today. In those days you didn't get paid. Probably it was on a Sunday afternoon because I had the good dress on. I think Mum probably bought it for me. She was very good at shopping. She would come back with a dress or something from Melbourne. It was during the war or just before. Eddy Tudor, Auntie Min's stepson used to work at Dimmeys in Richmond, and he'd tell Mum when there was a cheap sale. She'd buy sheets and things. Whether she actually went to the store, I don't know.

The older ones had to pay their board when working and living at home. At one stage it was one pound, I think. The boys would be working around at Rothe's and so on, they had to get to and fro. You didn't get much sympathy if you weren't helping.'

Now I was perplexed. Bessie elaborated. 'If you didn't have the energy, you'd be lazy! The general opinion was you have to keep up.'

We returned to the task of giving this photograph some colour, some meaning. The context of the click which had preserved a moment in time.

'Were you working on the farm then?' I encouraged.

'I'd left school twelve months before.' There was an abrupt finish to the sentence. Then silence. I pressed on for more detail. Bess obliged.

'Housework! Feeding the chooks, animals, milking the cow, picking up spuds and helping like that. Was early during the war. Helped at harvest time, stooking the sheaves. We used to cart it in and George used to build a haystack. I used to be helping or getting in the way or something!' Bess laughed.

'Picked up spuds at home for George and Percy. They had Jack Wickham's paddock, Wick's. George had a paddock he rented behind Swaby's. Just part of being on the farm.'

'Entertainment when you were sixteen?' I asked.

Bess was never one to talk much. Now she looked tense, lips in a thin line. She seemed to be at loss for further words. I felt I had to fan the flame of our barely ignited discussion.

'When George took me. I used to nag him into taking us, Percy and I. Mostly I suppose it was more me. We'd go to see a picture at the Trentham hall and sit on little hard stools. Don't know whether Dad knew or not, but he didn't speak up at all, and he wasn't made to feel that he could speak up. George was in his twenties then, and in charge. George had the motorbike and sidecar. A lot of times we'd just ride on the pillion. If Perce came too, he'd ride in the sidecar. I don't think he was that keen. We'd go to church at Trentham, lash out, go to the Presbyterians or whatever. Reckoned we were very brave! That motor bike and sidecar was a real family vehicle. Mum would go in the sidecar, and I would go on the back behind George sometimes.

I used to like going into the bush. Sunday afternoon people would come and we'd walk down to the bush. Anybody that was around. Frankie Attwood in later years would say, 'We'd get so bored on a Sunday. What will we do? Oh, go down to Bruton's I suppose.' I think he was living with Prices, his aunt and uncle, at that stage. Prices and Justices on the right side of the road down near the creek. The Stephens were in two houses on the left up the back of the Little Hampton School. Oh. They'd have a social evening at the church sometimes. Think they had a dance in the school and that was a bit of a no, no. Jack Talbot was MC. I'm not sure if he played an instrument.'

'The socials at the church. What did they do?' I said, realising that dances were out of bounds for Harry's children.

'Sunday evening at the church. Just party games.'

Bess's face lightened up; her mouth relaxed a bit. 'Bike riding when I could get hold of a bike. The first bike I bought was a boys' bike because they reckoned they were better than the girls' bikes. I was seventeen or eighteen. George had been up a few times to Mildura grape picking, and I went on the motorbike with him. It was dark when we got there. The people that we worked for had done up a tin shed with two beds and painted it all over with yellow. Called it 'Canary Cottage.' Probably painted inside with calcimine. I stayed there with their niece, and the boys stayed down somewhere else. We used to go in and have tea, and then they arranged to have it all outside. A lovely little sort of a bamboo place with a big table. It was so nice out there in the evenings. My bike? I've got a vague idea I got it in Swan Hill. When grape picking. That's 200 miles from our place. But how I got it down to Little Hampton I have no idea! I'd ride it into Trentham sometimes, do some shopping for Mum, get some messages for her. It was nicer riding around Swan Hill. Flatter than Little Hampton!'

'Where did you sleep at home, at age sixteen?'

'In the front bedroom. I think it was the single bed, because Daise would have been working away most of the time. Min and Rose were married then, of course too.

I went grape picking with Daise as well, once to Mildura. Run by the YWCA. Arranged because they couldn't get pickers during the war. Daise wrote and asked Mum permission to go because she was under twenty-one. Mum initially said 'No.' I said, 'I want to go too!' So Mum said if we both went together that would be alright. Daise was highly indignant about that. 'The only reason I can go is because of you.'

In my mind's eye, I was looking at that snapshot again. The vivacious smile. I glanced across the room. Here was another photograph. A dazzling jewel. Among other family portraits, including Bess and Fred's four children, there it stood in pride of place, enlarged. Bessie radiant. Her wedding day. I had been privy to that special time. My sister Grace was a small flower girl along with Minnie's eldest, Judith. Bess and Fred made an attractive couple. Both blackberry eyed brunettes, they sparkled with happiness. Fred became my dream of a man when he gave Bess the longest kiss on record after they were pronounced wedded.

We must have spoken for some hours that day, roaming like the Bruton children through the bush of Bessie's memories. We must have imbibed many cups of tea. Walked too, several times into the expansive garden, rich with Bessie's green fingered florals, herbs and collectables. Probably Bessie gave me a plant or two, which was her penchant. Frequent gifts for visitors. She and Fred, being welcoming and hospitable, may have offered me a bed for the night. This was also a thoughtful gesture, which I had with enjoyment partaken of on many occasions.

We soon ran out of any further discussion concerning Bessie's sixteen-year-old activities and environment. I pressed into another area, endeavouring to start a slow engine.

'What are your earliest memories?' I remember asking.

Bessie's voice was definite, like a blunt axe. It wasn't the abrupt mode of delivery which caught me by surprise. This was inimitably her. I looked at Bess, her face impassive. The axe fell, and I gasped with the pain of it.

'Suicide, I wished I'd never been born. Rosa told me, 'And you haven't gone to school yet.' I thought, maybe I'll die before I go to school. But Daise had said to me,' If you die, you go to heaven or hell'. I wasn't sure if I would go to heaven. Life was hard going—I wanted to get away from it. Had ten bosses.'

Daisy. Percy. Harold

Time had sped like quicksilver. It was after the new millennium that I asked Bessie again if she would share her memories with me. Bess was nearly eighty. Still a handsome woman, I thought.

The answer hung in the air, perilously, unexpressed. Bess suddenly disappeared. 'This will explain,' she said, offering me a page of a church newsletter. My eyes took in the poem. Bess's message. The edge of the silence felt jagged.

Memory Lane
I walked in Memory Lane today

It was roses all the way—
Until I heard a voice that said 'Walk not the path ahead...'
But on I pressed till suddenly –
Thorns and nettles tortured me.
My fingers bled; my sleeve was rent –
As down the tangle track, I went.
Go not too often or too far –
Along the road where memories are –
But find contact and pleasures new,
In what the present finds for you.

I was grateful that Bess eventually changed her mind. Those painful areas previously touched upon momentarily were thorns too deep. Too raw. Not to be revisited.

We embarked on a journey not taken lightly by either of us. The path was defined. Scary. We seemed like Hansel and Gretel in the dark forest. To stray from the path could mean death in the fiery furnace.

This day, a new day. Summer. The bees were busy on the Geraldton Wax resplendent with small nectar filled pink flowers. A bloom along with a plethora of other plants at the front door. I'd tried unsuccessfully to grow it. I pondered earlier as I stepped up to the open door. Perhaps it preferred the black coastal sand. This soil, where Bess and Fred lived at Mentone, had supported many a market garden. Now, crammed with houses, it seemed amazing that during the earlier era, tea-tree, robin redbreasts and bandicoots had somehow existed there. A short dash across Beach Road, down a steep enclosed concrete path, and the Drummonds could walk on the Mentone beach. One child Ross experienced some thrills and spills when speed testing his billycart on the neck-breaking incline. All four children, now parents themselves had enjoyed many a dip and frolic on its sands.

This is the same beach where a century earlier, Bess's forebears, her Bruton and Bluhm uncles and aunts picnicked on a Sunday outing. Sometimes in the twenties through to the forties, the more daring Brutons would sleep overnight in Grandma Elizabeth's bathing box.

The Mentone pier, with the tall lights from which the Bruton boys climbed and dived, no longer existed. The sand was now rarely decorated by the seaweed nutrient gathered in earlier years by horse and dray for William's renowned asparagus. The thick layer of tiny, almost transparent shells which echoed the tracing shimmer of water line, gone. Dark rocks were now polluted. No longer were they lush with molluscs, the large green periwinkle snails, or in the deeper water, shiny black mussels. All gone. Now the sand was coarse, yellowed, pumped to the shore from areas deep within the bay.

Bess and Fred attended the same church as had many of the Brutons. Not so William, her grandfather. A charismatic individual who, although contributing supplies of sand for the church foundations, according to vestry records apparently left the brotherhood 'denying the faith.' The Drummond couple had served within this community for many a year—Fred a church elder. Both were friendly visitors for the shut-in, usually attending together. There were many quietly considerate gestures contributed by them.

As I crossed the threshold after a 'Hey! Anyone home?' I recalled Fred's parents had lived in a house with a wide verandah on this spot. Now Fred and Bess were living in their new home, comfortable brick with no fireplace. Times gone by. Perhaps this house would one day give way to high rise millionaire dwellings as seemed to be now occurring along this valuable Port Phillip Bay shoreline.

We sat around the corner from the hallway where hung an oil painting, a waterfall, in a dark heavily carved wooden frame signed R.C.T. 1907. This painting, by Bess's great Aunt Rose Teagle, I had seen in the Bruton farmhouse, and later our home. Two or three other paintings, some of Fred's maritime water colours, an oil sea painting of Rosa's, one of mine, hung around us in the lounge. We talked, watched by the many family faces adorning another wall and spilling below over small tabletops. Central to all stood that wedding photograph of at least fifty years vintage.

Today as we talked Fred dozed in a chair. A veritable extrovert. He had retired— somewhat reluctantly from the job he'd enjoyed, manager of a large supermarket. His ready dry sense of humour, I knew, would surface sometime and he'd contribute his 'six pennith.' 'You ought to write up my grocer's story!' he'd said earlier. 'How we picked the weevils out of the dates and wholemeal flour!'

Bess and I sat at the table accompanied by the tape recorder. She seemed to have reconciled her nervousness and looked fairly relaxed. 'Who did you play with at home?'

'Daisy or Percy and Harold. Most of the time I fought with Harold. I remember saying to him one day 'Don't come at me as though you're going to kill me!' 'I wasn't going to but I am now!' Fortunately I was bigger than Harold. One day we were arguing about something in the paper. I was about ten. Dad banged our heads together. He was lying down and he couldn't stand it any longer. Mum came in and said to him, 'What do you think you're doing?' Off he went to bed.

As for Percy coming to the rescue. There was this young boy Collyer, same age as Perce. We were swimming at the Trentham pool. I could not get my breath. I was under the water, in too deep. Someone said, 'She's in trouble. She might drown!' Percy believed nothing could go wrong. 'Oh let her be, she's alright.' he said. It's a wonder we didn't die of infections or drowning. Harold was always doing something silly. Very determined. Used to skite. I vaguely remember pulling swedes, and Mum used to spoil Harold and pick out the nicest swede and peel it for him.'

Bess spoke with no passion, and her voice held no surprises. It was as though she had accepted her individual fate in this large family years before. The fairly neutral tone continued.

'Daise was three and a half years older than me, Bernie in between. I used to think, she's older than me, so she must know everything. She'd attached herself to Min and Stan. Apparently, she said to Min one day that I was so pretty. That she had straight hair and Bess had wavy hair. Rosa used to put my hair into rag curls, and Daise wanted the same, but it didn't look the same! Daisy had about three crowns in her hair! She felt pushed out when I was born.

Daise always wanted to be grown up. Mum was wrong. She thought Rose and Min did things together, tried to make us do things together. Daise didn't want to. I thought Mum should have known what to do. Sometimes I felt angry with Rose too. Thinking about it—silly really. I said to Mum 'I don't know who I should listen to! You or Rose! She says to do it, you say no.'

Daise argued with everyone. Dad threw her against the door. She argued with people at school. She had it in for Mum and Rose. Minnie was her confidant. Stan, Allan and Daisy were a little group to themselves. Daisy never forgave Stan for hitting her with the mattock, though he warned her.

She wanted a different sort of dress—wanted a cowl collar. I remember Rose saying, 'I don't know if I can make it that way.' but she did. I used to try Daise's clothes sometimes, then Daise thought they looked better on me. Clothes weren't that important to me. As long as things fitted and were tidy. That was the main thing. Someone said to her 'You're thin.' Then Daise said 'That means I'm skinny.' Someone gave Daise woollen gloves because she looked so miserable and cold. No one gave any to me!

Daise tried to lose me in the bush. I was quite little. But I could run just as fast as she could. Another time she and I went to Miller's through the bush to get some cream. I think she might have nicked off again. So I took off. Scooted for home.

I remember Daisy saying one day, 'I've got imagination and you've got none!'

A story Rosa told me came to mind. The young ones picnicking on the kitchen floor, replete with several pounds of sugar and jam, had quite amused me. It seemed that Bess did not remember what must have been a great time.

'What I heard about it was that it was mostly Daisy and Allan. Allan might have had the idea, and Daisy had to do the deed. We were probably just enjoying the fruits of it.'

Allan

A frightening picture emerged through the monochrome. 'I vaguely remember Allan pulling himself along the floor with one hand. I remember him falling into the fire. I remember screaming to Mum, who was in the kitchen. I tried to lift him but—big

251

blisters on the legs. Probably just fell into the ashes. He had to sleep on the couch for a few nights.

Allan was a stranger in our home. We used to expect a lot of him, to adjust to hospital then home. Allan was even more pigheaded than his father. Dad had to fit into the family, but Allan didn't have to. Allan and I used to argue a lot. He used to pick on the side you were against. He'd go the opposite. People would take offence at him. If he could just debate. Dad hated the wireless and I remember Allan arguing with him and Dad picked it up and threw it in the fire. And Allan said, 'I hate dictators!'

I think we all had a garden and I remember Allan had one too. He decided he wanted white stones around it. And he got Percy to go down to the side of the hill where there was some quartz rocks. Percy took down a hessian bag. He filled it up. It was heavy. He took one out and then took another one out. He was quite a little bloke then. That was before he started school. He was a skinny little fellow with soft straight hair. Allan would tell others what he wanted them to do. I think he used to sit there and paddle in the dirt in his garden.

One of my first memories of Allan was when Mum took me to Mentone to Grandma's. She went to see Allan, who was staying there. I was little. All I could see was this little boy in bed and those big eyes.'

Suddenly Fred, who had been snoozing, opened his eyes. 'Allan? I can tell you a few stories about Allan.'

It was before Bess and Fred's marriage in 1949, that Fred began riding his bicycle weekly from Coburg three or four miles or so across the city, to bath Allan. Stacking and lighting the chip heater was part of the process. This he did regularly for over ten years. Before her marriage, Bess stayed with Allan sometimes, upstairs at his shop in Rathdowne Street, Carlton. She cooked for him, knitted some long woollen leggings for his misshapen legs, which were often tinged with blue.

Fred with a propensity for amusing anecdotes recounted. 'This evening, I turned up and Allan was sporting a black eye and chipped front tooth. 'What happened?' Allan felt ashamed to say. He said he had offered to transport a gas stove along Bourke Street to Spencer Street, on his wheelchair. He had forgotten about the hill. Got out of control. 'Me and the stove parted company, then me and the chair!'

He'd tell me he wanted to go to the Richmond Temple. I'd carry him up on the tram, shuttle him off in the city, and then on the other tram to Richmond. He used to tell the tram conductors how to lift him up. 'You ought to see what my friend does. He picks me up under the arms and dumps me down. You people do it the wrong way.'

On the Tuesday nights when I'd take him to the Richmond Temple, I'd go and meet him. I was in the army at Royal Park. It was just before my discharge and we used to get off early. Allan would be selling papers on the corner of Spencer Street and

Burke Street, just a little way across from the railway station. I'd see him other times too, like when I'd meet Bess on the evening train from Woodend.

Sometimes Allan would say, 'I'm not going to be able to sell all my papers. So many left.' I'd call out to people getting off the tram 'Save you walking down to the newsagent Come on! Tuppence for the paper!'

Allan would say, 'I might get in trouble from the newsagent for calling out.'

I'd say, 'Tell them it's the army!'

People would pay tuppence for a Herald, the evening paper. He made half a penny per paper. Often people would give thrippence. Same with a four penny one, a weekly paper. People would give sixpence.'

Even the train-focussed traveller hurrying by could not ignore Allan's heavy wheelchair and misshapen body. At the least of it, whether buying a paper or not, a quick glance would take in the big guileless dark eyes, and tiny twists of hands. I had observed his best hand miraculously hold a pen and write an awkward spidery scrawl.

'How did Allan actually pick out the appropriate change? Separate a tiny silver thrippence from a large penny?' I now asked Fred.

Fred smiled that slow smile. 'As little as possible. He had a small purse, brown leather, round his shoulder. He used to empty it into his hand. Nine times out of ten he could pick out the change with his fingers.' He chuckled. It was obvious Fred enjoyed talking about Allan. Scoundrel as Allan was, it was clear Fred had some affection for him.

'Allan used to go slow, rarely gave the change out. They were in a hurry to catch a train. He would mumble very slowly and give a smile. People would say 'Forget it.' Even the paper boys carrying the papers over their shoulders didn't worry about giving change. Sometimes people would say when Allan was getting the change, 'Keep it mate, you need it more than us.'

Fred paused, staring through the side window into the past. 'But there were some crafty people around. One fellow used to come and straighten Allan up and tuck him in at the back. Allan said, 'My friend will help me.' I said, 'He'll help you alright. Get rid of him!' 'He helps me. He's alright.' 'Give me all the money you've got and I'll give it back tomorrow.' 'Oh No.'

The next time I said, 'Where's your mate?' 'He's gone.' 'Yes, and he took all your money, didn't he?' 'Yes. I should've listened to you.'

Fred opened his eyes wide, making a point. 'But. He wouldn't listen to anyone!'

Bernie. Daisy

When Bernie died, Bess must have been two months over two years old. Surprisingly she seemed to remember her sick little brother. 'I said to Mum 'I don't think it is right. Bernie should come home because I want him home.' Mum said, 'Yes I do too, but he's not coming home.' The impression I got was that Mum wanted Bernie home and there must have been something there that Mum couldn't do. And I remember Mum being upset and saying, 'My poor baby, my poor baby,' around this time. I think I remember playing with Bernie.'

Bess sighed. She was remembering another stress.

'Allan would get Daise to do things then tell Mum on her. Daise didn't feel much for Allan. He and I used to play draughts.

Daise managed to get things her own way. She'd growl till she got it. Min gave me a suit. Daise swore it was given to her.' Bessie's voice was heavy. 'I let her have it any way.'

'What do you think Daise would have liked to have done in her life, differently, perhaps?'

'Oh music! After they found that she was sick with Alzheimer's a part of her therapy was painting. And when I visited her in hospital in Queensland there was a painting hanging over her bed. It was very nice. I asked Paul after she died if they had got the painting and Paul has it at his place. The great idea was the violin, and Mum used to say, 'I wish I could afford to send her to learn.' But Daisy may not have liked the lessons because 'I've got to do it my way!' But you have to learn the discipline first then you can vary it.

Daisy always had bronchitis. Caught everything. Daise told me in later years 'Why was Mum always taking me to the doctors—I always seemed to be going. And Mum could ill afford it.' She kept getting a pain in her side and constipation. She had her tonsils out. They thought it could be appendicitis and then this and then that. When she was in her teens, she used to say to Mum, 'I can't understand why you stay with him.' Mum said, 'When you've got three or four kids, you can't leave them, you just stay and have more.'

Daise could see things others didn't see. Pick out details.'

My mind was elsewhere. I thought of the two little sisters, Bess and Daise. Innocent babes. Surviving each in her own way. Daise defiantly vocal, her need beneath her noise. Bess quietly bottling. One expressing, the other suppressing. The wind screamed for them both. It whined and wept their woes. It called wildly. It called softly. The windmill creaked and groaned their pain. The laurel tree rocked its branches. A gentle lullaby. And in the hush of an exhausted silence a yawning gap remained, an unfilled void of longing and loneliness.

And Bess kept smiling. A smile that hid a thousand hurts. And Daisy kept shouting for someone, somebody, to hear.

'What was it like, being a girl in those days?' I asked.

'Mum said 'Boys will be boys and girls have to make up for it!' We had to pick up spuds and so on, if they were stuck or they needed us.

Oh of course a girl's lot was different. I don't know why because the boys had opportunities I didn't. I could have done all sorts of things if I had been a boy.'

'What?'

'They got looked after. Came home, their bed was made and their dinner was cooked. They worked very hard too. But when they didn't work, they'd nick out to do rabbiting. Yes, I did go sometimes, but wasn't necessarily appreciated. I was only in the road. I think, for the times, Mum was quite enlightened. What would you say, considering the issues? I don't know. I think she was quite impartial.'

The Big Kids

Presumably the really big kids according to young Bess, would have been Tom, Rosa, Min, Bob, George and Stan, Daise. A formidable bunch when one considers the lack of power a young child may feel. Bess was a little sister to delight in or to dominate.

Bess smiled. Her voice hinted at irony. 'The younger ones were taught you must do what the older ones tell you. The older ones were always right. So that meant we were never right!' said Bess smiling again.

'Mum said, 'The older ones find the younger ones quite a worry.' I said, 'But the younger ones find the older ones a worry.' 'Yes' Mum said, 'but it isn't quite the same.' Mum was an oldest too.

As far as I was concerned, Rose was the voice of authority. I was aged thirteen. Rose said, 'You never have friends over. Why don't you have your friends over?' 'I don't have any friends, because I'm the only girl in the grade. Two boys and me. Too many boys. I don't like boys.' 'Don't be silly. All girls your age like boys!'

A girlfriend said, 'I'll come on condition you walk home with me, not the boys.' When it came time to go home, Rose said, 'Stan will go with her, he has the afternoon off. You feed the chooks.' The girl didn't speak to me again. I eventually became friends with Ann Swaby, we became good friends. She was five years younger, also June Belyea, another neighbour.

Tom told me that Rose was to a certain extent black and white. I didn't agree with Tom at the time because what Rose said was right. Tom had some radical ideas, theories about all sorts of things. Whatever was being discussed, he felt he knew the answers.'

Bess returned to Daise, a deeply imbedded thorn. She had boiled, brewed and bottled her feelings concerning this troubled relationship, memories of which seem to have dogged her footsteps forever.

'I remember we were down the mineral springs. Rose told Daise not to cross the river on the log yet. She was to stay there till Rose could help her over. But Daise kept going and fell in, then was very cross with everyone, especially Rose. She always took offence very easily. She was determined the whole world was against her.

'Everybody's got bare feet. I've got boots on—because my ankles are weak.' Just one more thing that made her different to the rest of us.

She told me when she was living away from home, she had a dream. She was feeling no-one loved her, and everyone 'agin' her! In the dream she died. Her mother was sitting on her grave crying like anything.

I remember Mum telling her one day, 'The only name I really wanted was Daisy because I always loved that name. And it suits you so well, you're a tiny little Daisy.' Then she spoilt it! 'I loved it so much. When I was a young girl, I called a cow Daisy.'

No. Daise didn't see it as a compliment. 'You named me after a cow?' I think she might have come round later, that it was something else. Oh, she was probably a teenager. We were working in the kitchen doing something or other.'

'And going back to Tom?'

'As a child, I don't have memories of Tom.'

She returned briefly to that major dominating force of her youth.

'Daise had vivid memories of Tom putting the earphones on her. She heard music for the first time, and he was important ever since. Made an impact on her. Daisy thought Tom had a good ear for music. She said to me, 'I could never forget the time when Tom put the earphones on me—it was the most marvellous thing that happened to me.' This was his crystal set. Daise remembered too, when she and Ted had the potato farm at Eidi, in South Gippsland. Ted was away when Tom visited once, and the roof blew off the cow shed. She didn't know until Tom was gone that the roof was back on.

Before he went away, he fiddled with the wireless a lot. He had a high aerial at home, big high one. He was a natural for the army signals. He experimented with different ways of doing things. He made his own electricity. He was an inventor. He made a wireless for our wedding present. A little box about a foot square. We traded it in after five or ten years. Got a little mantelpiece one.

I think I was there when Tom came back from working in NSW. Mum went to the door; this man was there with a suitcase. Mum thought 'I wonder who it is.' 'Oh cripies, don't tell me you don't know me either.' Tom said. I remember Percy, Harold and I, being down the paddock discussing what Tom's like and if he's coming home for good.

Stan was a bit like Tom. George and Bob would come straight in and sit for tea, but Stan would have a good wash in the bath and change his clothes after working. Stan had bronchitis. He was fussy. He'd have to wash his hands between dirty jobs. George would not understand. He would get impatient with him. The others would wash when they had to.

Mum was told that Stan would develop T.B. if he didn't leave Cheltenham too. Mum, Bob Min and George didn't seem to get bronchitis but got diphtheria.

Stan always had the job of shooting the animals, he didn't like doing it. In his late teens he said to Mum, 'I'm the only one has to do that. Why always me?' He was always helpful. Knew where all the birds' nests were. 'I'll show you on condition you don't show the little ones, you are not to touch them' and so on. Must have been slashing ferns, and Percy sat down, and a rabbit jumped out from under him. He taught us to be thoughtful of those things. He got that from Mum. She loved the birds.

Uncle Will Bluhm's cockie was Mum's originally, then Grandma got very fond of it. Ron and Dorothy looked after it. Ron's son Allan let the cat in. Cockie would have been sixty years old. George and Stan were in the Gould League concerning birds. Got the magazine.

When Tom was a baby, he was allergic to cow's milk. They gave him sago and all sorts of different things. I wonder how they heard he was allergic. He suffered with tiredness. Also, the T.B. would not have helped. It was very sad when Tom was taken prisoner in the war. Stan was overseas at the same time. We'd have prayers in the morning. Always had prayers at night for the boys.

Dad would go to Red Hill to Tom's orchard and stay and work hard for him after Tom married. That was before the war. Tom spent a lot of time with Uncle Will earlier. He could have learned about growing fruit trees from him. He would go to Red Hill with Uncle Will, probably on business. Uncle Will had the truck. He could have been an influence on Tom's life in other ways. Uncle Will's son, our cousin Ron, liked electricity too. Inventing things for the orchard, things like that, same as Tom. Mum was interested in mechanical things. Allan, Ron's son is too.'

'By the time you were a teenager, had family rules changed a bit?'

'Went out with the big boys. Dad had given up standing up to them. The older ones weren't allowed to go to the pictures. We did. There were still some things. We said we were going to a social, didn't let on it was a dance. He was very upset because of the deception. We told Harold off. 'I'm not going to tell lies too!' Harold said.

'Who were 'we'?'

'Percy, George and me. Only us at home by then. Harold was about twelve. I'd be fifteen or sixteen. We'd inferred it was the social. Harold started talking about the dance. Dad was upset, not so much with us. Didn't say it to us. He'd take it out on Mum. 'You encourage them to deceive me.'

I wanted to hear more about this clandestine activity, this devilish dance. 'Where was it held?'

'Only within the local district, Little Hampton School. Forbidden fruit, so it had to be good! Not as often as once a month, every few months. The school master had to get special permission from the Education Department each time. Several teachers did it, including Mr Collyer. When I was at school and there was going to be a dance, we'd still have lots of fun beforehand. The school kids grated up candle grease. This and sawdust was spread on the floor to make it slippery. We'd jump on it, slide around, rub it in with our feet. We might have helped sweep it up too.

I remember walking home one night before the dance was finished. Scared? What was there to be scared of? I think perhaps I should have been more scared than I was.

When I was older, I had a lot of contact with George. Harold was not very responsible. Before he'd have a fit, he'd be very cantankerous. George was the only one—Mum, Perce and I–the more we'd say to Harold the worse he'd get. George would say, 'Go and lie down.' He knew George would not fuss, and when George spoke Harold realised it was the right thing to do.

I was fourteen when Bob married at twenty-four. With the war, George took over. When he took me to the pictures, he would bring some Minties and he'd laugh at the film. Every now and then he would come home with a block of chocolate for Mum. Whenever they'd ask me to go out, I'd go, because another time they mightn't.! When the tennis was on, he'd take me. He'd play. He liked it. He and Freda were much into it. He was conscientious and kind. We'd get out and mix with people.

At church he would often sit in the back seat with Freda, their family. I remember sitting in front of him and listening to him sing. He had a good singing voice. Sang in the paddock, he and Percy. Percy used to yodel. When he got off the bus after school, we'd hear him through the strip of bush. Daise would play the mouth organ and sometimes whistle. Bob used to play the mouth organ as a kid. Think he probably encouraged Daise with it. George played too, and Rosa a little. Stan would whistle a lot.

George. He could have been rigid. I was arguing about going to church, that it was too hot to wear a hat and stockings. He said you can go without the stockings, but you have to wear a hat! He had a temper, but not a destructive one. He'd get frustrated, and he'd say some funny words that meant nothing. He didn't swear. Bob and Tom would swear. George and Stan wouldn't.

George stood up to Dad, but not aggressively. Went quietly his own way.'

'Who do you think George might have been closest to in the family?' I asked.

'Probably Percy. Bob and George took him under their wing. George would say in answer to a question about what to do on the farm that week. 'Wait till Perce, the boss, comes home from school.' Percy was very placid and confident in himself.

'And who did you share your inner-most secrets with?'

'Oh,' Bess laughed 'That was never the thing to do.'

'With George, perhaps?' I persisted.

'George was eight years older. We must have talked. We'd lunch together in the paddock and he was into the community too. He was one of the instigators to get the tennis courts built.

He may have felt guilty about not going to the war. The place would not have been paid off if George hadn't been there. When he married, he had nothing. Probably would have had a lot more if he hadn't helped Mum pay off the mortgage. He bought Dagg's. Bought it off Ted Shelden.

I cried a lot when George died. Ian was a three-month-old baby. I was feeding him. Ian was very upset. Someone said, 'Perhaps he's grieving for George.'

The shock of George's untimely departure. We were visiting my grandmother at Avonsleigh with Min. I still remember. Perhaps it was a telegram that brought the news. Olive's body was bent over with the shock. She had to sit down. Min and Rose's arms were around her as she wept. A pleasant summer's afternoon had changed to a dark chill. I removed myself from this sorrowful scene and walked slowly up the bush track at the back. I was sadly aware of having had very little contact with my Uncle George, whom I would never see again.

Bess continued. 'The week George died, he had made arrangements with Percy to go to Kyneton on the Friday. He was insured and going in to stop or lower his insurance policy. He was buried instead. The insurance policy cost a lot, but it certainly paid off. I think it paid the farm off. He'd made his will and everything. He would get tired, and Mum would give him Clement's Tonic. He had it a long time. On and off for at least ten years. Later on Mum went to the chemist, said she was worried about Harold. The chemist said, 'No! Don't give him Clement's Tonic. It has strychnine in it! It's a heart stimulant. Last thing he should have!''

The 'Outhouse'

Now a happier memory surfaced for Bess. 'I remember George sitting on the fence whistling or playing the mouth organ when us younger ones had to go to the toilet at night. 'I'll come with you' he'd say. I think he did the same for Daisy. At one stage there was this mopoke on the clothesline. In the early days we'd have a lantern.'

'Those outside toilets have become things of the past,' I said.

'Hopefully.'

'What did you call it?'

'Mum always used to call it the closet. When we started school, we found other names for it. What you could whisper. Dunny or W.C. I thought a lavatory was one with a chain. The seat, we used to scrub with phenyl regularly. People would say, 'You've always got a clean toilet.'

Grey and weather-beaten. It was visited by many prior to bedtime. Not necessarily bravely. A last walk before sleep, along that endless, often wet gravel path, accompanied by the dank odour of decaying leaves. Thankfully, during the night, the white crockery bed chamber pot would suffice. The quick dash in the dark, usually with Rosa, never engendered heroism in me. Rather, it fuelled my fantasies. After passing the austere washhouse, there were the dark bushes. They often rustled and swayed. Green leaved homes of mischievous gremlins. The kerosene lantern played tricks, casting even more mysterious shadows. The small building backed onto an even longer expanse. An enormous paddock that stretched down the hill to the 'never never' of the black brooding bush. I would shudder to think of it. The thought of being pursued by the dark-cloaked stealthy creatures I had read about in my first school reader, terrified me. The horrible hopyars!

The shadowy world of the lantern's flicker masked hiding places for the various insects, small creepy inhabitants of this small house. Sometimes they ventured out between draughty gaps or below the roughhewn seat, amid a sharp shout of discovery. On arrival, it was not always easy to feel the nail on which the strip of leather from an old boot, or a shoelace, secured the door. Once inside we would leave it ajar, grateful for the comfort of the waiting companion and a sliver of light. Enough illumination for cold fingers to grasp a neatly cut square of newspaper. This hung with string to another nail, inside, on the right wall. A hole made with a skewer through the corner, the paper had probably been folded then cut with a sharp-edged knife.

Too bad when nature called if there was the sting of rain or cut of wind. Too bad if during a period of concentration one is startled by a sudden back stiffening slither, or a creeping black spider. As one returned, the soft, safe lamp-lighted house beckoned. Not before passing the windmill. The regular creak, companionable during the day, could become ominous during these times. It seemed to signal the sinister dark well by its side. Though this was covered, I feared that any stumble on the path may result in fearful consequences. Especially as I had heard that the lady up the road in the corner house had jumped into their well to finish herself off.

Bess recalled more about these nocturnal expeditions. 'Sometimes we'd take the lantern. I've got the memory of a carriage lantern with a candle in it, probably from one of the jinkers. It was a hurricane lantern after that. I think there was a bit of a knack to lighting them. You'd hear foxes calling down in the bush. The owls used to come. Sometimes we'd all have to go and have a look. The toilet seat was up higher, and there was a stool so Allan could get up. And those trees on the way. Stan planted lucerne along there, along the fence line, the windy side, to the toilet. Before the war, I think. He was always interested in planting things. He said, 'Because you can feed the lucerne to the cattle if short of hay or something.' He had it all worked out. In later years Percy built a replacement toilet, closer, on the outside wall of the wash house.

And those other trees on the way. Mum tried to grow the shiny leaved mirror bush. It used to grow at Mentone. Apparently, it didn't like being cold and exposed. And the golden chain laburnum. It's still there. Mum tried so hard to get those trees to grow! That laburnum grew into a huge tree. I got a lot of seeds and I've planted a few here, but they don't do well. It likes the cold. I gave one to Doreen. It's near the paddock at the front. They put a fence around it because apparently it's poisonous to animals.'

Bess now sounded as though she was relishing the best meal she'd ever had. 'But they are.... Beautiful.' The word rolled slowly as she savoured every syllable. 'The pea flowers hang down in pinnacles.'

School

'I was just over five when I started. Stan took me to school. Don't remember George being at school. Must have left before I started. Stan used to show Daise where the birds' nests were, didn't show me because I might frighten them. Nests in the bracken fern. Chat's nests. Little black and white bird.'

'Allan?'

'Allan going to school? Yes, I remember. Stan told me they borrowed a pram off Belyeas. Daise and I had to take turns to push him. Stan must have left school, and Percy and Harold were smaller. The loggers with half a dozen horses would go past, sometimes only with one big log. One man, a logger used to say 'Oh you are such good girls. Here's an apple.' Sometimes it would be one apple, sometimes one each. I wasn't allowed to push it when he was around. Daise would want to! We'd go along the side of the road around the quagmire. After the war they gravelled it. We were very pleased. Jim McKenzie's son doing bread deliveries got bogged near the gate. I remember Allan saying one day, 'It's alright for you. I can't do that. You can run.' It didn't occur to me because he was just Allan and that's how he was.

We'd be just running late already for school, and Dad would say there was to be prayers first. He mightn't get up in time. You had to fit in with him. Don't think it took very long. Five or ten minutes. Dad would go to bed early and sleep in sometimes, then we'd get off without them.

I remember telling Rose not to put butter on my sandwiches because I liked the honey to soak into the bread. She used to make porridge for us. Lumpy. Told me I had to eat it before going to school. I vowed I will never have porridge when I grow up.

When I was older, we'd cut our lunch. Though there was usually somebody older who did it like Rosa and Mum. Jam or whatever else.

Mr Dunell. I was always scared of him because I could see what he did to the other kids. Oh, but I don't know that I was, really. I think he had migraines. He just used to put one of the kids in charge because he had such a bad headache. He used to complain because the sparrows made so much noise. I was very annoyed with him because he would put poisoned wheat around in the gutter.

When he left, the new teacher, I felt he took a dislike to me straight away, Mr Cagill. He and Mr Dunell gave the strap. I think the sight of it was enough for most of the boys. The worse thing about him was his sarcasm, wasn't so much the strap. I don't know if he took a dislike to me or I did to him. He wasn't a well man either; he had polyps in the stomach.'

'Friends?'

'Ann Swaby later on, they were younger than me. I just got a letter from her the other day. I always send Christmas cards. The two girls in the house over the road between our house and John Rothe's, Nancy and June Belyea.

Harold developed fits while I was at primary school. I remember the teacher saying he had read it up. He hadn't fainted. It was a fit. He was about six. I was about ten.'

'Daise?'

'Daise did not play with me particularly, but with the older ones. I got on with Nell Rothe, she always looked after me. Daise was friendly with Freda off and on. I think Nell used to protect me from Daisy. Nell would say, 'Leave her alone!' Daise tried to boss me. Nell was my refuge. She told Daise off when she picked on me. Nell had it in for Daise for years—all her life.

Got my Merit after Phil Collyer came. He was a funny man, but he did teach. Didn't give the strap. The boys used to hide the strap on him, and he would get Mum to get another one from the boot makers when she did the mail run. He'd say, 'I can understand sometimes you have to talk to each other.' When upset he'd jump up and down, he'd shout. Then everyone would be quiet for a few weeks and it would gradually build up again.

At the school were the Rothes, the Thorpes, Swabys, Moloneys, Scanlans, Gillises, Hourigans. They used to call the Belyeas 'bellyache.' Altogether there would have been ten or so children.

Instead of leaving school, I could have gone to Daylesford Tech. Mum wanted Percy to do carpentry. By that time the bus fare was subsidised by the Government, and the cost was halved. He didn't want to be a carpenter he wanted to be a farmer! 'You can be a farmer and still learn carpentry, is something to go back on.' There was no free bus in my day. It wasn't considered I go to Daylesford. After all, I was a girl.

I loved school the last few years, when I was the eldest in the school and had a nice teacher. Harold fell foul of Mr Dunell—I didn't. Mr Dunell would threaten Harold or give him the strap. Harold had a fall from the school roof. He walked around the spouting. He was very adventurous. Had to do what the older ones did. He was tall, they possibly expected him to be more mature than he was.

I remember Daise arguing with Mum because Mum wanted her to stay at school. 'And you let Rosa leave school and you don't let me.' Think she was thirteen and a half when she left. I don't think she could have got her Merit. Was probably while Dunell was there. I don't think he was a particularly good teacher.

I've got a feeling that George may have left school before the Merit exams. His birthday was in October. He didn't put any value on it. I can remember Bob leaving school. I remember him coming in and putting his hat up. 'I'm not going to school anymore. I'm fourteen today!' I guess he worked on the farm and where he could. John, that is Ginger Rothe, gave him work, and George worked for Fred Rothe. Bob would come home late. Mum would say, 'It's such an effort to keep his tea hot.' Apparently, Mum told Dorrie Rothe, Ginger's wife this. Dorrie said, 'But he's had tea already at my place.'

At the back of the school there were two houses. A sister and a brother lived together, and a sister lived in the other one, a widow. They were lovely old ladies and the old fellow used to take the wheelbarrow and he'd collect wood. One lady was deaf and the other one was lovely. She said, 'I could have married, but I promised Mum I'd always look after Steve.' Old Steve, he used to go down the bush there and get firewood near our place. He'd go a little way, he'd sit. At church he always sat in the second front seat and he always took up the collection. One Sunday he came when church was nearly finished, and someone else had to do it and everyone felt bad about it. He became a bit vague, did well to get there. He used to have a beard and once a year he'd go and have it shaven. Beards were unusual when we were kids. Short back and sides.'

'The climate. Walking to school in that biting cold, even snow!' I exclaimed.

'The snow would press into the tender parts of the horses' hoofs and they wouldn't be able to walk. So George would have to sometimes go and collect the mail on his motorbike. The climate. Coldest spot in the district, even. Where the house was, it was so cold and wet. Our bare hands used to get cold.'

The blanched numbness of cold hands! Not surprising in that bone chilling climate. I remembered something written in an historical account about the local school. It was in 1881 after parents' complaints that the school was lined. The children had often been unable to write due to hands too cold to hold a pencil. This, even though a fire was always burning.

'Glad I didn't grow up in Little Hampton.'

Bess was unmoved. 'I don't think the climate worried me that much. I had never known anything else. Mum had tepid water to put our hands in when we came home from school. Things were lovely and green in the Little Hampton climate, even when there were droughts elsewhere.

Stan, Allan, Daise and Bernie came to Little Hampton and none of them were very healthy. Mum was friends with Freda's mother who told her, 'They're so much healthier since coming here.'

We used to come home from school and pick up spuds. No pay! That was part of life. George was in charge. Me and Mum depended on George so much, especially with Perce and Harold. She'd noticed in Harold's bank book he'd drawn out all his money. And George spoke to him. And Harold wouldn't tell George what he had done with all that money. And when George got married, Harold gave him a beautiful rabbit fur rug. Very handy in the sidecar. I think Freda probably still has it. George felt awful. Terrible.

My happiest memories are coming home from school. The people you meet. Dorrie Rothe's niece, Claire. We enjoyed walking together. She'd turn right, and I'd walk up with her to her place.'

Fun

Bess was hesitant. 'Fun? Singsongs at Little Hampton church. When we were little and Mr Dunell was the Little Hampton schoolteacher, Mrs Dunell ran the Sunday school. She also had an after-school children's' meeting at the church. At the end of one year, she'd put on a concert with the kids. I think Dorrie Rothe helped too. The concerts were okay. I remember Rose dressing us up with fairy wings and muslin. Rosa and Min used to recite at concerts at home and at socials at the church.

'Family concerts?'

'Didn't appeal to me. Rosa used to be the main instigator. I remember her deciding Percy was to take part and Min and Rose teaching him 'Hi Diddle Diddle.' I used to try and get out of them. I'd hide under the table and watch. Don't think Harold minded it much. Later on when we had them at the Sunday school Harold was stubborn, he wouldn't want anything to do with it. 'I won't be holding a girl's hand,' etcetera!'

'Dolls?'

'I'm not a real doll person. Played mothers and fathers. George would teach us how to play with dolls, show you how to dress it. Made a clay doll for me once. Not very satisfactory. When I tried to wash it, just melted away. He was about thirteen. So, I put a wish to Santa Claus to bring me one. The school committee used to have Santa near a fir tree that was growing there. Got a celluloid one. Santa commented that it had no clothes on, and I felt embarrassed. 'Santa Claus just sounds like the Minister.' Everybody laughed when I said that. Had it for years and years. Could still be around there for all I know. In those days it was lucky to get anything without worrying about dressing it.

George would sort of join in with us. Stan would like going on his own. He'd take Daise, show her where the birds are. He was friendly in that way; he'd show us what he wanted to show us. George would try to meet us on our ground.'

'Us?'

'Me and Daise, Percy perhaps. I don't know.'

Bess rose suddenly and stretched up. She opened a glass sliding door on the top of the tall cabinet against the wall. Carefully, smiling with pleasure, she showed me her prize.

A doll. The pink celluloid of yesteryear. It stared at me with big brown eyes and a fixed smile. Delicately clothed, it wore a wisp of gold mesh, now tarnished, and a big pink ribbon bow, barely concealing its nakedness. In its day, it would have been a child's delight. I carefully held it in my hand. I wondered about the origin of such a pretty gift.

'It was Auntie Min Tudor's neighbour. I reckon I was about four. I think I came down with Mum before I started school. I think Lorna and I were playing with the little boy next door. His mother called me in and gave it to me. She didn't have a girl.'

I gazed at the doll again. I felt its limbs. Firm cold celluloid, but somehow soft and easily injured. There was a dent or two in the side of its head where perhaps an overzealous, ignorant someone had squeezed it, inflicting a wound. No warm clothes, marks of comfort and nurture. Seemingly unaware of its vulnerability, the eyes almost defiantly surveyed the world. Paradoxically, it held a shepherd's or bishop's hooked staff. Its gold hat, reminiscent of a bishop's, was flat above the faded fairy face.

'You've had it for a long while,' I observed.

'Rosa kept it in her glory box for me. Probably gave it to me when she thought I was old enough to look after it. When she got married. I was about fourteen. She'd take it out now and again. Everyone thought it was beautiful. At different stages of my life I'd play with it. Other times, good to have it put aside. But if she didn't put it away, I wouldn't have had it.'

Tucked away, aired rarely. Not unlike Bessie's memories.

Bess was continuing. 'My impression is the older ones weren't allowed to have dolls. 'Graven images.' I was Rosa's doll, I think. I don't think we were into dolls much. I think Daise was a bit keen—she'd use toys to make plays. I remember her playing school with toys up against the wall. I don't remember her babying them. When I was a teenager, I was making dolls' clothes to send to the mission. Stan was watching. He said, 'I don't remember you playing with dolls when you were little.'

Auntie Eva had a doll. Rosa would go and play with it there when our family lived at Cheltenham. And one day when she went Auntie had given it to Eva Clayton, our cousin. Rosa was very disappointed. But Rosa had a lot of babies instead to look after. Whereas Min wasn't allowed to have dolls either. It didn't worry her. To have a doll and dress it nicely would have been Rosa's thing. Not having dolls didn't worry me either.'

'Perhaps Rosa might have gained some enjoyment in keeping your doll carefully for you.'

'Possibly yes. She was so rapt on how beautiful it was.

But walking down the bush was something I really did enjoy. Oh. Running wild, I think. If you didn't like what was going on inside, you could go outside, find something to do. I was interested in the chooks, I think and feeding the calf. Put our fingers in the milk, then into the calf's mouth to get it to drink. Perhaps after half a dozen times or so they'd get the idea of drinking. But you had to hang on to the bucket because they'd butt it.

We used to feed the pig, usually had one at a time. I don't remember them killing them, they'd get it into the spring cart. Don't know how they kept it in there. Take it to Beattie the butchers in Trentham. If it was being done at home, they'd keep us right out of the way. Daise lived in Trentham for a while when Jan was little. Jan would say, 'We'll go down to the meatie, see Mr Beattie.''

'And what did you enjoy the very best?' I was thinking that it must be the bush.

'My fun was being on my own! Do you remember that laurel tree? I'd climb up. You'd take a book up there to read. Lovely cool spot, and the branches just the right angle to sit. Oh, I'd be thirteen or so, possibly before that. Goodness knows. I did it for a long time. I had to be old enough to be able to climb the tree. It had a lean to it. It went over the house at the front near Tom's room and shaded the verandah.'

Bess paused, enjoying the memory, ever green. 'But they were lovely, lovely trees. There aren't many laurel trees around now. Some around Emerald in the Dandenongs. I'd go by myself down the bush too sometimes, but mostly in a group. I remember Stan shimmying up the trees. He'd get up to have a look, skite.'

The laurel tree was special to me too. 'Those lush, shiny leaves. I'm glad it survived the axe. What did you read up there?'

'My reading? 'Anne of Green Gables' of course, and similar, and the various Anne books. Later on I was more interested in the boys' books, like cowboy westerns, rather than the girls.' It was cool in the tree. We used to complain about the heat in the summer. Mum would say, 'You get hot north winds at Cheltenham, like a hot oven. We don't get it that hot.' '

Bess in the laurel tree had fuelled my imagination. I felt a kinship as my mind's eye surveyed this languid picture. Bess as one ablur with branches and leaves, sunshine and shadows in dappled dance. Light playing upon silky shoulder hugging, softly waved, honey brown hair. Bare feet and strong brown legs spliced into dark branches. The tree whispering its support silently.

Bess and her book. A special world within, and without. Her house of dreams.

Horses

'Ride? I was nervous. The two youngest boys rode Little Doll. If anybody heavier got on her, she'd buck. Found out that's what the big boys taught her to do—probably for the fun of it.

Was lots of horse accidents those days. Little Doll was so old when I knew her—mostly she was just in the paddock as a pet. When I was young, Con and Big Doll and Little Doll were all old. Con had a tummy that rumbled a lot, just wind. Would sound like a motor when he was in the jinker.

Robert, he was the horse man. I'm not sure who taught Little Doll to buck, but maybe it was him. I was on Little Doll one day and she bolted. I pulled so hard on one rein, which broke and she stopped. Think she was trying me out. I can remember George leading a horse and me sitting in the saddle. I think he paid two pound for this horse and it was so skinny. I think he took pity on it. It came good, but it hadn't been trained. 'Darkie' became too hard for us to handle.'

Bess held a flat table knife upright between thumb and index finger, balancing handle then blade. Up and down. Down and up.

'Any horse accidents you recall?'

'Percy and I went in the horse and jinker to the mineral springs. I said, 'The tree's over there to tether him.' Percy said, 'Oh that's too far away I've always put him here.' He was going to move the horse and I don't know if it was distracted or not. The horse reared up on his back legs. Percy was holding him. The horse was way up high. He moved backward. He put the jinker wheel over the edge of the concrete near the dozen or so steps which went down into the mineral springs. Then the other wheel. The jinker pulled the horse over the sheer ten feet or so drop. He was screaming on his back. Must have been on top of the jinker, on the concrete at the bottom. I don't remember. 'What are we going to do!' Percy was about ten. I was about thirteen. Percy said he had seen someone in Spurling's paddock. I ran along behind him. Percy was well ahead of me. I don't know what the fellow did, but he got that horse on his feet.

We helped push the jinker up the steps and out. One of the shafts was broken. He got a sapling and tied up the harness where it was needed. I think the horse was a fairly new one they had bought in the sale yards. Probably a cheap one.'

'And the horse?' A question I had to ask.

Bess spoke with her inimitable bluntness. 'The horse was none the worse that we know.

Another time I went to pick up somebody at the station in the jinker and I only got as far as Moloney's, past the church at Little Hampton. I realised he didn't have a bit in his mouth. I couldn't control him! It didn't dawn on me till I got there what it was. Bob was playing tennis in the courts near the church, fortunately, and he put a bit in the horse's mouth for me. I tied it up at the station. A train pulled up. A steam engine. The horse had fire in its eyes. I didn't know till then what it meant. Plain terror! By the time they came out to the cart and the train had gone, the horse had settled down. Of course, if I'd had enough sense, I'd have tethered it up further in the yard.

There was a horse accident with Mum and the jinker when she was doing the mail. I was at home getting the lunch. I don't know what horse it was. It came and put its head over the gate. I remember George tearing out. I didn't know he'd got a fright. Mum had bounced out on to her tail. I don't know if the horse was still in the shafts when it got home. Mum hurt her back. We kept up the mail run. We took turns. I used to do it, and I think George did it sometimes. Bob was married. Some people said Mum's mail job wouldn't pay the horse feed. She said, 'I'm very glad of it and I have to go into Trentham anyway to do shopping.' I think it was about thirty shillings a week, ten shillings a trip.'

Now Fred appeared, having spent a considerable time on the telephone. He'd told me that if unable to fulfil his usual friendly visitor schedule, he telephoned instead. Perhaps that was what Fred had been doing. He heard the end of our conversation about horses. Flopping comfortably into his armchair among cushions with Bessie's crocheted woollen covers, he now contributed a horse story.

'When my dad had the grocer's store at Coburg, he used to deliver to various homes with horse and cart. Tommy was the horse, and Dad reckoned he was more intelligent than me! One day Dad was sick, and he told me that I had to do the delivery. Dad said, 'You don't have to worry about what houses to go into. Tommy will show you.' We went along Sydney Road, turned the first street at the Baptist church. Tommy stopped there. So I picked up the box of groceries and a lady came to the door 'Where's Pop?' she asked. 'He's not well.' At another place I told him to 'get up.' I thought he was deaf, so I called out again. I suddenly woke up Pop always had a cup of tea here and Tommy must have had a bit of time off. Eventually we crossed over the road to a house. I thought 'Tommy has made a mistake' then, but he didn't.

Two days later on the Wednesday there were more groceries to deliver and Tommy went to the same street but to different houses. On the Saturday I said to

Tommy 'I have to play soccer. Don't have time to stop to have a cup of tea.' I got Tommy to move when he shouldn't have been moving. I told Tommy, 'I'm jumping off the back here because I've got to play soccer. Home you go.' Tommy pulled up at the gates at home. Mum yelled out, 'Pop, where are you?' She just left Tommy harnessed up to the cart. Pop came out red and wild.' Fred changed his purposely deadpan expression into an eye twinkling smile. 'When I got home Dad said, 'The horse is more intelligent than Freddy!' '

Bessie was smiling. Laughing. 'He tells that story but it's often a bit different!'

I returned on track to Little Hampton. 'Remember any other animals?' I asked.

'The boys caught an echidna down the bush one time and they made a little sling and they brought it home so the little ones could see it. But it buried itself and we couldn't. Wombats were a nuisance. They used to make a hole in the fence, come in and scratch in the potatoes. You'd patch up the hole, but they would find somewhere else.

First dog I remember was old Bob. Black and tan-ish. I don't know whose dog it was. I know once Bob had a dog, and Harold used to have fox terriers. Dad would let the dog in if he was around. Mum always wanted him out. Dad couldn't stand the dog whining at the door. We always seemed to have cats. They'd have kittens and often they'd disappear down the bush.

Old Bob disappeared one night and never come home. Eventually they found him down the bush, dead. They said he was very old and very frail. He could not have walked that far normally.'

Of a Domestic Nature

'Churning the butter churn! I remember Rosa telling me she'd give me a penny if I churned the butter. Bob and George offered to help and asked, 'Does Bess still get the penny if we help?' Rosa said, 'I don't mind who does it as long as it gets done.'

Oh, I remember George used to eat a lot of butter. Put it on very thick. He'd use it like cheese. Mum told him before going to the Bluhm's 'When you go you take one pound of butter with you.' Auntie Min said, 'I love them to come, but I don't know how to keep the butter up to George.'

Rose was not good with the cooking; she liked the dripping. Mum usually cooked, mainly stews, and a little bit of meat to flavour the vegetables. We always enjoyed a roast. Min and Rosa liked to make cakes and scones and things, especially Min. She always reckoned she was going to be a cook, a cake and pudding maker. If Mum was away, the boys used to cook their own breakfast before going to work. Fried potato they might heat from the night before. They might put eggs on it.'

That cast-iron black and what seemed, ever-burning stove. Summer and sweat seemed synonymous. A hot stove on a hot day. Heavy iron saucepans and many mouths to feed.

'Cooking in the summer must have been horrific.' I said.

'The wood stove was always going. Later, when I was older, Mum did have a little primus stove. You pump it up. She used to boil up a kettle on this. Dad was scared of it. He hated it. When it was hot weather, he would rather go without a cup of tea. I think he was frightened it would explode.'

'Evenings?'

'By the time we got tea out of the way it was dark, and it would be time to go to bed. If it was a Saturday night, we'd have a bath. Get the water drawn, light the copper. Used to be a tub before Tom built the washhouse with the bath. We thought the big bath was beaut. It seems the boys were always in bed about 8pm. Be dark when they came in, have tea and go to bed. Percy used to be down there getting bags, etcetera as it became light at dawn, organising for the day. Frost would be on the ground often. He rode his push bike over to the paddocks where they were working. When we were married and Fred was working for Percy a bit, Percy would come and wake him up with a candle. He probably had the ute by then.

We drank a lot of mineral water. Especially the boys. They would have competitions about who could drink the most. Dad used to get thirsty and drink a lot of 'coffee and chicory' essence.

Mum used to paste brown paper and pictures on the wall instead of wallpaper. There was hessian underneath and paper. Miss Stephens an old lady said she used to go to our house to play, and it wasn't a new house then. We had curtains on the doors. Mum used to worry about fire with kids running around with candles. There were some close misses, big logs falling out of the fire. They'd be pushed back with a stick. On the floor there was lino. We had crochet rugs, potato bags. The blankets were patchwork, or anything we could get hold of, sewn on both sides of a bag. I know after Min married; she was expecting a lot of people and had to hurry up and make one once. I remember one day Min polished the floor and Dad skidded on it. He threw a spade of dirt on it then. It was better not to polish it, anyway.

We had a wire safe, big one, standing on legs. Three or four foot wide. The frame of a cupboard around it. I remember going out to it for cream. Possibly bought at a farmer's auction—a clearing sale.

Mum bought oatmeal, flour, and so on in cloth bags. We only had white flour, but weevils get into the wholemeal quicker. Mum used to make self-raising flour with carb soda and cream of tartar. She'd get a sack of flour and mix a big lot at a time on the kitchen table. Sift it two or three times, I think.

I was remembering the other day when we had an open garden scheme for the Cheltenham Church, and I made scones. When we were on the farm, we used to save buttermilk for the scones. Some people don't know what buttermilk is. I don't particularly remember doing it; I remember others doing it. If Min was home, she would have made the scones.

Mum used to make jam, often strawberry, from the ones she grew. Come to think of it, Mum used to make quince jam too. The quince tree stopped bearing and someone told Percy to drive some nails into it, and it bore. Some people say drive copper nails in it for nutrition. Later on we used to get the boxes of oranges.

When I was older, they started bottling fruit. When doing the jam Mum used to get lemonade bottles that we'd find, usually down the bush. She had a little circle of iron she'd heat and drop over the bottle, and the top would fall off. She'd then file it so that it would not be sharp at the edges. She'd cover the jam with brown paper, which she stuck with paste she made from flour. And the mice used to love it! I only remember this because the flour would make the paper more attractive to the mice. We were always checking the bottles.'

There were other opportunistic intruders besides mice.

'Rats. Always fighting the rats. Mum put bricks around the hob of the stove in the kitchen, smashed up bottles and put down to discourage the rats. She would use bait. It would smell the house out. Like a syrup that you put on bread.

I was telling Esther the other day Mum used to smash up bottles, put the ground glass under the kitchen hearth to stop the rats digging their way in there. She said, 'How did Grandma know all this?' Well. She was her father's son until her brother grew up a bit.'

There were other interlopers.

'Blowflies? Oh. Do I remember blowflies! Blowflies everywhere and little flies as well. You just had to ignore them, more or less. It was shutting the door. No wire doors to keep them out. But with a lot of people coming and going, impossible. Stinging march flies too. Not many mosquitos. Used to be mosquitos with the slow flowing creek and the damp. We reckoned it was too cold for mosquitos and fleas.

You know those old green glass bottles we found down the bush? You know they have a dimple in the bottom. They'd sit the gate pole in the little cup or something or other. I don't know how.'

I was mystified and asked Percy one day for more details.

'They'd bury the bottle in the ground and stick the gate in the dimple. They'd make the gate out of wood and sharpen the end of the corner. Then it would open and shut real easy. Probably everybody did it. There was no such thing as buying a gate. They used slip rails to keep the cows in. Put a horse shoe at the end of the post and put a pole through that.'

Another sort of gate came to mind when talking with Bess. 'The mallee gates?'

'A hunk of wire over the post. Oh yes, they were horrible.'

These gates I disliked too. The struggle to pull the wire over the post. Then pull back the gate which was a continuation of the fence. This without becoming entangled in barbed wire.

The wood heap was a stone's throw from the ornate front garden gate. Small chips spilled around the chopping block. The much-used necessity, it's wooden handle shiny-smooth with use, sat propped against a log for instant action. On a stand conveniently nearby stood a grinding wheel. The handle of this would be turned after wetting the grindstone with water from an old tin for a finer cutting edge. No one liked a back-breaking blunt axe!

'Who chopped the wood?'

'Probably anybody if the firewood was running out. I remember Rosa chopping some wood. She was chopping wood and a chip, or the axe hit my eye. And Mum cried because it was her baby! And she already had another baby then. I was toddling. Rosa said, 'I'd already told her to get out of the way.' Mum thought I'd lost an eye. Have a little scar on the corner of my eye, now.'

There was another piece of equipment, now outdated. I had seen it in the gloom of the closed in back verandah enroute to the wash house. Made with heavy dark iron, its flat feet shapes protruded awkwardly. Nowadays some people use these shoe repairer's lasts as door stops, ungainly as they are. I wondered who in the family was the fixer of shoes.

'Mum did. She would sole the shoes. Sometimes you use shoe tacks to put on the soles. Later on you could buy stick-on soles. Mum was very versatile. She could do all sorts of things and she enjoyed doing those things. She showed us how to use a saw and a hammer. I don't remember seeing Dad with a saw or hammer. But then probably I kept out of his way. He wanted to make a mud brick stable. Had a cherry case lined with tin and he was making the bricks with clay soil. He made about twenty.'

'Remedies?'

'Oh, rubbing garlic on chilblains! We all had them, and Harold's were bad on his feet. Rubbing them with the garlic, don't know if it helped or not.

Eucalyptus and olive oil. Eucalyptus for the hankie. Or a couple of drops on sugar and suck it for colds. There was a milk tin on top of the dresser with some dock seeds and that was for the horse, Little Doll, when she got asthma. Never saw them use them, how they were used. Boracic acid we used to bathe our eyes, if we got a stye, and peroxide was handy to put on wounds. Mum had a little medicine box with a small container she used to put on sores for the horses.'

I was now recalling a comment made by Rosa one day when we were visiting Bess. She'd commented, 'The only time you'd hear Mum sing was when she sewed. She made all the clothes for her family before she was married.'

Bess had replied, 'I don't remember her making clothes for the family. Remember her mending plenty of socks, boys' pants.'

Rosa then exclaimed, 'Bess used to wash the socks. She offered. Because Mum was so tired.'

Washing socks! An irksome task. No washing machines. 'Where and how?' I asked Bess today.

'Hot water after everything else was washed. The muddy socks were put in the running water, used both hands and scrubbing board. And later, when I went to work, I bought a wringer for Mum. Mum used to knit woollen socks. When the boys got older, they bought their socks. She had a big enough job.'

In the early years, I'd seen Bess knit socks and leggings for Allan. As a teenager, under Rosa's tutorial eye, I made some socks of a similar brown colour for my father, laboriously turning the heel. The first and last. The complexity of this task was an unnecessary challenge. As for the colour, I now heartily dislike it for anything. 'The socks were brown with earth, I suppose. And probably brown anyway,' I said.

'The ones I remember most were mauvy-pink, ones they'd bought. They were common. They'd wear them several days. Be stiff with dirt. After the war when I went to Trentham, I was working there for a while, as a house help for a lady. Her husband had a clean pair per day. I thought if you didn't have to wash all those socks you might not have to have a house help.'

'Who do you think in the family had it the hardest?'

'I dunno. Apart from Mum, I dunno. Yere and Allan, I guess, but we didn't see it as that.' Bessie's voice trailed away in a smile. 'But ah—yere... I dunno.'

Parents

Bessie's perennial pleasure, always inviting whatever the season. A leisurely stroll, something interesting to discover. 'This garden reminds me of your mother's.' I observed.

Bess was seated on a chair, straight-backed, tan vinyl. She looked comfortable. Her right hand slowly smoothed the floral tablecloth backwards and forwards.

'Mum used to say her garden kept her sane. I know she had a lot of tulips one year. I remember watering her stock plants. They grew beautifully, then came out single white! Probably because I fed them up with horse manure or cow manure or something and didn't give them a balance. I used to cart barrow loads to the garden. The cow would get in sometimes just when Mum was expecting some particular flower. The cows get in and destroy it. But that was just a part of life. We had one who would get a run up and straight over the fence. She didn't get over the garden fence, though. Wire netting. Mum had asparagus and various vegetables too.'

Her tone hinted of irony. 'Mum and Dad both used to work in the vegie garden. Not always in conjunction with each other!'

Clear before me was a picture of Olive's flower garden. A light dusting of snow over some patches of red brown. Bare earth, kissed by spring, slowly stirring. Olive always watched her bulbs from their first tentative appearance. My eye alighted on some favourites. The first time I had seen hyacinths. Difficult for her to afford, these few shoots were bulging already with promise as they pushed upwards. The heady perfume from these exquisite candles of tiny bell-like shapes and their bright colours has enchanted me ever since. A special reminder of Olive.

Bess was continuing. 'I remember the story of Daisy. She was very small. She used to go and nick Mum's flowers and put them behind her back. She'd say, 'No I didn't!'

We used to pick the wildflowers. Put the gum tips in a stone or glass jar in the fireplace in the summer. They made the house smell nice. We'd pick mostly heath. There were a few little orchids, but we left them alone. We'd pick the more common flowers. White heath was prized because it was not as plentiful as the pink. When we wandered in the bush, we quite often came across an old garden—daffodils—plenty during the gold rush. Even an old chimney. An old lady had told us that there were thirty houses in the bush there between our place along the road.'

Now I ventured from the comfortable to the more compelling. 'Cuddles?' I asked. For a moment I balanced perilously on the razor's edge.

Bess was looking at the square piece of white paper in her right hand. Having absent-mindedly folded it into four, she was alternatively balancing each corner on the table. Now her fingers hesitated and stopped. 'Not very.... I remember Rosa saying, because I was running to Mum, 'Don't do that because Mum's tired.' Or 'Mum's got the baby so you leave Mum alone!' We resented Rosa saying that. Mum was always there when we were little to hear us say our prayers at night. I think.

When Lois was a baby, and we were visiting up home, Dad would sit her on his lap and tell her stories. Then when his feet started playing up, he couldn't do it. I remember sitting on his knee before I was old enough for school. There were two or three of us fighting about who was going to be nursed, I guess. He'd tell stories about Sammy, the handicapped Aboriginal boy he'd met when he was up in Queensland, that time, and the interesting things Sammy used to do. He'd go and get the eggs, 'the cackle berries.' Dad did have a sense of humour, and it was a dry one. Even kids would understand it and he'd laugh too. I don't think Mum appreciated it. 'He's making fun of the little boy. Poor little boy, he couldn't help it.'

A poem Dad recited sometimes about a dog.

Poor tired Tim,
It's sad for him
He wags the whole morning through
Ever so tired with nothing to do.

Auntie Elsie and Auntie Eva Bruton. I'd heard all those stories about Auntie Elsie being so savage. She must have been under a lot of stress when Allan was there. She didn't put up with any nonsense. I'd expected to find a savage old lady, but she was so nice. And Auntie Eva was lovely.'

I dared another delve. 'You remember sitting on your father's knee more than your mother's?'

Bess's voice was firm. Final. 'Mum was busy.'

She continued. 'Nobody sat in Mum's chair on the window side of the fireplace, and she usually had knitting or sewing. Her father taught her to darn. Her mother didn't sew, and I don't think she knew much about housework at all.

We'd ask Dad, 'Tell us stories.' Sit on his knee. Something else he used to tell us about was going down the beach and swimming. He missed the beach when they moved. As he got older most of the time, we got on pretty well, I think. If he was in a bad mood, we kept out of the way. Don't think we talked directly. Not much person-to-person contact. I remember Mum saying, 'If you think that, why don't you tell him.' I didn't. Was too scared to tell him. Don't know why I was too scared. He took me to Drummond, and we had a nice day at the Andrew's place. I didn't really have friends when I was young. I think he realised this, and that's why. I'm not much of a letter writer.'

'What else did you like about your father?'

'He was quiet. Seemed to be capable. Gentle. But all of a sudden, off he'd go. I was hearing about manic depression the other day. I wonder about Dad and his father. They blamed Grandpa Bruton on the drink.

Qualities I didn't like? Inability to communicate. I remember Dad banging a chair on the table when I was quite small. Wouldn't talk about controversial subjects. Rigid black and white. Feeling intimidated with him.'

'Scary?'

'Oh yes. The act was bad enough. The emotional feeling for a child to see an adult angry was very frightening. We always had to be careful not to upset Dad. Became just a way of life and you don't recognise it is a strain. You think what happens is normal! One night, Mum raced off into the dark. She was sitting behind the front gate wanting to kill herself. Bob came looking for her. She heard him say, maybe to George, who was probably looking too. 'If anything happens to her, I'll kill him.' So Mum came in. No. I've no memory of it. I reckon I would have been very young when that happened. Probably in bed. Mum told me.

Dad was a lot like Allan. A bit like Stan. Stan's kids could have had the same impression of Stan as we had of Dad. Douglas was ordered out when he was fifteen or so.'

Harry's hide bound hell. His and their heartache. His heavenly vision, an ill fit with reality. Then his bone tiredness and struggle upon a struggle. Unknown to him, he carried the genes of coeliac disease.

'Who encouraged you?'

'With a big family, if one doesn't encourage, somebody else will. I think Min was pretty good at it. P'raps. I don't know. The thing that does stand out as far as encouragement goes, you say 'I can't do something.' 'I'll do that for you.' I suppose that was encouragement too.

Bess had that paper again. Up and down. 'I remember feeling upset with Dad for chopping down trees. Mum pleaded with him. 'The kids love playing in the trees.' No. he would not listen! Then it fell on the pigsty and he had to rebuild it. He never did damage to the laurel or the elm tree. Rosa remembers Minnie climbing to the top of the elm tree, right to the very top. The trunk was very wide. It would have been a hundred years old. They were all yelling at her to get down. The more they yelled, the more Min stayed. She was quite a tomboy. Dad had said, 'I'll fix you! I'll throw stones at you.' He didn't hit her on purpose. I'm not sure that was successful either. The elm tree? Percy eventually chopped it down. It was the height of praise in those days to congratulate someone for clearing their block.

Dad was a market gardener, not a farmer. He'd work for someone and not take payment. Then they'd work for him and he would try and pay them—he had nothing. The Child Endowment they only got for Harold. It was a new thing. Mum didn't want to get it! Pride. Independence. She had to be talked into it. Then Dad had difficulty accepting the pension. I think part of Dad's reluctance to get the pension was that he believed that his children should support him. George or somebody explained to him. 'The pension comes from the taxes. Your children have to pay taxes, and we can't afford to pay taxes and support you as well,' and he saw that. 'I've never paid taxes' Dad said. George said, 'But we, your children are. So you should get it.' I don't think any of the farmers paid taxes during the depression and war. Dad's income was very little.

He didn't have it many years before he died. Mum was convinced before Dad about getting the pension. He didn't handle the money. Mum handled it. But everything was in his name, and it was a matter of the head of the house applying for it. Mum had all the responsibility and no rights! In those old times, the men were independent in their own way but were dependant, really.

Mum and Dad voted for the person rather than the party. That's when Dad voted. He didn't always vote when we were children, because he didn't think he should. But I think he did sometimes. I remember him discussing how you choose the candidates. I remember at Little Hampton Mum being worried, because the police might come because Dad hadn't voted. Worried they'd be in trouble and costing her money she didn't have. When he was old and at Avonsleigh, he wrote a letter to the Council or Government. He said he was old and couldn't get in to vote and that his citizenship was not of this world. There are still people who think they shouldn't vote.

Tom commented about Dame Enid Lyons. 'She's telling people how to manage money and her husband is Prime Minister. What would she know about money! Dame Enid Lyons gave advice on, 'How to prepare budget meals.' In the 1930s, I think. She had twelve children and was sort of implying that she was poor too. In later years she lived next door to Stan at Devonport, Tasmania. Very nice lady. She gave Ron pocket money jobs, mowing her lawns, like that.

Dad could not stand to hurt anything. But his behaviour did not live up to his ideals. He didn't put the bit in the horse's mouth because he thought it was cruel, but let the kids ride the horse without the bit. That day when the horse played up, I didn't know why it did not do what it was supposed to do. It was not a predictable horse. We had not had it long.

With us younger ones, we were frightened of him because we'd heard the others rowing with him. Think it was more that than the direct experience. Same as going to Grandma's. Auntie Elsie. We were told she was crabby, and she was so nice. We were living in fear.

We'd get out the road and leave the big ones to stand up to Dad. Dad took to Harold one day and Daise stood up to him. She was more a hindrance than a help. He threw Daise against the wall one day too. She was going on and on. Harold would run to Dad each time he got into trouble, but he must have gone too far. But Harold asked for it, he really did. He had hold of Harold. Don't know what happened. If he took his belt off or not. I kept out the road. You knew if the belt came off it was time to disappear! Perhaps the older ones controlled the younger ones by telling them 'Mum or Dad will growl at you,' etcetera. Don't know if I remember Bob standing up to him or not. Oh, I do remember him very upset with Dad about something. 'If I ever marry, I will never treat my wife like you do!' Bob was so angry he barred the door to the bedroom. Dad was lying down. 'Don't take in his tea, if he's not prepared to get up and get it!'

I remember when Hazel Bruton was up there staying. She was thirteen. An old thirteen, me going on thirteen. She wanted to borrow Min's bike and told me to say it was for me. Dad said, 'It doesn't matter what someone tells you to say, you just say the truth!' Min said later. 'I wouldn't have lent it to Hazel. I thought it was you who wanted it.'

The boys, George would go crook. 'Whenever it rains, Dad wants to plough.' That's what you did in the sand at Mentone.

Mum said, 'Dad's getting on. Tired. But he's always been like this.' She could remember him lying down in the paddock at Mentone. 'Be different if he's a weakling, but he's big and strong, and he should be able to keep going.''

'I wonder if he ever got over the loss of Katie, his first wife,' I shared with Bess.

'He spent three months up in Queensland sugar cane cutting after he proposed to Mum. He had proposed to Mum, but Mum said she would not marry him yet. Wanted to get to know him better. Didn't seem to want to know her better. He went away. He came back in January, and married in May, 1910. Dad came back from cane cutting with some money and put a headstone on Katie's grave, and married with no money. Katie died in 1907. He would not talk about it.

During the war George bought a horse, called it Katie. Dad was very upset about it, held his head in his hands. 'Why?' George said. Mum said, 'He used to know someone by that name.' I'm not sure George ever knew the tie-up. It was years later that I learned what Mum meant. I sort of have a vague idea he was taking Katie to the midwife in the jinker, and whether the baby came too soon or not the way it should have, I don't know.'

Now, I recalled that Dorothy, Bob's eldest, down from their wheat farm in mid NSW, had called on Bess and Fred during the past week. Bess and she had visited Olive and Harry's final resting place in the historic Cheltenham cemetery. There they lay in the company of the earliest pioneers of the district. Many of these, like Harry's father, were among the first to till the soil of the sand belt. I discovered today from Bess, that Harry and Olive shared their grave with Katie Dawes.

Bess explained, 'No. Mum didn't know about it. Didn't know you could. It was a grave for two, and the first one had been in so long it was alright to add another. Dad said to her. 'I've been thinking. You know, I think perhaps you could go in with Bernie.''

'That must have cut her!'

'Yes it did. Dad died only six months before her. Dorothy said, 'Grandma's on top for the first time in her life!''

'If Olive had known she could go in with Harry and Katie, I wonder what would have been her attitude.'

'I don't think she would've objected. Oh no. That was her place to be with him. Dad's first wife was her friend, and it was such a short marriage.'

Bess's mother, my grandmother. In my memory, this quietly spoken woman with the gentle smile seemed to be a shadow in the background of the Bruton family. Never overweight, she was nearly as tall as Harry, who was well over six feet.

When Olive took on Harry in 1910, she was twenty-six, he thirty. Close to her father, she had been a major support. Bernard told Harry proudly that he had the best of the Bluhm bunch.

'Mum considered the Bluhms were more refined than the Brutons,' Rosa said one day. 'The Bluhms washed their hands before their meals, the Brutons would spit. Mum hated that.'

I wondered what the white bearded Bernard in the large, framed photograph felt as he heard the clip clop of his beloved daughter's carriage fading into her new future. A marriage for better or worse. The Brutons, albeit a respected family. Were his heart strings pulled with the loss? Was there some trepidation when he looked into Harry Bruton's burning black eyes?

Olive and Harry's sepia wedding photograph had always puzzled me. Harry with thick black moustache and Olive, long hair with soft bun, and long high-necked gown exquisitely pintucked. It was the dress which looked incongruous. Olive's dress was not radiantly light or frothy with celebratory frills. Not like wedding dresses she'd made for her two sisters. She, with her skills, could have designed the biggest fashionable splash in Cheltenham. Instead she had chosen a dress, beautiful in its way I suppose, but greyly sombre.

'What colour was your mother's wedding dress?'

'Olive green, I think. Mum made it herself. It had to last. She got married at home. 'I'm not going into the church. Only putting on a show for people.'

'Shy?' I wondered out loud, hoping the answer was that simple.

'Yes. I think so.'

'Grandma never said much,' I commented to Bess and Fred. Fred's love for his mother-in-law had always been apparent. Like many, he respected and adored her. He was quick to respond in her defence.

'Never had a chance to say much. Whatever she'd say were gems. I never ever heard her say a bad word about anyone.' His mouth changed to a hint of a grin. 'My mother was talkative. Within a couple of hours, I'd be wishing she'd go home. Olive could come and stay for a week, and I wouldn't know she was in the house. Our Lois is quiet like her.'

I turned to Bessie. 'Your mother always seemed in the background. I'd like to gain more insight.'

'Well, for one thing she was always there. That's why we don't analyse it. She was our mother and that, and she was the anchor. We didn't appreciate her properly, I suppose. We knew she was always going to do the right thing. She didn't express things as well as what she should have done.'

'Anything come to mind in particular?'

'Not at this stage. She didn't value words as much as Dad did. I think this is a difference between Mum and Dad. Dad used to enjoy words, I think—though he didn't use them much!'

'He used to read.'

'Mum told me her father would say if she was sitting down crocheting, 'Haven't you got anything better than that.' If she had been reading, it could have been worse. She felt it anyway.'

'A woman needs a man,' Olive told me, as I in my twenties discontinued another relationship. It was when she was ill with breast cancer in her eighties and living with my family. A few months previously she had said 'a man only wants one thing.' This, born no doubt of resentment. The years of childbearing and drudgery and fulfilling her sexual duty at great cost. Caught up in a labyrinth of duty and economic necessity. Pity help a woman who left her husband in those days! No pensions then. The road for many was even more desperate than the sad situation they had fled.

'But she loved him!' Rosa asserted one day. 'They'd hold hands always when they went to the polling booth to vote.' Grace felt some sort of connection not claimed by myself. I never felt I knew her. She always seemed busy in her kitchen, or quietly engrossed in some handwork. I well remember those convivial times spent around the cosy Bruton fire. My grandmother sat in her dark leather chair, head down and fingers active, usually with some darning. I would usually be focussed on some handwork myself. Taught by Rosa, I learned to knit in my third year. 'She's like a little old lady with her knitting,' someone commented.

It was at one of these such times, though I was older. The context has been well forgotten. So much for the convenient vagaries of memory. A comfortable feeling, disrupted. Like the startling crackle of the fire, Olive suddenly looked straight at me. 'You have an inferiority complex.' A truth maybe, the symptoms were probably evident to all except myself. Not a particularly palatable one, I felt, after asking Rosa to explain it to me in eight-year-old language. My image of Olive has been blurred with this bluntness. Her lack of eloquence, her lack of endearment. An inferred lack of sensitivity.

On reflection, there are clues which indicate this fixed image to be a misrepresentation of Olive. Not eloquent of speech perhaps, but an eloquence of another type. An alchemist! Transforming flour and potato bags into beauty. Cotton into crochet. A house into a home.

Unable to afford picture frames or wallpaper, she did what she could. Undaunted, she decorated paper patched walls with poems and pictures cut from magazines, occasional gifts to the family. Silver star starch, used for stiffening collars, blouses, muslin dresses, was mixed with boiling water for the glue.

There are both expansive and dainty doily sized creations of beautiful, crocheted lace, some fine as thistledown, which have emerged from Olive's multi-dextrous hands. Couturier par excellence, too. A sweep of design and finely crafted tiny pin tucks on the long ornate dresses of her era. Architect of buildings, paths, gardens. Olive's creations speak of an artistic woman, versatile, inventive. This artistry represents a crucial part of her profile, the biography of her life.

Olive's personal collections add colour to this portrait. An old decorative 'Sweetacres' tin with rusted lid, found at Rosa's, yielded some small treasures. Poems cut from newspapers. Biblical texts mostly on love. Two or three letters. A condolence card. Spray of white velvet flowers, still with soft sheen.

The red tuppeny stamp stood out, portrait of bearded King George 1. The letter, dated 1922, from the Infectious Diseases Hospital at Fairfield, Melbourne. This, a sorry marker, would call upon Olive's resilience and creative abilities. The words cut curtly. 'Allan is now able to return home. Paralysis has remained stationary. The only improvement is in his arms.' The last sentence would have stung, 'He is, of course, not able to be out of bed.'

Some twenty years later, 16th November, 1943. Wartime. A red cross on the top of this letter. It signalled an end to a personal cross. The gnawing pain suffered by a mother when her soldier son is missing, presumed dead. The last two sentences of this short letter, a reply to Olive, from the Victorian Division of the Australian Red Cross Society, bore good news. Tom, who had been a prisoner of war in Germany was on his way home.

There were several pretty postcards. I turned over a floral picture and read. 'A regular attendance card. October 1895. Olive Bluhm. State School Number 1111, Moorabbin.' Another post card 18th December, 1919, written in childish hand in black ink, from Tommy.

Pleasures and pain! All pointers to Olive the person. It was the poems and quotations which spoke most clearly to me. Edged in red 'A Hymn of Love,' copy of the Biblical text. Two small texts embellished with garden flowers and brown spots of age. These were probably given to Olive at Sunday school, which was the wont of the day. The taller one, an arch of flowers, 'The land whither thou goest is as a garden. Deut 11.10.' The square smaller card with red roses, and the first letter of 'He' ornately embellished in blue. 'He that overcometh shall inherit all things. Rev 21.7.'

Almost missed, humbly hiding against the rusted bottom, was a tiny piece of yellowed newspaper. A small poem carefully cut along the surrounding border. On the back was part of a 'Persil' washing soap advertisement.

As I read this poem, I pictured Olive. It seemed to typify her. She must have engraved it upon her heart.

The Quiet Hour
A Prayer

Help me to smile when hills are steep,
Find cheer when things go wrong,
And bank a store of courage
To help frail folk along.
Let me the art of living learn
And practice it each day,
And share whatever strength I have
With others on the way.
Give me a braver heart to find
The little chinks of Light,
That Thou dost always shew to those
Who trust Thee through the night.
Mary Eversley

My mind returned to Olive's many and varied pieces of hand work. Offerings of opulent and skilled intricacy. Crafted by love. Beautiful. As if these small pieces of finery were not enough, Olive had crocheted in white cotton a large bedspread for each of her two eldest girls. When living at our home, her hands were still busy. When I admired another bedspread she was making, at Grace's request, I recall she smiled gently and said, 'I hope I will be able to get it finished before I die.' That quiet acceptance did not result in a wish fulfilled. Rosa finished the last three squares of it. The same pattern, but the white was slightly different.

There is something else Olive made. To my mind, the most intricate. And stunning. Another large project. This double white cotton bedspread may have been crocheted after her marriage. Likely, it represented many hours of toil after daily chores were completed and children in bed. She probably sat, head bent under the soft glow of an ornate kerosene lamp. Her long hair, light brown with reddish tint, twisted as it was in those early days into a burnished bun at the nape of her neck, a chiaroscuro against the dark. A wedding present, for her youngest sister Min. Ten years her junior. It was given to Rosa by Min before Min died. Rosa in her usual style had transported and supported Auntie Min Tudor in her last years. I am now the proud owner of this breathtaking piece. The work features roses which stand up at regular intervals upon a firm white cobweb-like pattern. I treasure it. This special piece made by my grandmother. A communication from her soul.

My eyes strayed to Bess's windowsill. There, silhouetted against the bluntness, the square frame and sunlight, were two very small vases. Tiny purple bush violets had been placed in them. The stems had been chosen carefully. Long enough to wave gracefully above the rims. Here too, was poetry.

Extended Family

Bess recalled again their extended family in the Mentone and Cheltenham market gardening sand belt. She reminisced too, about her mother's sister Min Tudor at Mitcham and brother Will Bluhm who owned an orchard at East Burwood. Both further north-east from the Cheltenham market garden. She did not recall the Bluhm grandparents.

'Grandma Bluhm I don't remember, or Grandpa. Grandma came to visit us at Taradale, to see me when I was born, and died. Daise told me in later years, 'I saw Mum crouched down crying. I didn't know why.'

Grandma and Grandpa Bruton I can remember before I started school. Must have been quite good with kids. They had a wash basin outside, and he showed me how he could take his glass eye out. He put it in a cup of water, like taking your false teeth out. I didn't go there very much. Grandma came up home once or twice. I can remember I liked her. Also remember her dodging Rosa's camera. Rose was the photographer. Uncle Joe or someone gave her a camera.

I stayed at Auntie Min Tudor's as company for their daughter Lorna. Stayed from Easter till December. I think it was either 1934 or '35. I don't know whether I was ten when I was there or later. Daise had been there and complained a lot. Auntie Min tried hard to get Mum to agree to leave me there. Mum said, 'If you want more kids, you should have had them.' Lorna was given sixpence a week. I was given threepence. I was keeping it to give Mum. They wanted someone there for Lorna, who got the best.

And Daise felt second best, too. Auntie Min reasoned the threepence would be better than we got at home. Lorna was in the girl guides. Had sort of leggings to protect the shoes. Lorna's was made with the proper material, mine with paper or something—looked okay, but there was always a difference.

Auntie Min said, 'It's only natural to put my daughter first.' Lorna tried to make friends with Daise and me—but it sort of came between us. I think Daise went there twice and slept in the spare room at the end of the verandah. She wasn't well at that time. When she got a lot better, she did not like it there. Mum said, 'You can go if you want. You don't have to.' I decided to go. I suppose I didn't believe what Daise said. 'You couldn't have stood it. You've not had to put up with what I've had to!' was a bit of a challenge. Uncle Norm teased us whenever we were homesick, and he'd duck us in the water. I didn't like him particularly.

I wasn't unhappy there. They wanted me to say that I wanted to stay. It was a bit embarrassing because I really wanted to go home.' Bess's grin was wry. 'Even at that age I said, 'I don't know.' I have been saying it ever since! Min and Fred took me home on the train. They were going up to Tommy's wedding at Little Hampton. Sally and Tom were married in 1935.

We felt part of Uncle Will's family. We'd go sometimes. We were always welcome there. There was Lorna, Ron and I all around the same age. I think they had Allan a lot too. Stan spent a lot of time at Uncle Will's. Wished Uncle Will was his dad.

I remember the bushfires on Black Friday, in January 1939. Percy and I were staying at Grandma Bruton's and went over to Uncle Reub's to stay. Hazel was the same age as me. I think Uncle Joe might have taken us over in the jinker. I don't remember a lot of ash around, just the heat. One day after the fires, Uncle Albert and Aunt Ina dropped in their daughter Margery, for Grandma to look after. This was while they went to Noojie looking where the fires had been. I remember Uncle Albert drawing pictures of the poor little echidnas that had got burnt. They had no quills. They looked like tortoises. I remember the same thing being described by Min after sugar cane firings in Queensland.

A gentleman who goes to our church, Bill Pearsell, used to work for Reuben's family and he's very fond of them. Bill also loved horses, as Reuben did.

The Mentone Brutons had nicknames for everyone. They called Harold 'Wag,' 'Little Harold is a wag. He always has a bag of Giant brand liquorice.' Joe called Allan, 'Jumping Fangs' because he always had a toothache, or 'Hoppy.' Mum never allowed people to use nicknames in our house.

The story went that Uncle Albert who was a builder built the house for Grandma. She didn't want him to put electricity on. He said, 'I'll make it so it will only be a matter of connecting it up.' She was so impressed with it when she visited Auntie Rose Daff, one of her daughters, when she came back, she had it put on.

A question you asked me. The most notable invention of my life. I just thought it has to be electricity. It altered the whole way of life. Day and night became equal. Apart from electricity, I 'spose the telephone.'

Bessie smiled as she recalled something else. 'I remember one day Uncle Moss Daff and Auntie Rose came with George to visit us at Little Hampton. Percy and I hid in a box in the garden. We sent Harold in to see what was happening. We were both shy. Percy was very shy. I don't know if he was worse than me. I think we had to go in the end. 'No good shutting your eyes. We can still see you.''

Employment

'Ambitions? I don't remember any possibilities of anything other than staying home and helping Mum and so forth. Otherwise it would have been paid housework. I had the idea I could work on the farm. I liked outdoor gardening. At one stage we used to pick a lot of peas. I remember the robin red breasts when we were digging potatoes. They'd be sitting on a fork, watching. The machinery used nowadays would frighten them off.

My first outside job? Could have been a friend of Ted Shelden's sister, Ada. They needed help in the house as she was sick with the third child. May have been in South Melbourne. Ten shillings a week, which was marvellous. First pay. I went out and spent it on fruit. This was a luxury. I'd never seen so much fruit... oranges and passion fruit. Homesick? Oh yes! This housework was different to what I ever knew. When asked to make a cup of tea, I didn't know when the electric jug was hot. No one said to me, 'This is what you do.'

Must have been 1940, '42, when Daise and I signed up with the YWCA and some organisation or other to go up to Mildura to pick grapes. Daise would say, 'I'm never going to leave home again.' She didn't stay at home though. 'I can't stand being home,' so then she'd leave home and go out to work. When she was older and lived in Queensland, she said she couldn't stand the Queensland heat. Then down south she said she couldn't stand the cold.

When I worked at Ballarat, I bought this beautiful baby rug for Minnie's baby. 'Just what I want. I'm pregnant too!' Daise knew I had it for Minnie. I gave it to Daisy. She always played 'poor me' and she got the best of everything. Just about. People would say 'Poor Daise.'

When I worked at the Trentham Bush Nursing Hospital, the Sister helped me make a bag apron. Bag aprons made of hessian. Usually they had cotton around the edge and cotton ties. They were useful when doing the washing. Often it was sugar bags, not as coarse as spud bags. You'd put a pocket on it too with colourful material. If it was cotton, it would be wet no time. Most people economised this way.

I used to like working outside on the farm. Manpower officials would visit farms during the war to see who was eligible for conscription. They were questioning George one time, whether there was somebody over sixteen to run the farm. A woman could run the farm if she had a sixteen-year-old boy. 'Only Mum' said George. Percy was around. He was fifteen. He piped up with, 'I'll be sixteen soon!'

The man said, 'What about the young fellow out there?' 'That young fellow happens to be my sister!' I was harrowing, I think. George was going to get the crop off and then enlist. Bob told him, 'You're needed so much at home.' Bob said he was wasting his time sitting around doing nothing. If Bob had owned a farm instead of working for others, he wouldn't have been conscripted. George did get called up; he hadn't gone for a medical yet. They got a letter from the local doctor that Dad had an enlarged heart. But before that he was considering going.'

There was a note of pride in Bessie's voice when she talked about the harrowing. 'Enjoy it?'

Her enthusiasm was obvious. 'Two horses and the big harrows. I knew how to drive them and go back and forth across the paddock. No I didn't know how to harness them; probably knew I couldn't do it. Had to be taller than my five foot four. Percy couldn't until he grew taller. He had a late growth spurt. I never considered horses as friends. I was always frightened to stand behind a horse. Nervous about putting the bit in the mouth. Wonder if that was why Dad didn't do it.

Oh yes. Daise said, 'I never knew you worked on the farm.' I think she did enjoy some things about it too. I wouldn't have minded staying home and working outside. But when you're a girl, you're still a girl inside the house! Though, if I was working outside, the boys would help doing the dishes. I'd have to have the day off to do the washing, things like that.'

'And looking back on your life, what would you have changed if you could?'

Bess looked into the distance. Smiling. Thinking. 'Goodness knows. Nothing stands out. Probably be everything. No. I think it was pretty good, really.' She pondered a moment. 'A regular income would have been nice for the family.'

War. Twenty-first Birthday

Bess was nearly nineteen when she joined the army in October 1943. Fred stirred at the mention of army and opened one eye. 'I don't have any idea why Bessie went into the army.'

'Why join up? Mainly because I went up grape picking with George and Percy. And the girl there, she had it all worked out. We were going to go nursing, join up together. She didn't, eventually. I think her family found out her plans. Later, well she wrote and said her aunt wasn't well and she was going to stay and look after her.

And Daisy was married to a soldier, Ted, and so she was getting an income. Mum thought Daisy should put some money into her keep, as Daise was staying at Mum's while Ted was away in the army. She was doing a lot of things for Daisy, who had a young baby Jan, at the time. Daise said, 'I'll ask Ted.' Ted said, 'Your mother's got a maid having you.' When they went to stay at Shelden's Ted's mother said they had to pay her.

I thought, well Daisy is going to be home. If I join, I'll get out of the army the same time as Ted. But I was away for three and a half years, discharged in April '47. I was one of the last ones in and of course one of the last ones out. I thought Daise was there to help out and that, and Mum didn't need me, and it was a chance to make some money. And I'm not sure Mum could have stood it if we were both home at the same time!

I thought I could get trained for nursing. I was in the Women's Medical Service. Did half a day in a ward. Just once. Whether I would have if I had the choice about actually going nursing, I'm not sure.

Initially, I had two months medical, then I worked in the kitchen in Ballarat. I learnt a lot, but I didn't learn what I thought I was going to learn. I learnt to take care of myself. Showers, changing clothes, and a matter of living in a community when I was in Ballarat. Not such a difficult thing. When we were there it was so cold, and we pulled a couple of beds together. A lady was horrified. We didn't know why.

I remember sleeping between Rose and Min. I also remember sleeping with Rosa one stage. Was when we were older. Had the double and the single bed in our room. Earlier on I think Daise and I slept top to tail in the single. I slept under the table with Daise, and the boys would sometimes sleep on bags on the chaff when we were short of beds for visitors. Min and Rosa shared the double bed. I was always getting told to go away while they'd sit and whisper. There was no privacy.'

Bess paused, continued matter of fact. 'As a teenager, I remember crying myself to sleep many times. Rose and I were in the same bed—she'd ask, 'Tell me why.' 'I can't.' As I didn't know why.'

A small pause, and Bess picked up her strand. 'When in Ballarat transport home was difficult. I got home once at 11pm. Mum said, 'You should not have come. George has scarlet fever!' Ballarat was closed down, that's when I was sent to the Heidelberg Hospital, was folding clothes in the laundry. A fortnight day duty and a fortnight night duty. It was very noisy. The army tried to keep you closest to home if you were under twenty-one, but the boys were sent off at eighteen.'

Comments from the armchair across the room intrigued me.

'A fellow rubbed stinging nettles on himself and made a rash whenever he had to go for a medical examination for call up. They kept sending him home! You had to be over eighteen to be sent overseas. I was called up six months before eighteen, for the Militia. The A.I.F. referred to the Militia as chocolate soldiers. 'Chocos!' Why? Because they didn't have to go overseas, but that changed after the Japs attacked New Guinea.

About the time I was supposed to start military service I broke my leg and they wanted to take the plaster off to check.'

'What?'

'Some fellows would put on a plaster to get out of going into the army. My dad said, 'You take that off and I'll take you off! He'll go in his own good time. He wants to go.' I joined the A.I.F. when I turned eighteen. Did jungle training at Bathurst, New South Wales.'

Fred grinned, 'Those twenty to twenty-five-mile route marches fixed my leg up. I lost two stone.' He was looking past me to those distant days.

'I was supposed to go overseas. My father, who never got sick, got sick, and I had one week's compassionate leave. My unit left during this time. I said, 'Can't I catch up?' 'No, it's secret.' I heard later half were shot dead. The Japs were waiting for them.'

Fred hesitated, 'So the Lord was looking after me.'

Now Fred had caught up with his usual genial smile. He placed his feet on the soft footstool and reached for his book. 'If I'd gone, I'd never have met Bessie! Oh, they sent me up near Albury to a supply station, sending hundreds of cases of ammunition. This went to Sydney and so on, to be put on ships, even for India.'

Bess had been listening attentively. 'The public did not know the extent of danger Australia was in. We didn't know until after the war.'

We returned to Heidelberg Hospital, around 1944.

'I hated it at Heidelberg! I tried to get to Bonegilla, I was told it was quite good there. Bonegilla was up in northern Victoria this side of Wodonga, two or three miles from the New South Wales border. I put in an application; I was transferred after six months. I was in the pantry there. Kept the supplies up, brought in wheat germ and so on to build up the patients. Had to clean toilets, baths, showers, etcetera in the nursing sisters' quarters. It was a T.B. hospital near the Hume Weir. It was a huge hospital when I was there. I was nineteen when I went. We had two weeks off every six months.

We were in the convalescent mess and supposed to get the meals ready for men with no limbs, and so on, but the boys helped each other. Couldn't keep their eyes off the girls. 'So long since we saw a girl with clothes on!' They'd been in the islands, Borneo. We made the tables nicer with tablecloths and flowers. The men were only used to bare necessities. They appreciated it. Civilisation again.

When Stan was in the army, he wanted to allocate five shillings a week from his pay for Mum and Mum would not let him. I said to her it was a good idea, and she said 'No.' She had the same attitude when given some clothes for us in the depression. 'To think that I've come to this...'

I don't think Tom went into the army till about '41. He was married then. Couldn't make a go of it at Red Hill. Things were tough. He told Mum they were having to plant the fruit trees, apples and cherries I think, and wait for them to bear. It appears he went into the army because he was short of money and possibly to get away from home. Because, as a primary producer, he would probably have been exempt. It was after he came home from the war that he sold this property and bought one at Kyabram.'

Bess's twenty-first birthday was spent in the army. By this time the war was over. She remembered this milestone birthday well.

'Was at Bonegilla. Didn't even get a card from the family. They clubbed in together later on. Rose wanted to get everyone a watch, but Auntie Eva Bruton had asked for me to have her watch after she died. I didn't know her as well as the others did. I think it might have been her suit I got too, one that Auntie Elsie made. Fawn.'

'Do you still have the watch?'

'I think so. Don't ask me where. I had to have it cleaned every twelve months. It became too expensive. Anyway, later on, the family asked what I would like for my twenty-first. I said I'd like a Bible at that stage. Well, they put in together and bought one. I have a feeling it may have been Min who collected the money. I don't know. Possibly her because she was the one who gave it to me. When it was near my birthday, Min asked Rosa. And Rosa said, 'Oh no, she's only twenty, not twenty-one.' If they'd asked me, it might have been more sense.' said Bessie spiritedly. 'I think they all wrote. Mum, Daisy, and I think Percy might have written once or twice, Rosa now and then. Dad didn't. I've thought since, it didn't occur to me then—I'd had the idea if you don't get a letter, you don't write one! I didn't write that often. I used to write to Allan when he was in hospital.

I think I went to the pictures or something. One of the girls made a cake for me. One of them became a good friend. We phone each other at Christmas, etcetera. She's older than me.

I remember going to Avonsleigh, to Rosa's. I had borrowed one of Minnie's dresses. Such an adventure wearing a floral dress. Even on leave, the army would not allow you to wear civies. When did we marry? 1949. I was twenty-five.'

Fred was sitting bolt upright. His dark eyes were flashing. 'It was at an army do that I met Bess! I said, 'Who's that girl in the doorway over there?' The fellow said, 'I don't really know that girl. She's shy.' Fred's voice was like warm treacle. He smiled gently with the recollection. 'Because I'm going to marry her!' '

We ambled through the garden on my way out.

'You haven't seen my sunflowers.' said Bess. 'I usually use cockie seed. This time I bought some Yates seeds. Little seeds. I thought only little seeds. They won't grow big. Each day I looked at them, the flower was bigger.' Bess beamed as we surveyed tall, fat leaved plants with faces the sizes of dinner plates. One leaned near the path, some golden petals bruised.

The garden! Bessie's passion. Always something in flower. Always a pot to give away. She introduced me to the blue of borage, and the tall hardy daisy petalled cosmos, a magenta. My favourite colour. The dainty pink rose buds of the thornless Cecil Brunner adorns our front garden. Enormous and prolifically flowering, it is as high as the house. Scented verbena, fuchsias, chives. All gifts from Bessie.

Sunflower smiles, swaying slightly. I stare at the flowers.

Was it a sound on the wind, perhaps? My fantasy. A lone violin resonating softly against the faintness of a symphony. Sad. A haunting quality. Sunflowers and sadness. A plaintive cry, a bird, cuts across my reverie. Bess is smiling.

Stan

Tasmania

That day in the 'Cat and Fiddle' Arcade, Hobart, Tasmania! It was probably about 1957. This pretty arcade with a myriad of small shops was famous for the clock over the arch at the end. We sat outside the small coffee shop at a rounded table. The aroma of fresh cappuccino hung in the air as we sipped and waited. When the hand was nearly to the hour, those breathless few seconds, the silence in the arcade was palpable. Suddenly Stan, Audrey and I we were rewarded with the performance. A short, jolly tune played by the cat on its fiddle. This spectacle seemed to fascinate the tourists, and I was a tourist too. Holidays at Stan and Audrey's were treasured by me. They were always punctuated by something or other, different and interesting.

This picture is not, however, the scene specially imprinted on my memory. It is hazy compared with the next, which seems like one of a series of slow film footage. The latter remains in my mind as clear as if it were yesterday. A man, tall, but not six feet, swinging his left arm boisterously. His right hand seemed to be in the pocket of his flapping, unbuttoned dark suit. An energetic walk, buoyant, optimistic. He was going somewhere and enjoying every minute of it. Dark straight hair, nicely groomed, with a rebellious strand or two on the top. We sat watching him, Audrey and I, on this other day, another coffee lounge, during our Hobart stay. As he walked towards us, he smiled. An engaging smile. Good-natured aliveness. The smile of a man who was used to communicating. His face lit up. An underlying force of personality could not be mistaken. Charisma I suppose I'd call it now, as I relive the memory. Dark eyes danced in tandem with the connectedness of his smile. Sparkling eyes interested and happy.

He was too far away yet to hear my comment. 'I think he is good looking!'

'Yes!' said Audrey, gazing at Stan. 'I think so too!'

I admit I was secretly pleased to have been told sometimes that I looked a little bit like my uncle.

It was not until I was nearly twenty that I really made Stan and Audrey's acquaintance. Holidays at their home in Devonport on the northern coast of Tasmania became a regular occurrence. Geographical distance had been the problem. They, and their three children, lived about one and a half hours' plane travel from the mainland. That large tract of windy, often treacherous water, Bass Strait, separated the 'Apple Isle,' Tasmania, from Melbourne, Victoria. My preferred mode for accessing Tasmania in those days was the regular single-engine and twin-engine propeller-driven plane service. And I saved carefully during the year for this special trip.

Stan too, flew across Bass Strait on a fairly regular annual visit to his parents and siblings. That is, between his letter writing. Conscientious, regular, especially at birthday times.

I fed voraciously on the smorgasbord of experiences open to me during these Tasmanian sojourns. The blend in my view was perfect. Exploring within and without. No matter if it was a dull, Tasmanian day. Many a book I devoured next to the fire. The Bruton book shelves were rich with philosophy, religion, and the natural world. Also smartly bound in maroon, red leather with gold lettering was a set of books I coveted, unaffordable by my family. A prized Encyclopaedia Britannica. Then there was the questioning, the conversations, the debating with Audrey and Stan. Sometimes also with Robin Burtt, Audrey's nephew, who eventually joined the teaching profession.

I enjoyed very much the painting with Audrey in her small studio. Flowers picked from their colourful garden were tackled on canvas with thick paint and palette knife. Flamboyant golden sunflowers expressed my jubilance and unreserved enthusiasm. Afterward we enjoyed evaluative sessions in the kitchen surrounded by our prodigious productions. Our plein air excursions were also exciting. We'd paint while Stan explored. Stan would return with a list of birds he'd heard or seen, carefully listed in his pocket notebook.

Our forays along high wind-swept roads and heavily timbered wilderness with dark valleys were rich too. Perhaps for me the quintessence of these holidays. Essential equipment for our trip was the picnic basket replete with thermos, sandwiches and a tin of various sweet treats. Audrey's enjoyable fruit cake was always especially tasty when embellished by the wilderness chill, as we stood by the car's open boot.

Audrey and Stan were never without their respective binoculars. The car would be halted, sometimes abruptly, to view a circling bird, an interesting fungus or vegetation, a distant mountain. It was a wonder we ever reached our destination! It was also a wonder that Stan could perform the feat of keeping the car on the usually rough surfaced road, given that his observant eye was often the first to catch sight of something interesting. When Stan was not providing an informative commentary, Audrey and I would often be talking about painting. We would gasp and ooh and ah at so many delectable scenes which we would have liked to capture on canvas. Sometimes we would discuss which recipe of colours we would use to mix particular hues for the terrain we were passing through. Once we likened all our family members to particular colours! Astonishingly, we often agreed on the minutiae concerning the mix.

Many years later, 1999, I sat at Rosa's kitchen table with Stan. He was still his indefatigable self, cheery and engaging as ever. Now a widower of some fourteen years, he was a frequent guest, sometimes unexpectedly, at many a table. 'Delish!' he'd say, smacking his lips appreciatively. He'd been to an Esperanto conference a year or two earlier in the USA. As he stroked his greying beard he recalled 'A man stopped me in the street! He said, 'You look the spitting image of Abraham Lincoln!'' In retrospect perhaps I could have asked Stan, he being of political persuasion, for his opinion of Abraham Lincoln.

Stan didn't need any association with a famous figure to be authentic. Neither could one manufacture Stan's individuality. He was an unscripted character who made one think twice about one's own parameters. Stan always pushed his limits, be it sweating and toiling in Rosa's garden or Percy's farm, or long daily bush walks or learning computer skills. After Audrey's death, he moved from Tasmania to an unpretentious home he'd purchased in Trentham, on the Victorian mainland. This, and another move later to Castlemaine, were both but stone throws to the old Bruton farmhouse at Little Hampton. 'Audrey told me to have a base,' he said. She had obviously recognised his predilection for a nomadic life. The next hill was always full of exciting possibilities and discoveries.

Stan's thirst for knowledge was great. Once mastered, it seemed some skills gained were no longer challenges. Over the years he had studied variously, as a surveyor, real estate agent, heavy truck driver, accountant. He'd owned a poultry farm, a cow and a few sheep and planted many pine trees on their Tasmanian mountain block. At one stage he had a job picking up rabbit carcasses for the local cannery. Now, in his early eighties, he was learning to use his new computer and continuing his daily rigorous walks. His home-grown silver beet and vegetables, in keeping with the Bruton tradition, were always larger than life.

A good talker, and a good listener, Stanley, an inveterate extrovert and communicator, waxed eloquent in letters, nowadays type written about his travels. He'd circulate these to his many friends, relatives and acquaintances. Included would be detailed, often lyrical descriptions of topography, flora, birds, and various fauna of the humankind he'd met. An enduring interest was the natural world. During the previous summer he had again visited his favourite isle. He climbed a mountain and also walked with a group into Tasmania's southwest world-renowned wilderness, from Cradle Mountain to Lake St. Clair. A five-day trek, replete with leeches, swamps, bitingly cold mountains. Among his latest exploits was the typing of his war memoirs into his computer. These had been penned some sixty years before, as a young idealistic twenty-one-year-old, in the Middle East.

For a while we talked amid the drum of Stan's fingers on the table. This nervous tapping, a Bruton tendency, I always found aggravating. Perhaps it assisted Stan's focus. It was a challenge today to ignore it.

The tapping left hand—Stan's only hand. As long as I'd known Stan, he'd had one hand. This one and only hand that accomplished so much. The hand of a determined and courageous person. It was easy to ignore Stan's lack of a right hand. I took it for granted, since he never complained, that he could accomplish anything anyone-else could. The critical loss of something as important as a hand seemed of no consequence. This attitude was I'm sure due to Stan's optimistic and debonair attitude. He took this challenge of uni-dexterity in his stride. He learned to tie his shoelaces, to write, then later to type competently with his left hand. Of recent months he had bought his computer. 'I took my 'Brother' word processor to Nellie's to share my holiday with me.' Stan had told me. This became an annual routine, when staying at Nellie's, one of Tom's daughters, in Queensland.

But, as with us all, perfection had escaped him. While Rosa marvelled at the work this dynamo could achieve, she detested his bulldozer tactics. His generous, enthusiastic assistance in her garden was a double-edged sword. 'He takes over! Mum had to keep an eye on him too. And now he's pulled out my blue iris! And he's taken the bee equipment. Just taken it. He's too rough with the bees, thinks he has to subdue them!' But while she bemoaned these losses, she did not seem to be able to confront him directly. When she did, she claimed Stan would override her. 'And it's my garden!' she'd remonstrate indignantly.

At any rate, the mountains of weeds piled high attested to a fast and efficient worker. In the cold weather, he sometimes covered his right-hand stump with a sock. Today, there was an extra protection, a type of canvas. This one handedness was a legacy of the Second World War. It was ironic that after surviving battles in the Middle East against high odds, Stan had lost his hand in a grenade accident in his home country.

'I was out on a training patrol in Queensland and they had little pieces of gelignite and they'd light those, and throw them. I was up a tree; I was trying to get the right position to throw it. Stan now looked straight at me, his tone rueful, 'And I held it too long! We were near Maleny. Number ten platoon were going on a special duty, had a couple of men short. Wanted volunteers.' Stan's voice, sardonic, continued. 'Of course, Stan used to volunteer for everything, and I went with the company down the slopes of Mount Tamborine, now known as Canungra Jungle Training Camp.'

A recent conversation with an old friend of Stan's, Colin Blume, came to mind. He had been in the Middle East Campaign too. We were talking about Stan's most unfortunate disaster. He told me 'Stan was always thorough. We were along the coast in Syria and a tank came up. We were in the gutter trying to duck, and Stan was up trying to get his rifle through the slit in the tank. He closed it down! They didn't fire.' Colin spoke warmly, enthusiastically. 'He jumped up on the tank. He thought and acted straight away. Fast thinker. They chiacked him a bit later. The tank cleared off and I think one of the British boats out on the sea lined it up and turned it over.'

I discovered, recently, in a book chronicling the Second 14ths adventures, that Stan had been recommended in despatches for the Military Medal due to this action.

That day Colin made another comment, 'We were training in Queensland in preparation for New Guinea when Stan lost his hand. Within a week he'd written to our platoon commander, and he'd written it with his left hand! He had the guts to do things!'

Colin's admiration of Stan, after a friendship spanning some sixty years, was unequivocal, untarnished.

Cheltenham

We started way back. At the beginning. Stan was born at Cheltenham, fourth boy, and sixth child of the twelve. His first five years were spent on Harry's, his father's market garden there.

Stan's voice was easy on the ears. Not gravelly or sandy, it was warm, timbered, smooth textured. Like richly hued soft Australian cedar.

'A video clip type of memory is of following the older ones, anonymous siblings, and our cousin Flossie Porter, as they followed Dad down between the vegetable beds of our market garden. They were singing 'Oh Harry you know—you mustn't do so! You mustn't! You mustn't! You mustn't do so! I'm always telling you this!' Dad had little tiny Daisy on his shoulder. I think what impressed, what went through my mind was the irreverence of that girl Flossie, no older than my older sisters, addressing Dad as 'Harry!' Perhaps even earlier, are the rather vague memories of riding in the buggy with my dear Uncle Will and Auntie Minnie Bluhm, and talking to them about how the moon seemed to be going the same way as us, and at exactly the same pace. I remember asking 'When will the green pineapples'—we were passing some pine trees—'be ripe?' They told me in later years that I'd sit on the dickie seat at their feet and talk all the way to East Doncaster. I was happily ignorant of the fact that their answers were quite irrelevant. They couldn't hear a word I was saying.

Strangely, I have no recollection of having seen Grandpa Bruton, although I have very fond memories of staying at Grandma's with Bob for maybe a week or several, while we were both schoolboys. I reckon that would have been three or four years before the old bloke died. I remember too, years before that, entering the low wide verandah of the old house at Mentone and hearing a strange new sound in the house. Not having grown up with radio, or even gramophones, I was mystified, and asked one of my sisters, 'What's that noise?' When told 'Its Grandpa playing the fiddle.' I was pleased, because I had heard about him playing the fiddle and now anticipated seeing this marvellous accomplishment. I must have been very young because when the older ones led off elsewhere, I unquestionably followed. So I never saw a violin being played for many a year. Later on, when he was aging, us older ones understood that Grandpa spent much of his time at the Royal Oak, across Point Nepean Road from his market garden. I guess that would have dated from the time Uncle Joe returned from World War I and took over the management of the garden. Mum told me once that Grandma would sometimes hide money in the house, so that Grandpa would not be able to spend it all at the pub. I do remember Grandma Bruton quite vividly. A kind woman with a warmth of personality. Yes. I too loved our Grandma Bruton!

Our other grandparents, the Bluhms, originally lived on their market garden on the corner of Chesterville Road and Bernard Street. Dad rented it off Uncle Will Bluhm after Grandpa Bernard Bluhm had died, and Grandma went to live with them at their orchard at East Burwood. Myrtle Porter, one of our cousins, remembers Grandpa Bluhm having several hives of bees. He never wore a veil, but smoked a pipe while handling them.

Myrtle remembered walking up Chesterville Road to the paddock where Uncle Will and his father used to grow asparagus in the sandy land next door to Robert Tuck's. The land worked, went from Chesterville road to Wilson Street. Everest Le Page's father lived on the corner of Bernard and Wilson Streets. I understand that Everest's grandfather, my great, great grandfather, Nicholas Le Page, bought it soon after coming to Melbourne from the Isle of Guernsey. Everest always addressed Mum, 'Cousin Olive,' and she called him, 'Cousin Everest.'

Grandma Harriet Bluhm was a very quiet person. Seemed to keep to herself. Her father Mr Moore had been an ex-convict! I found through my researching that he had been a ticket-of-leave man. Transported from England because of poaching. No wonder the Bluhms kept to themselves. Grandma had a father who was an ex-convict and a husband who skipped ship!

Dad's grandparents, my great grandparents, were Thomas and Selina Bruton, originally came out from England in the early 1850s. They were pioneers too, settled on land on the corner of Burke and Flinders Street, Mentone. They had nine children. Grandpa William and Grandma Elizabeth had ten children. Grandpa owned ten acres of market garden in Latrobe Street, Mentone not far from the railway line. In those days, Mentone was known as Cheltenham.

I do not remember about actually moving from Cheltenham to Taradale. I learned many years later that when the local Cheltenham doctor told our parents, that their eldest son had been cured of 'consumption' and could return home, he added the stipulation, that they had to move first 'somewhere north of the divide.' He would get it again if he returned to Cheltenham. 'You have another one such coming on there.' he said apparently, indicating skinny little Stanley! So that is why we all moved 'over the range,' to Taradale.

Mum kept all the receipts. I found an old receipt May, 1924. Dad had bought a ton of chaff paid by cash. Five pounds. Must have been about 1922, when we moved. Rosa was ten or eleven then.

'Possibly, about the time Rosa started to look after Daise, we got diphtheria. Min, Rosa and George and me. We were sent to Fairfield Infectious Diseases Hospital. One of my early memories was a nurse I loved. Literally. She was my life line of course; there was no visiting in those days. There was a nurse I was terrified of too, and a machine I was terrified of. Since then I have been told that it was a trolley with medicines on it. Perhaps they gave me castor oil, which made me sick. Which it did, even twelve years later. We learned songs in Fairfield.

'Oh you ought to go to Fairfield for a month or two!
A half cup of Epsom salts and liquorice powder too!
Nurses have a needle and they stick it into you.
You ought to go to Fairfield for a month or two!"

School. Taradale. Little Hampton

'Yes. I started school at Taradale. Our first day was on the 29th January, 1924. I was five. I must have been there about two years when we moved to Little Hampton. It was round about then I think that Dad, having sold his Cheltenham land to his mum to raise the deposit for buying the Little Hampton forty-acre farm, was in financial straits. I know Moss Daff had a mortgage on it. The interest on it accumulated during the depression years. I think it was 450 pounds, but with compound interest (about four and a half percent) it was re-mortgaged at 750 pounds, when I was big enough to have it explained to me—probably in the early thirties.

Found an old receipt, indication of our family's financial hardship at this time. One of many on a metal spike at the old house. It is dated May 1st, 1926, 'Beehive Stores Produce and General Merchant.' Would have been about four months after we moved. Generally the accounts had been paid in full, but this one stood out as different. Account rendered was four pound six and tuppence 'Mr Bruton can bring in a few potatoes when he's coming this way. No hurry for a month or two.'

Taradale. The creek. I remember this was where I learned to swim. Used a kero tin, with the lid on, which floated to hang on to.

I remember Miss Morgan, who taught us at Taradale School. One day she taught us how to dance the 'Loopy Lou.' 'Put your left foot in, put your left foot out, give yourself a shake, shake it all about!' This was okay until I discovered it was dancing, and wicked! Since I knew Miss Morgan was not wicked, that meant it wouldn't have been really dancing. I saw Miss Morgan with three girls bigger than her, all crying. She was well loved. This was because she was going away.

The headmaster there, Mr. McMillan. We would have to line up on parade in the school ground and march into the drums. I remember two occasions. Us lining up at assembly and he explaining what an earthquake was, because there had been one in the night. The other occasion was his lining up my brothers and sisters and telling us all to go home again as we had chicken pox scabs on our legs. The girls felt very humiliated. I didn't.

Leslie Gribbis, the son of the blacksmith at Taradale told me, 'My dad could belt your dad.' And of course, I knew my dad would not belt anyone because he was a Christian and pacifist! Even then at that age I knew this. So I hoped it would never come to a contest between my father and the big blacksmith!'

Stan's eyes were shining. He was enjoying communicating about his life. 'I'm tickled pink you are doing this.' he said. Stan's tapping continued unabated, but I had accustomed myself to it. I was thinking he would have probably been the strongest contender for winning the Bruton marathon tapping prize.

'I remember when we moved up from old man James Jackel's thirty-acre farm rented at Taradale, to Little Hampton, to live at Mr McArthur's place next door to Suitor's. It was about mid-January 1926. Mum and Dad with their already large family of ten children, ranging from Tommy, nearly fifteen, to Bessie, just over one-year-old.

Tommy drove the spring cart loaded to the top. The only part of the load seven-year-old Stanley remembers now, was the half fruit-case carefully lidded, with the black, white and yellow family cat named 'Tiger' and her kittens. This was furtively hidden under the more necessary things by big sister Minnie and others. Mum had the pony 'Little Doll' in the jinker, leaving later in the day for the thirty-mile trip. How the dozen of us fitted into the two carts, I don't know. But I do remember the long row of us spread out on the front room floor for that first night. Next day we explored. Thick bracken ferns around big black stumps, with dusty tracks winding between, was a seven-year-old's first impression of the road. At the gate there were three or four huge old poplar trees, and on the north side of the fenced drive there were the remains of a pine avenue, which must have been someone's pride long before.

We all had flannel shirts, and after going to Little Hampton we had grubs in our under-clothing. So Mum had to do all sorts of things to get rid of them! I remember her picking the things out of the flannel in the sun. Old Ted Isles had lived there in the house with two or three dogs before we moved in.'

Stan continued the thread of his school days, now at a different school.

'At Little Hampton there was a Mr. Myring for a while. He was transferred. I recall him pointing to the wall map and putting his finger on Croajingalong along the northern Victorian coast, where he was going. I remember bawling halfway to school. I think I was sick. I bawled to let them know until I got to school. Tommy Higgins asked what the noise was.

Then there was Mr Parker, Very nice, but he blotted his copy book. I was a bit wary after he lined up most of the boys. I think I was the youngest one. I got three cuts with his heavy leather strap. The others, six cuts each. For I did not know what. I learned later it was because we had been swimming in Justice's dam half a kilometre away, in the nude. The girls got away with a lecture, and the boys got the cuts strangely enough. I told George I'd only got three. George said, 'But you were the first. They are the hardest ones!' I will always remember the three strokes. The threat of it stayed with me all of my school days. It gave me such a terror of being punished. I was very submissive ever since. Min was still going to school then about 1927. I was about eight years. George and Robert and two Justice boys were there too, swimming in the dam. We had no togs, so we'd go in the nude unless you had bloomers on. It was all because Mrs. Parker had seen us when she was walking up the creek. Min remembers being greatly shamed by Mr. Parker, he lectured her. I had the impression she'd pinched something. 'Your parents would be greatly humiliated about what you have done!'

I only had four teachers all my school days, apart from a few months when I stayed at Uncle Will's at East Burwood and I went to the Forest Hills School. This was probably when Mum was having stress with Allan and his illness. Fred's sister was my teacher, Miss Mock.' Stan sat quietly for a moment. He looked pensive. 'School was a great experience for me.'

'Why?' I asked. I wasn't sure what Stan meant.

'Our home life was not very conducive to development. So much of our life is at school. Even though I only attended for eight years, they were the formative years of my life. So much of our home life was to do with church and religion. Even in my day, I accepted that what we were learning at school was the truth. I had accepted what I learnt at school was about the facts of life. Then I'd go to Sunday school and hear stories about miracles. I would then consider them objectively.'

Stan's expressive eyes were flashing. His voice took on a more determined tone. His hand forgot to tap. 'Home was not encouraging of intellectual development. For instance, I don't think I ever did any homework. The older ones didn't do it. So I suppose that was an established pattern by the time I went to school. There was never a table cleared, you'd have to clear a corner. Then there were eight or ten people in the room talking about their activities, and there was plenty of alternative reading material about, for example, the Weekly Times and so on.

Tom and I used to enjoy reading. I had to make a conscious effort to read when I was growing up. I used to read wild westerns. That was a real escape. When I ran out of them, and was looking for more, I thought, that's stupid. You read them, what do you learn. Nothing.' Any fiction I ended up considering to be a waste of time.

Reading in our family was more an escape thing than a sharing thing. When I was a teenager Bob got caught up with those wild westerns, quick on the draw stuff! Clarence Mudford, and Zane Gray was one of the better ones. I became addicted to these books. The Pelman self-improvement course made me aware I should direct my reading, not just read any exciting reading. We were all into the westerns. Probably Tom introduced them. I don't think I even bought one in my life; they went from hand to hand. Probably Ted Shelden was in the circle consuming them too.

It was when I was nineteen, I sent for the Pelman course. George would say, 'What's it for?' I was lost for words! 'It gives you self-confidence.' 'You've already got too much self-confidence!' I knew I didn't from the course I'd learned. I didn't!

After I left school, I would feel nostalgic about the other kids, their company, for the contact with other people. Soon after I turned thirteen, I did the Merit exam. Mr Dunell was there then. He knew I should have passed. He knew I was such a panicky little kid. There was a system whereby you could be recommended for the Merit. When the supplementary exams came up in March, I didn't have to go to Trentham to do the exam again. He recommended me for the Merit, and I had the Merit Certificate given to me. 'Cos I wasn't fourteen yet to leave, I had to go on. Well, I wasn't particularly anxious to, but he put me on to doing the more advanced arithmetic at the back of the textbook not usually touched. This was in the hope that I would get a scholarship to get to high school. Tertiary education was really unheard of.

My arithmetic was not through lack of understanding, I'd make instant calculations. I can remember my teacher calling me out to the desk. He asked me the question, and I answered correctly. 'It's not what you wrote.' he said, 'Stan. You are incorrigible!' This was the first time I'd heard the word. I'd read it plenty of times in books. At that time work was scarce. So I stayed at school till the end of the year— then I was a bit over fourteen.

Mr Jimmy Dunell. I got on well with him, but he was a poor mixed up fellow. I guess you could say I was a bit nervous of Mr Dunell. Not because of any threats to myself but because of the tension, evident sometimes. This was made all too plain near the end of my school days, by his frequent strapping of a pretty girl, June Belyea, about her bare legs. She was so dumb with terror that she could not respond to his demands 'Answer me. Answer me!'

But. I realise since he had T.B. or approaching it. He knew about it. What I found revolting was he'd cough into his handkerchief and look at it. No doubt to check for blood. But he was in very poor health. He used to get very angry.'

Stan paused, his expression troubled, voice rough-edged with feeling. 'But I do remember him hitting into little June Belyea. She must have been nine or ten, a buxom girl. He was strapping her around the legs, demanding she answer some question she was unable to answer. The more he belted her, the more panicky she got. So she just stood there. Must have been when I was the only boy in the eighth grade. Her father was in the paddock and he asked if the teacher ever belted June. He'd seen the marks on her legs. He wanted to know what happened. He was incredulous. I heard he'd gone down, Dunell was in the garden. Dunell got in first and said, 'Don't you come over the fence!' Mr Belyea started calling Mr Dunell all he thought of him. 'Don't you come in that gate or I'll have you for assault!' So Mr Dunell didn't get the thrashing he deserved.

I used to sit beside Jimmy Moloney in the higher grades of school, two or three years. Jimmy used to tell me stories about what he said to swaggies, that swaggies chased him, swaggies camping under the trees, and so on. I tried to believe him. Later years I realised he was a liar. I knew the swaggies were only ordinary people. I read about them 'Humping the Bluey' in the school paper and knew from experience they were intelligent enough to talk with my father for a whole evening. Whereas to Jimmy they were bogey men.

They walked along the road with swags. I had definite ideas about the swag. The classic picture was a blanket rolled up lengthways. This wasn't the picture I saw. The ones I knew had a short swag, rope around it three inches from each end, rope around one shoulder and under the arm. The 'bluey' was the bluey blanket.

A job I felt fortunate to have for several years, as a child, was delivering milk. Some neighbours, in an old farm near Frankie Attwood's, Percy Barthleson and his English wife. Had it for years—all the depression years, I think. I used to take milk from her to the schoolteacher's back door for several years. Threepence a week. I thought I was on to a good thing when someone, Jimmy Dunell I suppose, increased my wage by a hundred percent. After I left school, I helped Mr Worrall plant spuds a day or two, up above the spring with all the blackberries. Then when we were teenagers Bob Crozier from over near Hanging Rock bought the place. Fred Rothe still then used to call it 'Old Mrs Plant's place.' I believe she had two families, one or some by Mr Feely.

Crozier used to drive his two horses mercilessly, and starve them, so they became walking skeletons, such as we'd never seen in the district. I even felt sorry for wicked old black 'Nugget' that we kids were seriously warned to keep away from. On a related subject, I remember Dad felt somehow responsible for old boy 'Prince.' I think he may have sold him to Bartie or to Edgar Belyea. Anyway, Dad offered to buy him back just to give him a few good feeds and put some meat on his bones.'

Stan grimaced. 'I'm off the track. We were talking about school, weren't we? Little Hampton was a one teacher school. Being a one teacher school, I'd get more work done, but I'd be listening to the interesting things going on in the higher classes. Mr. Parker used to read, probably installing love of reading. He read 'Westward Ho.' This was a classic. Was a hum dinger pirate story. I used to enjoy the weekly sessions of history too. I would feel a bit guilty because I wasn't getting my work done. Reading in our family was more an escape thing than a sharing thing. To me it was an escape. Still is. Anything to avoid doing what I should be doing.

A few years ago, when I was driving a truck in the isolated area of the Savage River in the northwest of Tasmania, I remembered listening to Mr. Parker reading poetry. I think I got an eighth-grade school reader and learned off some of the poems by heart. 'The Sixth Stock Drover' 'Wreck of the Hesperus' 'Man from Snowy River.'

Mr. Parker stands out in my memory. He instilled in our minds the love of poetry and reading. While Mr. Parker was there, there was a fence which divided the residence from the school. It was made into a high paling fence. One of the boys said, 'It's only because Mrs. Parker's going to have a baby so we can't see her in the garden.' That was the first I knew that you could see a woman was going to have a baby! I thought they just happened.'

Obviously, school constituted an important academic experience for Stan. However, besides the teacher hazard, there were some other negative aspects Stan discovered.

'Teddy Gamble. He'd challenge me to fights. He'd hoe into me. My only response was to defeat him. But he could not be defeated because he was two years younger than me, and I did not want to take unfair advantage. Nothing made much difference—he'd just hoe in. Generally speaking, I never had any trouble with being bullied at Little Hampton, probably because George was an aggressive sort of fellow no one picked on.

Talking of bullying. I remember when a little boy, maybe seven or eight, I used to have an unhappy time sometimes, when walking home from Blackburn Church Sunday School to Bluhm's place, with my cousins the Porters and some others. I guess it was because I was a nervous little chap, that a much older oaf of a boy used to pick on me in spite of reproaches from his sister.' Stan was ruefully half smiling, 'I must have been a prickly little coot! He'd twist my arm 'Am I a bully?' I'd say 'Yes!' I was too stupid to knuckle down and say 'No.'

The kid sitting next to me at Little Hampton was my special friend. In the eighth class, this one teacher school, we always had time to talk when the teacher was down the other end.

We rarely had contact with other kids except at school. No. I don't remember playing with my siblings at school. Girls played with the girls, and boys with the boys mostly, and very little organised sport. We used to play rounders, where you'd bat the ball and run, sometime boys and girls together. Once I got to school, my siblings were just school kids.

We were all called 'Broodies,' but when we went to Grandma's at Mentone, Uncle Joe would give us all nicknames. Allan was 'Bandy.' One of us was 'Nugget.' George, I think. I don't remember my own nickname. Nuggety in those days was solidly built. Min was apparently called Mrs. Tuck because she talked all the time, as did the real Mrs. Tuck. Rosa and Daise were the only ones who had dark hair—Daise's was mousy and Rosa's was black. All the others had blond hair earlier, which went darker.'

Stan's voice changed, now taking on an agitated quality. His hand commenced tapping an accompaniment, emphasising his words. His hazel eyed gaze was, as usual, direct.

'I know the reason why Harold didn't want to go to school. He was being bullied by Tom Thorpe. Tom was quite a few years older than he. Percy thinks to this day this was a triggering factor in his epilepsy. I know how he felt because Tom's older sister bullied me, fighting and belting me with fists. When I told the teacher, he said, 'Serve you right! Shouldn't be fighting with the girls.' Anyway, I must have run away in the end instead of answering back. This wasn't in my book to run away! Perhaps the teacher said something. I don't remember.

It was a couple of years after I left school, when I was about sixteen, that Harold must have started school. I was all for the idea he should go to school. Dad used to say, 'Let the boy stay home.' About this time someone said Harold had his first fit.

Daise was another one who suffered the misfortune of being bullied. The Rothe girls, Nell and Freda, held her down one day at school, and got hold of Tommy Swaby about the same age, and put him on top of her to make him kiss her. But he didn't. He spat in her face. He was a skinny little fellow like Daisy. Daise told me this story after she'd grown up.'

Trauma, as most victims of it know, can hone memory to a fine point that lodges like splinters in the mind. Now, Stan's voice was quavering, rough with indignation. The injustice, the unfairness of this tyranny of some seventy years previously, was immediately and startlingly real.

Stan's voice was now angry. 'The traumatic humiliation of being bullied in such a nasty way!'

Enjoyment. Siblings.

'My main enjoyment? There was no entertainment. My enjoyment seemed to consist of walking out in the bush both as a teenager and as a little boy. When I was little, we'd walk out in the bush as a group. There was George, Robert and I, Min, Rosa, and there may have been Daise or Nellie Higgins or someone. I remember once, three girls and four boys coming home from Ord's Mill. We were coming home past the second spring. Robert said, 'This way' and the girls 'That way!' The boys followed Robert, and the girls went the other way. When we came out, we had walked a mile out of the way. I gathered Dad was already setting out across the paddocks to find us because the girls had reported us going the wrong way.

Some people say that you can choose your friends but not your relations. If you are growing up in a family of twelve—pre-war, pre-TV, pre-radio, pre-cars and pre-rural prosperity, your family are your friends.'

Now the field naturalist Stan had surfaced, animated, eyes sparkling. His favourite subject.

'Last summer I went to look for a tree I used to know. It was a big gum tree. A big stringy bark. I saw it as a child. I looked for the tree last summer and found one. There had been another tree which was missing. Just after, I had heard from the Field Nats about a register of trees of significance. So I made a case for its inclusion. Not for my sake, but for the nation. I made the case by telling about how the farming land had been covered with huge dry dead trees in the twenties. There were no equivalent living big trees in the district. But these two trees were very big trees! They were about as big then as the giants that stood in the paddocks dead. So I went down and measured the location and made notes. Amazingly, the tree hadn't grown much in the last fifty years. Seeing and enjoying and learning interesting things about the bush. That was my fun.

Fun times—going places?' Stan was scratching his head, searching his memory. 'When Uncle Will came up, he'd usually take us for a drive, sometimes to Kyneton to church. Apart from that, we went on Sunday school picnics. One special one was to the Kyneton Gardens, which had a huge display of dahlias in blossom. Another time we went to Ballarat. I think we went on Fred Rothe's lorry pulled by two horses. In later years it was someone's truck. We also went to Hepburn Springs. That was when I was seventeen, I think. It was the first time I discovered that a girl was interested in walking with me alone!

After I left school, I went to the first pictures in Trentham. We just knew Dad would not approve; we didn't need to ask. He didn't express any objection anyway, and he didn't stop us from going. Mum never went, at least when I was at home.

When we were schoolboys, in the late twenties, there was Moloney's, and later Dave and Dot Rothe lived in the same place, about two miles from us. It had a wide verandah, was perched on the edge of the volcanic farmland with views over the auriferous forest northwards towards Mount Alexander, where the gold rush had started in 1851.

Not far over a small ridge was Jack Talbot's house tucked in at the foot of the steep hill, sheltered from the cold south winds. A different climate from his top paddock, adjoining Moloney's. It was to this paddock we Bruton kids liked to go, on rare memorable occasions, to look at the glorious panorama over the forest below. Then beyond 'Two Pine Hill,' Kangaroo Hill and Borlands Hill to Mount Alexander, blue and romantic in the northern distance. The distance was usually in sunshine, while we stood in cold winds, probably with a drizzly rain squall now and then.

I must have played with Georgie and Daisy. George was the more mobile of the two of us. He was two years older than me, and he was the brother I had most to do with when I was growing up. Robert and Tom were just the big brothers. I tried to emulate whatever George did. He was a bit of a challenge to me, and I think I was a bit of a thorn in the flesh to George.

I remember one particular day; we must've been out in the yard paddock picking up spuds. We were only school kids. Our boots were muddy. We usually went across the nearby fence into Bartie's bush, scuffing our boots over the ferns. George went rushing down the hill, making an adventure of it. I think he was trying to shake me off, and I wasn't going to be! We came up through the open forest, where we always got over the fence into the paddock below the house. I remember wearily climbing the hill.

George used to play a lot with Alec Justice in the same grade. Don't know what brought it on. Remember Alec saying, 'You Brutons. You Christians!' George said, 'What about that!' in an aggressively threatening tone. Stuck in my memory. I was confused, 'Was that a Christian reaction?' While I thought of what I should say. I think I had more than one fight with Alec. He'd put his head down so as not to get hit in the face and punch below the belt.

Play and work were all one thing, no distinction really to Robert and George. One memorable thing I remember, decades later. One moonlight night. Probably a hot night. We'd get up and go out and have a leak. Robert was starkers. Robert said, 'I want to go for a run.' We three wild young fellows, ten to twelve-year-old's, we all ran across the top paddock to the panels and back in the nude. The panels were two slip rails in the fence, halfway between our place and Frankie Attwood's, parallel to the road. This was our shortcut to school. Even when there was a crop, we'd make a track through it. We never went through our front gate.

George and I made caves. We started a cave in the very steep hillside above the spring below the cowshed. The cave was there for years later. It was big enough to crawl into. We had to lever ourselves on our sides and on our backs to make it. Fortunately the ground was firm. Clay subsoil.

George was a fellow of strong feelings. He was a great tease. I remember him teasing Allan. Allan would say 'torpit' and George would repeat the words back. Bob would never have done it, he'd no more tease than fly. In later years when I was at home, I visited them one morning. I went over to Rothe's, heard them talking about demonstrating the Myers spud digging machine. George said, 'Off I go to lunch.' and left me standing.

George felt like a closed book to me. Before he married, he was Mum's standby. Robert was married, Tom had gone. I remember George saying, when we heard Bob had got married, he was angry and resentful. 'He had no right to do that kind of thing.' We were brought up on the Zane Gray sort of morals. George had admired Nell. He should not have done that.

A most exciting thing as a teenager was when I got my own bike! George and I learned to ride on an Eadi Coaster free wheeler which was Tommy's. He must have got it second hand somewhere. When George and I saw a bike advertised in June 1935, for five pounds nineteen shillings and sixpence, Preston Star, it was by far the cheapest new bike we'd heard of. We both went and bought one each from the manufacturers in Elizabeth Street, Melbourne. I still have the receipt. These bikes were fixed wheelers. That's why they were so cheap. Would cost thirty shillings extra to put a free wheeler braking mechanism on the back wheel.'

'Any epic journeys?' I wanted to know.

'Yes. George and I used to ride down to Melbourne to the Royal Melbourne Show. We did this for several years. Distance? About sixty miles to the show, then another twenty miles or so. After the show we'd go to East Burwood to Uncle Will and Auntie Min's place. We'd get home there about 11.30, fall into bed. About eight the next morning Auntie Min would be saying. 'You came all this way to see Melbourne, and you're in bed.'

George used to go in the local bike races for a while. Held locally each Saturday in Trentham. He went in them two or three times. It must have been about that time I suppose, my bike was new anyway, and I could go by myself. I got to know the district. Discovered the little reservoir at Fernhill. Another time, I rode the bike to Daylesford and out to near Hepburn Springs where the creek flows under the hill. I've learned since it's where the gold miners tunnelled the creek, diverted it through the hill so they could wash for gold in the creek bed.

Our work and play seemed to be blended together. When we were working, there was no overseer. Pea picking lasted a short time. All hands-on deck! Even little Stanley. No one said, 'Come on you go too.' The others were out there and I just knew it was my job too. But I think I missed out on work that the others did because I was such a sickly brat. I remember sitting on the hobs inside the fireplace, shivering because I had bronchitis. I think the thing that impressed that occasion on my memory was that I could literally hear my breaths sort of rattling in my chest and back. I must have been very close to pneumonia at least. That was one of the reasons we went to Taradale. Tom and me. Although I don't remember much detail, I know I had a wonderful two years at Taradale.'

Stan spoke vehemently with great feeling. 'I hated the winters at Little Hampton!'

'And who do you think had the least fun in the family?' I asked, but Stan moved to a different track.

'My fun generally centred around Min and Robert. They were less serious. While at Taradale we roamed the country side as a group. Tom was the leader in the main, probably Rosa when Tom wasn't free. Tom and Rosa both being working people—she leaving school on the pretext of helping Mum—they were not so free to roam about and please themselves as the younger ones were. Georgie was a more serious one, didn't seem to laugh as much as the others. I have the feeling rightly or wrongly that when he laughed it was more derisive laughter at someone's discomfort. But he was still my leader in adventures like bike riding.

Who did I admire the most? Very hard to say. I admired Tom for his ability to know everything. I loved Robert because he was always such fun, and he could do everything. I didn't want to know how carbide lights worked and so on which Tom was interested in. Robert was not interested in such things. He'd walk to work even when he was a young man, but when he wanted to see his girlfriend, he reckoned he'd ride down to Croydon, over eighty miles to Melbourne. He'd never ridden long distances before so he set off, and he went for the weekend! He could barely walk. But he went to work on the Monday. Half of my siblings were older than I. I always loved Bess my little sister because she was such a sweet little girl.

Daisy was my main playmate when I was little. Mothers and fathers, 'You show me yours; I'll show you mine!' After she had grown up, she used to tell two stories, both indicating how even her closest brother Stan was not always kind to her. She must have been aged about three and a half when she was climbing in a fruit tree while I, aged seven, was mattocking in the garden. 'He said he was going to hit me and he did!' I was indignant when I first heard it. I've always remembered clearly the incident. I was 'working' and noticed that she was in the tree above me, so told her to keep away 'cos she might get hit, and went on with my work. Next thing I knew, she was yelling blue murder, and there was a nasty gash at the end of her eyebrow. I was not growled at, so I guess they knew it was an accident. I sure learned a lesson though!

Her other story was about a few years later, perhaps when I was ten or twelve. 'Stanley took me away down the bush and told me the wild beasts were coming, and ran away and climbed a tree where I couldn't get.' That was quite true too, but I was not to know she didn't understand that it was only a game, the core of which was to climb that lovely, leaning tree. Obviously, I was not as sensitive as I always imagined myself to be.

I doubt if she ever related another story of the bush, told by her younger sister Bessie. Bessie was very small then, but vividly remembers Daisy taking her 'for a walk in the bush' then running away as fast as she could. She must have been too young to tell what happened that day, but she still remembers her grim determination to run fast enough to keep Daisy in sight. I was less than four years older than Daisy, and it just seemed to me natural that Daisy should be jealous of Bessie. Because she was so much prettier than Daisy was, and Rosa used to take great pleasure in doing Bessie's golden hair in long curls.

I do wonder about the pre-natal influence on Daisy. Also, when she was a tiny baby, Allan would have been two years old. Daise was born July 1921, Allan, April 1920. And of course Allan caught polio.'

'Early recollections of Allan?' I asked.

'My memories of Allan?' Stan's voice was considered, perhaps slightly heavy. 'Memories seem to consist of family photos. He must have spent quite a lot of time at Grandma Bruton's. Auntie Elsie helped him a great deal. There was a photo of him when he was ten or twelve. He was walking between two rails, a hand on each side. Uncle Joe made it up for him, for his 'galloping track'. Allan used to practice with Uncle Joe's hands to steady him. He was stronger in those days. He had many operations to his legs, and the doctor admitted they should not have done the stiffening to that first leg.

I remember him getting around at school, must be before he went to hospital. Getting around. He'd put his good arm, his right arm, and drag his body sitting on his bottom, probably when playing marbles—he wasn't actually able to play. I sort of remember him being around the edge wanting to play, but I vaguely remember pointing out to him he could not play marbles unless he could do this and this.'

Stan paused, his eyes unusually slitted, crinkled up. He was trying to decipher an image. 'Something about being looked at. I used to lay in bed with my head just inside the door, and he'd lay in the bed across the narrow aisle. But he'd be looking at me. Just looking. Whether it was me who protested, 'Don't stare at me!' or may have been one of the older brothers. I think that must have happened before.'

He hesitated. Reflective. 'It's only in very recent years that I have realised that while most children are developing their personalities and relationships with others, by actively playing and choosing where and how they play and with whom, Allan had years of being alone. Amongst people perhaps, but alone, until someone chose to come to him.'

Stan had emphasised the words 'alone' and 'him' while looking squarely at me. His voice was slightly ragged around the edges. One could hear the empathy as he spoke of his severely handicapped brother, about twelve months younger than he. 'That initial year or two in hospital, a tiny two-year-old. It doesn't bear thinking about! His family were just not there.' Stan emphasised. 'Dad had the market garden to care for, for the survival of the family; and Mum by then had seven others to care for, and always another on the way. There's no way they could have been there often, at the restricted and very limited visiting hours allowed in those days.'

Stan looked down now at Rosa's cheery red patterned tablecloth. His voice did not echo this brightness. 'Allan of course had no memory of that period. I guess the reason most of us know so little about his later years of intermittent hospitalisation, is because Allan's memory shut out most of that time. Perhaps it has something to do with his just chopping off relationships with people too.

I had this job in the city of Essendon after my discharge from the army, July 1942. I was travelling from Kew. I used to see a lot of Allan in those days. Allan had recently bought a shop with an upstairs dwelling in the inner area of Melbourne, at Rathdowne Street, Carlton. That was where he was when Bessie thought of living with him. He fouled his nest by trying to dominate every aspect of her life! I knew he had a few hundred dollars saved up from selling newspapers, which he did from his wheelchair at the Flinders Street Railway Station. I suggested he buy a house. We could live in it and pay rent, and we could pay it off. The house cost 1250 pounds. He only had to make a deposit, say 125 pounds. Not many people could afford a house in those days. Colin, one of Aud's brothers, was just getting married, so we invited them to share the rent. Our rent was just the cost of repayment, twenty-five shillings per week. We each contributed one pound, so he was receiving more than the repayments.

Audrey and Daisy had become close friends after our marriage in April, 1942.' Stan pulled himself up laughing. 'But that's not about Allan.'

His recollections concerning Allan continued. 'At one stage, later, when we'd moved from Devonport to Melbourne, I worked for Allan as an estate agent. Allan was trained and had his business. He'd also, by the way, completed his training by correspondence as a pastor. He had three properties in Hawthorn. Would have been worth hundreds of thousands now. He used the properties he bought as collateral to get the loans.

Fred Mock used to get real angry because he was doing illegal and immoral things. For example, on a three month settlement period, knowing he did not have the money, he'd sell it before the settlement period, 'relying on the Lord to provide a buyer!'

I was thinking about family fun again. I wondered if Stan remembered the family concerts his older siblings had talked about. He only remembered two or three.

'I remember Bob and Min sang 'Lets grow old together, we'll have a life together you and I,' I don't remember if I did something in a concert. More often than concerts, usually one of the oldest three would ask, 'Tell us about Queensland Dad.' He'd tell us about going up to Queensland. This was before he married Mum. He must have humped the bluey for several days. He went by steamer up to Brisbane; he may have walked to Proserpine. He must have talked to us about when he was a boy. I seem to remember he said that when he went to school, he had to take threepence every Monday morning when he first started. Soon after this free and compulsory education became available.'

Bush

We returned to the solace of the bush. It was to the Tasmanian forest that Stan retreated for a week or two in 1988, after Audrey's death. The bush was his friend and comfort. It was not surprising, in a way, that Stan recollected so much detail concerning his youthful exploits through the Bruton fence into the indigenous forest.

'I think that my earliest memories of the bush, focus on that short track at Little Hampton, from our bottom fence, through the fairly open eighty metres or less of Souter's bush, to their plain wire boundary fence, and the road down to the creek. That was the way we used to go 'down the bush' for many years. Even after Dad ploughed up the grass for growing vegetables. We soon made a track beside the drain or between the crop rows, as we padded back and forth in single file.

The soil down there was grey, unlike the rich chocolate soil up around the house and indeed all around that farming area. I guess that it was because Souter's bush was as yet not cleared and cultivated, although a lot of it had been ringbarked. Perhaps also why there were more wildflowers down there. That bit of firm ground between two swampy bits was where we could find heath in bloom during the winter and spring. I remember that spot for its white heath, less common in that area than the red and pink varieties. It was at the road fence end of that short track that I encountered, when there by myself one day, the first of the few snakes that I ever sighted in the Little Hampton district. That too, is the only place in the whole district where we could find the yams that we used to dig up and eat raw. Not that they were tasty, but because we knew that's what the blackfellers used to eat before the days of spuds and so on. I have sometimes wondered, in recent times, did we hunt the yams to extinction in that area? I think now though, their recent disappearance would be the change of their environment, from the original grassy open forest, to the dense regrowth forest that we and succeeding generations have known.

It was usually my older sisters, Rosa and Minnie, who taught me such important things as how to tell the yellow yam flowers from those of the dandelions. Also, how to choose a strong enough stick to dig them up with. But I think now that it was Tommy who first learned all that, and ever so much more, up at Amhurst. He had been exiled there to the T.B. Sanatorium at the age of twelve or thirteen, and it seems the boys roamed wild and free in that healthy and romantic ex-goldfield district, south of Maryborough.'

'Any other discoveries?' I was sure this would have been the case, Stan being Stan with his penchant for enthusiastic exploration. Predictably, Stan was now enjoying himself. He was smiling as he talked. His eyes were shining.

'It would have been during my last years at school or that first half of the year 1933, before I went away up to Lockington to work at Mr. Mudford's dairy farm, that I often wandered alone in the bush. That was just near the home part of the Wombat State forest that adjoined our forty-acre farm on the west, and to a lesser extent part of Souter's or Barthelson's bush just through our south fence.

It was near the northern end of that long western boundary fence, the track out through the wattles. Here I discovered in a tiny grassy patch beside one of those two really big gum trees, several plants of a type I'd never seen or even heard of before. They had to be flowers. But unlike any flowers I had ever seen. They were grass green in colour, and of different, strange shapes.

I used to find them there each spring and was able to identify them from one of Charles Barrett's regular articles in the Nature page of the Weekly Times. He described and sketched two different types of species of green orchids that bloomed at the same time and in the same area as each other. So I learned the correct names, both common and botanical, of my first two discoveries! The common greenhood and the tall greenhood.'

I asked Stan if he would write down the names for me. His left hand carefully wrote 'Pterostylis nutans' and 'Pterostylis longifolia.' 'No. I haven't forgotten to give the second specific name a capital letter. The first, Pterostylis, is the name of the genus, which may include several species or indeed several hundred, as in the acacia genus or the eucalypts. The genus or surname is always spelt with a capital letter, but a specific name never. So every species of plant, once described and named by a qualified botanist, has the same specific name in every country of the world, regardless of the languages spoken, and the common names used. So unknowingly, I learned my first three words of an international language. Visiting the same spot in later years, I was disappointed not to be able to find them there again, although I still have a keen eye for green orchids.'

Some animated conversation followed between us. I too, shared Stan's enthusiasm for this small, dainty, very simple Australian native. They seemed to bloom during spring's first breath of warmth. I had never known their botanical name, and probably would not remember it, in spite of Stan's coaching.

Stan was fired up. His words flowed like a smooth stream. He did not have to rack his memory. All these images seemed burnt upon him.

'Another pleasurable discovery I made, probably years earlier, was only a hundred metres or less from that same northwest corner of our old farm. That way we used to go to Ord's Mill. I had followed up the small creek that runs about south west from the corner of the vacant property, known to us until about then, as King's place. Jack Wickham's father who lived at Sunbury bought it for Jack when he left school at fourteen, about 1929, and must have provided finance for rabbit–proof fencing and some cropping. I wanted to find the source of that permanent creek, that was crossed only a hundred or so metres down into the bush from the cleared land, by a pleasant bush track that I always thought of as the road to Ord's Mill.

The springs emerged from the ferns and blackberries which at that time made a half circle around the wee grassy flat.' Stan's voice had slowed. He was poised to tell something important. His voice sounded reverent. He was now staring beyond me through the double glass doors and Rosa's floral profusion. Staring at a past scene.

'About at eye level, as I peered into the bushes, I noticed a neat little nest which appeared at first glance to be empty. A more careful look revealed a tiny round hole in the centre of it, showing me that I had discovered the kind of nest about which I had somewhere read—a two-storied nest! The top story served the double purpose of protecting the little family inside and of deceiving any would-be predators into thinking that it was an empty nest! I could feel three or four tiny eggs in it, so stood back some little distance to watch for the return of the parent bird. I'd never heard of binoculars then. But I had such a good look at that little bird. Had we then any sort of field guide to Australian birds, I would surely have identified what kind of thorn bill it was. As it was, I had to be content to decide that it was a 'tom tit.'

To go down to Ord's Mill we had a short, well-worn footpath through the wattles and bracken ferns, from the north end of our boundary fence, along the western side of our property. Where the fence sagged enough, we'd squeeze between the wire netting and the top wires. Coming out on to Miller's Road, we'd turn right and go only a few chains towards the junction with Glenlyon Road. Then we'd turn left down the Ord's Mill track over the creek and up a short steep pinch into the real forest. My earliest memory is of looking up the steep bush track and seeing clearly two native cats on a tree that leaned right over the track.

At some stage of the thirties depression there was a camp of seemingly dozens of tents, just in the forest beside Ord's Mill track, at the top of that steep pinch up from the creek crossing. We never visited there, I suppose, because we had been told not to. But when I discovered that they had all gone, I spent quite some time fossicking in the rubbish they had left behind. That's where I first found newspapers or magazines full of praise for the Union of Soviet Socialist Republics, and depicting the mighty dams being built, and the holiday camps for workers by the Black Sea. Or what is the Caspian? I doubt if I took any home, in spite of my inclination to collect anything and everything, I certainly didn't show them to anyone.

They were known locally as the sustenance gang or the susso blokes. Their jobs seem to have been simply to thin out the dense stands of tall, straight young trees. So it was all axe work. No crosscut saws were needed. Except perhaps to fell big old 'useless' trees that have to be preserved these days as habitat for native fauna. Instead of being cut into firewood lengths and sent on the State Railways, to the poverty-stricken unemployed families in Melbourne, as we expected, those thousands of trees were simply left on the ground to rot!

It may have been only a year or so later that we had a very humid time. Whether winter or autumn, I don't know. I've always seemed to remember it as winter time, when I became aware of dozens of different shapes, shades and colours of growths on the rotting bark of the logs and stumps in that area near home. I doubt if I had yet heard of the word fungus. There were mushrooms and puffballs in the paddocks. All else apart from 'blackfellers bread.' This, a large white fungus, grew well up in old and generally damaged trees in the forest. I thought of all non-mushrooms as different kinds of toadstools. I've no idea how long it was before I read somewhere about Cole fungus. This immediately identified for me one of the several families of wonderfully coloured fungi that I discovered in winter. I counted up the variations in shape, colour and sometimes size. I think that my figure for the different kinds was well up in the twenties, but I doubt if all those variations counted were different species.

That track out through the wattles from our western fence was not the first nor the most vivid I remember. I think that my earliest memories of the bush centre on that short track from our bottom fence down to the creek. That was the way we used to go down the bush for many years. We'd also cut through the bush too to the mineral springs, straight through the bush from down near the hollow log culvert to and around old Ted Isles' hut in the corner of Jim Plant's farm. And still in the bush, right up to the springs lane, about opposite where the big chestnut tree was in Keogh's place. Years later, when I had grown up to be a farm labourer, I still liked to go to the springs in May, so that I could collect a few chestnuts to roast by the fire. But I digress!'

Tom

Perhaps we would still be enjoying the bush, if I had not changed the subject to another gold nugget of glow which emerged from the developmental crucible of Stan's childhood. Tom was a sort of oracle to him. Stan did seem to particularly enjoy his company. I had recalled Stan alluding to this earlier. But I didn't expect his first story.

'My first memories of him were—well, he was just one of the older brothers and sisters while I was at Cheltenham. We must have left in 1923. I remember walking up the creek at Taradale, exploring this back creek, which was down below us, with a high bank each side. Tom was pointing out the little rabbit pellets there and saying, 'That's kangaroo shit or poop,' whatever we used to call it in those days. I realised later he was wrong.' Stan paused, passing his hand over his eyes. 'But I think he was just having us on. None of the rest of us had that kind of sense of humour that some families have; we had a sense of fun, but we got no satisfaction out of misleading or deceiving each other.'

Stan was now talking quietly. Almost a soliloquy. 'One thing which gave him such prestige in my eyes were the things he knew. Strangely, the last few years I remember only the two or three things he told me that weren't true. Like that the people in Greenland are green, Chinese are yellow, and black fellers are black. I believed that for quite a few years.' he added, laughing. 'He knew a lot! A lot of his talk was when he was at Amhurst with T.B. What they used to do. I found in some old invoices, records of Dad paying for Tom's keep. Seven pounds paid to the Public Health Department, from 13th September to 19th December, 1922.

Amhurst was a gold mining town. When the sanatorium eventually closed down, the population moved to Talbot Town. About the size of Little Hampton. When Tom came back from Amhurst he was about thirteen, perhaps twelve. All they seemed to do all day was rabbiting and looking down mines, bush walking and all sorts. Tom was born 1911. This was 1923, would not be long after the 1914–18 war. It had been a big hospital in those days. It was a busy town. There were lots of men brought back from the war with T.B., or after it.

Tom skited about what he used to do. No. he didn't get visited. This was a period of Tom's life when he was exiled. If visiting had been allowed, I'm not sure if it was, Dad didn't have the money for travel. He and Mum had to work too.

Yes, I think, come to think of it, that we ended up at Taradale due to Dad's apparently making it known in the church. By some means he learned about Jackel's twenty acres to rent there. Dad didn't do much with the dairy, he was busy making use of the property to grow vegies. The cows may have belonged there—must have bought them off Jackel. I remember three of the cows, Bryndal, Rowenie and Winksey. Some fellow said, 'She's a good one. If you can hang your hat on her hips, she's a good milker!' Rowenie was strawberry, Bryndal, brown. Winksey was brindle, half jersey, black with sharp horns and quick movement. Some years after we moved to Little Hampton, Dad sold her to Harry Barrow. He wanted to get rid of her. She'd bellow and bellow in a high-pitched voice. She may have been answering Barrow's cows across the valley. Mr Barrow said he didn't mind her noise, but I think he became tired of it eventually, and sold her. May have been five or six cows at Taradale. I remember taking shelter in the open planked shed facing the north, which was the shelter shed for the cows. Only thing Dad put up was the stable at Little Hampton. And he did a good job of it. Amazed me and some others too.'

After a contemplative pause, Stan continued. 'Tom was more adaptable. What impressed him on the family were the things he did with Mum. Put windows up where the stove had been on the northwest wall. I don't know how long the kitchen was dark for, but it must have been for a while. When we went there, there was a stove next to an open fireplace in the kitchen. He shifted the stove to this fireplace and made a wood box where the stove had been. Tom might have done some lining to the boys' room and back room. The great achievement was building the wash house out the back! Had been a lean-to between that and the well originally. I wondered why it had been built out there instead of on to the house. I realised now, there was no place that it could have been added to conveniently. Tom was Mum's right-hand man in many respects after he came back from being away. He was the handyman.

'He's only fourteen, He's gone off like that by himself!' Mum said when he left the first time. Apparently, Dad said, 'You know, if you're going to talk like that to me then you can get out!' Or something like that. Mum was dismayed about it. He went to about thirty miles north of Bendigo for about twelve months with his bike, which was his only possession, and worked on a farm.

No. I don't remember his home-coming. That must have been when he built the wash house because when he went again, the next time he was away for about four years. So I was grown up when he came back, about seventeen or something, and the wash house had been in use for years and years.'

It was my memory now, that flicked back, very briefly, to one of my few contacts with Tom. This was when he visited my family at East Burwood one day. Tallish, slender, salt and pepper hair. A likeable man, with a genial, slightly crooked self-effacing smile, and a slight stammer. I thought he must have been doing well from his citrus orchard at Kyabram as he drove off in his smart Mercedes car.

Stan was continuing the strand. 'The next time he went, I don't think he was particularly unhappy. Just a young man determined to have his own ideas and to speak his own mind. This was, of course, to behave the way he saw the rest of the community behaving, and not abide by father's precepts. That's what my young men did aged sixteen, and it's also the kind of thing that men did in those days.'

'A certain rebelliousness,' I contributed tentatively.

'Oh yes. Very!'

'He was the eldest child, wasn't he? Do you think Tom had anything to rebel about?'

'As I said, any, most young men would rebel a little. But ah—they don't all have to be so demonstrative about it. He was very rebellious. Sort of cocky. I remember Tom used to shout at the horses and you know, yell at them. Whereas Dad would take them quietly, he never raised his voice practically. Very gentle with them.

In later years, Tom talked about politics. When he came back from the four years away at Ungarie and West Wyalong in New South Wales, I don't know how long he was back, before he rented about twelve acres across the road from Shelden's in Lyonville Road. He and George planted it in spuds. Before that, he had been working with the Forestry Department. Whoever was responsible for employing men in the bush, called 'Sustenance.' Worked for very little. This was the first unemployment benefit. Had to be looking for work, had to prove they were looking for work in different places.

That's why there were a lot of swagmen. Very low wages—simply to exist on. There was that big camp across the creek I mentioned, where Jack Wickham built his hut later. That's where I saw that fantastic variety of fungi growing, including a coral fungus as big as your hand. I've counted at least six colours of this, pink tops, purple tops and so on.

Tom was a rebel—a free thinking type who liked to think things out for himself. I remember the one thing that gave him prestige in my eyes, was the things that he knew. He'd tend to like discussion. He would not have been able to discuss with his own father. One day he must have said to Dad that Mr. Belyea did something a different way. And Dad said, 'But I know I'm right!'

Bob and George were not interested in the wireless; they were busy men with day-to-day responsibilities. They were a bit scornful of Tom and I, because we were not as practical as them. Tom and I felt we were cut off from the world. Tom made a crystal set. Dad did not approve of the wireless so Tom and I clandestinely listened to it.

Dad saying 'I know I'm right' was typical of the relationship. The difference in age and personality. Tom was a Bluhm in most ways—an open mind. Though I don't think the rest of Dad's family did have closed minds. Tom connected himself with the Bluhms. Open mind, and a lack of temper. Dad, Bessie, Rosa and I flew off the handle! I don't remember Mum going off the handle, she'd get angry, complain, say angry things and not many of them.

I'm thinking of Uncle Norm, husband of Mum's youngest sister, Auntie Min. I knew he was a hard worker. He stuck on the job all his life though he'd been brought up on a dairy farm. His daughter loved him. I remembered Jean saying, 'Tall, dark and handsome, and he smokes.' I'd asked her why she smoked, 'I suppose because my dad is a smoker.' That didn't figure with us with our father. Dad was no-one's ideal man.'

We chatted about more prosaic matters. Perhaps this was for Stan a welcome relief. It was likely, I thought, that the all-encompassing and painful subject of his father would inevitably rise again during our later discourses.

Father

'In my teens I was a young man who thought that Dad was an old man and not with it. Then later, I realised that he had learned a lot in a short time, considering our moving from Cheltenham and then later from Taradale.

There are some good times I remember concerning Dad, mainly as a kid. Dad sitting at the fireplace with one of the swaggies. The swaggies would come to the house and ask to sleep in the barn. It seemed the normal thing was for them to come and have tea with the family. Sometimes Dad used to take food out to them and talk to them, and quite often too after this, he'd invite them in to sit in front of the fire. And it was quite interesting to me, even though I was a little boy, to listen to the conversation. I was puzzled one day, Dad told a fellow he could sleep in the chaff shed, and he didn't invite him in to sit by the fire and a yarn. Perhaps Dad sized him up as being inappropriate to come in.

Most memorable were the songs that Dad used to sing. During the Little Hampton days he used to sit with Percy or Bess, or the baby of the time on his knee, and sing songs. Sankey's Hymns and that sort of thing. I still remember it. 'Bringing in the sheaves,' 'There shall be showers of blessing.' It was generally when he was in such an expansive mood that one of the older ones would ask him about his Queensland experiences, and that was the high point of the year.

Min told me long after I had married myself, it was after our second child, Douglas, that one of my sisters saw a letter headed 'My darling,' from Queensland. We thought it must have been the cane season. He was away about four months.

In later years Dad found a letter on the mantle piece to an address in Sydney who advertised advice on birth control. He angrily said it was sinful and threw it in the fire. Mum told me that. That was before Daisy was born. The doctor had said, 'You must not have any more children.' It was too dangerous for Mum. I felt Daise was not wanted, and she subconsciously must have known it. Bernie was born after Daise, but took up a lot of Rosa's time because he was ailing. Daisy was about one year nine months old when Bernie was born, then Bessie, one year nine months later.

On the subject of Bernie, poor little fellow. I found a receipt concerning his burial and removing his body from the Children's Hospital to Cheltenham, conducting the funeral, a hearse, even mentioned a white covered coffin with white ornaments, cost six pounds. Sinking the grave and so on was four pounds fifteen shillings. The account was dated March 1st, 1927. Mum used to keep all receipts. It's surprising that they could have found the money to pay for this. Perhaps Grandma Bruton assisted.'

Stan's feelings concerning his father were obviously very mixed. I wondered what else he liked about him.

'Not a lot! I liked that family singing! And in some ways, I suppose when I was a kid, I respected him because he was Dad. I put quite a lot of store by that fact. I was interested in a story told to me by my older sister about a burglar who came into the house, and Dad pointed a toy revolver at him and told him to go or he'd shoot him. That added to my respect for him. But I was puzzled that he had deceived a man or threatened him with violence. The fact that he took manly action, made me feel more secure with the old swaggies coming around. There wasn't much I liked about him when I was growing up. But I used to be very glad I wasn't an orphan. He was my dad, and my life depended on him. He supplied the food, the home. Not a matter of mother and father providing the needs of life, it was father providing them.

One thing I did like as a teenager about him. I used to enjoy his sitting and waiting for his meal at the table, or when he was eating. He might chuckle. 'What are you laughing about now?' Mum might ask. He'd tell about some funny happening and make an interesting story and usually a good laugh. But about half a dozen times only do I remember that kind of thing. And being a junior member of the family, I never initiated any of the discussions concerning Queensland. He never talked to me about himself.

Dad didn't seem to take part in the chatter of the family, but occasionally, when he'd be sitting, he'd give a bit of a chuckle. Mum would say, 'And what are you laughing about?' in a slightly putting down way. He might say 'I was up the paddock' and he'd tell us a story about a funny event. It made us aware that he was not only a thinker, but he could talk. But instead of trying to communicate with him, we'd have conversations through Mum. His communication with his whole family, except perhaps with the two older ones, was through Mum. 'Dad thinks you ought to do this.', 'Dad thought you should be doing something else.' It was something I detested.'

Stan was fidgeting. He seemed almost embarrassed, disquieted. 'I was afraid of him! I used to know real fear when my dad's voice was raised in anger or when I heard his footsteps approaching rapidly as only happened when he was angry. In later years I realised he was always heading towards the bush. I don't know, I wonder if he went into the bush sometimes when his wife got pregnant, and he found himself unable to restrain his sexual urges. Urges he would not want to yield to. Might have been his way of handling it.

I suppose my fear of my father wasn't necessarily for myself. It was for us! In a big family, you think more in terms of us than me. Dad never used a stick. I don't remember ever having seen him use his belt, but I feel I have seen him unbuckling it when he felt an older sibling was due for it. I didn't like his shouting because I was afraid. I don't think he ever laid hands on me. Mum gave me a belting once I think with 'the stick.' I don't know when or why. I must have been a timid little brat. I was afraid of violence when he started shouting. You'd think I'd have learned from that, but I didn't, did I?'

Stan looked down at the table. He looked uncomfortable again. His tone was rueful, rough with remorse. Typical of Stan, his compulsion to be scrupulously honest overrode any concern about exposure. He looked me straight in the eye. The words seemed to tear out of him. Jagged. 'My poor little coot! I came over fierce, belted him occasionally. I felt well justified in doing so.'

Stan's voice trailed away, now softer. 'George went the same way, I think. The eldest, anyway.'

The moment, painful, poignant, passed too slowly. 'Not one of us is perfect,' I said.

Stan's mouth was momentarily set in an uncharacteristically crooked line. He cleared his throat, a sudden staccato highlighted against sombre shadow.

'I've thought about my father all my life. Especially in later years when I could see him in everything I did myself. I remember wishing in my school days, that one of my uncles could be our father. Different uncles at different times. Joe, Norm or Will. Even in later years Fred Rothe. Except for Rosa, I don't think he was ever close enough to talk to us. I suppose he was a bit like George in not getting close to anyone. Dad was very repressed.

Uncle Will was completely different from Dad. He was literally a father figure to me. I lived with them for those several months. I never felt Dad fulfilled the part of father to me and I know Percy would have felt the same. George was Percy's father figure, and I think Percy felt a responsibility to help George's family when George died.

Uncle Will was very much like my mother. That was possibly his great charm. You always knew where you were with him. He didn't joke like Uncle Norm, Mum's little sister Min's husband, and Uncle Joe, who were our favourites. I remember one day with Uncle Will. I was pulling boxes off the front of the truck, and he was getting them off the back. I must have kicked one, saw uncle dancing around, it must have fallen on his foot. 'Boy oh boy, I don't know if I've broken my toe!' he said. I'd have been terrified if I had done it to my father. Probably wouldn't have been as expressive. I loved uncle all the more; that he could be justifiably angry and still wasn't to be feared over it. When I went to work for them, I must have been sixteen or seventeen.

I remember getting really impatient, and I didn't say anything to Uncle Will about it. He'd say, 'Put the collar on old Bonny will you.' And then he'd say, 'And the hames, this goes round the collar the chains are hitched to.' Then 'Put her in the sledge will you.' 'Now get half a dozen of the pine cases and put on.' 'Put on the cases and go to the lemon patch and pick the lemons.' I found this annoying because I felt he had no idea of my mental capacity or experience!

Uncle Will had a white cockatoo when I was little, and he died at a very old age. He'd tell Auntie Min, 'Cocky wants a cup of tea.' Was milky tea cocky liked. We'd feed him with a teaspoon through the bars of his cage. Cocky would say, 'I want a drink.' 'I want a potato!' We'd give him a cooked spud, and he'd eat it in his claw. But now I'm getting off the subject.

I remember Uncle Norm in later years. He was such a friendly man. He was an outgoing man. He wasn't a father figure, but I admired him greatly. He was a role model. What I liked about him; he wasn't a demanding sort of a person. I didn't feel I had to be on my best behaviour, though you actually did. Strangely, one of the things I remember was him telling George and I, 'When you use the toilet, pull the chain.' I think I was saving water by not doing it. It was so different from the toilet at home.'

Stan was looking down, tapping his fingers again. 'So many memories of my father were what I was told by my mother, all second-hand dealings with my father.

After I got married, I realised how Mum had influenced the boys against their father to despise him. She'd say about planting spuds 'I said to Dad we ought to do that, but he says I'm too old for experimenting. Fancy saying that. He's only forty-five!' And Daisy did the same to Ted.

Looking back from more mature years, I've had the sneaking feeling that Mum, whether unconsciously or not, set all her family against their father, just by criticising things which were justified. But it wasn't wise to tell all his children all his sins. He never did about her.'

Family routine

'Everyday family routine? No such thing in our family. We'd go into the front room where the open fireplace is after finishing our evening meal. If you were sitting on the form on the other side of the table against the wall, you'd slip under the table. And go to the fire. Although we didn't start our meal until someone said 'grace.' Apart from breakfast, for all other meals we had to be sitting around the table before 'grace' was said. Where breakfast was concerned it would be one after the other as we came in. There was no bedtime by the clock. We'd each go off to bed as we felt like it.

In my early school days Rosa would wash and Min dry. In later years Min would wash up and Robert would dry up. Later years still, there would be arguments about whose turn it was! It was generally the matter of seniority. The elder one would wash up and the younger one would dry. I definitely know that when I was drying up, I had pains in my legs. My legs used to literally ache when I stood up to dry up. My older siblings would call these deviously 'drying up pains' because it happened when drying up. Mum told me later they were 'growing pains.'

In spite of his leg pains, it seemed that Stan had run and walked a lot as a child. And he's never stopped! Not even now, in his eighties.

'We were active kids. We usually ran to school because we started late, and if we came home for lunch, run a good bit of the way home. And if we got the meal early enough, we'd walk, if not run, back. So, the only time we dawdled was going home from school. We'd walk or run two to three miles a day. But then, I do remember some leisurely walks to school. Perhaps in later years when we were older and more organised.

Sometimes we took our lunch to school, however my memories are more about running home for lunch. Bread and jam was the standard thing. Rosa or Min must have prepared it. Probably Rosa, who was at home. Looking back, I suppose Rosa did quite a lot of what I accepted as Mum's work.

I don't know whether I missed many school days, but I seemed to have very often, bad colds, more so than the rest of the family. The Christmas holidays were wonderful. I must have experienced several before I realised that they were things that happened at a set time each year; that they could be anticipated, and that they inevitably ended. I thought at first, like summer, they were a way of life that just went on and on. I'd still like to exchange winters for summers.'

'Looking back, what else would you have changed if you could have?' I asked.

'I have to think back to Taradale days to remember when I didn't wish things were different. As to how I would have changed them if I had been able, that's rather hard to say.'

Stan was licking his lips as though, I imagined, he was being offered an ice cream but was not sure whether to devour it. But now, he thought of something.

'I would have liked good waterproof boots to walk to school in! I suppose it seldom happened, but I seem to remember the cold wet days when I sat in school with wet feet. We were pretty skilled at avoiding puddles though, and mud. I realise now that our soil at Little Hampton is of the freely draining type. I would have liked that metal road from Trentham, that went up past Belyea's, Barrow's, Rothe's and Rainey's extended down to our front gate.'

'Some memories of the family fare?'

'Swedes and spuds seemed to be almost a staple food for us. Something fried seems to have been part of every meal. Fried eggs were a big thing. Often there was nothing else, I feel sure. I remember we were not allowed to spread butter on our 'tato because it was extravagant. Only when we could afford to were we able to eat it. We used to sell the cream to the butter factory at Taradale and Little Hampton. They called for it. We had two or three cows at Little Hampton for some years. Us kids used to make the butter when we were older. The kids had to have so many turns of the churn each. Mum didn't like making too much butter because she wanted to sell the cream.

We didn't eat rabbits a real lot. Might have them for a while. I can remember a pig being killed a couple of times. I think Rosa said one a year was killed. I recall leg bacon hanging from the ceiling. They used to roast the legs too sometimes. On rare occasions Uncle Norm Tudor came. He killed a pet lamb for us. He worked for a sausage manufacturer. He had grown up on a farm. Not the kind of farm of my father. It was mixed, he'd gone in for everything. He killed the pig. It was too big for the bath. We decided to pour boiling water over it and had to scrape the hairs off.

Breakfasts? Probably porridge. When we were older it was a wheatmeal, called digestive meal.

Stews made of carrots, parsnips, we had sometimes, and occasionally, other kinds of vegetables from our garden. I felt I had wonderful food when I went to the army, though a lot of people used to deride it.

Who cooked? Seemed like Mum's work. In later years when I was still at school the girls would make cakes, sponge cakes, that Mum never made. We'd appreciate the luxury of those. Probably only after they had been working as domestics had they learned something of the culinary arts. We never used to understand about recipes till we saw them in the 'Weekly Times'. Mum would just put a bit of this and that in.'

Stan's use of 'we' in relation to recipes was intriguing. This apparent interest was, I suspected at best, academic. Stan's contribution lay in appreciatively consuming, not in cooking. Much to Audrey's chagrin, as I recall. In later years, when visiting his bachelor abode, although always welcoming, it was 'everyman for himself.'

Stan was continuing. 'Mum used to buy flour in bags. These were fabric as I remember, and she made them into pillow slips. Then there were sugar bags, about the same size as the flour bags. Tightly woven hessian. The spud bags were more roughly woven, thicker, heavy duty hessian.

Toast and dripping was a big thing. Sometimes butter. Dripping was always piled into the same bowl; the bottom was probably inedible. Audrey's family used to eat gravy, and that was called dripping by them. Dad used to cook up wheat. He'd boil it. It was quite nice with syrup or milk, if properly done.

We used to supply milk for the teacher's domestic use when the Dunells came. I used to have to go in the gate into the teacher's place with the milk. They had a big collie dog and the darned thing was about shoulder high to me. He barked fiercely; he had a long narrow snout. It was a test of my courage to go to the door in spite of the dog. From quite young we had to turn the separator. It wasn't my job until George had to milk the cows. He'd bring in the milk and put it in the separator. It just seemed to happen, the separating. Never organised. When I was older, George would go to work. I would milk the cows. Bess and Daise had a job too—I remember them washing and drying up.'

Illness

'I don't remember the frosts being any worry to me when I was a kid, although I used to suffer from the cold terribly at school. I think that was largely because of having wet boots, not waterproof. Ill-fitting boots too. No, I don't remember chilblains. But I do remember as an older child having chilblains on my ears—terribly bad!

I remember the snow. The ceiling in our bedroom wasn't lined. It had been a small shed that had been hauled over to the end of the verandah, and the door was off the verandah. But when it snowed, the snow just used to whirl in those flutes between the corrugation and the wall. So that I do remember on at least one occasion, waking up and there was a fine layer of snow over the blankets where we were sleeping.

I remember laying in bed and sensing the rain in the wind that was blowing from the north. I still remember it was June. And sure enough there was very heavy rains either after that or the next day, for two or three days, but it wasn't a cold wind on that occasion. I suppose it was the humidity, really. You could sense the coming of the rain in the autumn. The front door was always open practically. I suppose in later years we probably used to close it. I doubt it was ever closed for some time, when I was a kid.'

Rosa was passing our chairs. 'Mum used to try and look for something to put on the ceiling in the boys' room to stop the weather. When she got a bit of cardboard, she'd use this. She didn't have money for anything.'

'That must have been in later years. I don't remember anything there. I do remember laying watching on the frosty mornings, lying in bed late. As the sun shone through the drips that were forming on the corrugated iron on the eastern side, it would send shimmers of light up the corrugation. It was a beautiful sight!' he exclaimed; eyes warm with this remembrance.

Typical of Stan, I thought. He saw poetry in this inhospitable scene.

'You suffered with a cold a fair bit as a child?' I asked.

'Yes. That was probably why I was sent down to Auntie Min and Uncle Will Bluhm's place when I was very little.' Stan was clearing his throat again, like a half cough. 'I do remember I used to have Hypol. First of all it was cod liver oil. Hypol was a great discovery, thick white with the oil in it. Much nicer. Especially if you got a lolly with it.'

It was clearly the cold that thrust its frosted knife into Stan's memory. The cursed Little Hampton cold was indeed the winter of his discontent. Once again, he voiced his despair and distress.

'I have miserable memories of Little Hampton. Sitting on the hob in the corner of this pokey little fire because they were short of wood at the time, hearing my breathing. I know now it would have been real bronchitis. And shivering. Trying to get warm. Oh, I was chronically unwell.'

'Yes, he was. Never seemed to get rid of it.' added Rosa, her skirt brushing Stan's chair.

'Oh,' I said. 'Little Hampton's climate would have made it all worse.'

Stan concurred with vigour. 'Yes. Well, it did! We were at Taradale for that two years. That was heavenly. I used to love Taradale.'

'Mum hated it too,' added Rosa as she returned to the kitchen.

'The hob?' Stan was answering my question. 'The sides of the fireplace are raised up about six inches on each side so the logs can rest on that and leave a flow of air underneath to supply the oxygen for the burning of the fire. It's right in the fireplace, literally. There was a big fireplace but only a little fire in the middle.'

'Should have been burning all the time!' said Rosa.

I recalled the fender protecting the floor at the front of the fire. It was made of brass. The fire would dance in the reflection of this shiny metal.

'But,' said Stan. 'It's more important to have a concrete strip up to the fire. The amazing thing was our house never burned down. Because I remember that there was at least one place in later years where you could see right down through the floor boards.'

Stan was reminiscing about Taradale again. 'I must have thrived in sunny Taradale, but at bleak old Little Hampton I often missed out on adventures of the older ones, because of my frequent 'colds.' That must have been why I was not with them the day that Tom, Robert and George went with Ron Justice and I think Tom Higgins, away out in the bush near Ord's Mill. They came home eventually carrying a huge old wombat that they'd killed, suspended like a New Guinea pig, from a pole carried by two at a time of the biggest boys. In those days' wombats, like rats, mice, rabbits, sparrows etcetera were officially declared vermin, and it was the responsibility of all landholders to eliminate them.'

Stan looked at my widened eyes intently. 'It seemed to me though, a bit unfair to kill the poor thing away out there in the bush.'

Employment

As was common in those days, Stan left school at aged fourteen. Now slower and more deliberate, there was a hint of sadness in Stan's voice. 'It was the normal thing to do. I would have liked to have gone on to technical school, not high school, which was the only alternative. The working people went to tech. High school was for the academic people, and wealthy. No one from our school went to high school. The reason why I did not go was that Mum and Dad had to sign a paper to say they'd provide two and ninepence per week for the bus. The education was free, but not the bus. I don't know if Dad even asked. I know it was impossible, because we could not even afford to buy food or clothing.

Actually, I would have liked to be a cabinet maker. I think that was furniture making. Creative carpentry. No, I never made anything at home. Mending a shed. That was the first thing I did when I came home after I started working. The first thing I bought was a file, because in my growing up days there was a lack of implements. Always a blunt axe! But Tom seemed to manage. He was more adaptable.

A while after I left school, one of my farm labouring jobs was to work for Mr. Mudford at Lockington, north east of Bendigo. I think Miss Stephenson over at Drummond may have been instrumental in my getting this job. I used to work long hours and enjoyed it. Weeding strawberries. It was hard on the back, and very hot, and I was only a youngster and by myself. Five bob per week and my keep. We'd break the ice on the dish to wash our hands, and when we'd finished, we'd have to break the ice again. It was a bit hard to keep going. I used to write letters home. A letter came and it might have enclosed my fare home. Mr. Mudford had a letter from Dad to say he wanted me to come home to help him plant the spuds. This both surprised and impressed me, as Dad had never done any organising like this I knew of. Just at that time, after I had given a week or two or fortnight's notice, Mrs. Mudford went into hospital to have her third child. I had my fifteenth birthday while I was there in the spring. I didn't know she was expecting, and they had employed me to make work less for her.

When I got home, after a few weeks, there was still no preparation for getting seed or planting spuds! I expressed to Dad disappointment that I'd come home to plant spuds. Dad was surprised. He said, 'Why? I thought you were too hard worked up there. I thought you'd be glad of an excuse to come home!' So he thought a lot, even if he didn't say much.

He'd read my letters. Mr. Mudford was left with a sticky situation. Lots of cows and a wife sick. Dad didn't ask if I wanted to come home. I felt rather angry. Yes, I had been terribly homesick. But that did not necessarily mean I wanted to come home. Though I was homesick, I felt that I was working on my career!'

Stan had mentioned the bone chilling conditions at his workplace, about 150 kilometres north of the Bruton home. I was thinking again of the bitingly cold climate of Little Hampton. Legendary among locals, it was known as being even more intemperate than the surrounding districts. Cold and spuds. Probably Stan had partaken of this mix too.

'When we went out digging spuds early in the morning after a frost, we'd fork the top layer off, just like a sheet of ice. Put that aside. Sometimes the frost used to lift the surface, the hard crust of the earth. It would be raised up half an inch, and an inch of frost under the surface. In the sheltered spots where the sun wouldn't get all day, the frost stayed. I saw this more particularly over in Tasmania.' Stan cleared his throat, as he was prone to do. He had done this as long as I remembered.

'And the spuds you came home from Mr. Mudford's to plant? What happened?'

'The spuds didn't get planted till Bob finished his temporary job planting John Rothe's spuds. We got going on the plough and between us we planted the top paddock, five or six acres. It had all been in swedes, which had gone to seed. They were four to five feet high. The plough didn't actually bury these tall swedes. So there were rows of swedes lying on their sides and some rows with flower seeds still coming on. So we harrowed and harrowed between the rows of spuds to within an inch of their lives. Then we scuffled them. But there were still a lot of self-sown swedes up between the spuds.

Another memory I have from my teenage years. It was one of those grey mornings when clouds seem to hang down low. I was digging spuds for Mr. Davies. That is the place Max Bruton lives on now. Must have been 1936, or '34. A twin-engine monoplane flew very low over my head, perhaps 200 feet up, to win the Victorian Centenary Air race. London to Melbourne. When we read in the newspaper, it said the plane had to fly very low to get over the dividing range. It wasn't an uncommon thing for planes to crash into mountains in those days, or lose their way because of poor visibility.'

Now Stan was grinning. Not usually adept at telling jokes or amusing stories, he was about to tackle one. 'A legend passed down to Ted Shelden from his father about old Steve Stephens. When working with the thrasher at Rothwell's place, Steve produced a startled hush from his workmates by saying in his loud, deliberate manner, 'Can I sleep in May's room tonight, George?'

Stan's eyes were dancing. 'They didn't know, as Steve knew, that May was away from home, leaving a vacant room in the house.'

Now Stan remembered something else which tickled him.

'Bill Moloney, born about 1913, told me about Harold Beattie. He used to walk up through the old Moloney's, Con and John's farm, from the north end of Coliban Road, to every dance they had at the school. Bill's grandmother, probably an original settler, was ninety-six when she died. Bill used to go and visit each day, the survivor of the two old bachelors, Con and John. The first to die was anxious as to how the other, who had always worked with him and depended on him to make all decisions, would get along without him. Right up till they gave up work, they'd plough with two men, one driving the horses. When they had a truck, one did the gears, and one the steering! The remains of their house are still there. It was only about 200 yards from Bridgee Moloney's. They'd milk about a dozen cows. The cows never went into a bail, they'd just sit under them in the yard.'

'Your twenty-first birthday?' I asked.

'It just came and went. I was probably visiting Audrey at Boort at the time. I was twenty-one in October 1939. In September '39 Mr. Menzies announced we were at war. The only birthday present I remember was when I turned fifteen at Mudford's. They gave me a satiny shiny pure black shirt. I was only getting five shillings a week and my keep. I was quite impressed. The shirt would have cost seven and sixpence or so. I wore it for Sunday best. It was the first new thing I ever remember having. I usually had hand-me-downs from Bob and George. Grandma Bruton would send things down with Dad. Dad came home from Mentone; he was a bit amused. They'd given him a set of shoes, fairly old. He put them on his seat next to him while he was waiting for the train. When the train came, he discovered they had disappeared!'

'Did you talk to anyone about your inner-most feelings when growing up?'

'Not really. On religion I sort of joined in, probably silently, on a discussion or some with Rosa and several of us. I would have been ten or twelve when, at Drummond Church Sunday School, where we regularly attended, Mr Bischoff, our student preacher, conducted the whole Sunday school session as a preaching—evangelistic meeting. He wanted commitment to baptism, according to the Church's teaching. George and Robert and our friend Fred Bremmer did. I resisted the impulse to do likewise, having decided that I'd do that when I was grown up enough. That is, when I turned fourteen and left. We also attended Sunday school at Little Hampton sometimes. Mrs Dunell was the Sunday schoolteacher.'

Pre-war

'A memory that stands out in my mind was when George, Tom and I, rode on our push bikes down to the Royal Melbourne Show. I think it must have been the first expedition that Tom had come on. Tom had a free wheeler bike, you put your foot on the wheel to stop. We had fixed wheels and toe clips. I can still see Tom freewheeling down the hill leaning over like a racing cyclist, and on the wrong side of the unsealed road! I was worried it would have been all the same if a car had come. That was near the Cororoit Creek. Fortunately, in those days there wasn't much traffic. The major memory of that time was standing on the parapet at the newly built Shrine of Remembrance admiring the city lights along St. Kilda Road, which I had never looked down on before. There were decorations of some kind. Some of the lights were like festive lolly pops. I think it was for the Centenary of Victoria, possibly about 1935.

We were all impressed by the beauty of this scene. Tom expressed concern that all this beauty was threatened by the possibility of a war, which would threaten our freedom as a nation. We had no idea then. He first started rifle shooting. He joined a rifle club, which was a Government sponsored arrangement. A rifle and ammunition was provided for volunteers to practice shooting at a rifle range. This was only about fifteen years after the First World War, 'The war to end all wars!' Then he joined the militia a year or two before the war. Volunteers trained about once a week. They would go to the drill hall in the evening, and once a year to camp for about two weeks. I joined about one year before the war. Tom and I joined for the same reason. We followed the news with interest and heard about Mussolini, one of the three dictators in the world then. We were both idealists and saw the need of world government as the only way to achieve peace. We could see these dictators were going to gradually take over the world if they were not stopped.

I learned from Tom about the reality of the situation. It was 'worldly' as my father would say, and not for Christians. Tom had an interest in politics. He didn't talk a lot about this, though. I always knew he had communist leanings. He was never a member of the Communist Party. He never spoke about being atheist until he came home from the war. We did listen to 'The Watchman,' a political commentary on the news. This man, Thomas Mann, that was his nom-de-plume, was a very wise, a brilliant commentator. Probably the first one we ever heard in Australia. This man also influenced me. He saw war as likely. So I joined the militia, which Tom had been in for some time. Ted Shelden was also in the militia, then later he joined the A.I.F.

Then of course Tom had been in the rifle club, which had some tie up with the military. I don't know if this organisation eventually became the militia. Tom and I must have been listening to Mr. Mann while Mussolini's mobs were invading Abyssinia. I think they had already invaded Libya. Then sanctions were imposed on Italy through the United Nations, which were useless of course. No darn sense in trying to appease or deter by means of sanctions these power-hungry countries. We saw the inevitability of war.

Tom saw a historical film about Spain he identified with. This fuelled his belief that we should be prepared and trained. The film showed the French invading Spain and the peasants going out with their pitchforks and being laid low by the troops' rifles.

When I was eighteen or nineteen and up fruit picking, I must have seen in the paper, there was going to be a meeting at Tatura about eighteen miles away. A recruiting meeting for the militia. There was going to be a couple of MPs there, so I rode over from Merrigum. John McEwan and Robert Menzies were the guest speakers. They convinced me of the value of this organisation. You just had to go regularly to a drill hall for two or three hours every week and once a year into camp for two weeks. So I joined. John McEwan and Robert Menzies were both very bright young men then.

Tom did a heroic thing one night when he was coming home in uniform. A bloke murdered someone. Shot him. Tom took the gun off him!'

War

The next time Stan and I met was in the winter at Percy's. Stan frequently drove along a rough back road, a shortcut from his home twenty kilometres further north at Castlemaine, to see his younger brother. He was trying to be supportive of Percy, now physically weaker, also Doreen. 'I'm proud of my little brother,' Stan shared one day. Also, he had major activities which challenged and absorbed him on Percy's farms. These were to do with planting and maintenance of trees.

His other many interests and involvements were hard to keep up with. Amnesty International, Voluntary Euthanasia Society, Esperantists, Bird Observers, Field Naturalists, Aboriginal Advancement League. These were but a few. His mind seemed crammed full of interesting details.

He was probably too busily focused elsewhere to remember the mundane things of life. As long as I'd known him, he'd forget. He would announce, ruefully, again, 'I've locked my keys in the car.' He became quite expert at crawling through the boot of his car in the early days. Like a tunnelling wombat. Honesty would get the better of him, and he always seemed game enough to own up to Audrey, who sported an excellent memory. 'Oh Stan.' she would say with quiet resignation when he shared this annoyance with himself.

During the next couple of days Stan and I sat by the wood heater while it snowed outside. We talked about his experiences in the Second World War. Having joined the A.I.F. he was trained, then posted to the Middle East.

'When I joined, I think it must have been round about when war was declared in September '39. Tom was in the A.I.F. too, and only the A.I.F. served overseas. No conscript man could serve overseas until the Japanese came into the war. Conscription was very controversial. The Prime Minister wanted to introduce conscription, but the Catholic Church and the Labor Party opposed it. Appropriately, I thought. It had to go to a referendum and failed. Men were still conscripted, but therefore into the Citizens' Military Service, 'Militia,' but were not allowed to serve overseas. This force was home based and protecting Australia. Kept here in case Australia was invaded. That is why they raised a second force, a second A.I.F. for overseas deployment. After I left the army, I discovered that prior to the Jap invasion of New Guinea there were militia boys up there. Papua was part of Australia then.

Most went to war because it was the accepted thing to do. Heroism and all that. Before the antihero. It made no difference to me whether Tom had joined or not. Tom left Sydney about three weeks after I did. I was content to go on training. I wanted to get my training done when I heard about France falling and Dunkirk.

I was still in the militia earlier, when Ted Shelden got in touch with me. Said he'd joined the army, and I said, perhaps he might of told me more about it. I was thinking that somehow or other that the authorities directed one into the second A.I.F. I had felt that the militia was doing a wonderful thing in training the nashos, and I felt I was doing a good thing being a part of them. I must have got an exemption from the weekly drill parades because I was an itinerant worker. I never thought of that before. I was working up at Boort, bag sewing with Audrey's father, when the announcement came that England had declared war. 'And consequently we are at war!' said R. G Menzies. After war was declared there was a period there called 'Phoney War.' England declared war—had to keep out of it as long as possible in order to build up an army and navy etcetera.

It was when France fell, and consequently the British troops that had been sent to France had to escape via Dunkirk. This was when I realised 'It's alright staying here and doing what I'm required to do by the Government, but that's not solving the world's problems!' So when Tom told me he'd joined the second A.I.F. I thought I'll join too.

When you talk about motivation to join up. Tom was leading a life which did not seem to be leading anywhere and not happily married. The appeal of adventure, a life young men expect! We had grown up to admire the people who were the heroes we had read about.'

During subsequent discussion, Stan indicated he had been somewhat different. He had been prepared to leave his girlfriend for his ideals. Stan became aware it was not a black and white matter.

'My only conflict was admiration for the Quakers, and my father would definitely have been a conscientious objector. During the First World War before the referendum, Dad was so determined not to be conscripted to kill people, that he looked into the possibility of emigrating to British Guyana on the East Coast of South America, Mum used to tell us. That was before I read about Dame Mary Gilmore and people who established an ideal community. It didn't appeal to Dad because it was a socialistic thing. At that time I was not a socialist. No, we never heard the word. It was only communist. I happened to be visiting Audrey, probably the first time I went to Boort, just when there was an election. I knew where to vote, not how to. I said to Pop Burtt, 'It doesn't matter much who you vote for as long as it is not Labor. They are communists! I voted for the Country Party. The only time I think I voted for them ever!'

This admission from a staunch dyed in the wool, Labor voter, left me gasping. Stan's partisan approach to this party was renegade in the eyes of the Brutons. They were, I believe, more conservative Country Party voters, perhaps occasionally Liberal. That is, apart from Tom. I, being of the swinging voter breed, questioned this unwavering allegiance from time to time. Stan's and Rosa's too. She was a staunch Liberal supporter. Interestingly, late in their old age, they both switched to the Greens.

George had been the family's main stay during the war. He had worked the farm. Kept the home fires burning. 'What was George's attitude to the war?' I asked.

'His response after the war had been declared—I might have tried talking about it, 'In my opinion soldiers are all mad or anyone who joins the army is mad!'

Passionate words. I was about to discover that others felt equally passionate in another direction.

'A long time after Ted and I had joined the A.I.F, Ted said, 'I wonder why George didn't join up.' I quoted what George said to me. I didn't know at the time Ted had transferred his comradeship to me. He had been George's best friend. When I came home, or discharged, I found he'd written George an abusive letter, accusing him of avoiding his responsibilities so as to stay home and get rich on the land he, Ted had been working on and had to leave. That is Dagg's farm. George bought it from old Ted Shelden, Ted's father. I wasn't there, so I don't know much about it. It was when I was in the militia learning to be a soldier. I felt shocked and embarrassed.'

Stan was pensive for a moment. Then he added quietly, 'Looking back, Ted must have been 'unselfconfident'. Perhaps getting that medal in New Guinea convinced him at last his country had acknowledged he was somebody worthwhile.

If George had gone into the army, he would have had a better diet. The army diet was healthier, more plentiful. At home George's diet was heavy in fats and dairy produce. There were veggies, but fruit was a luxury.'

A better-balanced diet perhaps, I was thinking, but an enormous smorgasbord of risk. A young man could have his life suddenly snuffed out in a bulleted bloodied second. Even worse, the painful process of his dying could be agonisingly protracted, a slow and sad suffering.

Stan, Tom and Bob, all experienced the rigours of war, but surprisingly survived. The results remained seared into body and soul. The capriciousness of life. George, the brother who remained to till the earth, to tend the family, was the first to die, relatively young. Perhaps though, Stan's comment had been fuelled by a more discriminating interest of late in diet. His cavalier attitude had come at a cost of dangerously high cholesterol. Perhaps he was trying to make sense of George's ironically early death.

Now Stan led back to his war experiences while Percy snoozed on the couch. 'I remember writing in my diary, after actually winning a cross country race while in the Middle East, something like 'I now know I'm as fit as any man in this company!' Big thing for a skinny lad. I was a chesty little coot—felt a bit self-conscious.'

It was on 19th October 1940, that Private Stan Bruton, an infantry man, embarked on the SS Aquitania bound for the Middle East. As the boat headed northwest of Perth to 'who knows where' Stan turned twenty-two years. He returned in March 1942, married Audrey in April, and was transferred to Queensland in preparation for his re-deployment to New Guinea.

'We were in Adelaide after we returned for three weeks. They gave us ten days' leave. I married Audrey and took her home to see my mother at Little Hampton. The honeymoon was AWOL at home! It was probably the next day after the wedding that we went to Mum's. At that stage quite a few fellows went AWOL! After we came back, I went to report to the Watsonia Army Barracks. They said because I had been AWOL, I had to go up on the train to Queensland. I stayed at the army camp at Yandina near Nambour. We were near Maleny which is mountain-like and beautiful.

That's where I blew my hand off. I ended up in hospital at Ipswich. There was a fellow in hospital with me who had an appendicectomy five days before. The unit told him he had to return because they were on the move. While I was still there, I presume they went down to Brisbane, and then on to Port Moresby New Guinea. Our battalion the Second 14th became one of three battalions which made up a brigade. This was sent up to reinforce the thirty-ninth battalion, who were already fighting the Japs at Kokoda. So it was about 27th of August 1942 that our battalion went into action at Isurava. My friend Col Blume, who I went up to Queensland with last month, will be revisiting the Kokoda and Isurava. I'm absolutely delighted that I have been included in the list. Although I was not in action there, they just had another place left. We will be going by plane and helicopter. They are counting on changing Australian history. They want to put Isurava back into it. The vital battle was at Isurava.'

'That grenade accident could have saved your life.' I said.

'After returning from the Middle East, the minority were as healthy as I was. Lost lots of mates in New Guinea. I used to read the casualty list in the newspaper at Castlemaine. I had photographs taken when I was on leave in Jerusalem with Stan Ellery. I saw his name. Killed. Col told me the story about Mark Kilburn. When they were retreating from Isurava Mark said, 'I don't feel right about going up that track.' Col said, 'What are your orders? We had better go up there.' Last time he saw him. He got killed! Mark had told Col while on the boat when they were going to New Guinea. Mark said, 'This is my last trip.' Col said, 'Yes. We could be sent anywhere after this.' 'I don't mean that, I'm not coming back.' He said this less than a month before. Col was an officer. He was in charge of the composite platoon—a few from various companies.

Yes blowing off my hand extended my life quite a lot! I was still very unhappy about not being with the boys.'

I realised we had begun unravelling at the wrong end of Stan's war experience. Perhaps this reflects my tendency to read the conclusion of a book first. I never like the suspense and always hope for happy endings. In Stan's case this sudden devastating accident, given the tenuousness of a soldier's life in war time, may have been fortuitous. Due to this catastrophe, he was spared further danger in New Guinea and discharged from the army. This was mid way through the war in October 1942, the month of his twenty-third birthday. Nevertheless, this irretrievable loss constituted a burdensome privation to be endured, a fetter for an adventurous spirit.

Stan spoke almost without breath about his recollections of the Middle East. 'I seem to have no difficulty remembering various details,' he said, surprised.

The acute remembrance of names, descriptions of towns, the topography of differing terrain, and other details could only have been collected by a person with an observant eye.

War. Middle East

'We had embarked on the Aquitania at Sydney on the 19th October 1940 and arrived in Kantara, on the Suez Canal, Egypt, about the 26th November. Then we went by rail to Palestine, took about twelve or twenty-four hours, to a prepared camp at Julis. It was beside an orange grove near an Arab mud village in the south of Palestine, between Tel Aviv and Gaza. We were there training for quite a few months and were still there in the springtime. It was fairly cold but pretty much fairly Mediterranean weather similar to our own. No snow was visible, except when we went on holidays and saw it on Mount Hermon, looking up at Jerusalem.

I do remember the spring. 'The lilies of the field!' I remember sitting listening to an army lecture and counting thirty-two or thirty-six kinds of wildflowers and recognising familiar ones amongst them like hollyhocks. The name because it came from the Holy Land. They were only ground cover at that stage, weren't in bloom.'

Now, I shared two of Stan's letters with him and Percy, as we sat by the happy crackling fire. These two letters, still in their browned envelopes, the blue ink almost as fresh as the day, had lain silently for six decades. One had been given to me by Rosa. 'I saved all Stan's letters and gave them back to him, as he wanted to type them up. But I found this the other day!' she'd announced proudly. Then Min had discovered a letter too and posted it to me.

'I'll read Rosa's first,' I said. 'It's dated 5th May, 1941. Min's you wrote exactly three months later!

VX47264
Pte. S. J. Bruton
'B' Coy 2/14th B
A.I.F. Abroad
Monday 5th May

Dear Rosa
I've owed you letters for a long time and was going to write very soon now, and so when the cake arrived the other day, I decided it was time to

start. Thanks very much for the cake Rosa, it certainly is a beaut, but I haven't been able to quite decide whether or not it is home made. Quite a coincidence, I opened it today, and printed on the bottom of the tin was use before May 5th 1941! Wasn't that good judgement! It was shared by the gang as is usual and was voted very good. Cakes are always enjoyed, especially out from civilisation a bit like this.

I've moved a bit since I last wrote to you. I'm out in the desert in Egypt now. We had a great trip up around northern Palestine one day about the Saturday before Easter. We went about 350 miles but we manage to get time enough to enjoy every minute of it. First, we went up through the new Jewish settlements around Tel Aviv and around the foot of Mt Carmel, near the sea to Haifa the main port of Palestine and a nice big new city. From there to Acre or Acco where we spent a half hour looking around the old huge fortifications or city wall built by the Turks, with still traces of the Crusaders. One too, I think is up a long valley with a lot of olive groves, right up to the top of the Galilean hills where we could look down on the Sea of Galilee, which looked just like the Malmsbury reservoir away down between steep hills, and wasn't it a beautiful blue! At one spot I could see behind us just a glimpse of the Mediterranean, and in front Galilee. I was surprised when our bus driver told us that it is not a sea but a fresh water lake, but afterwards I saw a herd of cattle wading in it and drinking. It is also 600 feet below sea level.

We paused on the side of Mt Ezmon or maybe Acmon to look at the snow-capped Mt Hermon about 40 miles away. I was very glad to see that, as it is at least one fine sight that is exactly as Jesus saw it 2000 years ago and is as the old psalmists used to write about it. We could see Mt Tabor from here too. We went through Zefat then down the hills to the valley above the lake, and such hills too! We passed near a low hill which is supposed to be the Mt where Jesus preached the sermon on the Mount, and around a bit, away from the lake around the tiny villages which is all left of Capernaum and Magdala (where Mary Magdalene came from), and then the road ran along the rugged shore, cut into the mountains till we came to Tiberius, an old town on the shore. There we saw a flying boat—of all things!—between the gum trees that were growing beside the water there. When we stopped in the town Ted and I went straight down to the miniature 'wharf,' just in time to see the flying boat take off and go sailing away over the mountains. I reckon that was a real interesting sight. When we left the town, we went straight or rather twistingly up the steep hills until we could look down on the lake which was as blue as the sky, and the mountains beyond it all bare and brown, and away up beyond the valley was old snowy Mt Hermon; a very pretty scene. I saw a lot of beautiful views that day, mountains, fertile valleys and water. From Tiberius we went to Nazareth through Cana of Galilee, where there is a village on either side of the road. One side is ruins from of an old village destroyed about 10 years ago by an earthquake and the other side is new, even though it doesn't look like it. The Arab villages never do. There was an old-fashioned well at the side of the road. We never stayed long in Nazareth but it is a pretty place when you come down out of the hills in which it is nestling. It has quite a lot of trees and greenery, of which the hills themselves have none. In the town is an old stone well which is the same one as Jesus would no doubt go to with his mother, as a boy, to draw water.

From Nazareth we went up to the edge of the Galilee hills where we could look down on the beautifully fertile valley of Jezreel with settlements dotted over it. It is further down this valley to the east of there that the Valley of Megiddo is, in which people seem to be so interested.

We went along the side of the Galilean hills passing through several little forests planted by some far-seeing Jews and several little Jewish settlements, till we came to where the Galilean hills and Mt Carmel meet, then through the little valley separating them back to Haifa again. Haifa is not mentioned in the Bible at all, but it is now the 3rd largest city in Palestine. It looks pretty when you approach it from the way we did, with its white stone buildings up the side of the Mt and tall cypress trees making it look like a picture of some Swiss town.

When we were going 'home' we met crowds of people out on their evening stroll—the whole population of the settlements seemed to be out on the streets, happy looking people so unlike the Arabs—then we remembered it was their Sabbath evening and I guess they were going home from church. We had left before daylight and got back to camp after dark. The next week we shifted down here to Egypt, another interesting trip.

We arrived at our new camp on Good Friday—what an Easter. We were only there a few days but had several dust storms, and the dust is so light and thick that it penetrated everywhere and was choking too. We are in nice heavy white sand now and though we've had several sandstorms; they are not solid when we have a pair of celluloid goggles.

We still have not seen anyone to fight except one lonely aeroplane which bombed a place a few miles away and fled with anti-air craft shells making white puffs near him away up in the sky. Thanks for the photo of Joy. I love it. It makes me homesick! Give my love to Ernie and Ern. Cheerio Rosa, old sis.

Lots of love from
Stan.

VX47264
Pte. S. J. Bruton
'B' Coy 2/14th B
A.I.F. Abroad
5th August 41

Dear Min

Just a li'le letter from your little brother to let you know he's still alive and well. I suppose you hear that much from home, but that doesn't make you want to write 'cos you've no letters to answer. I'm sending a little handkerchief as a souvenir of this country. All through this campaign I was puzzled by the way the mulberry trees were kept cut back to 3 or 6-foot-high, because having no old branches on them I knew that they couldn't bear fruit.

A week or so after it was all over, a boy who speaks English showed a couple of mates and I over their silk factory! That solved the problem; they were mulberry trees all right, but the inhabitants of this country call them 'silk trees.'

In this little factory was a row of benches with about twenty women and girls, each with a dish full of hot water, kept hot by steam pipes. The cocoons are soaked in this, then the girl gets the end of the silk thread, connects it to a wheel (or reel) which winds on the threads from about 6 or 7 cocoons all into one thread. They showed me a hank of gleaming yellow silk, just as it comes off these reels. He said that it is then sent to Damascus to be woven.

That is why I was interested to see these little silken things being sold. By the number of 'silk trees' throughout the considerable portion of Lebanon that I've seen, I'd say that silk must be an important thing in the lives of the Lebanese people.

These people with whom I have come in contact all seem to be peaceful and comparatively clean living, and healthy compared with all the other Arabic-speaking peoples I have seen in Palestine and Egypt.

I'm becoming a much-travelled man aren't I! I'd like to be able to write a book on these travels—and adventures—of mine to send home to all you people, but I'll have to be content to wait till I see you and by then I will probably be talking about and thinking of other things.

I bet people will think I'm a little bit of a liar when I do start telling yarns, I've some beauts to tell. There is a sheep beside me now that has to be seen to be believed. It's a fat tailed sheep which are common throughout the Middle East, and having just been shorn I can for the first time see what a wag it is. Not only has it a wide flat tail as big as its head, but also another dainty little white tail growing on the end of it. I've seen several nice spots in this country but this where I am writing is about the best yet.

By the way this page's date is 8th of August. We are camped nearby here doing a bit of guard work and this little open-air café is the best idea I struck yet. It has a concrete floor and from a fine spring, 3 times as big as ours at home, there is a good little creek winding in and out amongst the tables, then out along a vine covered concrete floored sort of patio. I guess that's the name for it because, the proprietor has been to Brazil; I s'pose that's where he got such a bright idea from.

I'll send you a post card I bought in Beyouth (or Beirut). I bought a lot at 3d each but I have a lot of places to send them to also.

I think I'll buy a camera one of these days, the trouble with them is that they are so very easy to lose in the army and they cost so much—I reckon I could get some wonderful photos in this country.

There have no doubt been lots of photos in the papers at home of places that I could recognise. I've noticed one at least, that is the big wireless mast outside Beirut which can be seen from very many miles away. I've been seeing that a lot since a day or so before the campaign finished. I've been to Beirut several times, but it's not a very interesting place, probably only because I'm losing interest in towns after seeing more interesting things. Too much excitement is inclined to make a bloke easily bored.

There is another little place about 8 miles up in the hills that looks very interesting though. Aley is the name and it is where anyone from Beirut who has money, lives in the summer, being up in the mountains.

Some of us went to the pictures (to see 'King Kong') one night and it was all lit up like the Paris of story books. It's only small, but bright and it was crowded that night on account of a swimming carnival at a little freshwater pool in a brilliant setting of concrete and gardens. I had my first milk shake since before Easter and my first Koko Kola ever at one of the several big, cool cafes or casinos or 'whatever-they-ares.'

Speaking of cameras, Ted bought one in Beirut but the first film was a blackout and the second is mostly pretty blurry. It helped to knock off my conceit considerably though. I had a photo taken of me stripped to the waist, and I look exactly like Mahatma Ghandi! Spoiling an otherwise good photo of Ted in typical Syrian scenery. I used to think Syria was a desert, but the country I've seen is not, it's all hills where I've been except for a narrow flat up to a few miles wide by the sea.

It was on such a flat where we had our real 'baptism of fire.' I had heard bullets zipping close before that, but that's where I first really felt the fear of death. Believe you me Min, it's no joke even when you're fresh like we were then. The bullets were really as thick as hail, and I'll never be able to understand why they missed so many of us. I don't know whether or not I'm religious, but I've discovered a genuine faith in God during this campaign. That day, I just prayed hard that I wouldn't be hit! Silly, I knew, *but I did. Since then when I feel that scared, I pray instead for courage, and believe you me Min, God really is there to help me then. When the scrap was finished Ted and I were 2 of the only 4 of our platoon who had come right through without being sent back wounded or sick, though a lot have arrived back with us since. Three chaps, all from our section were killed at the flat that day. One was 'Ginger Bill'—one of the best! It makes me mad when I think of fools like Masso who glorify war, which kills the best of men without letting them even fight back.*

That's a cheerful note to finish on, isn't it Sis? We don't often look at things that way, thank God, we enjoy the present when we can and hope for the future when we can't.

Let's hear from you at times Min, I don't even know your address! Being boat mail, I'll wish you Many Happy Returns of the 18th too!

Cheerio

With love from Stan

Stan's face was glowing. 'I'm so utterly delighted they thought enough of those letters to save them! It's just great! I'd forgotten about the silkworms. Haven't typed up any of them yet. I'm still typing the diary material, with the help of my friend Ern Perkins from the Field Nats, he's a computer wiz. Well, that's until I go to New Guinea, and then I'll be going to Queensland. Nellie's at Woombye.'

It was one month after he returned home from his sortie to New Guinea in June, that Stan visited us on his way to Queensland. Out of the blue his buoyant optimistic voice was on the telephone. 'I'm here nearly to Bairnsdale. Have a bed for the night?'

Over morning tea we again continued the strand of Stan's Middle East experiences. He had risen early and walked several kilometres around and through local farmland, returning with an inventory of local birds in his well-thumbed diary.

'In the spring, about February or March, we moved down across the Suez Canal again by train. I think the train must have gone right through Cairo. We went through Alexandria. Paused there, long enough for the more rebellious to get off and to interact with the natives trying to sell us something.'

'And you were one of the rebellious ones?' I asked.

'No, I was a good boy! We left the train at Alexandria and camped at Amreya for a day or so, and that was when I saw my first and only really thick dust storm. Visibility was down to about fifteen metres. Couldn't recognise the mess tent. In the night you would pull the blankets over your head and in the morning, you'd shake the dust off everything.

I think it was there we had our hair cropped, and the hair was only half an inch long. You put steel helmets on the hair. It was very uncomfortable. Poked the head like little spikes. It was the only time we had our hair cut off too, I think. Then we were on the train again. We knew the Germans had landed and were coming down, already getting near Tobruk. They were coming down from the west along the coast. I remember travelling through the night, but I think we might have travelled all day as well. And it was then......

You spoke about adventures. Well, I got sick of being cramped up hour after hour during the night. Perhaps about twelve midnight, the other chaps were asleep, I walked out to the end of the carriage and then there wasn't much satisfaction. And I found I could in monkey style swing myself up to the roof. It was nice and flat. And then I could jump across from the front carriage. It was a steam train. I could see the glow on the next carriage. Then I thought, they are Egyptian drivers no doubt, and they might stop if they see me. And that might be it. I didn't go near enough to worry them.

I remember about eleven o'clock one night, probably the same night, they stopped the train. All off! As a private, I didn't know why they stopped. 'Take up defensive positions!' We had no shovels, no trenching tools. It was hard soil. All we could do was to stay in our sections. We were only there about half an hour. So then we went into the night. It turned out afterwards, we were told on the grapevine, they'd had word that the Germans had broken through, they had armoured columns at this time. It was at that time we were heading towards them and they were coming towards us, so they must have got the opposite message later. We must have travelled many, many miles. I think it was after dark in the evening that we got to Mersa Matruh. This is in North Africa along the Mediterranean coast, just out of Egypt. The sands were white, and the sea, a real blue. It was a pretty sight.

Our company was allocated to what looked like a factory. Bare concrete walls and bare open windows. The final thing you are supposed to do at night is to check your rifle. As I did! I must have accidentally pulled the trigger—fortunately it was pointing to the ground! I remember my utter confusion at the explosion! Within a few seconds everyone was out of the windows, etcetera. The next morning we formed up in a column instead of back into the train. While we were forming up, there was a cloud on the horizon to the north of us. And when we started moving, we discovered these were big white sand hills, coastal sand dunes. We spent the next three months there.

There was a row of trenches also, facing out to the west, which had been used in the First World War. They were boarded up. So the battalion took up these trenches, and they were enjoyed by all.

I had a couple of adventures there. It was an adventure in itself to learn what was under the ground in that place. The water supply was collected by underground tunnels which had been built by the Romans probably 2000 years before, and it extended for miles from where we were, not far from the coast. Where it went, I don't know. We were told it was about three and a half miles, and that they had discovered they had been built from two different directions, with only nine inches out! So they must have had some pretty good engineers! We were told it was subsurface water coming down from the escarpment, on the horizon many miles away. I wondered if it could have been sea water being purified, going through the porous terrain and being accumulated in this channel. It would be interesting to read my diaries and letters. I have not read them for sixty years since they were written.'

I marvelled at a young man's foresight in writing a diary of his war experiences. I was delighted that Stan had written this diary. A few weeks after our earlier discussion, I had received a note from him with some typed pages from it.

'I rediscovered your letter regarding info re my wartime experiences, while looking for a comparatively recent diary and I came across one dated August, 1940.

I then decided to copy it on to a floppy disc so that I can make print-out copies of it. I have intended for years to do so with all my diaries, but I realise now that it will probably take more years than I have at my disposal. So I'll just go on with this one, sending you a few pages at a time as I get them filed.'

Today, Stan's voice sounded rueful again. It hinted at some self-castigation I suspected. The twinkle in his eyes betrayed a smile at himself.

'Another terrible story! Usually wherever the troops are moved to, they establish latrines, a trench in the ground wide enough to straddle. But in the shifting sand it is not possible, so we'd scratch in the sand like a cat. I thought, why not rig up a seat for comfort? I could see two or three steel pickets, probably there since the last world war. I drove in a picket, I struck something, and dug up a First World War mine! I thought I must show my mates. I took it to them. Carried it carefully. I was told 'Get that bloody thing away from here!' There were concrete posts open, sharp as teeth, fifty metres away, from the First World War probably to stop vehicles, about one metre from the ground. I sat the thing on top of one of those. Probably had been built earlier by the Egyptians, for modern warfare, modern tank defences. And I forgot about it, of course.

But it was the next morning or a week or two later. Each morning a roster—had someone on guard, always. At a certain time, you had weapon testing. The person on guard duty would fire a few rounds into the desert. This morning the whole mile or so of trenches heard the same as me. I heard this violent explosion! I saw the tent was intact, but I hit my head on the top. All I could see was a cloud of dust just settling from the explosion. Apparently, Jackie Adams thought instead of firing out to the desert, he'd take a pot shot on that! Jackie Adams was one of my section. Whatever section you were in, you were always like a family. Jackie Adams got a mention in the history of the battalion. The first unit history written after the First World War. He is not alive now.

I think it was the lieutenant himself who came down from headquarters. Without saying 'Who fired the shot?' he said, 'It must have been hit by a stray bullet!' The company commander wanted to know what happened in B Company area. Our lieutenant Kyffen 'Kyffo' sent back word 'It was an explosion due to 'an act of God!' It was known, we were warned, there were mines still there since the First World War and no one knew where they were. One of the adventures was going out on patrol. I was very scared, but apparently they sent a patrol out every night to stop anyone wandering from the camp.'

War. Action

A year later, another snowy sojourn. Another companionable crackly fire at Percy's. Stan took up the subject with hardly a hesitation.

'But Jackie Adams! I used to go to Newsreels when I was in Melbourne on leave and sometimes, I'd see actions in New Guinea on the film. One time there was a documentary on the fighting in New Guinea, the Ramu Valley. It was based around a corporal taking out his men. The corporal was Jack Adams. In The History of the 14th Battalion, towards the end of the book, the author said, 'There are always men in any history that don't get mentioned and much has occurred and will never be mentioned. As an indicator of what I mean, there was one soldier that was in every action in which the battalion took part, but he's not mentioned in this book. His name is Jackie Adams.'

I shared a tent with Jackie after the Syrian campaign. I like to think of him as the typical digger in his personality. Though in appearance he was not long and slim, he was short and broad. I remember him saying after our first action, when he was abusing the corporal, he was probably in his cups. 'Once a corporal, never a man!' I found it amusing that he became a corporal. This happened in New Guinea—a private may have to take over in an infantry action. They were all leaders when the time came. Jackie for instance was always agin' the government and a bit of a grumbler.

The next time we moved back into Palestine about three or four months later, we didn't call at Julis. We kept going. Somehow, we were transferred into trucks and we went up to a place in Vinymina which was a delightful little village. It may be a kibbutz now. A little village but the shops did not have shop fronts. You just went into these private houses amongst the orchards. One place would sell trinkets, another fruit and lollies and so on. The next day we headed north. I had read enough about Palestine from when I was there before, to recognise we were going up through the land of the Samaritans. We went past Afula and camped there for several days. We had happy memories of Afula after having been out in the desert for months. I took a trip through Nazareth, up through a cleft in the hills. I could write a book on this! I took a bus to the Sea of Galilee. I walked along a road right through the city of Nazareth but I noticed a cutting, perhaps a five-foot cutting on the left of the road as I went up the hill. It was a masonry roof of a church. The roof was at ground level and the church floor ten or twelve feet down. The earth around it must have accumulated over the centuries.

Then we moved to near the coast, the border of Lebanon. We must have travelled at night and we were warned not to move out from under the olive trees. This was because the border guards, the Vichy French had powerful binoculars. We were going to invade. Our battalion history book tells about this invasion and I think I probably wrote about it in my diaries. When we invaded Lebanon and it must have included my section, instead of steel helmets, we were told to wear our dress felt hats. The idea was that they might welcome us with welcome arms, make it easier for the Free French to take over. Lebanon was under French dominion. France had been allocated Lebanon by the League of Nations after the First World War so it wasn't really a colony of France. And Germany had of course invaded France and subdued it, through the Vichy French who were subject to the orders of the pro German Government. But by this time De Gaulle had quite a strong Free French Force, and they went with us to different areas.

The Vichy French accepted the German, Hitler rule, after France was overwhelmed, and the Free French did not. They sabotaged the Germans and the Vichy French whenever they possibly could. Helped prisoners of war who broke out. Bit like the Scarlet Pimpernel! There was many an airman taken by the Free French and conveyed across the English Channel.

Our lieutenant Kyffin was one of the party who walked deep into Lebanon. This was to try and prevent the Free French from exploding a device which would block the area around the sea cliffs.

There were several different sections. Each had a Jewish guide because the guides knew the road. Kyffo's guide was with them when they went into Lebanon. It was after this that Kyffo lost an eye. He survived the war. He left quite early because he lost his eye, or the sight of it, anyway. The Jewish guide wore a black patch over his eye. And he used to write letters to Kyffo. Finally the guide came to Australia to visit many years after, when he was Minister for the Defence. Moshe Dayan. And he did come out here not long after Kyffo had died, but he visited Kyffo's widow. I wrote this story for the Esperanto delegate in Israel six years ago.

The next day we were wearing our helmets. I think I have most of the action in my diaries. I think we were in action for six weeks. It would only be two or three days of close contact with the enemy, and even less of that in the firing line. The fighting would move on. Sometimes we had time to catch up and do our washing and have a rest. I remember how desperately tired I was. It was the first time in my life that I was quite content to sit around, eat, drink and sleep, for three or four days. This was during the Armistice. We had to maintain our positions in case the Armistice broke down while the agreement was being worked out. When the Armistice was signed, we were at that time up in the mountains overlooking Beirut in forward position.

We went about thirty miles past Tripoli, past the great high mountains, along the foothills. It was the longest day in June. We stayed there till we could see the snow on the mountains. The snow kept coming down a bit lower each time. Then one morning there was about six inches of snow all around the tents. It was soon after that we moved down to the coast. Then we camped at a pleasant place out of Tripoli on the coastal plain for a short while. Must have been there for quite a while, because we were still at Tripoli in camp during Christmas. I don't remember anything about Christmas.'

I was remembering Stan's many letters and daily diary keeping. 'I would be surprised if there were any others in the company who wrote as much as you.'

'One fellow wrote letters every day to his family and friends in Bairnsdale. Artie Longmore. He lost his arm eventually in New Guinea. We used to ask what on earth do you find to write about? He used to write plays and send them to his friends. There were wonderful talents among those boys! One of our blokes, Tapper, we used to call him Tuppy. I thought it was just a joke, but I found out he was 'Nicky and Tuppy' from a radio program!'

'See any Bedouins?' I asked.

But Stan was thinking of something else.

War. Tom.

Stan was tapping with a frustrated hand up and down. He was on a different tangent. 'I'm trying to remember. I visited Tommy! He was at Gaza. We shifted to hill sixty-nine about twenty miles or so from Gaza, and while I was there Tom got in touch with me. Being in the First Corp's Signallers, the communications centre for the many units, thousands of men in Palestine at the time, he knew that we were camped only a few miles from Gaza where he was. So he wrote to me from there, and told me, in spite of the censorship, how to find his camp. I hitched a ride. He wasn't in the Arab city, but at the Camp of Gaza. He was at the centre of the camp because he was in the 'sigs'.

I have very few memories of that visit. Tom did tell me, well, I had already received newspapers telling about the Australian troops taking Bardia, and retaking several other Egyptian forts from the Italians, who had surrendered in thousands. Great long columns. I read about our troops, privates, delegated to be their guards, handing over a rifle to an Italian while he went to the toilet! While in Palestine we used to get a local paper that was published in English. But the only thing I remember about Tom's reminiscences, were that he confirmed that this was a true story about the Italians surrendering in droves. It had sounded unbelievable. I was a bit suspicious about propaganda. But it was a matter of tens of thousands who surrendered to a few hundred Australians. They didn't want to fight under Mussolini. Their hearts were not in it. The memorable thing to me was, Tom must have been up further. This Bardia was in Egypt. Tom must have been in Cyrenacea which is now Libya. My sympathy was with the poor old Arabs who had been subjugated by the Italians. But Tom's sympathies were with the Italian settlers. The Arabs did nothing with the country except herd goats off it and use every blade of grass. A good Mediterranean climate there. The Italians were settling there and, in any terms, would have been pioneers. They made farm lands of the area. It showed how Tom thought about things—without believing too much of what he heard in the newspapers and the news.

I find the army records of Tom very interesting indeed, especially the dates. He ended up a prisoner-of-war for nearly two-and-a-half years. In July 1942, when I left the army, Tom was still 'missing' before he was reported a prisoner-of-war in Stalag Camp 18a. I discovered he had embarked for overseas service the same month that we, the Second 14th Battalion, embarked from Sydney in October 1940. We disembarked at the same place as his unit. That was at Kantara, where the railway line, from Cairo to Palestine, now Israel, Turkey and Europe crosses by punt, the Suez Canal.'

Stan was whistling as he tried to find words. He often whistled. I was never quite sure whether it was a nervous whistle or that he was enjoying some sort of melody. The whistle was usually off key and decidedly out of tune. Stan looked up and saw me watching. 'Did I whistle?' he said, laughing.

My thoughts were not of the moment but of early morning when Stan visited Bairnsdale. This familiar sound was not a particular nicety at dawn. Along with Stan's clatter as he prepared himself for his routine ramble, it was a shock to one's slumber. In desperation, I requested a quieter departure. Unfortunately, Stan's enthusiasm seemed mostly to get the better of him, and he continued to whistle, bang and clang in the wee hours.

'The visit to Tom was about one hour. Tommy and I had a lot in common.' Stan was pulling his dark, slightly grey beard. 'I didn't see much of him since I was fourteen. It was because of Tom I got into the militia in the first place. It was because of Tom's interest in the radio that we knew there was going to be a war.'

'He wasn't cut out for farming, do you think?' I said.

'He was a good orchardist and cane farmer but happier inventing and doing technical things.'

Now Stan pulled himself back and returned to war. 'Julis. It was summer time; we were told to get into full uniform. We had not worn it since Australia, and they marched us with full packs down to the beach. I could see no reason for this. It could have been to fool the spies in the local city. Soon after this we went to North Africa. Then about the time of Pearl Harbour we came from Tripoli back to Julis. From Julis we went on the train to the Suez Canal and then embarked on a big ship, the 'City of Paris,' on February 15th.

Stan was now tracing with his index finger a map in the air. 'Think we may have called at Colombo but we didn't get leave. At one place either Bombay or Colombo, we went south. They would not tell us at any time where we were going. We were hoping we were heading for Australia. We discovered later we were. The whole convoy, which instead of its normal zigzag erratic course with one steady trend, changed direction suddenly. The wireless bulletin typewritten for us, announced a full naval battle near

Java, which our ship was avoiding. I had been lying out on the deck watching the stars, and suddenly the ship made a 180-degree turn back where we'd come!'

One day I'd commented to Bess that I imagined Stan would have been a very good tree climber as a child. Bess replied, 'Percy, Ted Shelden and I had been chatting. Ted said, 'No different shimmying up rocks and mountains, or shimmying up a German tank! That's one thing I saw him doing. Shimmying up a German tank.'

A story I recall, which perhaps defines another aspect of the rigour of Stan's war experiences, was something he told me once. Stan and some of his mates had fancied some meat. They killed a pig, which was roaming around their camp in Syria. It was after they had eaten, they began to feel very sick in the stomach. And sick at heart. This pig had apparently been seen eating the corpses of some of their dead comrades.

'There were a lot of American soldiers in Australia during the war, weren't there?' I said.

'Have you heard this?' said Stan, as he launched into a poem with some gusto.

Is 'e an Aussie, is 'e Lizzie?
Is 'e an Aussie, is 'e eh?
Is it because 'e is an Aussie that 'e keeps you busy, Lizzie?
As 'e jazzy ways and does 'e make you go all fuzzy wuzzy?
Got you dizzy 'as 'e Lizzie?
Is 'e an Aussie is 'e eh?'

I was nonplussed. 'Never heard it before.'

'Well, the Aussie boys didn't like the Americans stealing their girls! There was a lot of angst about that.'

The falling snow had greyed the dusk as Stan headed off home to Castlemaine, driving through the back roads. Darkness was falling fast. The weeping cherry could be seen soft pencilled with pearl against the smudged black of garden greenery. Stan could have slipped into his night shirt under the pillow in the spare room, but he had a field naturalist excursion the next morning. No doubt he would be up with the birds and spend time meditating and writing his diary. His standard prelude to a usual busy day.

'What are these trees Stan's been planting?' I inquired of Percy as we sat around the fire after Stan's departure. Perce talked as Doreen napped.

'Stan's been flat out. He wants to get some trees in before he goes to Queensland. He's been planting blue gums and manna gums at Ray's, and he's put in a row of blackwood's along the fence up over Meuser's hill. At the old place he's put in chestnuts, a special kind that flower early. Had an expert graft them.'

Percy drew breath for a moment. He added somewhat bemusedly. 'He's planted fourteen giant American Redwoods down there. One for each of his brothers and sisters and Mum and Pop. I said, 'But they don't mature for a hundred years, do they? You'll have to stick around a fair while!' Stan said, 'That's my legacy!'

Allan. Wilderness

That night, I spent an hour or so reflecting on a few of the many facets which made up the kaleidoscope of Stan's life. That he as a young raw army recruit, uneducated, formally that is, and untravelled, should have the foresight to consistently document his experiences, observations and reflections during his war service. These pocket-sized closely written diaries, until now, had lain dormant. I was glad Stan had rediscovered these treasures. For that matter, I felt pride in the proactive and adventurous spirit which had characterised Stan throughout his life.

The discovery of these diaries was, however, for him, a mixed blessing. He told me later, looking somewhat shamefaced, 'I find myself reluctant to record my diary verbatim with the pompous generalisations of the twenty-one-year-old, who was me! Some of my assumptions are distastefully ignorant!'

My mind flicked back to the conversation with Percy. The redwoods. According to my understanding of Stan, indigenous Australian trees, many majestic, represented the quintessential aspect of his interest in flora. A question was burning within me, demanding an answer. Fancying myself to be a protégé of Stan's, I felt every right to confront him! I imagined saying, 'Why plant American Redwoods, when we have the great 'Eucalyptus regnans,' king of the eucalypts or the very long-lived Huon pine?' Perhaps, I mused, Stan knowing the vagaries of human nature may have considered that a more exotic type of tree might survive the fickleness of the great predator, the chain saw. Maybe he had been introduced to the redwoods during his years in Tasmania. One day, years ago, he had proudly shown me the beginning of an arboretum he was helping establish out of Devonport.

Memories were aplenty that night. Some stood out with cinematic vividness against the velvet darkness. Those jaunts with Stan and Audrey into the Tasmanian wilderness. Stan's unbridled enthusiasm. Stan surrounded by a conglomeration of greens, the solidity of lichen covered trees and the untidy Australian bush. A caricature. Stan had told me, as we surveyed this dark, damp, mysterious tangle beneath the towering dense myrtles near the Savage River. 'Men have ventured in here—only a few yards and have lost their way. Never been seen again!'

In those days people like Stan were an endangered species, especially on this beautiful isle with the rich diversity of flora and fauna. It was the timber men, the cutters and millers, along with the tamers of the wild rivers who built enormous dams for the generation of hydro-electric power, who had the prestige.

My mind returned to the myrtles and thick rain forests. Myrtles could be seen towering on both sides of the roads. These rain forests would alternate with open blond button grass plains. The rivers and streams draining from the peaty soil of these plains ran the colour of tea. Stan admired this special beauty too, but somehow, I associated him with the more rampant lushness of the bush.

Our travels to the mysterious rain forests on the west coast were my special enjoyment. These, in comparison with the drier, less dense eucalyptus forests on other parts of the island, engendered feelings of being in another world. A world unfamiliar to me, saturated with new and different arrays of scents and secrets. Along the way Stan would point out native laurel, the red spidery flowers of the waratah. On one of his sudden brake jamming stops, he ran to the side of the road, grabbed two or three leaves, dark green on top, pale underneath, crushing them. 'Smell this!' he said. That was my introduction to the cinnamon fragrance of the sassafras.

He explained that the upper stratum of the forest was generally dominated by the myrtle beech, the sassafras, the blackwood. Also gracing this canopy was the old stalwart, the King William pine, loosely called by locals, 'King Billy.' Then there was the understorey, the shadowy inner sanctum where scrub grew, with the distinct feature of lying horizontally often many metres from the ground. Added to this were blackwood's, laurels and leatherwoods.

Stan always pointed out the leatherwoods if they were in flower. And always, I felt fortunate to be a partaker of the spring symphony of smells and sights of this special favourite of Stan's. These trees, very popular with the bee keepers, yielded honey, heady and aromatic. Dipping liberally into the sky-blue ceramic honey pot which usually graced their Bruton table, had been a precursor for my preference too, for leatherwoods.

Sometimes the road wound hair-pin bends above the deep gullied, damp dewy havens of the leatherwoods. Although the perfume was not new to me, I recall standing transfixed at the sight, and distinct sweet scent, wafting from a gully of leatherwoods in full bloom. Exotic! It was like the Arabian Nights. Stan picked and gave me a small branch, festooned with single four petalled soft cream flowers, their centres bright with small yellow pollened brushes.

One of life's highlights for me ever since has been to repeat this sensory treat, of standing above a stand of leatherwoods in full florescence. These leatherwoods, together with the sassafras, evocative of those trips, have become inextricably linked with my recollections of Stan.

'Those big, beautiful grass trees,' he had said. 'The ones with the long leathery green leaves. The dead leaves underneath are always dry. Good in the wettest weather for a source of something to light a campfire.'

Yes. With Stan's tuition, the Australian bush, which at first appearance was a bewildering display, seemingly without form, took on a new meaning. Suddenly the jumble of plant life revealed structures and beauties hitherto unseen. Stan used the term 'beautiful' frequently, and stood there amongst the profusion with great awe, reverence even.

Stan's appreciation of the landscape went further than simply knowledge of his geographical whereabouts. He connected with it deeply, physically and spiritually. He loved the intrinsic nature of the environment; it seemed to permeate his very being. It seemed to me a particular type of courage was necessary to enter an unknown place, the wilderness. Be it the wilderness of the mind or of nature. Time and again Stan was drawn to these untamed areas. And there was something untamed about Stan, too.

'I don't think I have ever met such a fit man as Stan.' was a recent admiring remark from Col Blume, Stan's long-time army friend. On pondering this, I was reminded of an entry in Stan's war diary. Way back there in the Middle East, he had maintained his fitness too. He hadn't told me any details about that compulsory cross-country race he'd won. In his diary, an entry indicated he'd run 3.5 miles in 23.5 minutes. On thumbing through it further, I found some more salient comments.

'This army life, especially action, has completely destroyed my self-pity. I prefer now to pretend to be fitter than the fittest always, and it is always the best way too. It's a matter of auto suggestion, of course. There is no doubt though, that I am as tough physically as any man in the company, which is undoubtedly the best in the battalion. I'm glad I always kept off the smoking and the drinking, and that decision I made when in Palestine to keep tough, has certainly had its good results.'

The image of Stan's heading off earlier that night, from Perce's warm fire into the inclement weather, was momentarily before me. Stan wearing his woollen tweed hat with the small front verandah and head hugging back. Pulled down firmly on his forehead, it shadowed his piercing eyes. Wiry, not an ounce of fat, and not as tall as he used to be, he was, as usual, dressed in his tweed jacket. A favourite. Mostly earth browns, a touch of sage, with the small green triangular badge displayed on the lapel. He'd worn this badge identifying himself as a member of the Aboriginal Advancement League for well over fifty years. Many years before, while staying at Stan and Audrey's, I had met their friend Pastor Doug Nicholls, a kindly aboriginal who in his time had been an icon in the football world. Then, there were those months, or years, when Audrey and Stan laboured at an Aboriginal mission at Carnarvon, in faraway Western Australia.

My mind travelled back to Stan's feeling for the bush. Perhaps his connection with the original naturalists, these first custodians of the land, was, in part, due to this shared affinity.

Now, staring into the darkness, I reached for the light and added another woollen blanket, pulling it closely around my neck. Snow outside, cosy and comfortable in the big high double bed. Content to continue my cinematic experience, I settled back against the feather pillow and watched what came to mind.

A double bed! Stan and Audrey's. They, sitting up, leaning against flower patterned pillows. She in her short-sleeved floral nightdress, he probably in his nightshirt, sewn by Audrey. My focus wandered to stare at Stan. He was still wearing this type of night attire, I noted, when he stayed at Rosa's in later years. I'd smile to myself at the sight of skinny pale legs protruding from knuckled knees. Stan would be quite unaware of course of this amusing spectacle. Probably he would be putting his false teeth into a glass of water. Not the first time either, that he had absentmindedly deposited his teeth in my favourite cup on the kitchen bench. I suspect one day I may have, in haste, gulped his teeth water.

Back in those early days now, I see myself sitting on the foot of their bed; me talking. Of course! But then all three of us never tired of this activity. Sometimes we openly contemplated the inexplicable, or shared my endless ruminations about religious imponderables.

On a particular summer's evening I recall very clearly, their patient listening, as I shared a lonely dilemma which was hounding me like a dreadful nemesis. 'God's will.' Ridiculously, I believed that if something was hard and disliked, like nursing, it must be 'God's will.' Some sort of test of one's allegiance. Surprised and confused, I noted that my nurse roommate's claim of God's will for her had happily coincided with her own desires.

In truth, looking back, I believe I'd have made a decent teacher, and had a much easier lifestyle if I'd chosen more wisely. In all fairness, the choices weren't wide for many girls of that fifties, sixties era, especially from a cash strapped family. The major choices were nursing or teaching. Somehow there was a compulsion in the nursing direction. It wasn't my cup of tea. A gross mismatch. I hadn't developed the armour plating for it. The lack of freedom, the harshness, the physical and emotional rigours, long hours and bone sapping tiredness. Drugs, drips, difficult days. The gasping, rasping and lonely struggles of the dying. Staring eyes often pleading, fearful. Worse on night duty, when those sounds permeated the whole ward. And my very soul. Their traumas. Mine. Lifeless bodies, or pain wracked. These distresses are marked indelibly upon me to this day and were for many years the subject of nightmares.

Aud and Stan were unable to help me that night. I discovered later, it was indeed 'Mother's will' I was grappling with, enacting her unfulfilled ambition to be a nurse.

'If you aren't successful getting your university scholarship, I'll finance you!' Stan told me one day. I suspect looking back, his heart was many times bigger than his pocket. It was during a summer stay with them, that I received the affirming letter, my deliverance. Stan and Audrey were as thrilled as me.

There were no 'holds barred' in those discussions back there. Fortunately for me, no censorship on sex and religion either. The human body was somehow disgraceful to my mother, and nudes unacceptable. I struggled with the limitations and needs of my own flesh. My first book on painting was given to me by Audrey. A small paperback, it sported nude portraits by the masters, amongst other gems. Her sensible approach was refreshing, as were our discussions on sex sometimes. 'Isn't she beautiful! Look how she's proudly, almost defiantly sitting.' Audrey commented, looking at Monet's 'Olympia.'

And seeing Audrey and Stan together. Their open display of affection, touching, talking, was a breath of fresh air to me. My English father, an older man, brought a subdued air to my family, and he was emotionally remote. Not sensitive to my needs, he saw any further education as unnecessary.

Later, when Audrey and Stan moved to Victoria, our Potpourri of pow-wows and painting continued. It was around this time, with their encouragement and participation, that I bought my flat.

Life after death? We discussed this for many moons. Audrey and I were the most interested. We read prodigiously on the subject and performed little experiments like staring at clouds and making them disappear. Audrey and Stan introduced me to erudite books by Raynor C Johnson, then Master of Queens College, Melbourne University. A physicist, Dr Johnson had explored various subjects. The psychic, mysticism, religion, the nature of time. Life after death. I devoured them and have some of these carefully researched treatises in my collection to this day.

Audrey died. She'd asserted years before that she was unafraid to die. 'Not since that experience when a staircase of light, of love came upon me one morning in bed.' I dreamed she was speaking to me in two vivid dreams. As though she was communicating. Stan had no such dreams.

During our sojourn at Percy's, the last few days, I'd asked Stan, 'How did you educate yourself about the natural world? Apart from your own observations, that is.' His answer drew us way back there again to those earliest experiences.

'It started off with the Weekly Times. Photos in the middle of it. Fancy it was the naturalist page. Also we used to read a bit in the 'Pals' which was a periodical magazine Tommy got. Not so serious, more sensation. Things like letters from someone who saw the ducks pushing the ducklings out of their nest from the tree into the water below.

We didn't start getting the Weekly Times until just before I left home. Charles Barrett was the naturalist who wrote a quarter page in each issue. There was a colour page. A pretty crude colour picture of a bird! Later on, the Weekly Times published a series of glossy photographs. I remember a particular series on Birds of Paradise.'

Obviously, I thought, this Weekly Times was an important paper. It seemed to this day that farmers considered it an essential source of information. But Stan said the Bruton family had not received it until Stan was well into his teenage years. I'd asked Stan 'Why?' once again.

'In the early 1930s it was dearer. Four pence, I think. The only newspaper we got in our house was the Leader, cost maybe threepence. We used to get the Leader when Maggie Price would come with the mail, be a sugar bag full of newspapers. After Maggie Price died unexpectedly with peritonitis, Mum tendered and got the mail run. Probably the school master backed her up. The newspaper people said, 'You don't have to pay for the Leader because you are carting the papers for us.'

Mum would take the jinker to the Little Hampton Post Office and leave at about 9.15, generally just after we'd gone to school. Then she'd wait till about eleven o'clock when the train came in and the mail to Little Hampton had been sorted, and they'd give her the mail bag suitably stamped. It was the proper canvas mail bag, sealed up with wax and stamped at the Trentham Post Office. She'd go to Wall's newspaper shop more or less across the road and pick up a sugar bag full of newspapers. All neatly rolled up with a name on them. They were tipped out on the verandah of the school house and people picked up their newspaper. The tiny post office, about half the size of this table, was inside the school house then.'

'Besides the written word, any person influence you?' I said, returning to the original subject of Stan's interest in nature.

'It started with going for walks at Taradale, my first year at school, when I used to hold my big sister, Rosa's hand. My memories of Rosa picking the wildflowers, to take home a bunch for Mum. I must have liked flowers even before that. I remember to my astonishment seeing a tree with flowers on it. Thought flowers only grew in the garden. Then, of course, us kids would go roaming around the district and see various flora.'

Somehow though, Rosa's close connection, her love of animals, did not seem to have influenced Stan. Feathers, but not fur. His response came as a surprise that day when I shared a favourite Sioux Indian saying I had read. 'They say, 'All animals are my brothers!' There had been a silence. Unusually, Stan was at a loss for words. 'But they are animals.' he replied, nonplussed.

Sleep was beckoning, but a last image, entirely different, pressed against the darkness. Two faces. Stan and Allan, both dark-haired, dark eyed, in their seventies.

Over the years, Allan spent quite a few holidays at Stan and Audrey's. This was usually instigated by Stan. There seemed to be a sort of camaraderie between them, in spite of Allan's penchant for preaching at every opportunity. Audrey said one day with a glinting eye. 'The kids asked me, 'What can we do when Uncle Allan starts preaching at us?' I said, 'You can run faster than him.'

It was the day before Christmas, in 1994. Stan had arranged to bring Allan over to Rosa's at Emerald for the night. He often called on Allan, assisting him in whatever way he could. This included dressing him, bailing him out of various financial deals, and listening to Allan's stories and concerns about his ill-chosen, often shady house-sharing tenants.

I well remember it. Rosa was tired. She had been preparing her usual delicious Christmas sago plum pudding and moving furniture. This was in order to put down a non-skid carpet runner she'd bought so that Allan's crutches could grip more easily. I had brought her the inimitable cup of white tea, having persuaded her with difficulty to lie down. Stan had just pulled up in his apple-coloured sedan with Allan aboard. Typically, there were noticeable gaps between the cessation of car engines, the squeaks of car doors, and the laboured 'stomp clomp' of Allan's crutches. Allan always needed someone, hopefully strong, to manoeuvre him out of the car, position his crutches, and haul him to his feet.

Suddenly the predictable pause was shattered. Stan was calling loudly, 'Some first aid required!' This quiet interlude was transformed, taut with tension, as I opened Rosa's screen door to the front concrete patio.

Blood was what I saw. Two scarlet pools, the size of my hand. Wet, rich and glistening. My eyes risked further, to encompass Allan's head, face down on the concrete, and then his body. A body misshapen, with a heavy built-up black boot clumsily protruding. It seemed as if now no one was there to pull the strings of this puppet body. No one to orchestrate the precise and laboured movements required to accomplish even the smallest task. The man with an iron determination, who overcame obstacles, had been overcome. He lay on the concrete like a broken doll, seemingly discarded by life itself. I saw his hands. These small twisted and inadequate tools lay naked on the concrete in their truth. The one marginally functioning hand which awkwardly held a pen, wrote the long spider scrawl which used to embellish religious book gifts, unwelcomed by the family, was now still.

In those split seconds, I became aware of another. Stan! Stan was leaning with head against crossed arms, his pale stump starkly vulnerable against the rough red brick of the house wall. Desperate sobs tore from him. The brother he cared for must be dead.

Thankfully, I noted on turning Allan's head to the side, he was breathing. I think I muttered 'Uncle Allan' and stroked his forehead. There was no time to worry that I remembered precious little first aid. The trickle of red from the jagged cut in Allan's forehead soon stopped with the help of a clean towel. But not before Stan had distractedly used Rosa's smelly dish cloth on Allan's head, after mopping up the red stained concrete.

It was after a long couple of minutes that Allan half opened his one visible brown eye. It was not long before he was sporting a wry grin and asking for a mirror to view his wound. This punctuated by some hymn singing. Stan accompanied him in the ambulance for a hospital check, Allan sitting up smiling and carolling, as though he was going on a Sunday school picnic.

Fortunately, this accident did not appear to produce any repercussions for Allan's long-time polio ravaged body. He lived for four years after this. Stan read a eulogy at his funeral. Allan was seventy-eight. 'I never thought Allan would make old bones!' Stan told me.

Stan's handless arm. His handicap. Minor compared with Allan's cataclysmic ordeal, but in itself an unremitting challenge. That accident during the freshness of youth. An unfortunate event which suddenly and irrevocably changed his life.

This was to be eclipsed only by an accident of equal suddenness in Stan's eighty-fifth year.

We were unprepared. He'd said he was going to live to a hundred and we sort of believed him! In July 2003, Stan enthusiastically joined a four-wheel drive trip with a group of field naturalists. An epic journey, they ventured many days into the dry, red-earthed spinifex heartland far west of Alice Springs.

Later, Stan realised a lifetime ambition of visiting Kakadu National Park, one of Australia's special gems at the top end.

Then Litchfield National Park, two hours from Darwin, had beckoned. Serene fresh water pools surrounded by an abundance of lush jades and emeralds of monsoonal rainforest. Florence Falls fed by breath-takingly beautiful ribbons of lace from the majestic plateau high above.

A tropical day. The day before Stan was due to return. With typical panache he pointed his arms to the mysterious wild dark green depths and dived into a circle of silver. Warm and balmy on the top. Icy below. Claimed by his beloved wilderness, he did not surface.

AFTERWORD

Robert 'Bob' died gently at home, on January 1, 2001.
He was 86 years old.
Lung cancer.
His funeral, like all the Bruton funerals, was large.
Cars lined the streets and a big country afternoon tea was served in the packed Trentham Hall.

Minnie suffered a stroke and passed away five months later in the Nambour Hospital, Queensland on May 20th, 2009.
She was 96 years old.
Her husband Fred pre-deceased her, by about eighteen months.

Percy was cared for by his wife Doreen and family for many years.
He suffered a slow progressive form of Motor Neurone Disease.
After several months in the Trentham Hospital, he died peacefully on July 5th, 2015.
He was 89 years old.
Twelve months later, almost to the day, Doreen collapsed and died.

Rosa suffered many falls and breakages. The last two or three years, my husband Geoff and I took care of her at our home. She passed away serenely on April 22nd, 2011, Geoff's birthday.
Bob was proved right when he asserted, 'She'll outlive us all.'.
She died at almost 99.
Rosa was buried with her forebears at the Cheltenham Pioneer Cemetery.
The historic Cheltenham church overflowed with as many mourners outside as inside the church.

Bessie cared for her husband, Fred, who had become dependent.
He died in a nursing home.
Eventually she moved to an aged care facility. After catching the flu, she died peacefully on October 7th, 2016. She was 92 years.

Stan, energetic and enthusiastic to the end, drowned after diving into a natural lake in the Northern Territory on July 31st, 2003.
He was 85 years old.
Stan was buried in Trentham, after a shocked and sad farewell at the Little Hampton church, which had been an important part of the Bruton lives.

ACKNOWLEDGEMENTS

To Bob, Min, Percy, Rosa, Bess and Stan who shared aspects of their life stories—all important contributions towards the overall Big Australian Story, thank-you.

To those who have enthusiastically encouraged and recognised the importance of these historical narratives, thank you.

My husband, Geoffrey de Jonge's keen eye and practical support, have been invaluable in a myriad of ways. There have been special contributions from others, all appreciated. Dib Bluhm, Vane Lindesay, Doreen Bruton, Eleanor Weekes, David de Jonge, Ann-Marie Teasdale, Lorna Piper, Grace Rainey, Arie Wetsteyn. I thank you all.

APPENDIX

The Bruton Family

Children of Olive and Harry Bruton

Thomas	b 27-02-1911	m	Sally Plant
Olive Rosa*	b 13-07-1912	m	Ern Rainey
Minnie*	b 18-10-1913	m	Fred Mock
Robert 'Bob'*	b 29-03-1915	m	Nell Rothe
George	b 28-10-1916	m	Freda Rothe
Stan*	b 23-10-1916	m	Audrey Burtt
Allan	b 18-04-1920	m	Rosa Stephanovic
Daisy	b 30-07-1921	m	Ted Shelden
Bernie	b 23-03-1923		
Bessie*	b 21-12-1924	m	Fred Drummond
Percy*	b 03-08-1926	m	Doreen Hoopell
Harold	b 02-07-1928		

* Narrators of the Bruton story

Shawline Publishing Group Pty Ltd
www.shawlinepublishing.com.au

SHAWLINE
PUBLISHING
GROUP

CPSIA information can be obtained
at www.ICGtesting.com
Printed in the USA
LVHW041515090321
680995LV00012B/2109